Library of
Davidson College

EXPANDED TUNINGS IN CONTEMPORARY MUSIC
Theoretical Innovations and Practical Applications

EXPANDED TUNINGS IN CONTEMPORARY MUSIC
Theoretical Innovations and Practical Applications

Enrique Moreno

Studies in the History and Interpretation of Music
Volume 30

The Edwin Mellen Press
Lewiston/Queenston/Lampeter

Library of Congress Cataloging-in-Publication Data

Moreno, Enrique.
    Expanded tunings in contemporary music : theoretical innovations and practical applications / Enrique Moreno.
      p. cm. -- (Studies in the history and interpretation of music ; v. 30)
    ISBN 0-88946-485-5
    1. Musical temperament. 2. Tuning. 3. Musical intervals and scales. I. Title. II. Series.
ML3809.M76   1990
781.2' 6--dc20   90-6025
                                                                                      CIP
                                                                                       MN

A CIP catalog record for this book is available
from The British Library.

Copyright   ©1992 Enrique Moreno.

A tape cassette has been produced to accompany this volume. Consult your librarian for details.
Individual purchasers of the volume who require additional copies of the tape should contact The Edwin Mellen Press.

All rights reserved. For more information contact

The Edwin Mellen Press	The Edwin Mellen Press
P.O. Box 450	Box 67
Lewiston, NY 14092	Queenston, Ontario
USA	CANADA L0S 1L0

The Edwin Mellen Press, Ltd.
Lampeter, Dyfed, Wales
UNITED KINGDOM SA48 7DY

Printed in the United States of America

This book is dedicated to my parents:

Dr. and Mrs. Enrique Moreno

A TAPE CASETTE HAS BEEN PRODUCED TO ACCOMPANY
THIS VOLUME. CONSULT YOUR LIBRARIAN FOR DETAILS.

CONTENTS

Foreword i
Acknowledgements iii

Part One: **Objective Approach**

Chapter I   General Structure of Expanded Tunings.......... 3
Chapter II   The Question of Chroma and Its
               Hypothetical Expansion..................................... 25
Chapter III   Implementation of Expanded Tunings............. 37
Chapter IV   Expanded Notation.. 49
Chapter V   Probability of Expanded Chroma..................... 59

Part Two: **Aesthetical Approach**

Chapter VI   A Theory of Expanded Tunings and
               The Western Musical Tradition......................... 85
Chapter VII   Expanded Tunings and Composition
               Today and Tomorrow.. 101

References 115

Appendices

Appendix I   Music Examples (Scores)................................. 121
Appendix II   Tables.. 135
Appendix III   Recorded Examples

Index 201

FIGURES AND MUSICAL EXAMPLES

FIGURES

Figure 1	Functions of Oct-12, A-12, A-16, A-20, and A-24.............	19
Figure 2	Functions of Oct-12, B-12, B-15, B-20, and 8-24.............	20
Figure 3	Functions of Oct-12, C-12, C-14, C-17, and C-21.............	21
Figure 4	Simple Helix of Pitch..	26
Figure 5a	Coincidence of Harmonics on The Musical Staff.............	29
Figure 5b	Table of Coincidence of Harmonics...................................	31
Figure 6	Initial Steps to Use Different Tunings for Music Performance...	43

MUSIC EXAMPLES

Scores:

Music Example no. 1:	Ave Maria..	123
Music Example no. 2:	Melody..	129
Music Example no. 3:	Chorale..	131
Music Example no. 4:	Theme with Alberti Bass...............................	133

Recordings:

	SIDE A		SIDE B
I.	*Ave Maria*	V.	*Concert Adagio*
II.	Melody		
III.	Chorale		
IV.	Theme with Alberti Bass		

INDEX OF TABLES

Part One: **Reference Catalog**

Table 1   Tunings from the Families Oct-n, A-n, B-n, Cn, and D-n

        Octave-Based Tunings (Oct-5 , ... Oct-24).............. 137
        Family A-n (A-8, ... A-27)...................................... 146
        Family B-n (B-12, ... B-31)...................................... 155
        Family C-n (C-12, ... C-40)..................................... 164
        Family D-n (D-12, ... D-48).................................... 176

Part Two: **Comparative Tables**

Table 2   Constants in cts and TU.. 193
Table 3   Proximity of Tunings.. 194
Table 4   Originality of Expanded Tunings in
        Comparison to Octave-Based Tunings 195
Table 5   Foreign Croma Interference in The Family A-n....... 196
Table 6   Foreign Croma Interference in The Family B-n....... 196
Table 7   Foreign Croma Interference in The Family C-n....... 197
Table 8   Foreign Croma Interference in The Family D-n....... 198
Table 9   Chroma Originality.. 199
Table 10   Total Originality... 200

Foreword

The object of this book is to present composers, performers, music theorists, music psychologists and educators with the most elementary facts and conjectures relating to some hitherto unknown or at least mostly unexplored groups of possible tunings. Expanded tunings are equal tunings organized upon exponential progressions in which the bases are numbers other than two. Consequently, expanded tunings are not organized in cycles defined by the octave relationship. From this, it follows that **the present work is not directly concerned with any historical or modern form of tuning in which the octave is divided in any number of equal or unequal parts.**

One of the aims of this book is to investigate whether expanded tunings may be perceptually coherent, and whether their mathematical and acoustical properties may constitute a sufficient basis to support the hypothesis of an amazing perceptual phenomenon elicited by tonal compositions in expanded tunings - expanded chroma. In reference to this problem, psychoacoustical problems are considered, and the scores of original musical examples in expanded tunings are discussed, analyzed, and also illustrated with the set of recordings that accompanies this book.

Of no lesser importance is the relevance of expanded tunings as a new technique for music composition. For this reason, the present study places a strong emphasis on descriptive aspects and on technical and musical problems related to the implementation of these new tunings. In order to

further facilitate an immediate application of expanded tunings to the practice of music performance and composition, a comprehensive example of a methodology has been developed and complemented with pertinent numerical tables for analysis and for reference. Thus, interested readers without a mathematical background (in this case, college algebra) sufficient to enable them to derive the tunings themselves may find that some of the tables will enable them to program a considerable number of expanded tunings into a digital music instrument, provided that the architecture of the instrument supports this option.

An attempt has been made to demonstrate how expanded forms of intonation seem to be a logical step in the evolution of musical practice within the Western musical tradition. In this respect, the subject of expanded tunings is related to several problems of contemporary music and aesthetics.

Acknowledgements

Several grants by the University of Kansas stimulated the progress of this study, especially two major grants obtained by Jeffrey Weinberg, associate director of Financial Aid; I wish to express my gratitude to him for his support for my project, and to Dr. Stanley Shumway, professor of music theory at the University of Kansas. I am indebted also to the College Honors Program of the University of Kansas for two research awards during the years of 1987 and 1988, and to Dr. Edward Mattila, professor of composition and music theory, in connection with these two awards. I would like also to express my recognition to professors Earl Schubert and John Pierce of Stanford University for their careful reading and experienced suggestions in the areas of psychology and psychoacoustics.

The insight, criticism, and help of a group of friends from various fields has been a major force behind the present work. Aerospace engineer Dr. Rainer Suikat has generously devoted a considerable amount of time to assist in several stages of this project. Dr. Willard Remmers, engineer Miguel Gutiérrez of IBM, and Russel Hodge have contributed to this book with invaluable encouragement and criticism. Many thanks are due to Dr. Michael Kimber and Dr. Carl Johnson for proofreading my manuscript, to Steven Trautmann and Scott Van Duyne at Stanford University for their

helpful commentaries, and very especially to engineer and economist Juan Cisneros, whose extraordinary help and intellectual enthusiasm have accompanied the progress of this book from the early stages of the coffee shop discussion to the latter stages of computer typesetting.

A word of acknowledgement and gratitude goes to singer Bethany Hodges, the performer of the vocal musical example illustrating tuning A-12 (appears as no. 1 in the recording that accompanies this book), and to my wife, pianist Laura Goehner-Moreno, whose encouragement and musical assistance have been instrumental in the completion of this work.

Excerpts from the books *Memories and Commentaries* (Doubleday & Co., Inc.) by I. Stravinsky and R. Craft, *Introduction to The Physics and Psychophysics of Music* (Springer-Verlag) by J. Roederer, and from the article "Intervals, Scales, and Tuning", - edited by D. Deutsch in *The Psychology of Music* (Academic Press) - by E. Burns and W. Ward are quoted by permission of the authors and their respective publishers.

PART ONE:

OBJECTIVE APPROACH

CHAPTER ONE

General Structure of Expanded Tunings

The expression "expanded tunings" represents an undetermined number of equal tunings with expanded characteristics. In the context of this study, the term "expanded" will be used in reference to the standard tuning of contemporary Western music, which is the twelve-tone-to-the-octave equal tuning. In consequence, from the point of view of their mathematical description, expanded tunings and the standard tuning are structurally identical, and the adjective "expanded" will denote any such structure with larger values than those that determine the particular characteristics of the twelve-tone-to-the-octave equal tuning.

Then, since both, the twelve-tone-to-the-octave equal tuning, and expanded tunings are equal tunings, we may observe the characteristics of their common structure by establishing a mathematical description of a system to calculate equal temperaments. Subsequently, we may observe how the same structure yields expanded versions as we assign larger values to the parameters of the structure. Such a mathematical description of a system to calculate equal temperaments may be briefly and concisely expressed as a formula. In this case, the formula must include the following variables and constants:

1) The frequency of any degree of the scale (f_x) to be calculated

2) The frequency of the first degree of the scale (f_1)

3) The exponential base (B) of the scale

4) The number (n) of scale degrees between powers of the exponential base (B)

Thus, to calculate the frequency of any scale degree of the scale (f_x) we establish a formula in the following manner:

$$f_x = f_1 [(\sqrt[n]{B})^{(x-1)}]$$

where f_x represents the frequency of scale degree number x to be calculated, and x can be any integer; f_1 is the frequency of the first degree of the scale. This number must correspond to a pitch; n represents the number of scale degrees in a subset, or cycle of the scale, and must be a natural number. B is the exponential factor of the scale and must be also a natural number. Observe the following formula:

$$f_x = f_1 [(\sqrt[12]{2})^{(x-1)}]$$

The twelve above the radical indicates that there will be twelve equal divisions between the interval of an octave. The two within the radical indicates that after a cycle of twelve equal degrees the frequency will have increased by two - reaching an octave, and this arrangement of values shows that the formula immediately above corresponds to an abstraction of the standard twelve-tone-to-the-octave equal tuning or simply *standard tuning*.

Thus, suppose that we want to calculate the value of the second degree

of a standard twelve-tone-to-the-octave equal scale whose first degree (f_1) is 440 Hz (here, f_1 is arbitrarily chosen to equal 440 Hz, but obviously f_1 can be any pitch). Plugging our desired parameters into the formula in order to find f_2 - or the second degree of the scale in question, gives:

$$f_2 = 440 \, [\, (\sqrt[12]{2} \,)^{(2-1)} \,]$$

$$f_2 = 440 \, [\, (1.05946)^{(1)} \,]$$

$$f_2 = 466.162$$

Now we know the values of the first (f_1) and the second (f_2) scale degrees - 400 Hz, and 466.162 Hz, respectively. To find the value of the following upper contiguous scale degree we continue in the same manner:

$$f_3 = 440 \, [\, (\sqrt[12]{2} \,)^{(3-1)} \,]$$

$$f_3 = 440 \, [\, (1.05946)^{(2)} \,]$$

$$f_3 = 440 \, [\, 1.12246 \,]$$

$$f_3 = 493.882$$

And our list becomes:

440
466.162
493.882
... etc.,

for as many scale degrees as we wish. We can now present a formal definition of a generalized equal tuning, which we will symbolize with the letter T.

Definition of An Equal Tuning T

$$T = G(x).$$
$$G(x) = f_0 \cdot C^{(x)}$$

where f_0 is any arbitrary frequency corresponding to a pitch, a pitch is any frequency capable of being perceived by the human auditory system, $x \in \{Z\}$, $\{Z\}$ is the set of all integers - i. e. x is an integer - and C is the principal - positive - n th root of B : $C = \sqrt[n]{B}$, and both, n and $B \in \{Z^+\}$ - i. e. n and B are non-zero positive integers.

Notice that the index of f has been changed from 1 - in our general formula - to zero, above, so that for convenience $G(0) = f_0$. Notice again that f_0 is not necessarily the lowest useful note in the range of a scale. Both f_1 and f_0 point at an arbitrarily chosen starting pitch.

In consequence, we determine that:

a)   our traditional musical scale is based on the constant defined by the twelfth root of two (1.05946 to five decimals), and that

b)   in order to accomplish our proposed expansions, we could obtain different musical scales by assigning new values to the n and to the B in the first general formula above.

It should be clear now that by assigning a value of, for example, fifteen, to the n in the first general formula above we will obtain a scale of fifteen equal steps per cycle of the scale. It may not be so clear, at first sight, what kind of relationship, among cycles, appears when we assign the

B a value other than two. It is evident that if B equals two, the first degree of each cycle (whatever the number of degrees of each cycle) will be a power of two (an octave), and if B equals three, the first degree of each cycle will be a power of three (which is not an octave), and so on; but, in what kind of musical relationship are two tones related by a power of three, four, five, etc.? We will see that this relationship is a cyclical exponential progression related to the harmonic series, and that ultimately all expanded tunings - indeed, all possible equal tunings $\in \{T\}$ - are related to each other through a hierarchy established by the harmonic series. This fact deserves to be expressed more formally, which entails that we must work out a few tautologies implied in our definition.

First, we will show that an exponential base of a tuning T is a primary interval that generates exponentially related cycles.

Primary Interval Lemma

The exponential base (B) of any tuning T is an interval $b_2 : b_1$, where $b_2 = G(n)$, and $b_1 = f_0$.

Proof

By definition, $\quad G(x) = f_0 \cdot C^{(x)}$, so

$$G(x) = f_0 \cdot \left(\sqrt[n]{B}\right)^{(x)}$$

solving for B:

$$G(x) / f_0 = \left(\sqrt[n]{B}\right)^{(x)}$$

$$\sqrt[x]{G(x) / f_0} = \sqrt[x]{\left(\left(\sqrt[n]{B}\right)^{(x)}\right)}$$

$$\sqrt[x]{(G(x)/f_0)} = \sqrt[n]{B}$$

$$(G(x)/f_0)^{(1/x)} = B^{(1/n)}$$

$$\left((G(x)/f_0)^{(1/x)}\right)^n = \left(B^{(1/n)}\right)^n$$

$$B = (G(x)/f_0)^{(n/x)}$$

which implies that when $x = n$, $B = G(n)/f_0$. Also, $G(n) =$

$$f_0 \cdot \left(B^{(1/n)}\right)^n$$

consequently, B is an interval:

$$\left(f_0 \cdot \left[\left(B^{(1/n)}\right)^n\right]\right)/f_0 = 1\,B/1 = B,\text{ so}$$

$$B = G(n)/f_0 = b_2 : b_1,\text{ q.e.d.}$$

Next, we show how how the primary interval of any tuning T relates to the harmonic series.

Harmonic Location Theorem

For all tunings T, the primary interval (B) of T, composed by two

tones b_2 and b_1, is an interval of the harmonic series; moreover, b_1 corresponds to the fundamental, and b_2 to the n th harmonic.

Proof

First we will note that the first tone of an interval formed by a fundamental tone and a second tone related to it by a factor of two, three, four, etc. can be considered a tone of frequency

$$f_0$$

and the second as a tone of frequency

$$f_x = f_0 \cdot (x+1),$$

where $x \in \{0, 1, 2, 3, ... N\}$.

Considering the variable value of the second tone in relationship to the constant value of the first tone, if $x = 0$, both tones are equal and the interval is a unison. If $x = 1$, the second tone will be two times greater than the first, and the interval is an octave. If $x = 2$, the second tone will be three times greater than the first, and the interval is a pure twelfth. We continue in this fashion and confirm that this sequence is the harmonic series function:

$$H(x) = f_0 \cdot (x+1)$$

which indicates that an harmonic interval ($h_2 : h_1$) is a function

$$I(x) = f_0 \cdot (x+1) / f_0$$

By the primary interval lemma, B is the interval $b_2 : b_1$, i.e.:

$$G(n)/f_0$$

and since

$$G(n) = f_0 \cdot \left(B^{(1/n)}\right)^n$$

$G(n) = f_0 \cdot B$, and therefore B is also the interval $(f_0 \cdot B)/f_0$. Finally, since by definition, $B \in \{1, 2, 3, ... N\}$, and $x \in \{0, 1, 2, 3, ... N\}$, $B \in \{x \mid x \in \{0, 1, 2, 3, ... N\}\}$, and the interval

$$(f_0 \cdot B)/f_0 \in \left\{(f_0 \cdot (x+1))/f_0\right\};$$

it follows that any $B \in \{I(x) \mid I(x) = f_0 \cdot (x+1)/f_0\}$, q. e. d.

Now we can establish that for every number assigned to the B in our first, general formula for the calculation of equal temperaments there is a correspondent harmonic in the harmonic series. In musical notation, an inexact although approximate illustration of this series may be shown by:

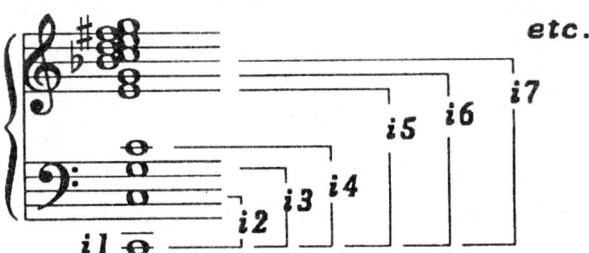

where the letter i stands for the word "interval". We observe then, that in our general formula for equal temperaments:

$$f_x = f_1 [(\sqrt[n]{B})^{(x-1)}]$$

the value of B represents an harmonic interval (i) whose geometrical progress increases in powers of its value. In the case of interval one ($i\,1$), where $x = 0$, $f_x = f_0 \cdot (0 + 1)$, there is no progress, since $f_x = 1\,f_0$, and, given that B takes on the value of $(x + 1)$, B will be equal to one, and the resulting interval ($i\,1$) will be a unison.

In the case of interval two ($i\,2$), where $x = 1$, $f_x = f_0 \cdot (1 + 1)$, $f_x = 2\,f_0$, and, given that B takes on the value of $(x + 1)$, B will be equal to two, and the resulting interval ($i\,2$) will be an octave - a power of two. In the equation for the standard tuning:

$$f_x = f_1 [(\sqrt[12]{2})^{(x-1)}]$$

the 2 represents powers of two (octaves), shown by representing ($i\,2$) in musical notation below:

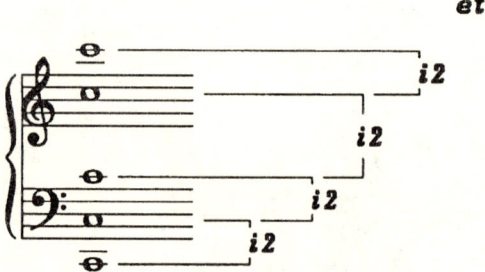

where each ($i\,2$) is to be divided into the same number (n) of equal steps.

In the case of ($i\,3$), where $x = 2$, $f_x = f_0 \cdot (2 + 1)$, $f_x = 3\,f_0$, and, given that B takes on the value of $(x + 1)$, B will be equal to three. Then, in the equation

$$f_x = f_1 [(\sqrt[n]{3})^{(x-1)}]$$

the 3 represents powers of three (pure twelfths), approximately shown in common notation by the following illustration:

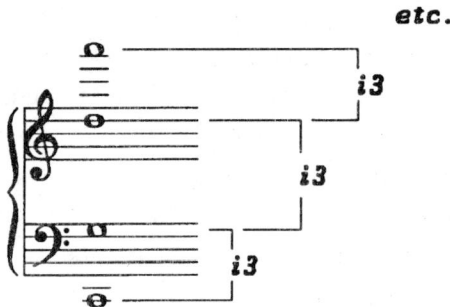

where each ($i\,3$) is to be divided into the same number (n) of equal steps. Summarizing, in the equation

$$f_x = f_1 \left[\left(\sqrt[n]{B} \right)^{(x-1)} \right]$$

the B represents a logarithmic interval defined by the distance between f_0 - the first, "fundamental" tone - and $f_0 \cdot (x+1)$, - which are the second, third, etc., harmonics - to be divided into a number n of equal steps.

It is now clear that our traditional twelve-tone-to-the-octave equal tuning is the result of dividing the interval between the fundamental of an harmonic series and the first harmonic, and that many new tunings can be obtained by dividing the distance between the fundamental of an harmonic series and any other harmonic like the third or fourth or fifth, etc.

However, all scale degrees of any tunings whose exponential bases (B) are equal to 4, 8, 16 or any other power of two are already contained in some tunings where the exponential base is 2, and therefore, the resulting tunings are redundant. Let us see this more carefully.

We will observe that when the individual size of the intervals n - in a tuning where $B = 2^y$, (y= 2, 3, 4, ... n) - is compared to the individual size of the intervals of a tuning with exponential base is equal to two the

comparison reveals that the size of the intervals of the tuning with base 2^y is a multiple of the size of the intervals of the tuning with base = 2. These redundant relationships can be expressed as a theorem.

Redundancy Theorem

For all tunings T, if the exponential base (B) of a tuning T_s ($T_s \in \{T\}$) is a number β, such that $\beta = (W^y)$, ($W, y \in \{2, 3, 4, ... N\}$), then all intervals of T_s are contained in a tuning T_t such that $T_t =$

$$G_t(x) = f_0 \cdot (\sqrt[n]{W})^{(x)}$$

Proof

By the definition of a tuning (T), $T_s =$

$$G(x) = f_0 \cdot C^{(x)}$$

where $C = \sqrt[n]{B}$. Now, let $C = \sqrt[n]{\beta}$, then

$$C = \sqrt[n]{(W^y)} \qquad \text{(since } (W^y) = \beta)$$

$$C = (W^y)^{(1/n)}$$

$$C = [W^{(1/n)}]^y,$$

and since $T_s \in \{T\}$, $T_s =$

$$G(x) = f_0 \cdot C^{(x)}, \text{ and}$$

$$T_s = G(x) = f_0 [W^{(1/n)}]^{y(x)}$$

$$= f_0 \cdot (\sqrt[n]{w})^{(yx)}.$$

By the definition of y, $y \in \{2, 3, 4, \ldots N\}$, and since $x \in \{x \mid x \in Z\}$, then $y \in \{x\}$; consequently, $T_s \in \{T_t\}$, and $n_s \in \{n_t\}$, q. e. d.

Finally, we observe that y being a coefficient of x, the value of y shows the frequency with which the intervals of T_s will appear in T_t. This means that, since the intervals are numbers to the power of x, multiplying x by a y is just adding a number y of intervals. For example, an interval x of a tuning T_t is y times the size of an interval x of the corresponding tuning T_s, and adding y times the interval x of the tuning T_s will give us the interval x of the tuning T_t. This can be easily visualized by imagining that, on a keyboard, an interval x of a tuning T_t where $y = 2$ goes from C1 to C#1. Imagine again that an interval x of a corresponding tuning T_s goes also from C1 to C#1. We will find interval x of tuning T_t mapped onto the corresponding tuning T_s noting that interval x of tuning T_t is found at yx of T_s, in this case at $2x$ of T_s. Then, if the interval x of T_s went from C1 to C#1, that is, one half step, interval x of T_t will be found at two times one half step, i.e., it will be the interval that goes from C1 to D1 in T_s.

A simple inspection can reveal these redundant relationships, especially when it comes to identities. Consider a tuning where the exponential base is equal to 4, and the number of equal steps is 24. Its formula, compared to the formula of another tuning where the base is 2 should indicate the presence of repeated intervals:

$$f_x = f_1 [(\sqrt[24]{4})^{(x-1)}]$$

In it, the relationship between the exponential base and the number of steps is given by

$$\sqrt[24]{4},$$

which is equal to $4^{(1/24)}$.

Now, $4^{(1/24)} = (2 \cdot 2)^{(1/24)}$

$$= 2^{(1/24)} \cdot 2^{(1/24)}$$

$$= 2^{[(1/24) + (1/24)]}$$

$$= (2)^{(2/24)}$$

$$= (2)^{(1/12)}$$

$$= \sqrt[12]{2},$$

which is showing us that the tuning whose exponential base equals 4 and is divided into 24 equal steps is just the tuning whose exponential base is 2 divided into 24 equal steps. Therefore, considering all tunings where B is equal to 2 is considering all tunings where B is equal to 4.

Likewise, tunings where $B = 9, 27$, or any other power of three are repetitions of some tunings where B equals three, and the same situation occurs with the numbers 16, 25, etc. Thus, a restriction established to avoid redundant tunings could be expressed as: "the value of B must not be equal to

$$(W^y)"$$

where W and y are as defined above. This restriction helps us to determine the value assigned to the constant B in order to obtain original tunings. Obviously, the series of natural numbers which are not the power of a lesser natural number other than one begins like this: 1, 2, 3, 5, 6, 7, 10, 11, 12, 13, etc.

We have seen that when B equals one, no progression occurs. Therefore, we discard the number 1 for our purposes of calculating expanded tunings. Tunings whose exponential base is 2 produce a cyclical organization in powers of two (octaves) and cannot be considered as *fully* expanded tunings even if they contain more than twelve intervals. Then, in reference to fully expanded tunings, and only in reference to fully expanded

tunings, we label all equal tunings whose exponential base (B) equals two, and that contain more than twelve equal intervals as *semi-expanded* tunings. Should their exponential base still be equal to two and their number of steps less than twelve, they will be labeled as *contracted* tunings. Semi-expanded and contracted tunings are also a wonderful and barely explored resource for new music.

In a recent and monumental study, Blackwood (1985) has given rigorous mathematical basis for the definition and study of a multiplicity of historical forms of tuning that posses a recognizable diatonic structure. In addition, the diatonic structure of some semi-expanded tunings is explored. The terms "semi-expanded" and "contracted", however, are used only in the context of the present study.

Yasser (1932) and Mandelbaum (1961) have elaborated, with foresight and precision, respectively, upon the particular advantages that the nineteen-tone-to-the-octave equal tuning offers to tonal music. Pierce (1966) discussed a contracted tuning with eight equal steps to the octave. To our knowledge, Pierce has been not only the first, but also the only one to have ever formally discussed a contracted tuning.

The reader is also referred to the dated but historically interesting findings of Busoni (1911), and Carillo, the Mexican theorist and composer whose artistic production includes many small and large works in third-tones (eighteen to the octave) quarter-tones (twenty-four to the octave) fifth tones, etc. for various instruments and for orchestra. His foremost theoretical study, the book *El Sonido 13* (1948) is still an obscure source, possibly due to very limited editions. Benjamin (1967) presents a comprehensive list of Carrillo's compositions and theoretical writings. Although in terms of quantity and magnitude of production Carrillo should probably be the most studied composer and theorist of semi-expanded music to the present, Haba, much better known than Carrillo, is also very notable for his many compositions in semi-expanded tunings and for his pedagogically oriented *Neue Harmonielehre des diatonischen, chromatischen, Viertel-Drittel-Sechstel-Zwoelftel-Ton Systems* (1927), which deals in a practical form with various rational semi-expanded tunings (rational in the sense that, provided that the octave is divided into twelve

equal semi-tones, there are six equal whole-tones to the octave; consequently, we say that each of these six whole-tones can be rationally divided into two halfs, three thirds, four quarters, and so on). For period views on Carrillo and Haba see respectively, Meyer (1929) and Overmeyer (1927). We will proceed here with our discussion of fully expanded tunings by discarding the number 2 as a possible value of B.

Also, according to the restriction mentioned above, we shall discard numbers that are powers of smaller natural numbers.

We obtain the following introductory list:

EXPANDED TUNINGS:

Value of B	Type	Number of Intervals
3	A	variable
5	B	variable
6	C	variable
7	D	variable
etc.	etc.	etc.

For example, a tuning whose exponential base (B) equals five and contains seventeen intervals per cycle will be labeled as "Expanded tuning type B-17".

In order to avoid a confusion in terminology when making reference to the musical intervals corresponding to the value of their exponential base

(*B*), we will refer to them as the following illustration shows:

Harmonic Interval	Value of *B*	Name of interval
	7	morenoctave *D*
	6	morenoctave *C*
	5	morenoctave *B*
	3	morenoctave *A*
	2	octave
	1	unison

Of course, in the context of our usual twelve-tone-to-the-octave tuning, it does not make any sense to call a twelfth a "morenoctave", but on the other hand, in the context of an expanded tuning, it becomes absolutely necessary to have a special name for the primary interval of the tuning (*B*, or the interval to be divided into *n* steps). Since the present author is apparently the first one to propose a *generalization* whereby the exponential base of an equally tempered system *T* is assigned a value from the series 3, 5, 6, 7, 10, etc. in order to yield generating intervals for different families of expanded tunings, then the generating, prime interval of an expanded tuning may be humorously designated with the expression "morenoctave" followed by a capitalized letter - where "A" corresponds to the number 3, "B" to 5, "C" to 6, "D" to 7, and so forth.

For example, in the following three pages, Figures 1, 2, and 3, show graphs of the functions of several expanded tunings. The reasons for the choice of the particular functions shown in the graphs will be discussed in Chapter Five. Notice how, due to the fact that all considered tunings are equal temperaments, the curves of the functions are smooth, whereas, in the case of unequal temperaments the functions would show zig-zag movement. In order to establish a comparison between the selected expanded tunings and the standard tuning, each graph contains also the function of the standard tuning, Oct-12.

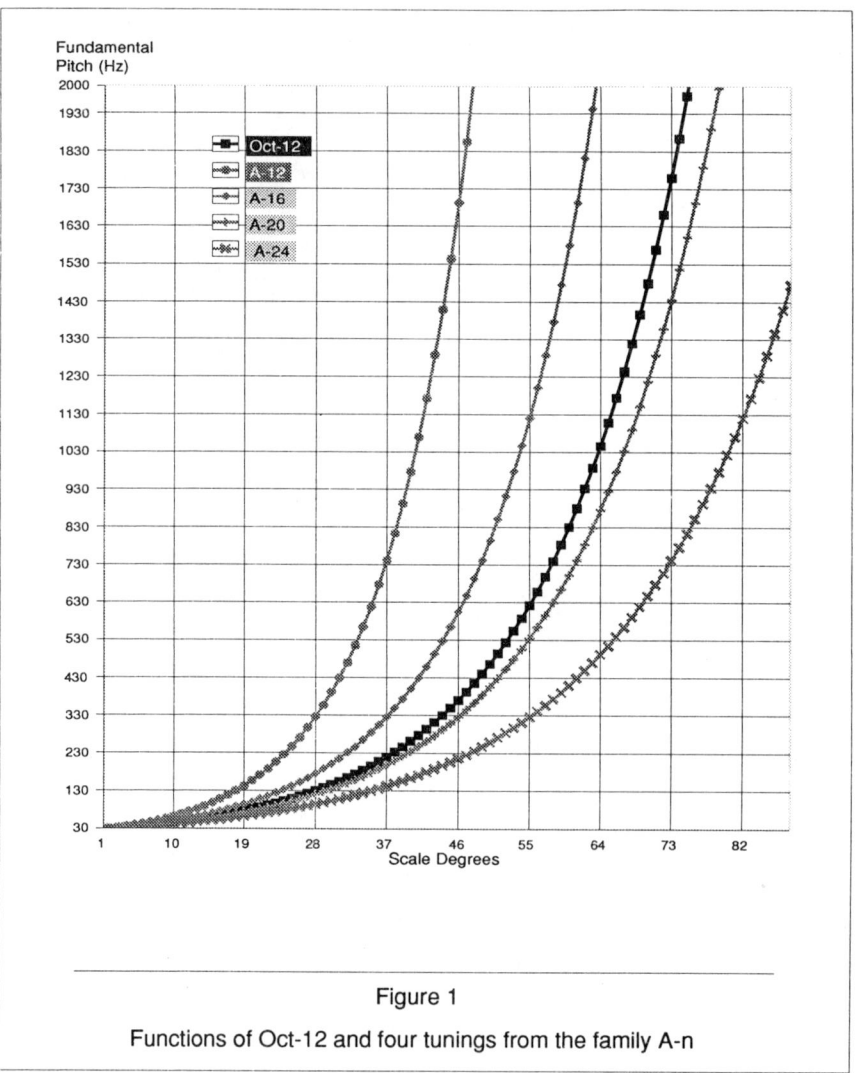

Figure 1

Functions of Oct-12 and four tunings from the family A-n

To our knowledge, there have been at least two different prior attempts to propose a name or a designation for an expanded base, and this only in connection with the particular case when $B = 3$ and $n = 13$. In the first attempt, Bohlen (1978), in a study on consonance based on

combination tones proposes the scale A-13 and calls the exponential, generating interval a *Duodezeme* ("twelfth", in English).

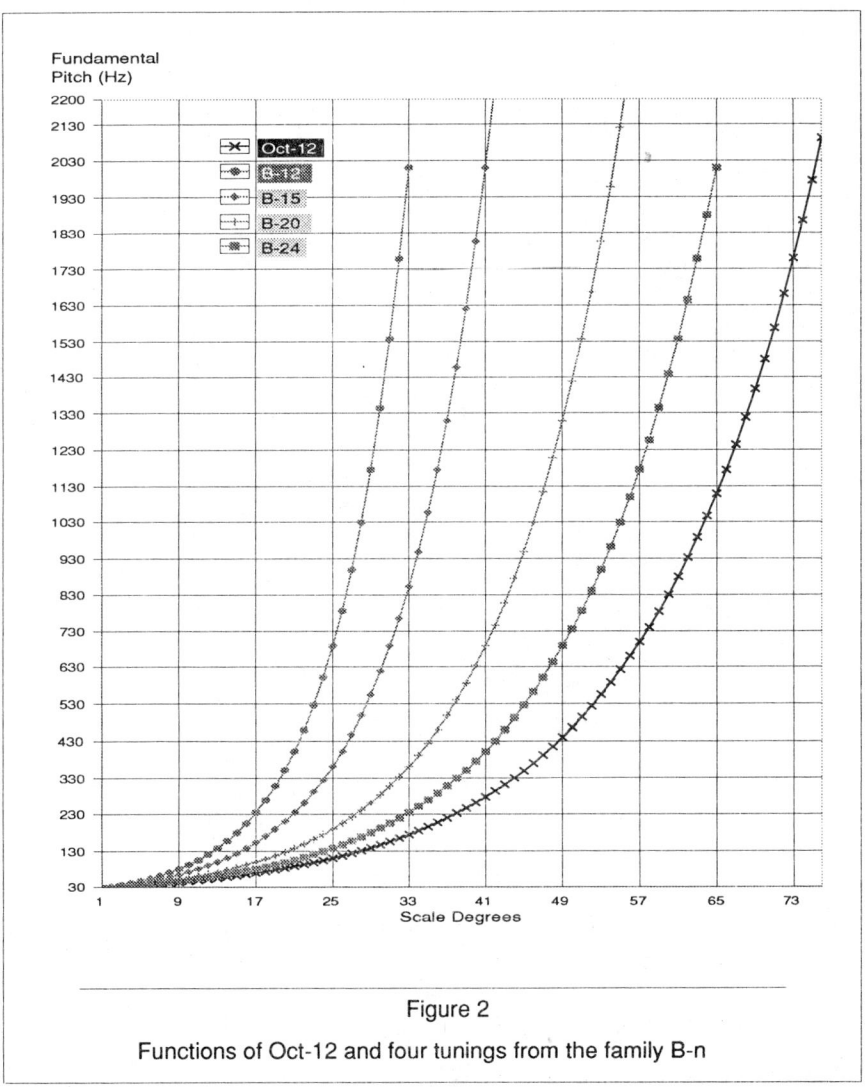

Figure 2

Functions of Oct-12 and four tunings from the family B-n

Alternatively, Mathews, Pierce et al. (1988) arrive at the same scale quite

independently from Bohlen as a result of their intonation sensitivity studies for chords with frequency ratios 3 : 5 : 7 : 9. They call the generating interval "Tritave". This particular expanded tuning - A-13 - was named by Mathews, Pierce, et al. "The Bohlen-Pierce Scale".

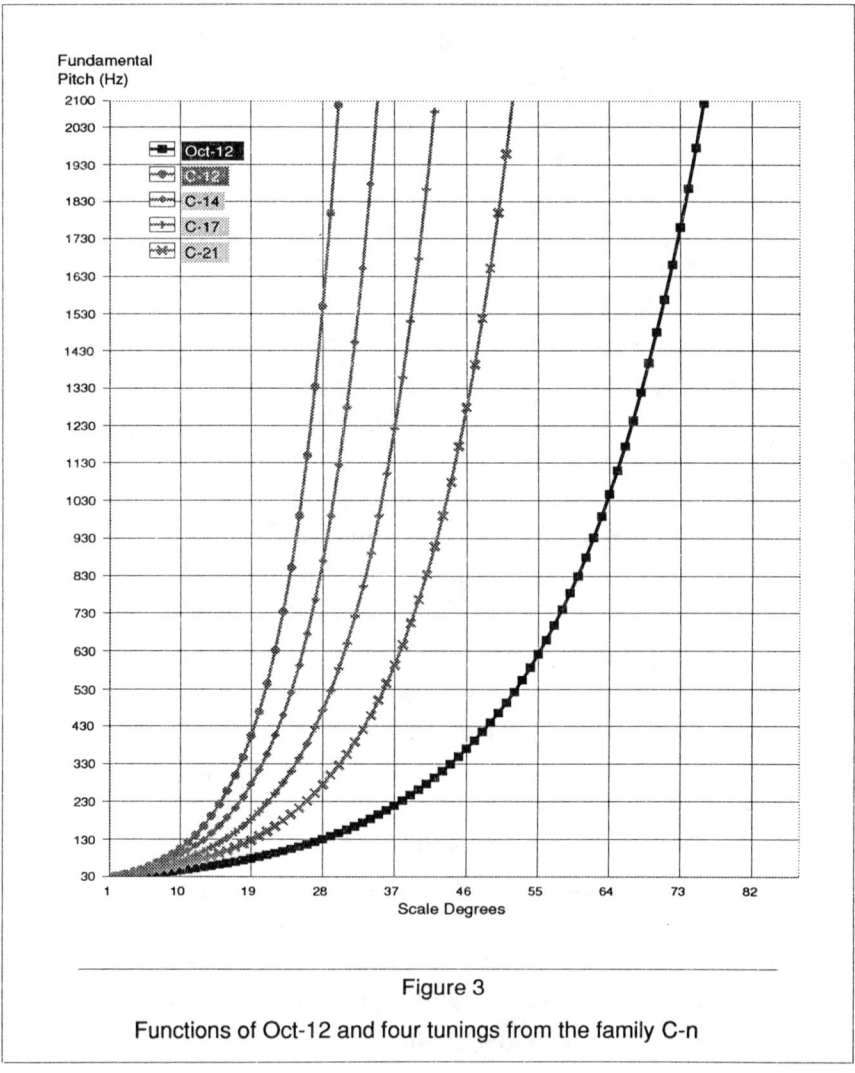

Figure 3

Functions of Oct-12 and four tunings from the family C-n

The present author worked for some years on the idea of a general set of families of expanded tunings, and had no knowledge of the two sources cited above until 1990. An original terminology had been developed, which will be kept here. This is mainly due to the desirable connotations that the word "octave" possesses - evocations of perceptual similarity - and in part to be consistent with earlier work (Moreno, 1987). Furthermore, by prefixing the word "octave" with a neutral prefix we aim to avoid using a prefix with quantitative connotations (like "twelve" or "tri"). We hope to be able to evoke conceptual images of new types of psychoacoustic similarities (expanded octaves) yet we want to avoid a straightforward confusion with the specific similarity associated with octaves. In using, for example, the arbitrary term "morenoctave" we try to make the reader think of a "different" kind of octave (a similarity) of a certain type "B", which is hierarchically associated with types "A", "C", etc., and with octaves. Our next chapter will modestly explore this similarity business. Before leaving the subject, it will be interesting to note professor Earl Schubert's (1991) comments apropos these names:

> It might be noted, in conjunction with this discussion of the term "octave" that the word itself has only indirectly to do with the number or concept "two". As nearly as I have been able to discover, it derives from the fact that the steps of the scale repeat at the eight tone - in other words, our conventional scale, from the layman's standpoint, would be modulo 8. Nor is the term directly related to the twelve equal divisions of the equally-tempered scale. By now, of course, the term is associated firmly for psychoacousticians, physicists and some musicians with the frequency ratio of two. I suggested Pierce and Mathews that, their scale should be labeled a "nonave", the Latin equivalent for designating nine, noting their adoption of nine [diatonic] scale steps before repetition rather than eight - but it didn't take.

At this point we are ready to present a formal definition of the generalized fully expanded tuning.

Definition of Fully Expanded Tunings T_e

$$T_e = G_e(x).$$

$$G_e(x) = f_0 \cdot C^{(x)}$$

where f_0 is any frequency corresponding to a pitch, $x \in \{Z\}$, and C is the principal root of B: $C = \sqrt[n]{B}$, where $n \in \{Z^+\}$, and $B = \{3, 5, 6, 7, 10 \ldots N\}$.

Evidently, there are many possible expanded tunings (from now on, the expression "expanded tunings" will be used as it should: only in reference to fully expanded tunings) most of them with a distinct harmonic organization. Some tunings manifest an acoustico-psychological signature of their own. These new tunings are psycho-geometrical structures capable of producing a sense of harmony and enharmonicity, and, in some cases, of tonality, depending on the characteristics particular to a given tuning. The exact geometrical organization of the tunings is consistent with the conditions - non-linearity of perceived stimuli, cyclical progression, equal temperament - under which the human perceptual-cognitive mechanisms are able to learn to simplify and organize physical stimuli into simpler patterns that produce a psychological sense of symmetry. We affirm this by a direct inference resulting from the consideration that expanded tunings, as shown, are structurally identical to our standard twelve-tone-to-the-octave equal tuning.

In this moment, an interesting question arises: can we predict any psychological phenomenon resulting as a consequence of physical stimuli produced by the interaction between tonal music composed using an expanded tuning and the perception of such a music? What about the dissimilarity or similarity of tones separated by one or more morenoctaves? We shall examine these central questions in the next chapter.

CHAPTER TWO

The Question of Chroma and Its Hypothetical Expansion

One of the most intriguing features of certain expanded tunings is the possibility of expanded chroma. In expanded tunings, the prime, generating interval (B , or the exponential base of an equally-tempered scale) is not an octave; instead of octaves we have other intervals from the harmonic series, here labeled as "morenoctaves". Can we predict something about the psychological implications of a system of physical stimuli defined by the equation of an expanded tuning, and very particularly, about the perception of music organized not in octaves, but in morenoctaves?

One important point here is to call attention to the fact that all Western music is organized around the phenomenon of chroma, or octave generalization, and that due to this characteristic, among others, our great music is possible. What is the nature of the chroma phenomenon? Why is it so basic to our Western musical tradition and to many more (in fact, to almost every known musical tradition)?

In the Simple Helix of Pitch (adapted and modified from Shepard, 1965) we find an illustration for the concepts of octave, octave equivalence, octave circularity and chroma (Figure 4). The characters progressing in an ascending helicoidal direction represent pitches of the twelve-tone-to-the octave equal tuning. Octave generalization is represented by any vertical

line intersecting the abscissa - or *X* axis - i. e. a group of pitches labeled always with the same letter. One commonly found definition of chroma is equivalent to the concept of octave generalization or pitch class (Forte, 1973).

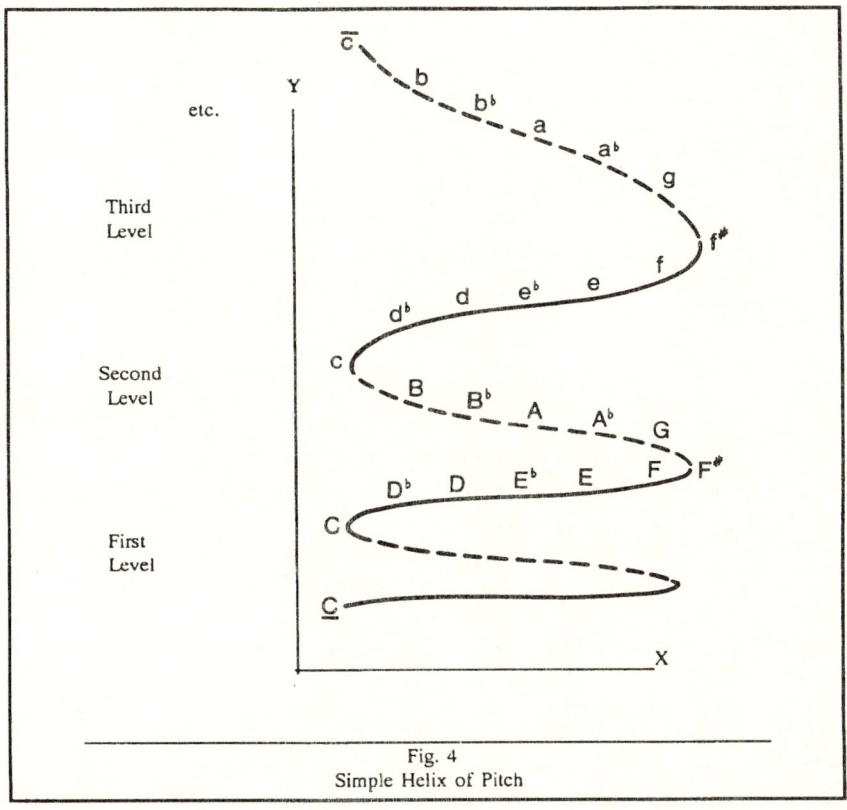

Fig. 4
Simple Helix of Pitch

Octave circularity refers to the perception of pitch in two dimensions, specific pitch level - or height- and relative chroma. Specific pitch height is exclusively correlated with frequency. Relative height - or tone chroma - is correlated with the position of a pitch within a particular octave, and it is represented by a line intersecting the ordinate - or *Y* - axis. The helix, first suggested by Drobisch (1852, 1855) is only a graphic representation of the commonly accepted idea of bidimensionality of pitch (Bachem, 1948;

Shepard, 1964). However, it has been pointed out that there is no physiological evidence that this model corresponds to an actual neural mapping of pitch in the auditory cortex (Deutsch, 1982). For the purpose of this study, we shall describe with a single term, "chroma", the concepts of octave generalization, tone chroma, and especially octave circularity.

We arrive at the crux of the matter when we consider that octaves are groups of frequencies related by powers of two. Concerning this fact, the main question is: why do we perceive octaves as different versions (different in tone height) of a same pitch class? And the next obvious question follows: Is this a natural phenomenon or the result of a learning process? Perhaps these questions should not be posed as a logical exclusive disjunction (an either-or), taking into account that the learning may come about *because* of the existence of the natural phenomenon. The importance of these questions is directly proportional to the weight of twenty-five centuries of music theory and practice in the West (and apparently in other advanced cultures) where octave similarity is one of the most basic assumptions.

Let us imagine an individual for whom the psychological mechanisms for the perception of chroma had not, for some reason, established a correlation of functional similarity for all tones separated by one or several octaves. This individual would not be able to perceive the harmonic structure of traditional music; instead, the perception of a continuum of unrelated pitch classes would take the place of our cyclically repetitive scale. However, we take it for granted that if an individual is physically and psychologically normal (for example, not mentally deficient), and provided with a more or less prolonged exposure to music that is harmonically and structurally organized on the assumption that the listener will perceive tones of the musical scale as psychologically organized by the perception of their chroma, this normal individual will learn to perceive the harmonic and structural organization of traditional music by developing consciously or, as in most cases, unconsciously, his or her associative capacity to simplify and categorize sensorial information.

On the other hand, Nettl (1956) and Sachs (1962) have pointed out that octave similarity may not be assumed and perceived by some

"primitive peoples"; thus, evolutionarily, octave similarity does not seem to be a necessary or inherent trait of very early and archaic music (Burns and Ward, 1982). Experimental evidence (Allen, 1967; Thurlow & Erchul, 1977) indicates that the concept of octave similarity is apparently the result of a learning process. Francès (1968) and Zenatti (1969) (cited in Risset, 1978) present evidence indicating that young children do not show a natural or innate sense for musical intervals. The former evidence is reviewed by Burns and Ward in Deutsch's *The Psychology of Music* (1982). Burns and Ward conclude that "octave generalization is probably a learned concept with its roots in the unique position of the octave in the spectrum of the sensory consonance of complex tone intervals" (Deutsch, 1982). But what is this "unique position" of the octave that induces the perception of chroma; and more important, is the perception of chroma limited to octaves (powers of two)? A review of current psychoacoustic experimental evidence and theories reveals that

a) there are some theories to explain the phenomenon in question, but that
b) there is no conclusive experimental evidence that any of these theories may be an accurate explanation of the chroma phenomenon.

Here is one list of theoretical explanations for octave similarity, or chroma, along with some observations. All of them are presented by several scientists and follow a line of thinking that permits loosely structuring them into a more comprehensive theory. We will examine them following Roederer (1975) and Burns and Ward (1982).

1. Coincidence of Partials or Total Consonance

Roederer (1975) affirms that octave generalization "is obviously related to the key property of the almighty octave - that of having all its harmonics coincident with the upper harmonics of the fundamental. There is no other musical interval with this property (except the unison, of

course)."

Burns and Ward (1982) state that "the exact octave is unique in that all of the partials of the tones will coincide exactly. Therefore, the octave interval will be no more dissonant than the lower frequency complex tone alone."

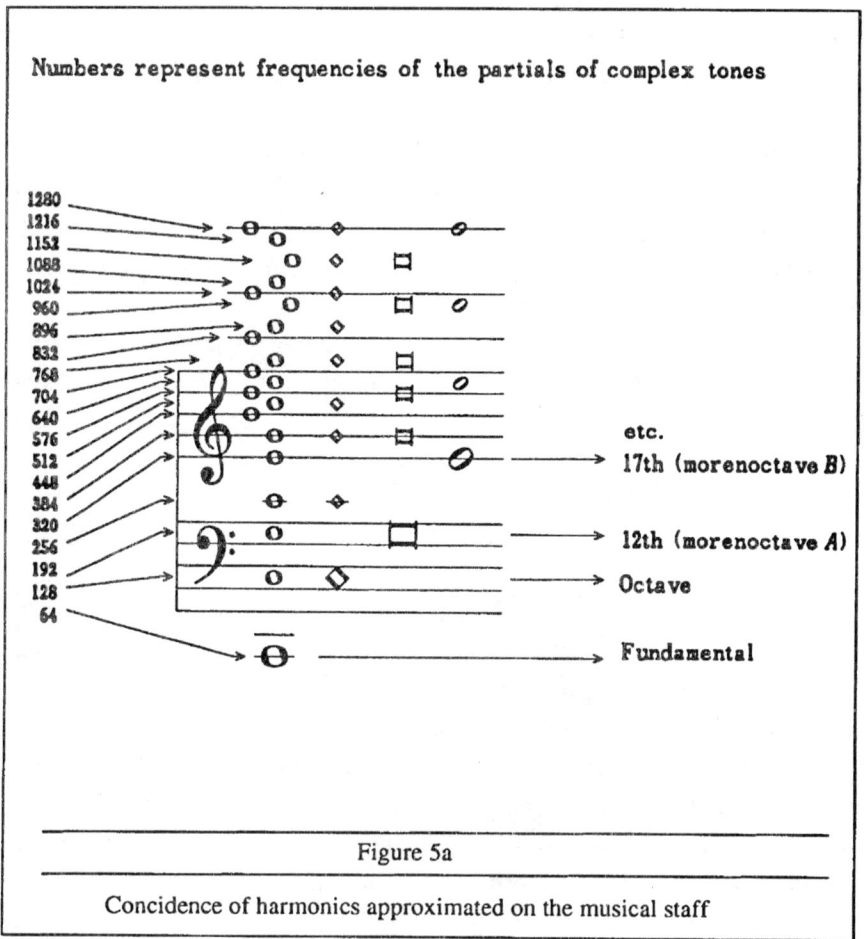

Figure 5a
Concidence of harmonics approximated on the musical staff

1.1 Observation

Both Roederer and Burns and Ward are obviously thinking within the boundaries set by our familiar assumptions about intervals when they affirm that the *only* interval that has all of its harmonics coincident with the upper harmonics of the fundamental is the octave; a closer inspection reveal that this inaccurate. Observe Figs. 5a and 5b.

In figures 5a and 5b we may see that there are two problems with the last statements of our three quoted authors. The first is that, if both tones consist only of the odd harmonics - fundamental, 3rd, 5th, etc. - and, if both tones are sounded simultaneously an octave apart, their harmonics will never coincide. A number of variations of this case will show us that even if the fundamentals are an octave apart, the particular absence of amplitude of one or more particular harmonics (as it is more likely to occur when dealing with acoustic instruments) may cause many combinations of non-matching harmonics, thus making this explanation for chroma similarity dependent on specific spectral content. But let us assume -as Roederer, and Burns and Ward actually do - that both tones are complex tones, and that they consist of their fundamentals and their upper partials. Then we have a problem again with their claim that the octave is the only case in which all the partials of the tones will coincide. There are intervals other than the octave in which all harmonics of the upper tone will coincide exactly with harmonics of the fundamental. As shown in Figures 5a and 5b, a complex tone whose fundamental frequency corresponds exactly to that of one of the harmonics of another complex tone will produce - when sounding simultaneously with such other complex tone - a series of tones that will coincide exactly with harmonics of the other such tone, provided that at least the lower tone consists of the fundamental and all its upper partials. This coincidence will occur with an incidence given by the ratio in which both complex tones are (i. e. if the ratio between the two complex tones is, say, 1 : 3, we will have a match of harmonics for every third harmonic of the fundamental tone).

Series of the fundamental	Series of the octave	Series of the pure twefth	Series of the pure seventeenth
64			
128	128		
192		192	
256	256		
320			320
384	384	384	
448			
512	512		
576		576	
640	640		640
704			
768	768	768	
832			
896	896		
960		960	960
1024	1024		
1088			
1152	1152	1152	
1216			

Figure 5b

Table of coincidence of harmonics for four complex tones

2. Repetition Rate

Roederer (1975) presents a colorful and interesting exposition of this explanation (repetition rate):

Quite generally, the existence of the chroma, i.e., the fact

that pitches differing by an octave have a degree of "similarity" that is considered identical to that of the unison, indicates that the pattern recognition process in our auditory system must respond in some "special," perhaps simplified, way when octaves are presented. Note again that the octave is the first interval in a harmonic series, and that the associated repetition rate is *identical* to that of the lower tone. Any other consonant musical interval (fifth, fourth, etc.) has an associated fundamental repetition rate that is *not* present in the original two-tone stimulus. If we remember how the pitch processor might work (Section 2.9 and Appendix II), we realize that, whenever presented with two complex tones whose fundamental frequencies f_1 and f_2 are a musical interval apart, the output from the pitch processor should contain two prominent signals representing the pitch of each tone (corresponding to f_1 and f_2), *plus* the other less prominent signals representing the repetition rate corresponding to the pair of first harmonics f_1 and f_2 and its multiples. Under normal conditions these additional signals are *discarded* as pitch sensations, a process that requires an additional "filtering" operation. Note, however, that this additional operation is not needed whenever an *octave* is presented, because no such third output signal is present. (See also page 182, *op. cit.*).

2.1 Observation

If this is true, we here notice that any of the intervals labeled by the present author as "morenoctaves A, B, C, etc." have also an associated repetition rate identical to that of the lower tone; therefore, the octave is not the only interval free of "parasitical" signals.

3. Activity of a Central Pitch Processor

Burns and Ward (1982) continue their exposition saying that:

> Another explanation is a consequence of the perception of the pitch of complex tones. Current models of complex-tone-pitch perception (Gerson & Goldstein, 1978; Terhardt, 1974a) assume that complex-tone pitch perception is a pattern recognition task in which a "central pitch processor" attempts to match the partials of the complex tone with the best-fitting harmonic series.
>
> A consequence of this type of operation will be a certain amount of octave ambiguity in the model predictions of fundamental pitch. For example, a complex tone consisting of all harmonics of 200 Hz might also be estimated as even harmonics of 100 Hz. Such ambiguity has indeed, been found in complex-tone pitch-perception experiments (Gerson & Goldstein, 1978; Houtsma, 1979).

3.1 Observation

In regard to this widely accepted model, we observe that if the second harmonic is weak or missing, a progressively less probable, but nonetheless possible, amount of ambiguity in the model predictions of fundamental pitch could be elicited at the twelfth and at those harmonic intervals here labeled as "morenoctaves". Following their example, a complex tone consisting of all harmonics of 200 Hz might also be estimated as every third harmonic of 66.666...Hz.

4. Uniqueness

Burns and Ward (1982) conclude that "...octave generalization...has its origins in the octave's unique position in the range of sensory consonance

of complex tone intervals."

4.1 Observation

As we have seen, the position of the octave in the range of sensory consonance is not so clearly unique, perhaps it is just *preponderant*. In view of the preceding arguments and their correspondent observations, the author advances the following initial hypothetical conclusions:

Conclusions

1. Perception of the chroma dimension seems to be achieved by a neuropsychological mechanism that learns to re-categorize lower-level neurophysiological processes into a simpler, more abstract higher-level perceptual function.

2. Prolonged exposure to music in which the octave is a common and reiterated interval seems to trigger the spontaneous operation of the mechanism.

3. Perceptual neuropsychological processes related to the psychological dimension of chroma seem to include factors such as:

    - coincidence of partials or total consonance
    - activity patterns of a central pitch processor
    - repetition rate

    all of which indicate that perhaps the chroma phenomenon may not be exclusively restricted to the stimuli elicited by octaves, since there are other intervals that may elicit stimuli with similar consequences (similar coincidence of partials, similar activity patterns of a central pitch processor, and equal repetition rates).

4. Perception of chroma dimension as given and determined by intervals (of an harmonic series) other than the octave does not seem to be impossible. The term "expanded chroma" is applied to this type of hypothetical expanded perception of the chroma dimension, and the names "morenoctave A, B, C, etc" are given to the harmonic intervals if they refer to the prime intervals of expanded tunings.

5. Given the facts that the octave is the first interval of the harmonic series, that its harmonics coincide with those of the fundamental in a 2:1 ratio, and that historically, the octave has been the first interval of this type to be consciously used as a chroma-inducing factor, it seems reasonable to conclude that the intervals labeled as "morenoctaves A, B, C, etc." would produce an increasingly less spontaneous perception of the chroma dimension due to the fact that every new expansion would stretch the perceptual associative capabilities of the neuropsychological mechanisms responsible for the perception of the chroma dimension. The perceptual limit remains to be determined by future musical practice, if perception of expanded chroma is possible at all.

6. The intervals that could induce perception of the chroma dimension would appear in a strict hierarchical dependence given by the form:

Traditional chroma:
octaves

Expanded chroma:
morenoctave   A
morenoctave   B
morenoctave   C
etc.

Therefore, in a tuning organized in octaves, no other interval than the octave would induce a spontaneous perception of such hypothetical expanded chroma. If a tuning is organized in morenoctaves type-A, the tuning would induce perception of expanded chroma type-A, if, and only if, no other interval of the tuning is an octave or closely approximates the octave; consequently, in a tuning of the family A-n and containing no quasi-octaves, no other interval than the morenoctave A would induce perception of an increasingly expanded chroma. This process would continue on hierarchically.

To summarize, for every equal tuning, the presence of octaves would inhibit the perception of morenoctaves; the presence of octaves and morenoctaves type-A would inhibit the perception of morenoctaves type-B, C, D; the presence of octaves, morenoctaves type-A, and morenoctaves type-B would inhibit the perception of morenoctaves type-C, D, E, etc.

7. Finally, it seems reasonable to expect that conclusions judging the practical musical value of such hypothetical expansion of chroma perception could emanate only from a substantial period of musical practice or from conclusive experimental evidence.

CHAPTER THREE

Implementation of Expanded Tunings

Now that our discussion has reached a modest but consistent degree of theoretical insight, we can begin to approach certain practical problems. Our goal in this section is not to exhaust all possible solutions to the problems in question, but to demonstrate that these practical problems are rather insignificant. By proving this statement, we expect to cast out the seemingly pervading view that composing music based on different forms of intonation involves enormous mathematical and technical problems.

If a composer decides to work with expanded, contracted and semi-expanded tunings, the following group of problems may require the implementation of a method destined to minimize the amount of time to be spent in mechanical tasks and to optimize the process of decision-making that will probably have to precede the composition of particular music materials or even improvisations (due to the immense quantity of options available for exploration). In this approach, we will divide the whole group of problems into two overlapping but distinguishably separated groups: problems related to machines, and problems related to information. Consequently, we have:

a) **Mechanical problems**

    1. Instrumentation

    2. Calculation

b) **Decision-making**

    1. Selection of a tuning

    2. Determination of initial scale degree's value for a selected tuning according to timbre

    3. Notation

    4. Harmonic organization

By instrumentation we mean the process that involves the selection and use of the instrument or instruments capable of total tuning control. Naturally, the level of accuracy must be very high. For this reason, the only practical alternative is to use a musical instrument whose intonation can be carefully and rapidly controlled by computerized tuning tables.

The first step in developing a method for the implementation of expanded tunings is, then, to become familiar with the possibilities and operations of a selected computer-controlled instrument or instruments, particularly with three operations: individual tuning of each scale degree, global transposition of an already value-determined tuning, and memory storage of an already value-determined tuning.

The individual tuning of each scale degree demands the consideration of two factors: units of tuning, and the actual act of programming the value of each scale degree in tuning units. Units of tuning may be determined nonlinearly or linearly. The conventional linear units for sound frequency are Hertz (Hz). The conventional non-linear units for pitch are cents (cts).

A single cent is equal to a one-hundredth of a semi-tone in twelve-tone-to-the-octave equal tuning; that is, there are 1200 cents between two tones separated by an octave. However, cents are only one among the many possible kinds of non-linear units, and some computerized musical instruments may be preprogrammed to work with other types of non-linear units, for example, 1024 tuning units per octave (that is, 85.33 tuning units per twelve-tone-to-the-octave equally tempered semi-tone). From now on, we will perform calculations and analyses in these two types of non-linear units, cents (cts) and tuning units (TU: 1024 per octave). It is of certain practical relevance to become familiar with the particular psychoacoustical meaning of the tuning units with which the selected instrument or instruments work.

The second aspect of the individual tuning of each scale degree includes two possibilities, direct programming of previously calculated values for each scale degree, or automatic programming by transferring data from a computer interfaced to the computerized musical instrument; the interfaced computer runs a program that calculates the value of each scale degree. In the first case, it is necessary to learn the particular procedure to access the computerized musical instrument's tuning tables and program the values of each scale degree. The second possibility is obviously much more practical, given that a considerable amount of time is saved by having an independent program that calculates the values of every scale degree and automatically transfers the data to the computerized musical instrument. Since such a program running on an interfaced computer (or on the computerized musical instrument, if it has this capability) is related to the problem of calculation, we will discuss it further ahead in more detail.

Global transposition of an already value-determined tuning is a very valuable function in case the tuning tables of a computerized music instrument may not be automatically returned to a transposed position by a program running on an interfaced computer. Ideally, every computerized musical instrument should be able to perform this operation.

Similarly, in the absence of a program automatically tuning the tuning

tables of a computerized musical instrument, the memory storage of a value-determined tuning (or many different tunings) becomes an important time-saving requisite. In case the computerized musical instrument's internal memory is insufficient, it is convenient to know whether the instrument is able to transmit the tuning's data to a storage device from which they can be later instantaneously retrieved. The storage function in coordination with the transposing function may perform, in terms of time economy, as a less successful substitute for the aforementioned calculating program. It is now evident that a calculating program with automatic access to the tuning tables is highly desirable. Therefore, the second step in developing a method for the implementation of expanded tunings should be devising a system to tune the musical instrument instantaneously, whether it be by means of internal or external memory storage in coordination with global transposition, or by means of a calculating program controlling the tuning tables. This being clear, we may determine that the third step is the development of a method of calculation.

Logically, we need to know the value (in whatever tuning units the selected instrument may require) of every scale degree of a selected tuning in reference to the value of an initial scale degree. Hence, unless the musical instrument's tuning units are Hertz, we need to know how the instrument or instruments relate their linear tuning units to an absolute scale in Hertz, for example, observing that with a particular instrument 440 Hz are equal to so many cts, so many TU, or whatever. Once this is determined, we select a formula and proceed to calculate each scale degree of a chosen tuning, and again, we have to notice that in the absence of a computer calculating program, we will have to spend some time calculating by hand with the help of pocket scientific calculator. This task is tedious but simple and requires no further comment, since it has been already illustrated by means of the tutorial on page five of the first Chapter.

The best solution is, of course, to have a computer program specifically written to calculate the value of a number of scale degrees in any kind of equal tuning. The program, which may be called the "Music Scale Generator," should be written having in mind the specific kind of tuning units in which the user is interested. Upon entering the program, the

user will have to define the desired tuning in the following terms:

    a)   Exponential base of the scale

    b)   Number of equal divisions between exponential powers of the scale

    c)   Total number of scale degrees to be calculated

    d)   Value of initial scale degree

    e)   An option to transmit values to the tuning tables of the music instrument (if possible)

In other words, the program should prompt the user to:

    1)   Enter the base of the scale

    2)   Enter the number of divisions

    3)   Enter the value of the first degree

    4)   Enter the number of scale degrees and ask,

    5)   Do you want to transmit data to synthesizer?

    6)   Do you want to print data?

    7)   Do you want to calculate another scale (start again)?

A music scale generator program is most useful when it can transmit its data to the tuning tables of the music instrument. This strategy solves the problem of storing tuning data by avoiding it altogether.

Let us make a summary of the problems presented so far by reducing them to two abstract cases. In the first case, we imagine a composer restricted to a totally tunable musical instrument and a pocket calculator. In the second case, we imagine a composer able to use an independent computer program in addition to a totally tunable instrument or instruments. Figure 6 is an illustration of these two abstract cases.

Now we consider problems related to the systematization of a decision-making process. Before going any further in this chapter, the author wants to reiterate that all suggested solutions to be presented here are merely examples, the basic idea being that a theory of expanded tunings calls for a method of implementation and that this is an easy and relatively simple problem. The first of our decisions will be to select one or more from among many possible tunings. Naturally, we can do it randomly, or we may initiate a systematic empirical exploration, but this is a poor approach, and redundant, since that will be necessary anyway. In short, we want to know how and why we decide to select a tuning. This demands a method of analysis of the comparative properties of tunings, that is, a comparative analysis of a group of tunings. In turn, a comparative analysis of a group of tunings presupposes that we have already made a selection, choosing from an unlimited number of possibilities. Once we have selected the group, we must establish clearly what we want to know about the relationship of a tuning with respect to the other tunings in the group. Finally and obviously, we devise a system to obtain this information in the clearest way and in the shortest time.

Let us develop, then, all of this as an example and devise one possible system of comparative analysis. First, we decide the size and the members of the group. A little more than 120 tunings seems to be enough to include a great variety of tunings (many more in fact, than we could reasonably and empirically explore in a short time) and yet not great enough to make the analysis impractical, too theoretical, or even meaningless.

I	II
- Select appropriate instrument(s)	- Select instrument(s) and /or computer(s)
- Learn to use individual tuning and transposition functions	- Find out tuning units requirements
- Find out tuning units requirements	- Write calculating program
- Calculate scale with pocket calculator	- Interface calculating program to the instrument's tuning tables
- Input scale's values	
- Save in storage medium	
- Retrive scale and adjust values using transposition	

Figure 6
Initial steps to use different tunings for performance

This number allows us to select twenty or more tunings of five different families of tunings. A great deal of interesting data would result from the comparison between expanded tunings, and contracted and semi-expanded tunings (octave-based tunings). Accordingly, we decide that our first family of tunings will be the family of contracted and semi-expanded tunings. The other four families will be the families of tunings A-n (where the capital letter stands for the morenoctave to be divided in a number of

equal steps, and the letter "n" for the number of steps), B-n, C-n, D-n. How many steps per octave or morenoctave will each of the twenty tunings have? Our decision may seem arbitrary again, but let us suppose that we have the feeling that a tuning with less than five steps per octave or morenoctave is practically useless, and that a tuning with more than fifty steps per octave or morenoctave begins to be a little too complicated to handle. Then, we decide to determine the members of the set in the following way:

1. **Family of octave-based tunings** (20)

    Members:
    > All tunings from 5 steps to 24 steps to the octave

2. **Family A-n** (20)

    Members:
    > All tunings from 8 to 27 steps to the morenoctave A

3. **Family B-n** (20)

    Members:
    > All tunings from 12 to 31 steps to the morenoctave B

4. **Family C-n** (29)

    Members:
    > All tunings from 12 to 40 steps to the morenoctave C

5. **Family D-n** (37)

    Members:
    > All tunings from 12 to 48 steps to the morenoctave D

We proceed to determine what we want to know about this group of tunings, having in mind that the resulting information will guide our particular compositional interest. Let us suppose that we want to know the following:

1. **Intervals existent in each tuning**

    Purpose:
    Consonance-dissonance analysis

2. **Constant of each tuning**

    Purpose:
    To elaborate a list of all 126 tunings ordered according to their perceptual proximity.

3. **Perceptual proximity**

    Purpose:
    To estimate how similar or dissimilar the perception of one tuning is from another.

4. **Comparative Originality**

    Purpose:
    To compare each expanded tuning to all twenty contracted and semi-expanded tunings in order to elaborate a list that shows which expanded tuning are more original (different) in comparison to contracted and semi-expanded tunings.

5. **Approximation to chroma intervals** (interference of foreign

chroma-inducing families of expanded tunings)

Purpose:
>To know whether an expanded tuning contains an interval that so closely approximates the chroma-inducing interval of a different family of tunings that the chroma of the tuning in question will not be perceived by the listener. According to our sixth conclusion at the end of Chapter Two, a approximation to a chroma interval of an immediately preceding different family of tunings (within a given expanded tuning) would obscure the clear perception of the chroma of the tuning in which the approximation occurred.

6. **Total chroma originality**

Purpose:
>To know which tunings among all 106 expanded tunings are freer from the interference of chroma-inducing intervals foreign to their own family, and consequently more likely to produce a sense of expanded chroma, if this were possible.

7. **Total originality of an expanded tuning**

Purpose:
>To compare the results of comparative originality analysis with the results of total chroma originality analysis in order to elaborate a list that shows which tunings are more original according to the results of the comparison.

Accordingly, we proceed to devise a system to obtain these data. The system will consist of three consecutive steps:

a) Elaboration of a set of instructions

b) Calculations

c) Elaboration of tables

The instructions will have to be written in such a way that subsequent data may be derived from former data. Obviously, a computer program has to be written in order to calculate and compare thousands of numbers.

The calculation process is irrelevant to our discussion. We will present the results of this example in the form of tables containing all the data we have decided to find (see Appendix II). A more detailed discussion on the manner in which this set of tables has been elaborated, and on some of the most obvious practical applications of these tables, will appear within Chapter Five in connection with the examination of the tuning A-12.

It is a good idea to have these or similar tables always at hand so that whenever we decide to work with expanded - or contracted and semi-expanded tunings - we may be conscious of our reasons for selecting a particular tuning, the implications of this selection, and some of the characteristics of the tuning. The reader is encouraged to analyze carefully all of our tables' and make judgments on the musical possibilities of the tunings that most interest him or her. Meanwhile, we should keep in mind the fact that these tables are very useful in many respects. For example, in musical practice, and only in musical practice, there are tunings that are more interesting than others. The tuning A-19 is revealed to be utterly uninteresting from a practical point of view, because perceptually, it is extremely similar to the usual twelve-tone-to-the-octave equal tuning, the difference between their constants (C in our definition of the generalized equal tuning - see page 6, Chapter One) being the difference between 85.421052 TU and 85.333333 TU, that is, 0.087719 TU, and of course, due to the presence of quasi-octaves in each cycle of the scale, the possibility of expanded chroma perception is ruled out.

CHAPTER FOUR

Expanded Notation

Our next point to consider is to decide how to notate expanded, contracted or semi-expanded tunings. What exactly is the problem? Musicians use a system of notation in which conventionally lines and spaces represent the position of the notes of the diatonic scale. This system has been used for so long that it has evolved to a stage of great perfection. There have been, within the Western tradition, however, other systems of notation called tablatures. Eventually, lute and keyboard musicians decided to notate music for their instruments exclusively on the traditional staff. Musicians who played on instruments of fixed intonation realized that, as far as their instruments were concerned, the staff could as well be considered a tablature. For a singer, a notated pitch is an instruction that means: "find (within the continuum of your register) this pitch, determine its exact intonation in regard to the harmony, and sing it". For the player of an instrument of fixed intonation, like a keyboard, a notated pitch means "activate the mechanism that corresponds to the notated pitch." There are no decisions to make concerning the intonation of a notated pitch; thus, in the case of a keyboard player, the reading becomes the mechanical process of depressing the keys that correspond to positions on the staff. This is the tablature principle.

A musician who is not activating an instrument of fixed intonation depends on the subtle mechanism of a very well trained musical memory. The player must know exactly what is the desired pitch before producing it. When we think of the great amount of different intervals characteristic of different expanded or semi-expanded tunings, we immediately realize that a musician singing, or playing on an instrument that does not have fixed intonation is at a great disadvantage (as far as expanded, contracted, or semi-expanded tunings are concerned). Even if the instrument has integrated sensors that control a synthesizer (as some do) the player still has to determine the pitch, which means that the player knows or must know the desired pitch beforehand.

Leaving the human voice aside, the problem leads us to considerations regarding the expansion of music instruments. An extensive application of expanded, semi-expanded, and contracted tunings to the art of music composition demands that every music instrument be capable of total control of pitch and timbre. We see now that, in addition to this, every expanded instrument (a musical instrument with total timbre and tuning control) must provide the means to ensure programmable fixed intonation. Otherwise, and provided that instruments were adapted so as to be able to perform in any kind of intonation, the player would have to learn each interval of every desired new tuning, a monstrously paramount task more appropriate for a computer than for a human memory.

At the time this book is being written, the only expanded instruments are synthesizers or computers, and, in terms of intonation control, only a few synthesizers are truly expanded instruments. Most modern synthesizers are in actuality music computers. A music computer may be programmed to play by itself or may be played through a mechanical controller. All acoustical instruments are mechanical controllers, and in principle, as such, can control or be controlled by a music computer. The marriage between the music computer and the acoustical instrument is, in the present author's opinion, the next step in the evolution of music instruments.

Computer control can provide the means that allow an instrument of non-fixed intonation to perform as an instrument of fixed intonation and to

predetermine such intonation according to any tuning scheme. At the same time, the mechanical instrument can control the music computer to obtain a variety of timbral schemes. As mentioned before, this is a matter of digital, and instrument, and miniaturization technology. Since these hybrid expanded-acoustic instruments are theoretically possible and a logical step towards the next stage of their own evolution, it is not farfetched to consider the possibility that such instruments will be produced in the future, specially if a large repertory of music in expanded and semi-expanded forms of intonation is written within the next centuries.

Consequently, in view of the fact that at present the performance of almost any piece of music in expanded intonation has to be realized through a synthesizer or a computer, and that if acoustical instruments ever become expanded, programmable fixed intonation will emancipate the musician from depending on pitch memory, then we may conclude that the performance of music in expanded intonation is most probably to be realized exclusively on instruments of programmable fixed intonation (unless it is sung). This conclusion is of importance because from the point of view of an instrument of fixed intonation, our present system of notation can be considered as a tablature.

Illuminated by this reflection, we may reasonably decide that notation of expanded, contracted and semi-expanded tunings will have to follow the tablature principle - a notated pitch on the score does not correspond to any pitch in particular, but rather to a mechanism to be activated, the actual pitch being the result of the tuning of the instrument, which will have to be indicated in the score (we will discuss, in Chapter Five, and in connection with the discussion of our Music Example no. 1: "Ave Maria" a solution to the problem of singing accurately in expanded forms of intonation). What kind of a tablature should this be?

Our present system of notation is so perfect and so generalized that it is actually more convenient and certainly more realistic to retain it with all its features than to invent a new one. At the same time, our present system of notation will have to expand in order to include additional information.

The expansion may be accomplished through the use of a hitherto unused dimension of our system of notation (not unlike the way in which

the expansion of our new tunings is accomplished, that is, through the use of a hitherto unused dimension of our system of scalar exponentiation). What is the new additional information that the expansion is supposed to convey? In all tunings containing less or more than twelve pitches per cycle (per octave or morenoctave) and notated in conventional notation following the tablature principle, the *class* of a notated pitch becomes difficult to identify at first sight, and demands additional means of identification that allow the reader to identify its class affiliation at once in order to analyze the harmony.

Let us illustrate this paragraph. Suppose we have a five-octave keyboard tuned to the tuning B-15, or to the tuning Oct-15 (fifteen steps per morenoctave *B*, and fifteen steps per octave, respectively) or to any other expanded tuning with fifteen steps per cycle. Let us suppose that the first key of the keyboard is C, and that we will call it Cl. We decide to notate this initial Cl in the following form on the staff:

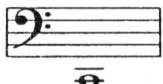

According to the characteristic of the tuning, the beginning of the new cycle occurs fifteen keys after Cl, (counting Cl as key number zero) that is on D#2. Therefore, whenever we want to notate the pitch that sounds when we depress the key D#2, we notate:

The beginning of the subsequent cycle occurs on the key F#3, and will be notated:

Evidently, in a fifteen-note tuning, the notes of the chord

belong to the same pitch class, although they do not share the same name. The dissociation between pitch class and name is a source of confusion when notating tunings of less or more than twelve steps per cycle in our standard tablature form and transforms harmonic analysis into an absurdly complicated and slow process.

On the other hand, due to the different varieties and to the great number of possible tunings, tablature notation is the only practical solution for the notation of expanded, contracted and semi-expanded tunings, and the possibility of inventing a new tablature (or for the same purpose a new keyboard layout) is probably too unrealistic (at least for our generation and a few more coming). Hence, we conclude that we have to apply a principle of expansion to solve the problem of dissociation between pitch class and name. In other words, we must expand the capabilities of our system of notation in such a way that the expanded notation clearly indicates the pitch-class affiliation of any notated pitch regardless of its name. A reader-performer-analyzer must understand immediately the pitch class of a notated pitch which he or she is seeing at any time. To this end, we apply our method of expansion, which consists in discovering an unused dimension of a basic characteristic of our Western musical tradition, in this case a new dimension of notation.

Our system of music notation makes use of the following elements:

- musical symbols (standard and non-standard, if necessary)

- spatial patterns determined by horizontal lines

- numbers

- words (traditionally in Italian, currently in any language)

It does not make use of a variety of colors. Only black ink is used. Introducing a variety of colors seems an excellent idea because:

- Color is not a commonly used dimension of our system of notation.

- The use of color does not alter the characteristics of our system of notation.

- Color works well for the purpose of identifying a pitch class at first sight.

These reasons are of such weight that they by far counterbalance inconveniences such as raising the cost of the edition or the extra time spent in coloring the score. In addition, we must consider that computer technology offers a practical and increasingly affordable solution to the problems involved in the process of coloring and the printing of a colored score. As a matter of fact, composers, arrangers, and music publishers have realized that the computer is a necessary tool in their trade, even to the point that currently the art of music engraving is literally disappearing. Furthermore, in the near future it may not even be necessary to print the score of a composition, since, evidently, it is more practical to keep it in digital form, and this means that "the cost of the edition" will not raise because of the price of color inks or fancier paper. The decision is made then, and we proceed to express it in the form of four rules and one

exception:

Rules for the use of color in music notation:

1. A tuning has as many pitch classes as it has steps per cycle.

2. To every pitch class, a different color, and only one different color shall be assigned.

3. Color represents pitch. No enharmonic spelling shall alter the one-to-one absolute correspondence between color and pitch.

4. Only note heads are to be colored.

Exception:

- Any tuning containing twelve steps per cycle shall be notated in black and white.

Naturally, in a tuning with twelve steps per cycle, the correspondence between pitch class and pitch name is clear enough, and we may dispense with color even if enharmonic spelling obscures this correspondence once in a while. Other points to be considered regarding notation of expanded, contracted or semi-expanded tunings are:

a) information about the tuning for which the piece is written,

b) the initial frequency, and

c) the correspondence between keyboard and staff. A way to indicate this information could be by simply specifying:

   1) Name of piece, etc.

2) Tuning family and number within the family

3) Initial frequency of the first key

4) Name of the first key

5) Position (on the staff) of the first key

We repeat, for the sake of clarity, that tunings are classified according to their family and number of steps, the first family being the family of contracted and semi-expanded tunings or tunings that contain equal division of the octave. The abbreviation "Oct-n" indicates that the octave is divided into n equal steps. Similarly, "A-n" indicates that the morenoctave A is to be divided in n equal steps. Examples of such abbreviations are:

- *Oct-19*   means:
    an octave divided into nineteen equal steps.
- *A-23*   means:
    a morenoctave A divided into twenty-three equal steps.

In the present author's experience, sight-reading at the keyboard is a surprisingly mechanical task. Sight-reading a piece in an expanded tuning has not presented any extraordinary problems when, during informal tests, the author has asked a professional musician to sight read a piece in an expanded tuning on a synthesizer - even if the musician has perfect pitch.

Finally, we will make some comments regarding our last two decision-making problems: determination of the initial scale degree value for a given tuning, and harmonic organization. The determination of the frequency of the initial scale degree of a tuning has to be made in accordance to the acoustical characteristics of the overall timbral scheme of the tuning. Many electroacoustically generated timbres will produce satisfactory results only within a narrow frequency range. Currently, if one intends to sound most synthetic timbres below their lower efficiency point, the results will be barely audible, in terms of pitch, or not audible at all.

If, on the other hand, one surpasses the timbre's upper efficiency point, the audible result will be side bands, aliases, or other artifacts of digitization. In any case, the specific acoustical characteristic of the timbre will be lost. Therefore, whenever implementing an expanded tuning into a specific timbral scheme, we should correlate the values of the tuning to the practical range of the timbre. This demands a certain amount of time spent in experimentation for each particular case.

Our last decision concerns the specific harmonic organization of a particular tuning. Evidently, at the time this book is being written, the vast and newly discovered world of harmonic organization of each possible practical expanded tuning remains open and virgin to exploration and experimentation. It is now the privilege and responsibility of adventurous composers to explore the harmonic possibilities of new tunings. We may expect that, as in the past, successful compositions will constitute the basis for harmonic practice and theories of the future.

So far we have been through a process of investigation that began in Chapter One with analysis, and subsequently proceeded to the establishment of a hypothesis - the possibility of expanded chroma - and finally to point to the development of a methodology based on the consequences of our investigation.

In the next chapters we will continue with a slightly different style. Analysis, and - in the last two chapters- the author's opinions on the subject of expanded tunings will combine with musical examples in order to relate the topic to the broader range of its implications in the context of contemporary and future art.

CHAPTER FIVE

Probability of Expanded Chroma

Perhaps the most evasive question in this study is that of the real perceptibility of expanded chroma. Let us begin with some experimentation by listening to our first Music Example: Ave Maria, a vocal piece written to illustrate a few basic characteristics of the tuning A-12 (please see Appendix I for the score of Ave Maria, and Appendix III for the recording). Tuning A-12 does not contain any close approximation to an octave *within any one cycle of the scale*, and according to the conclusions reached at the end of Chapter Two, since the harmonic organization of the piece is tonally oriented, the tuning could induce expanded chroma perception. By "tonally oriented" we mean that through most of the length of the piece we can at least establish a series of preponderant single tones which justifiably appear as "centers", even if the resulting harmony is too diffuse, extended, or vague to permit the positive establishment of "tonality" in any of its traditionally accepted definitions.

The piece consists of a melody on the Latin text of the Ave Maria, and of a chordal accompaniment. The span of the melody is one morenoctave *A* (approximately within and throughout the range of a professional soprano). Once the piece is played through, the melody is played again, but this time it is played and sung one morenoctave lower; the chordal accompaniment

remains in the same place. By playing the piece again with the melody displaced one morenoctave lower, we intend to find out whether the chords and the chord progressions remain "the same". Of course, if by the word "same" we understand an exact octave relationship, we are expecting something that will not take place because this is not an octave relationship. If, however, we contrive the meaning of the word "same" in the new sense of similar relationship (perceived similarity) or morenoctave similarity, we are on better grounds to judge the phenomenon taking place when the melody sounds a morenoctave lower.

The question "could this be a new expanded octave relationship?" would perhaps be better approached in these terms: "Do chords conserve their identity after the morenoctave displacement?" "Do chord progressions have similar harmonic functions during the morenoctave displacement?" "Do tonic chords, especially the first and the last, sound really like conclusive tonic chords during the morenoctave displacement?" This piece, although extremely simple, presents interesting chord progressions, but an analysis of the chord progressions should not be realized within the frame of harmonic analysis of a piece in twelve twelve-tone-to-the-octave equal temperament. The reason is obvious. The intervals of this tuning are not the intervals of our usual tuning. Shall we think that the interval of a second in this tuning sounds like a major third? We may think it does, but it is not a major third. Shall we think it is a version of a major third? It is understandable that the listener will try to match certain intervals of this tuning with the closest intervals of the twelve-tone-to-the-octave equal tuning, and that the listener will possibly attempt to catalogue certain intervals as out-of-tune versions of the intervals he or she is used to hearing. Nonetheless, all intervals in the tuning in question are perfectly in tune (in accordance to the mathematical characteristics of the tuning) and, consequently, they are not versions of anything else. Due to the fact that the tuning is an entity in itself, we have to judge it for what it is.

We need to see that the tuning has a unique organization, and that its intervals and chords are, in justice, as unique as the tuning itself may be, even when other tunings may contain very closely approximated versions of some intervals; The main difference comes perhaps not so much from the

intervals of the tuning themselves but from the *context* that the whole tuning as an entity provides for every interval in it. In this sense, to attempt analysis employing exactly the same procedures that we would employ for the analysis of a piece in twelve-tone-to-the-octave equal tuning would constitute perhaps a reasonable mistake. It would be reasonable because it is reasonable to attempt to understand unknown things in terms of the things we know, especially if there exists a certain resemblance. It is reasonable to judge the world according to the categories of our experience, but it is not logical to assume that our categories are the ultimate representation of reality. In a colloquial example, we may imagine an English-speaking person with no knowledge whatsoever of the Spanish language trying to read a book in Spanish. Having noticed that many Spanish words closely resemble English words, this person comes across the word "actual". It would be reasonable for this person to assume that the word means "real", in English, taking into account the immense quantity of cognates that exist between both languages. But at the same time, it would be illogical to assume that the word "actual" in Spanish means "real" in English given the fact that the same word, even spelled in the same way, may mean two different things in two different languages (the word "actual" in Spanish means "present" in English).

Following the same line of thought, we realize that notating this tuning with the aid of symbols that make reference to our usual twelve-tone-to-the-octave tuning or to historical tunings would be more or less absurd. Imagine having to interpret the signs $^{\wedge}b$, $^{\sim}\#$, as "not so flat" and "not so sharp", or $^{\sim}b^{+++}$ as "quasi-flat plus three syntonic commas", or whatever. In short, regardless that some of the intervals, chords, and even chord progressions may resemble certain well-known intervals, chords, and chord progressions, this tuning and many others (although not necessarily all) deserve a fresh departure point. We may need to begin by trying to assemble a theory of consonance and dissonance of the intervals of the tuning. In such case, each interval within the morenoctave would have to be classified as more or less consonant or dissonant. A hierarchy of consonance and dissonance would help to create the rules of a counterpoint

unique only to a tuning in question.

For example, we immediately notice that, in the present case of A-12, the level of beating in a morenoctave is zero, and the interval can be classified as totally consonant. On the other hand, a minor sixth, or augmented fifth (in terms of keyboard span) produces the highest level of beating, and can be classified as the most dissonant interval in the tuning. Next on the line of consonances, the major second and the perfect fourth appear quite consonant in comparison to the rough dissonances of the minor second and perfect fifth. It is a most interesting and pleasurable task to discover the consonance-dissonance relationships of a new tuning and to elaborate rules of counterpoint thereupon. All sorts of surprises may appear at any point of the process. The most bizarre forms of modality and the most strange possibilities of modulation are counterbalanced by the appearance of modes, chords and possibilities of modulation whose resemblance to our usual tuning is obvious.

Observe, for example, and listen to the beginning measures of the Ave Maria in the corresponding score. The piece intends to explore some obvious tonal possibilities of the tuning by employing a very small proportion of dissonance. In the first measure, only the most consonant intervals are used: morenoctaves and major seconds (remember that when we use the term "interval" or "major second" we are talking in terms of tablature keys [or "keyboard" if you will, see Chapter Four] *not* in terms of the *sound* of a "major second" in the twelve-tone-to-the-octave equal temperament). In the second measure, the new chord is composed of a major second and a perfect fifth in the accompaniment, while an E in the soprano - a non-chord tone - resolves to a C - a chord tone - in morenoctave relationship with the C in the bass. The third measure is a repetition of the first, in terms of harmony, and suggests that the progression from the first to the third chord is useful for tonal music. An interesting modulation occurs in the eighth measure by means of the pivot chord in the fifth and sixth measures; this permits repeating the material contained in the first three measures a major third down (again, in terms of keyboard span or pitch name) from the original position. Compare measures three and nine. The rhythm in measure nine softens the passing dissonances. Observe also

how the last note of measure ten is an anticipation of the next chord in measure eleven and how the note does not receive a beat. The dissonance of this note is due to the fact that it forms an augmented fifth with the C natural in the tenor, and as said, this is the most dissonant interval in the tuning. In measures seventeen and nineteen the augmented fifth appears on a strong beat to accentuate the drama of the name "Jesu Christe".

In measures sixteen and eighteen, the weak beats are employed to resolve suspensions, both, in the soprano and in the alto. Compare the transition from measures five to seven to the transition from measures fifteen to twenty; the same pivot chord is used to modulate to E flat. Finally, it would seem that ending the piece on the B flat of the penultimate chord of the piece (soprano) would be satisfactory. However, the point of maximum repose is on the G, which forms a perfect interval with the bass (last measure).

In this piece, the pervading quasi-major tonality creates a lofty and rarefied atmosphere, especially when the possibility of perceiving expanded chroma is brought about by transposing the melody a morenoctave lower.

To our knowledge, Ave Maria is the first piece ever written using this form of tonal expanded intonation in A-12. In the author's experience, a talented singer is able to easily memorize the pitches of her line (by ear), and, in a relatively short period of time, she will be able to sing in unison with the soprano voice of the computerized musical instrument. Now, if the singer is asked to sing without the help of the instrument's melody, a much longer period of time has to be expected before the singer may approach an acceptable level of accuracy.

An interesting trick can be employed, however, in order to produce a more musical effect. Two computerized musical instruments are used for this purpose; let us call them "instrument A" and "instrument B". Instrument B is tuned exactly as instrument A. The output of instrument A is channeled to loudspeakers. The output of instrument B is channeled to a pair of headphones. The singer wears the headphones. Having previously learned her part by means of doubling the melody at the unison, the singer is ready to perform with her accompanist. The accompaniment is played on instrument A, and the melody on instrument B. In this way, the singer will

be able to hear the accompaniment, the melody, and her own voice doubling the melody, while the audience will hear only the accompaniment and her voice. This method can produce results that range from satisfactory to excellent.

In the recorded example, the reader will hear soprano Bethany Hodges, a talented student majoring in vocal performance at the University of Kansas during the time the recording was made. She practiced the piece for about six hours. The level of accuracy that she achieved with only six hours of practice sheds light on both, the location of difficult intervals (either somehow a little bit out of tune due to incipient memorization, or justified towards a familiar twelve-tone-to-the octave equal interval), and the feasibility of singing in a different tuning (somehow eased by the fact that this piece is tonally oriented). Despite of its high signal-to-noise ratio, we have decided to keep the present recording, since it documents not only the above described process but also the first public performance of the piece.

Continuing with the question of expanded chroma, we will now consider examples in which a fragment, consisting of a few musical phrases, will be subjected to various types of morenoctave displacements and doublings. Since at this point we are interested in further discussion on the possibility of expanded chroma perception, we will consider short fragments rather than entire pieces.

The first, second, and third Music Examples (see Appendix I for scores and Appendix III for recordings) are still in the tuning A-12. In Example no. 2, three musical phrases are distributed over nine bars, and together form a period. From bars ten to eighteen, the period is repeated with only one change: the soprano line is transposed a morenoctave higher. In bars nineteen to twenty-eight, the soprano repeats the same material at the same register as well as the bass, but the bass is doubled at the morenoctave. This example permits us to better appreciate different consonant and dissonant intervals of the tuning. The bass and the outline of the higher voice usually move in parallel to avoid a general feeling of counterpoint. The questions here are still the same: do all three periods sound basically as the same one? Do cyclical displacements and doublings

change in any way the harmony? Particularly interesting would be the opinion of a naive listener with no knowledge whatsoever of music theory. Such a listener could be instructed to identify the beginning of each new period and subsequently asked to describe the difference between each new period and the former, or more cautiously (in order to avoid suggestions) the listener would be asked: "what happens now?" "Is this different or is it the same?" "If different, how or why?"

Notice that the timbre used in this example, synthetic electric violoncellos (or something like that), contributes to highlight the beating of certain intervals, particularly thirds and sixths.

At this point, we must pause for a moment and examine an important musical fact, the relationship between tuning and timbre. In Example no. 2, is it a good idea to use a timbre as rich in overtones and as sustained as that of a violoncello when many dissonant intervals are present? The answer, of course, depends on the intentions of the composer, and that is precisely the point: when working with new tunings, the timbres to be used will highlight or mask the beats produced by those intervals that are harsher than the harsher intervals in twelve-tone-to-the-octave equal temperament. Thus, awareness of the effect that timbres have upon consonances and dissonances is brought about by the novelty of intervals belonging to different tunings. Moreover, composers of music in expanded or semi-expanded tunings (at least at the time this study is being written) are confined to the electroacoustic medium, where synthesis of timbres seems to be the most general concern. It would seem natural that composers familiar with sound synthesis could take advantage, for expressive purposes, of the tuning-timbre relationship, as it has been already pointed out by Carlos (1987).

If harmonic tension increases with the level of dissonance, a timbral scheme that masks dissonance would apparently have a smoothing effect on harmonic relationships. In certain cases commonly found in electroacoustic music, factors such as the form of the sound wave, vibrato, echo, or time formants may prevent the unambiguous perception of the pitch of a tone. Naturally, in such cases, the particular acoustic and harmonic signature of a tuning becomes as obscure as the more or less individual ambiguous

pitches. Hence, the necessity of studying the kind of effect that a timbre or a combination thereof will have upon a particular tuning is revealed as a part of the compositional craft that new tunings demand. **The reader should carefully notice that if the perception of the pitch is not clear, the choice of a different tuning is meaningless.**

Timbre choice is a major component in expanded, contracted, and semi-expanded music, since it could render a whole tuning scheme merely theoretical by blurring pitch relationships, or it could contradict a stylistic principle by evidencing an excessive or an insufficient amount of dissonance. When dissonance is the desired effect, we should keep in mind two basic principles: first, that the timbral scheme should be clear enough, and that vibrato, echo, and other distortions should be minimized; second, that notes in the extreme ranges of the timbral scheme (too low or too high) should be used sparingly, because wide spacing tends to mitigate dissonance. The following example intends to call the reader's attention towards the tuning-timbre relationship, and at the same time to present a new instance of transposition at the morenoctave continuing thus with our discussion on the possibility of expanded chroma perception.

The first five measures of Example no. 3 are repeated exactly at the higher morenoctave. Let us call these ten measures "periods one and two". After a long pause, both periods are repeated in inverse order using a new timbral scheme. Let us call these second ten measures "periods three and four." Here, the reader-listener may try to weigh the effects of different timbres on the same music material. The first ten measures are played using a combination of timbres that more or less evoke a brass ensemble. After a silent pause, the second ten measures employ a combination of something like strings and celesta. Furthermore, during the third period, the celesta voice plays not simultaneously (in chords), but *arpeggiando*. During the fourth period, the celesta voice plays the chords simultaneously. The orchestration of periods one and two was designed to maximize the level of inherent dissonance. Conversely, the orchestration of periods three and four intends to minimize dissonances. This objective is approximately accomplished, due to the fact that the strings are kept constantly in *pianissimo* and are discretely modulated with a slight vibrato. At the same

time, the celesta sound wave has a very quick sustain and decay envelope, which means that the sound does not last long enough once it reaches its fullest point. In consequence, the ear does not have enough time to appreciate the beats produced by the more dissonant intervals. In addition, the harmonic content of the celesta sound wave is poorer than that of the brassy sound heard in periods one and two, and so, the inherent dissonances of certain intervals are masked by the timbres, their orchestration, balance, and by effects like vibrato and dynamics. Without any doubts, periods three and four sound relaxed and milder (in terms of dissonance) in comparison to the former two periods.

Example no. 3 intends to illustrate four-part voice leading in chordal style. Example no. 1 consists also of four voices, but the voice leading is not as cohesive as in Example no. 3. In Example no. 3, the questions concerning the possibility of expanded chroma become again questions about the harmony. Do harmonic functions permit the establishment of tonality all through the example? Apparently, each period unfolds along minor lines and evidently, each period ends in a major chord. Is the harmony of periods one and three perceived by the listener as the same as that of periods two and four? What kind of relationship exists between the last three chords of periods two and four? Are the final chords in measures five, ten, fifteen, and twenty perceived as the same chord with the same function?

In order to study morenoctave displacements in more detail, Example no. 4 introduces a two-bar phrase repeated at several morenoctave transposition levels. Observe measures one and two of Example No. 4. Consider the positions of the melody and the accompaniment in these first two measures as the original positions. The following displacements take place in measures three to ten: the last two beats of measures three, four, five and six drop down a morenoctave in the lower voice; the upper voice goes up a morenoctave during measures five, six, seven, eight and nine; the lower voice accompaniment goes up a morenoctave during measures seven, eight and the first two beats of nine; the lower voice accompaniment returns to its original position on the last two beats of measure nine and remains

there until the end of the example. Notice also how the last phrase comprising measures nine and ten of the upper voice is interrupted at the end of measure nine and continues down a morenoctave at the beginning of measure ten. Do all of these displacements affect the identity of the melody, of the harmony, of the tonality? If the reader is inclined towards a negative answer, it is possible that expanded chroma perception has taken place.

The reader may have noticed that, so far, we have only considered examples in the tuning A-12. There are two reasons for this preference. The first reason is that A-12 has its chroma axes in the same places (on the keyboard and on the staff) as our normal 12-tone-to-the-octave equal temperament, that is, morenoctaves in A-12 are to be found every twelve keys, and therefore, the reader can identify chroma axes with no unusual effort. This consideration has been important, since we want our readers to concentrate on the possibility of the hypothetical expanded chroma phenomenon. On the other hand, our particular preference for A-12 so far is due to the fact that this tuning occupies one of the highest ranks among all possible expanded tunings. A high rank means, in this context, that this tuning has been compared to many other expanded, contracted and semi-expanded tunings, and that this comparison reveals that A-12 is one of the most original, practical, and likely to induce expanded chroma perception, if this were possible. Exactly what we mean by original, practical and likely to induce expanded chroma perception can be further clarified by taking a closer look at the tables discussed in Chapter Three (see Tables 1 through 10 in Appendix II).

Table 1 is labeled "Tunings from the Families Oct-n, A-n, B-n, Cn, and D-n". It contains data about 126 tunings. For each tuning, the value of each scale degree is given in Hz, cts, and TU. The first scale degree starts always at 27.50 Hz, right on the practical threshold of audible pitch. Subsequently, scale degrees are given with their correspondent values until frequencies of 5000 Hz have been reached, or until the scale has reached a number of eighty-eight scale degrees, whichever occurs first. Frequencies beyond 5000 Hz are of very limited practical use in music composition, as far as *fundamental pitch* is concerned. The limit of eighty-eight scale degrees corresponds to the number of keys on an average piano keyboard

(or a professional piano-like digital keyboard used to control a synthesizer). Observe now the value of the last (eighty-eights) scale degrees of tunings Oct-22 and A-27. They are 426.35 Hz and 947.81 Hz respectively, which means that there are many more scale degrees before reaching frequencies of 5000 Hz (the extreme practical limit, depending on the timbre being used). However, our listing stops at the eighty-eight scale degree because most professional-size keyboards have only eight-eight keys. In consequence, more than one keyboard will be needed if a composer wants to use all practical scale degrees of a tuning with small scale degrees. This solution works well for an ensemble of keyboard players, where each keyboard is concerned only with a certain range of the scale.

In order to obtain the values in Hz for scale degrees belonging to an unlisted upper octave, all that is needed, in octave-based tunings, is to multiply the value in Hz by two. If the tuning belongs to the family A-n, the multiplication will be by three; if the tuning is of the family B-n the multiplication will be by five, and by six and seven if the tunings belong to the families C-n and D-n, respectively. To obtain values for upper octaves or morenoctaves in cts or TU we add the constant value of an octave or a morenoctave in cts or TU. An octave, as mentioned before, has a constant value of 1200 cts or 1024 TU. The constant value of a morenoctave A is 1901.96 cts or 1623 TU. The constant value of a morenoctave B is 2786.31 cts or 2377.65 TU. A morenoctave C equals 3101.96 cts or 2647 TU, and a morenoctave D equals 3368.83 cts or 2874.73 TU. With these preliminary rules, any interested person may use our tables to tune an instrument or to analyze the intervals of any of the 126 tunings here listed.

Table 2 shows the constant increment in cts and TU of a scale degree in each one of the 126 tunings in Table 1. This table is a quick reference to find the size of the scale degree of a given tuning.

Table 3 presents all constants in the former table ordered according to size from the lowest to the highest values. In this table, the different families of tunings considered in our investigation (Chapter Three) appear mixed, and their distribution shows the proximity of one tuning to another according to the size of their constants. In Table 3, we can see the tunings that more or less closely approximate the acoustical signature or proprieties

of another given tuning. Observe how the smallest constant of all is that of the tuning Oct-24 (50 cts), and the largest, that of D-12 (280.73 cts), which is 40.73 cts larger than Oct-5. Also, notice that the tunings D-34, B-28, C-31 and A-19 are so close to having a constant of 100 cts that they become practically undistinguishable from Oct-12, our usual tuning. Therefore, we judge that D-34, B-28, C-31,and A-19 are not true expanded tunings (from the point of view of perception). These tunings are not the only instance of very close approximations. Observe, for example, that D-48, A-27 and Oct-17 have a common constant of 70 cts. Again, for all practical purposes, D-48 and A-27 tend to be practically undistinguishable from Oct-17. In Oct-17, the octave is perfectly in tune. In A-27, the morenoctave A is in tune, but not the octave, which is approximated by the eighteenth interval of the tuning by 2.47 cts. In order to further investigate systematically more similarities and differences of this type, we have elaborated Table 4.

Table 4, labeled "Originality of Expanded Tunings in Comparison to Octave-Based Tunings", is the result of obtaining a match between the constant of every expanded tuning and the constant of an octave-based tuning that most closely approximates the value of a given expanded tuning, and subsequently ordering them, beginning from the one that produced the highest difference; the higher the rank of an expanded tuning in Table 4, the more original it is said to be in comparison to octave-based tunings. What could be the cutoff point in Table 4, the point below which an expanded tuning becomes (or functions like, i.e. is perceived like) a pseudo-expanded tuning by virtue of its similarity to an octave-based tuning? The author's guess is that when there is a difference is less than two cents between the *constant* of an expanded tuning and the *constant* of an octave-based tuning, the perceptual difference between both tunings begins to be blurred, and it is certainly blurred below one cent. Exactly where is the line dividing true expanded tunings (perceptually speaking) from pseudo-expanded tunings? This remains a matter of experimental research.

Table 4 shows that many tunings with lower constant differences have to be discarded from the potential list of "true" expanded tunings, if we were to use this term. A definition of truthfulness would establish that a tuning with a constant too close in value to the constant of an octave-based

tuning could not be a true expanded tuning. Another circumstance that would prevent a tuning from being perceived as a true expanded tuning (and that would complement this tentative definition of truthfulness of an expanded tuning) is the presence of an interval close to the octave or to a morenoctave belonging to a preceding family of tunings. How close to an octave? Again, this would have to be determined by experience. At this point, we must consider that even if a tuning does nor have a close approximation to an octave, or to a chroma interval belonging to a preceding family of tunings within one complete cycle of the scale, the presence of such an interval in other places along the practical range of the scale could cause an interference with the chroma of the tuning (except in the case of octave-based tunings, of course).

The present author suggests that the limit to determine if an approximation could cause interference may be found between one fifth and one sixth of an Oct-12 semi-tone, that is, between twenty and sixteen cts, depending on timbre. An expanded tuning with an interval close to an octave by a distance of less than twenty to sixteen cts would fall under the influence of that octave, and therefore would not have an opportunity to induce perception of expanded chroma, which means that such tuning would not be a true expanded tuning. In order to investigate systematically these approximations to foreign chroma intervals along the practical range of the 106 expanded tunings here considered, we have elaborated Tables 5, 6, 7,and 8.

Tables 5, 6, 7 and 8 are the result of a search for foreign chroma-inducing intervals, i.e. powers of two for the family A-n, powers of two and of three for the family B-n, powers of two, three, and five, for the family C-n, and powers of two, three, five and six for the family D-n. The search is conducted by families, and tunings are ranked according to the value of the difference between the value of the nearest chroma-inducing power of n, and the value of the interval that most closely approximates the value of such chroma-inducing power of n. Accordingly, those tunings in which the difference is less than twenty to sixteen cts would not be considered true expanded tunings, or at least they could not belong to their own family. For example, if a tuning of the family C-n had an interval whose value lies nine

cents away from a near power of three, the tuning would be perceived as a tuning of the family A-n, in which morenoctaves are powers of three.

In Table 5, we have determined that the first six powers of two (1200 cts, 2400 cts, 3600 cts, 4800 cts, 6000 cts, and 7200 cts) are potential foreign-chroma-inducing intervals for the family A-n. It might be that subsequent powers of two could interfere with expanded chroma perception, but this seems unlikely to happen due to the resulting distance. For the same reason, in Table 6 we are looking for interference produced by the first six powers of two, and by the first four powers of three: 1901.96 cts, 3803.92 cts, 5705.88 cts, 7607.84 cts; in Table 7, we look for interference from the first six powers of two, the first four powers of three, and the first two powers of five: 2786.31 cts, and 5572.62 cts; finally, in Table 8 we are concerned with the first six powers of two, the first four powers of three, the first two powers of five and the first two powers of six: 3101.96 cts, and 6203.92 cts.

The tables show that only one member of the family A-n is safely away from the influence of an octave by more than twenty cts (we are tentatively setting twenty cts - a fifth of an Oct-12 semi-tone - as a "safe" distance from the chroma-inducing influence of the octave, but perhaps this tentative distance should be increased or decreased in relation to the frequency of the octave in question, i.e. whether it is a higher or a lower octave, since the acuity of pitch perception increases or decreases at different places of the auditory spectrum), and no other tuning in this family passes even the sixteen cts test. The only surviving tuning is A-12. The remaining three families are not more successful: no tuning from the family B-n passes the sixteen cts test; C-12, C-14, and C-21 pass the sixteen cts test, but only C-17 passes the twenty cts test; not even one of the tunings in the family D-n passes even the sixteen cts test. In conclusion, among 106 expanded tunings surveyed, only two are qualified to remain in our tentative list of "true" expanded tunings, and possibly three more could be also included. It is important to mention again that these 106 tunings were selected because they are the most practical in terms of music performance. The findings of Tables 5, 6, 7, and 8 are summarized in the next table.

Table 9 is labeled "Chroma Originality". In it, expanded tunings

appear ranked according to their freedom from the influence of chroma-inducing intervals from other families. In consequence, the first five places correspond to the tunings A-12, C-17, C-12, C-21, and C-14. A graphical sketch of the functions of these five tunings appear in Figures 1 and 3 of Chapter One.

Table 10 compares the results of Tables 4 and 9. The result of the comparison is a rank number which represents the average of the two rankings that the tunings received in Tables 4 and 9 - i.e. "Originality of Expanded Tunings in Comparison to Octave-Based Tunings", and "Chroma Originality").

Table 10 is labeled "Total Originality". This label intends to express only the fact that both "originality" tables have been compared. The label should not lead any reader to think that tunings at the top of Table 10 are necessarily the most original in the true sense of the word. Table 10 merely expresses a relationship.

For the purpose of this Chapter, which is mainly concerned with an examination of the hypotheses of expanded chroma, Table 9 is the most important of all. Observe that, in this table, the tuning A-12 is ranked number one, and all the tunings that obtained higher rankings, with the exception of C-21, are tunings with fewer steps per scale than A-12. In effect, if we go to Table 1, we will notice that the first five tunings in Table 9 contain (within the practical range of their scales) the following numbers of useful steps per scale (according to our less-than-5000-Hz criterion:

    A-12 has   56   useful steps per scale.
    C-17 has   49   useful steps per scale.
    C-12 has   34   useful steps per scale.
    C-21 has   60   useful steps per scale.
    C-14 has   40   useful steps per scale.

This circumstance makes the tuning A-12 the second richest tuning within the list of the first five tunings of Table 9. A classification of all five possibly true expanded tunings according to their richness in total number

of useful steps will give us the following list:

        C-21 has 60   useful steps per scale.
        A-12 has 56   useful steps per scale.
        C-17 has 49   useful steps per scale.
        C-14 has 40   useful steps per scale.
        C-12 has 34   useful steps per scale.

One conclusion is that all possibly true expanded tunings in our tables are poorer in number of steps than the twelve-tone-to-the-octave equally tempered tuning, which has a standard average number of eighty-eight useful steps - quite a disappointing conclusion, indeed. Among all five tunings discussed, the average number of steps is forty-eight. Therefore, we may deem any of these five tunings with less than forty-eight steps as "poor" in step content. A classification of the five tunings according to their likelihood to induce expanded chroma perception would be linked to the hierarchy of the families, and to chroma originality rank (Chapter Two: conclusion no.6, and Table 9). A ranking of our five tunings according to their family likelihood to induce expanded chroma perception coincides with the results of Table 9.

In relation to our current performance, composition, and notation habits, a tuning with twelve steps per cycle is the most practical tuning with which we can deal. The more steps per cycle a tuning has, the more practical difficulties it is likely to present during the processes of composition, notation and even execution. Here is a classification of the five surviving tunings according to their practicality:

                A-12
                C-12
                C-14
                C-17
                C-21

The tuning A-12 is not only the most practical, but also is the first

tuning that most probably would induce expanded chroma perception. In addition, A-12 earned the sixth place in Table 10 (labeled as "Total Originality"), and its number of usable steps places it above the average with a good second place; hence our decision to select A-12 in order to illustrate our commentaries on the possibility of expanded chroma. By showing the thought process that led to this decision, we also hope to have illustrated the usefulness of tables 1 through 10, or at least one interesting approach to them.

A question arises here. Are the rest of the tunings useful? Apparently, all tunings not included in the list of the top five (in Table 9) are not "true" expanded tunings according to our tentative definition of truthfulness of an expanded tuning. However, with the exception of those tunings whose constant differed two cents or less from the constant of an octave-based tuning in Table 4, most expanded tunings should have their own particular distinctive features and harmonic possibilities. In some cases, the presence of a quasi-octave is not so obvious, and indeed, it does not need to be at all, if the composer insists on avoiding the particular interval that would evidence it. This is certainly a very interesting idea that now deserves some consideration.

If the perception of expanded chroma is really possible, we could systematically avoid those intervals (found along the scale of an expanded tuning) that could cause an intrusion of foreign chroma. Moreover, even if the safety limit of twenty to sixteen cts that we have established to distinguish the first five tunings (in Table 9) from the rest were not an accurate estimation, we could still make use of this type of systematic avoidance. In this way, provided that expanded chroma perception were possible, we could make most expanded tunings function like "true" expanded tunings; the rules to be observed would be:

1. Localize all potential problem intervals.

2. Organize the tonality of the composition around the chroma axes, and assume expanded chroma.

3. Avoid systematically through the composition any problem interval.

Let us consider an example. First, let us suppose that in the tuning A-12, intervals that are close to any power of two do cause a real interference with the hypothetical expanded chroma of the tuning. The value of such intervals -powers of two - would be:

1200 cts

2400 cts

3600 cts

4800 cts

6000 cts

7200 cts

8400 cts

Now we go to Table 1, localize tuning A-12, and look for values close to these intervals. The closest interval to 1200 cts is the interval formed by scale degree no. 1 and scale degree no. 9. This interval is close to a potentially troublesome octave by 67.9 cts, but since this is greater than an Oct-12 quarter-tone, we cannot consider it as problematic. Next, we have the interval between scale degrees nos. 1 and 16, close to 2400 cts by only 22.55 cts. This one could be a troublesome interval, a minor tenth in terms of keyboard or tablature span. Therefore, we may decide to avoid using any minor tenths in any combination, whether it be alone or within a chord.

Continuing, we find that scale degree no. 24 approaches 3600 cts by 45.42 cts, and since it seems a reasonable distance, we need not trouble ourselves with it. Interval no. 31 is 45.10 cts away from 4800 cts, and

similar remarks apply to it. Interval no. 39 is only 22.87 away from 6000 cts. This one may be a potential problem interval. The distance from the bass note is two morenoctaves A and a major second. This interval would have to be avoided too. Next, interval no. 46 is 67.65 cts away from 7200 cts, and it presents no problem. Finally, interval 54 is just 0.32 cts away from 8400 cts. Obviously, this is almost a power of two and has to be rigorously avoided. Interval 54 is four morenoctaves and a perfect fourth away from the bass note. In terms of twelve-tone-to-the-octave equal temperament this interval would encompass seven octaves:

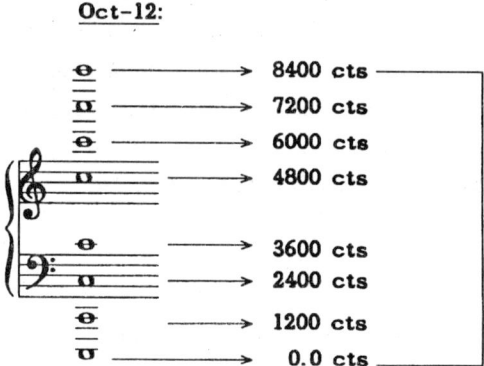

In terms of A-12, the problem intervals occur in the following proportion:

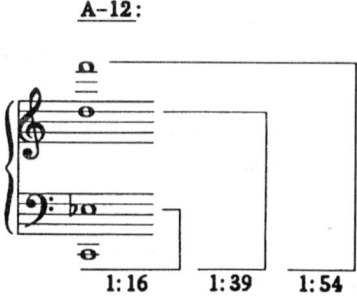

Observe that the distance between scale degrees nos. 39 and 54 is a minor tenth, a mirror of the distance between scale degrees nos. 1 and 16. Also, the distance between scale degrees nos. 16 and 54, three morenoctaves and a major second, is a mirror of the distance between scale degrees nos. 1 and 39. On the other hand, the interval between scale degrees nos. 16 and 39 does not constitute a problem interval, due to the fact that scale degree no. 16 approximates the closest power of two (2400 cts) by a default of 22.55 cts, and scale degree no. 39 approximates the closest power of two (6000 cts) by an excess of 22.87 cts. The default and excess distances add up in the interval formed by scale degrees nos. 16 and 39, which is 3645.42 cts, that is, 45.42 cts larger than a power of two, and in consequence it can be labeled as non-problem interval. The conclusion of this analysis is that, should we harbor any doubts about the capacity of A-12's integral scale for inducing expanded chroma perception, then we should systematically avoid the following intervals:

a) A morenoctave A plus a minor third

b) Three morenoctaves A plus a major second

c) Four morenoctaves A plus a perfect fourth

In case of similar doubts, we can apply similar restrictions to composition with other expanded tunings. Note that the first of these three intervals is usually a very common interval in tonal music. The second is not very uncommon, and the third is very uncommon. Is avoiding these intervals an extraordinarily burdensome requirement ?

Let us go back for a moment to our Music Examples nos. 3, 2, and 4, in this order. Of all four Examples discussed so far, only Example no. 3 makes a careful avoidance of any interval that could approximate a power of two. The span of the chords precludes the possibility of a chord larger than three morenoctaves, and all minor tenths have been avoided. Thus, Example no. 3 adopts the most extreme conditions to propitiate perception

of expanded chroma. Notice that in measure six, the bass line is susceptible of doubling at the lower morenoctave. We have avoided this, since it would cause problem intervals. If expanded chroma perception were possible at all, Example no. 3 would be our ultimate type of example. The reader is advised to listen to it carefully once more (as well as Examples nos. 1, 2 and 4) and decide whether he or she is able to perceive a new chroma dimension.

Example no. 2 contains four instances of close approximations to powers of two. All four of them are minor tenths (in terms of keyboard span). They are located:

1) on the third beat of measure seven,

2) on the fourth beat of measure eight,

3) on the third beat of measure twenty-five, and

4) on the fourth beat of measure twenty-six.

Of all these approximations, the most interesting one is no. 2, on the fourth beat of measure eight. Because of the fact that this quasi-octave is exactly near the cadence of the phrase, we would expect that its presence would inhibit the sense of resolution towards the ensuing morenoctave, but this does not seem to be the case. A similar situation occurs on the fourth beat of measure twenty-six. Listen carefully to measures seven and eight, and compare them to sixteen and seventeen. To what extent does the presence of the quasi-octaves affect the harmony of both passages? Do measures sixteen and seventeen (where there is no quasi-octave) sound different (in harmony) compared to measures twenty-five and twenty-six (where there is a quasi-octave)?

In music example no. 4, we have a recurring minor tenth (F to Ab) on the second eight of the first beat of measures one, two, three, four, seven, eight, nine and ten. Did the reader identify by ear the presence of these quasi-octaves during the first listening? Until this point, we have purposely

omitted a mention of them in order not to prejudice the reader in his or her efforts to decide on the question of our hypothetical expanded chroma. We will leave to the curious reader the task of identifying quasi-octaves in music example no. 1. It would be better if this identification were first done by ear. In this way, the listener could perhaps appreciate better the effects of the context surrounding the intervals in question.

We have seen that Tables 5, 6, 7, and 8, reveal that the presence of "problem" intervals is very frequent in every tuning. In this sense, no expanded tuning lacks in quasi-powers of two, or quasi-powers of three, etc.

Admittedly, to expurgate problem intervals seems a great annoyance for a composer. On the other hand, the process of avoiding problem intervals could be thought as an analog to the process of composing a piece according to a fixed set of contrapuntal rules in a given style. For example, in sixteenth-century polyphony, a rigid set of contrapuntal rules specify the allowed and forbidden combinations of intervals on a given beat. In this sense, a "problem interval" within a composition in an expanded tuning, could skillfully be treated in the same manner as a passing dissonance would be treated in traditional forms of counterpoint hoping that this treatment would protect the expanded chroma of the tuning against the possible interference of foreign chroma brought about by the problem interval.

So, what would happen if, regardless of these considerations on foreign chroma interference, we ignore all problem intervals and proceed to put together a long piece of music using a great variety of intervals in a great variety of contrapuntal situations? In order to illustrate this question we have included, along with our Recorded Examples nos. 1, 2, 3, and 4, Recorded Example no. 5: *Concert Adagio*. This is a piece of large proportions in sonata form. *Concert Adagio* is written for the tuning A-16 and should be performed by five totally tunable independent synthetic voices (the piece consists of five independent lines in constant contrapuntal motion) although it can also be performed by an experienced pianist with large hands on one totally-tunable polyphonic synthesizer.

In the tuning A-16, as it can be seen rapidly in Table 1, quasi-octaves

are very common intervals (a graphic comparison between the functions of A-16 and Oct-12 is included within figure 1, in Chapter One). However, *Concert Adagio* was composed without any intentions to avoid approximations to octaves. Since the piece is set in an extended form of quasi-tonal cromaticism, the chroma axes of the piece tend to fall under the influence of approximations to octaves, but the cumulative differences to perfect octaves form (in large chords) intervals with very particular acoustical and harmonic properties. Evidently, the themes and harmonies of *Concert Adagio* would have been impossible if all approximations to octaves had to be avoided.

Even avoiding problem intervals does not settle the question whether expanded chroma can be perceived by some or by all persons. Yet, in the present author's opinion, perception of expanded chroma seems a difficult occurrence to prove. One of the objects of this study is to expose the merely hypothetical possibility of this phenomenon, to place it at the core of a new compositional technique, and to trigger a desire to obtain the necessary musical experience and scientific evidence that will ultimately decide whether a sense of expanded chroma can be gained or developed by some or all individuals. This study must have at least demonstrated that, at this point, it is important for musicians and scientists to know why or why not expanded chroma can occur. Are audible frequencies separated by a power of two the only kind of frequencies that the mind associates with a function of similarity, or are there other relationships that may cause the same phenomenon? Is this a spontaneous neurophysiological process or does learning play an important (or even exclusive) role in it? Can we learn or train others to learn how to perceive expanded chroma?

The author must confess that he can perceive the symmetry elicited by certain expanded tunings, but that, nevertheless, it is a problem for him to develop a sense of functional similarity for tones separated by one or more morenoctaves. However, there is something intuitive and puzzling that makes morenoctave displacements or transpositions appear as "logic" within the context of tonality in an expanded tuning. Is this a form of functional similarity? It must be said that the author has received some interesting commentaries and reactions from persons (ranging from

musically naive to professional musicians) who claim to perceive (during informal tests) what could be termed as "functional similarity," (expanded chroma) or at least a sense of it. The test usually consists of playing several times a short piece composed in the tuning A-12 and then asking for verbal descriptions of it, especially concerning instances of similarity. Is perception of expanded chroma simply a function of unlearning our usual assumptions on similarity?

Perhaps the reluctance of the present author to accept morenoctave relationships as functionally similar is due to the habit of assuming the exclusive functional similarity of octave relationships. It is interesting to speculate on whether this omnipresent and strongly-reinforced assumption could inhibit or distract the mind to the point of incapacity for the perception of another not-so-obvious form of similarity. Finally, although it is the author's opinion that expanded chroma perception remains a problematical and rather difficult-to-prove event, we must preserve a state of openmindedness until enough years of musical practice and/or sufficient psychological experimental evidence elucidate why or why not expanded chroma perception can occur.

PART TWO:

AESTHETIC APPROACH

CHAPTER SIX

A Theory of Expanded Tunings and the Western Musical Tradition

Introduction

At this point, we expect that our readers may be aware of two fundamental facts concerning actual music in expanded tunings:

1) Expanded tunings are subtle psycho-geometrical structures whose perception as such depends on the organizing force of those characteristics which we commonly call "melodic constructs", "tonal centers", and "harmonic organization", which in turn demand a certain amount of perceived rhythmic periodicity.

2) Outside of this confined and perceptually sophisticated realm the use of expanded tunings - or for that purpose of any alternative tunings- is meaningless, because the perception of the particular structure of a tuning depends on the aforementioned conditions.

It is in light of this restrictions that we have endeavored to find an answer to the question: "What is the place of expanded tunings in contemporary music?"

The first part of our answer to this question - presented throughout the

rest of this chapter - is an exercise in trying to follow the consequences of assuming that there is still a Western musical tradition, and that this tradition is still capable of further growth.

In contrast to the utopian and prescriptive nature of our first answer, our second answer - presented throughout the next chapter - will explore some aspects of the immediate cultural environment facing the discovery of expanded tunings from a more realistic point of view.

Essay

The ideas behind expanded tunings can be primarily aesthetic, that is, of a philosophical nature. When these ideas crystallize in the form of two basic principles, conservation and expansion, practical music systems can be predicted by applying the concepts of conservation and expansion to the manipulation of formulae representing physical and psychological facts.

The idea of conservation responds to the necessity of retaining the basic characteristics by which a given tradition of music is identified. This idea may appear to contradict our main intention in this chapter, which is to investigate whether it is possible to stimulate the implicit growing potential of the Western musical tradition by means of applying a theory of expanded tunings.

A process of renewal or growth may include discarding, replacing, adding and expanding. Discarding and replacing are in direct opposition to the necessity of retention. Such a necessity becomes manifest when one reflects upon the individual successes of particular basic characteristics of a particular tradition, which in this case, as said, is the Western musical tradition from its beginnings up to the point where it evolves into twelve-tone, serial, textural, conceptual, concrete and randomized music. For the purpose of this section, these evolutionary departures are to be considered as anamorphoses of the Western musical tradition, because they reject or avoid the perceptual principles set by its basic characteristics. Let us consider then, an abstract of the basic technical characteristics of the Western musical tradition as it has been circumscribed above.

Basic technical characteristics of the Western musical tradition:

1) Accurate Instruments

   Our tradition uses preferentially musical instruments capable of producing mostly harmonic sounds (periodic vibrations) of sufficient frequency resolution to produce definite pitch sensations.

2) Musical Scales

   The whole continuum of audible frequencies is reduced to sets of discrete frequencies which, in the case of equal temperaments correspond to an exact logarithmic organization in order to obtain continuous subsets of contiguously successive discrete frequencies. In the case of historical, unequal temperaments, the frequencies correspond to an approximate rational (in the sense of ratio-oriented) organization in order to obtain subsets of discrete frequencies that are in a one-to-one correspondence with the members of a previously-defined system of at least twelve pitch classes, plus some other pitch classes that were considered as non-enharmonic variants of the twelve primary pitch classes.

3) Exponentiation

   In the case of the twelve-tone-to-the octave equal temperament, being the whole set of discrete frequencies divided into n contiguous subsets of twelve contiguous discrete frequencies each, at least one different pitch-class name is assigned to every member of all subsets that bears the same ordinal code within a subset. For example, the second member of each subset might receive the same pitch-class name, i.e., C-sharp; the logarithmic distance between pitch classes bearing the same pitch-class name is always an exact power of two.

4) Chroma

The psychological phenomenon of chroma is assumed in order to make possible the perception of exponentially related subsets as similar and perceptually equivalent cycles of the whole scale. Octave generalization is the organizing force providing perceptual coherence to the exponential divisions of the scale. This is a point which is usually overlooked, because the octave has been regarded as a natural perceptual identity.

5) Tonal Centers

Western music has made a systematic use of the fact that listeners can develop a psychological mechanism which assigns a dynamic quality to a tone according to the structural properties of the set of tones to which it belongs (Zuckerkandl, 1971) (Balzano, 1981). This occurs when the tone appears within a musical context in which a listener, already familiarized with the subset in question, is able to recognize the subset and associate it with a more or less culturally conditioned, variable musical meaning (Lundin, 1953). This phenomenon makes possible the perception of tonal centers.

6) Harmonic Functions

Theories of harmony that establish hierarchies of functions are used to regulate the simple or complex interplay of tonal centers according to an aesthetic position bearing a close relationship with the roles of consonance and dissonance.

7) Notation

A system of symbols permits the accurate codification of all pitches pertaining to the original comprehensive set of pitches along with

their harmonic relationships. The system should be of such nature that instantaneous sight-reading or performance of the encoded music must be always possible.

Evidently, there is a hierarchical interdependency that descends from the first to the sixth characteristics. This fact suggests that, if for the purpose of stimulating the growth of the Western musical tradition we decided to eliminate the first or the second characteristics, we would be unable to retain the rest, with the exception perhaps of a fragmented version of the last one. A detailed analysis of the seven afore mentioned characteristics leads, within this approach, to at least two important conclusions:

1) The identity of our musical tradition depends on the organizing force of all seven characteristics.

2) If we want to preserve the identity and continuity of our tradition, we must preserve - rather than discard - the characteristics on which it depends.

Some may argue that it is possible to reject characteristics five and six - tonal centers, harmonic functions - and yet continue with the tradition without rejecting characteristics one through four and seven, as it is the case of most twelve-tone and serial music. It could be said that characteristics five and six are a phase of the Western musical tradition, but that, however, they do not define it. This argument would be fallacious, because:

a) When twelve-tone and serial music emerged, the Western musical tradition had already been defined (historically) by characteristics one through seven.

b) A tradition is a continued practice that, while occasionally dropping some non-essential, secondary aspects grows mainly by successive additions (otherwise we have the beginning of what might be

another tradition).

c) Therefore, to reject characteristics five and six after they have been historically established as a common practice is to break ties with the tradition.

d) Most of the twelve-tone and serial music repertory rejects characteristics five and six.

e) Therefore, twelve-tone and serial music break ties with the Western music tradition.

Twelve-tone and serial music depart from the Western musical tradition. They do not continue it; to affirm that twelve-tone and serial music are part of *the* Western musical tradition is, as demonstrated above, a *contradictio in terminis*, - an inconsistency or a form of propaganda. At most, we could say that twelve-tone, and serial music, *et sic de similibus*, initiate a new, parallel Western musical tradition based on dissonance and rhythmic aperiodicity and not adopted by all serious composers as a common practice. Whether this incipient tradition will develop through the centuries remains to be seen.

For those who love Gregorian chant, Beethoven, Skriabin, Bartok, etc., but do not like serial, textural, concrete or random music, the answer to the question implied in the second conclusion is more likely to be inclined towards an affirmative: to preserve the identity of our tradition. For those who enjoy Stockhausen and random music, a negative answer may not seem too bad. For the purpose of this study, we opt for exploring to the possibility of preserving the identity of our tradition. Our intention to renew must exclude the suppression of any basic characteristic. As a result, we have established a principle: conservation.

Now we face our renovating task with the restriction that we should not substitute or suppress any of the seven basic characteristics. Then, if we do not want to substitute or suppress, we should consider the possibility of accomplishing our goal by adding new characteristics to the basic seven.

An analysis of many possible additions brings a disappointing result. Two considerations are enough to make this point clear. The first is that, the further a new characteristic is distanced from the first and most essential seven characteristics, the less psychological impact it has - the less power to produce a sense of invigorating and decisive renewal; and the proof of this is seen in the next second consideration.

Many possible additional basic characteristics have already been tried in order to stimulate the growth of our musical tradition. Usually, such additional characteristics remain peripheral, ornamental, and at the most they create hybrid styles and are apparently incapable of causing a true renaissance. Often, these additional characteristics follow two typical trends. One of them could be called the geographical and the other the temporal. The geographical consists of the borrowing or appropriation of characteristics of musical traditions foreign to the Western tradition. Examples of this are: the use and incorporation of musical instruments alien to the tradition - instruments that in many cases produce either inharmonic timbres or tones with a high degree of inharmonicity; the use of complex rhythmical structures that are borrowed from so-called ethnic musical traditions; the possibility of using musical scales from other musical traditions, such as the Indian, Persian, Javanese, etc.; the ornamental use of scale degrees smaller than a semi-tone; the imitation of the unimodal organization of some Middle-East styles; the copying of the so-called minimalistic musical form of certain improvisational styles of some Eastern traditions etc., etc. The temporal trend exhibits two directions: one looking towards the past and the other towards a Hollywoodesque future.

Examples of the revivalist direction are: the use and/or incorporation of ancient instruments to new music; the attempt to revive performance practices from the Middle Ages such as those from the trouveres and troubadours, and those concerning the ornamentation of melodic lines and rhythmic accompaniments: the revival of old tunings and temperaments such as the various forms of just, pythagorean, or mean-tone tunings etc.; the creation of improved mathematical models of just tuning and the proposed implementation or modification of instruments such as computers

and modified keyboards to supposedly facilitate performance in just tunings; the imitation of historical improvisational practices etc., etc. Examples of the futuristic direction are: computers used for real-time creation or improvisation, and algorithmic composition of traditional diatonic music; synthesizers, samplers and computers used to perform traditional music, etc., etc.

On the other hand, the most successful of all hybrids that surged from the fusion of several of the formerly mentioned additions with the Western tradition - jazz - exhibits at certain points of its evolution an extraordinary and promising vigor. Finally, the mixture of many of these additions and their hybrids with anamorphic branches that departed from our tradition (serial, concrete, random music, etc.) complete a vague, general picture of our present musical panorama, as far as creativity is concerned, and it is manifest in many new areas of musical development, like, for example, "pure" computer music, whose present output is almost exclusively oriented towards a further elaboration of the principles laid down by Russolo (1913), Schaeffer (1952, 1966) and the *musique concrète* school of the nineteen fifties.

These additions to the basic characteristics of our tradition are certainly stimulating and in many cases marvelous, but in the opinion of many (and this is such a commonplace that needs not to be proved) they have not prevented a visible "decrease" in Western music's artistic appeal of output (the present author does not necessarily agree with this opinion). Taking into account the enormous wealth of possibilities that the aforementioned additions create, how can we answer the question whether we have seen in the last 30 years works of the quality of, for example, the *Brandenburg Concerti*, Wagner's *Tetralogy* or *The Rite of Spring*? This question, however is not the same as to affirm that no music since 1960 will endure.

Evidently, this is a matter of opinion, but the lack of agreement, among music lovers and musicians, is a sign that points to the gap existent between musical works that are an integrated part of the Western musical tradition, and musical works that are not. Have the great composers of the past exhausted all the possibilities of the characteristics of the Western

musical tradition so that no more great masterpieces can be composed abiding by the seven basic characteristics (and additions) of the tradition? Before continuing with our philosophical investigation, we must stop to consider this question.

Let us suppose first, from a pragmatistic point of view, that the question is actually a pseudo-question and therefore not valid. We have to stop here. We must go to the desk and keep composing according to whatever we want to do, and to whatever aesthetic or anti-aesthetic goals we chance to have, and then we have to wait and see what future generations say. But since this is what we are going to do after our investigation anyway, the pragmatistic approach proves to be redundant and only suitable for persons deprived of philosophical intuition. As a result, we decide to move ahead and suppose that the answer is affirmative: maybe the resources of the Western musical tradition, as defined by its seven basic characteristics are still not exhausted.

How many composers of art music who have something to express would not like to compose at least one masterpiece that is appealing to those who can appreciate art music? Very few indeed, if any at all. Then, if a composer believes that the resources of the Western musical tradition are exhausted, he or she should follow the path of Xenakis and Boulez and sever all direct ties with one or several of the seven basic characteristics. But according to our principle of conservation, if we still want our desired goal, we must preserve the identity of our tradition. In order to do this with intellectual honesty, however, we have to have clear signs that our tradition is capable of further growth, so we now explore the possibilities of expansion.

How can the seven basic characteristics of our traditional Western music be expanded? And since they appear hierarchically organized, is it not true that by expanding the first, second, third, etc., characteristics the rest are affected? We propose the following measures in order to expand the seven basic characteristics of the Western musical tradition:

Proposed Expansions

1.1 Expansion of Accurate Instruments.

Let the most important musical instruments of the Western tradition be able to produce and control with automatic precision all possible gradations of pitch and all possible combinations of timbral spectra; let their only restrictions be:

a) those that according to the nature of their formants (resonance regions) and transients (attack, sustain, decay, release) are related to the particular physical design and performance technique of each instrument, and that

b) however increased the potential degree of inharmonicity of sound that the expanded instruments may be able to produce, they must use mainly sounds with unambiguous pitch resolution. Inharmonic sounds are to be considered as coloristic ornaments and to be treated in composition as harmonically non-essential atmospheric devices.

These two-restrictions ensure that the identity of the first characteristic be conserved. This proposition could be expressed as "expanded use of instruments" or "use of expanded instruments". In this study we are not concerned with the technical problems that are involved in updating and expanding instruments, which is an engineering problem.

2.1 Expanded (Equal) Scales

Let the whole continuum of audible frequencies be reduced to sets of discrete frequencies that correspond to a logarithmic organization in order to obtain subsets composed of a variable number of discrete frequencies; let the only two restrictions be that

a) the discrete frequencies must always correspond to an exact logarithmic scale, and that

b) the number of discrete frequencies must be a positive integer.

These two restrictions determine that all scales resulting from this form of organization will be equally tempered. The proposition could be expressed as: "expanded equal temperaments".

3.1 Expanded Exponentiation

Let any complete equally tempered scale be divided into n contiguous subsets of n contiguous discrete frequencies each, and let at least one unique pitch-class name be assigned to every member (of each subset) that bears the same ordinal code within each subset; at the same time, let the logarithmic distance between pitch classes bearing the same pitch class name be always an exact power of a positive integer other than 1. The only restriction will be that this number must not be equal to

$$(W^y)$$

where W and $y = (2, 3, 4 \ldots n)$. The restriction is established in order to avoid repetitions (see Chapter I). The proposition could be labeled as "expanded exponentiation".

4.1 Expanded Chroma

We would not be surprised if listeners of a system of expanded equal temperaments with expanded exponentiation could actually make use of an expansion of the chroma phenomenon, because the listener may try to perceive exponentially related subsets as similar and perceptually equivalent cycles of the whole scale - expanded chroma generalization as the organizing force to provide perceptual coherence

to the exponential divisions of the scale. Were this so, the only restrictions would be such that:

a) the perception of this phenomenon could only be induced in the listeners by pieces of music composed in systems of expanded equal temperaments with expanded exponentiation (expanded tunings), and that

b) the composer would have to organize the music around the chroma axis assuming that the physical organization of the tuning itself and the harmonic organization of the music will induce an expanded perception of chroma. This characteristic is best expressed as "expanded chroma".

This proposition is based on the listener's natural inclination to organize perceived information into patterns, and we think that the system will be organized psychologically in one particular way. In other words, cycles x and y of a same expanded scale would have to be judged as identical to a degree, and while we would agree completely with a definition of the listener as organizer, we think we will only be sure on this point after we had been able to create a generation of listeners trained to do it.

5.1 Expanded Tonal Centers

With the foreseen expansion of the fourth characteristic, a concomitant expansion of the fifth characteristic is bound to occur quite naturally. We point to the subtle appearance of chroma axes in addition to tonal centers. The same restrictions assigned to the fourth characteristic apply here. We could think of this characteristic as "expanded tonal centers".

6.1 Expanded Harmonic Functions

Similarly, the sixth characteristic becomes expanded by carrying on the consequences of having expanded the former characteristics. It could be redefined as follows: let composers use theories of harmony that establish hierarchies of functions to regulate the simple or complex interplay of tonal centers and chroma axes according to an aesthetic position that bears a close relationship with the roles of consonance and dissonance as redefined by increased beating *and* timbral parameters. Let the only restriction be that, as in the past, such theories must evolve from musical practice and not from the act of defining hierarchies of functions *a priori*, whether they are defined by scientists or by music theorists. Thus, we can speak of an "expanded theory of harmony".

7.1 Expanded Notation

Finally, notation, the seventh characteristic, must expand also, in order to accommodate to the necessities of the former expanded characteristics. Notice that, in accordance with our principle of conservation, we say "expand" and not "become something else". Notation should not change from its traditional tablature form (it must simply become more complex by expanding the possibilities that it already offers).

Notation must maintain at all costs the restriction that is inherent to our traditional notation: instantaneous performance of the encoded music must always be possible for any standardly trained musician. Ideally, notation should codify in a general form all parameters over which the performer has control, as well as clearly show harmonic functions. To this end, we propose the use of color to differentiate pitch class from the tablature name of a pitch class (Chapter Four). The only restrictions should be those that have been proposed in Chapter Four under the heading "Rules for the use of color".

If these expansions were possible, they would allow us not only to maintain our principle of conservation, but also due to their basic potential they would become a principle themselves. Then we may establish our second principle: expansion. Thus, expansion and conservation complement, rather than contradict, each other.

Our seven propositions for the seven basic characteristics, along with their restrictions, represent an effort to explore the *multidimensionality* of the seven basic characteristics of the Western musical tradition. Technology has brought to us the possibility of beginning to apply our proposed expansions systematically. Today, digital instruments that can be controlled from a keyboard or wind instrument, or from a stringed instrument (in fact, from any kind of mechanical device known as MIDI controller) are sold in the market. We particularly refer to the kind of instruments that give the user complete control over their tuning tables and, of course, over all parameters of timbre - although still in a primitive manner. We will now summarize the applications of our principles of conservation and expansion.

Observing the list of characteristics we want to conserve and expand:

- Accurate instruments

- Musical scales

- Exponentiation

- Chroma

- Tonal Centers

- Harmonic functions

- Notation

we may conclude that,

a) engineers have already begun to expand multidimensionally the concept of an accurate musical instrument.

b) Also, expanding the concept of equal temperament and exponentiation provokes a chain reaction that could expand hierarchically the rest of the characteristics in the following manner:

1) By expanding the number of equal intervals of a scale and/or by expanding the exponential base of a scale, one could expect to induce, in certain cases, the perception of an expanded sense of chroma.

2) An expanded sense of chroma could induce the perception of tonal axes, in addition to tonal centers, which in time would require

3) new harmonic systems, where consonance and dissonance would be linked to beats and timbres. This would demand

4) an expansion of the capabilities of our notation system. It should be evident that

c) our desire to stimulate the growing potential of the Western musical tradition could be accomplished with the expansion of equal temperaments and exponentiation, and that

d) in order to obtain expanded temperaments and expanded exponentiation we should establish a mathematical system to calculate musical scales (as the system shown in Chapter One), and proceed to calculate and implement expanded tunings (as we exemplified in Chapter Three).

CHAPTER SEVEN

Expanded Tunings and Composition Today and Tomorrow

Introduction

Independently of the question of expanded chroma, all expanded tunings produce a sense of symmetry. All expanded tunings are equal temperaments and, as such, they allow for transposition and modulation. Tonality and modality are possible in many expanded tunings. Of course, in case of an ultimate failure of the human mind to perceive expanded chroma, the chroma of expanded tunings would orbit around approximations to octaves, or if these were avoided, perhaps it would be assumed as being implicit in the harmony. However, their basic mathematical organization is an indicator of their perceptual cohesion.

As it can be easily seen in the tables, a substantial number of expanded tunings will not sound equal or even close to octave-based tunings. In this statement we include not only tunings from the group labeled as "possibly true expanded tunings" (in Chapter Five), but also many other tunings from the other larger group. This means that the intervals, chords and melodic possibilities of many expanded tunings are unique, which amounts to an immense number of new harmonic and melodic patterns. In light of these facts, the classification of tunings as "true" or not "true" expanded tunings

should not be a general classification, but a particular analytical classification referring *only* to chroma interference. A more meaningful general classification would include *original* and *pseudo-expanded* tunings. In the category of the *pseudo-expanded* we would include tunings that are (for practical purposes) perceptually indistinguishable from octave-based tunings.

Composition with expanded tunings is a possibility that will have to be exploited and explored sooner or later. The development of digital technology has opened the door to precise control of pitch. It is only a logical consequence that many composers will try to apply the resources of digital technology to their field. Furthermore, there seems to be a certain saturation point beyond which the harmonic and melodic possibilities of our usual tuning cannot reach. Many expanded tunings offer either novelty or subtlety or both. Once technology makes these offerings available with an acceptable degree of practicality, the challenge to make good use of them becomes too great to go unnoticed for many generations. Indeed, expanded tunings are an enormous resource for the music of the future.

Essay

At present, there are several important reasons why composition with alternative forms of tuning cannot promptly become popular or even widespread. The most important reason is that expanded instruments are still in an elementary developmental stage. As of today, commercial sound synthesis systems with total tuning control - with the exception perhaps of gigantic, prohibitively expensive systems - are not yet capable of producing timbres as subtle, rich and beautifully expressive as those of the traditional orchestral instruments. Composers of serious electroacoustic (from now on read also "electronic', "computer," "digital," etc. for "electroacoustic") music usually evade, deny, or are naively unaware of this problem when saying that traditional tonal or atonal music, or features thereof - melodies, tonal centers, rhythmic periodicity- are not *idiomatic* to electroacoustic music.

This attitude is strongly related to the now archaic medium of electroacoustic music: magnetic tape. Nonetheless, the dogma of idiomaticity should be understood and questioned in terms of the inherent limitations of sound synthesis systems of the recent past. It is true that during the past decades, the majority of powerful sound synthesis systems were not designed for live performance. Therefore, composers were less preoccupied with real-time control of synthetic sounds than with their assembly on magnetic tape. The result has been the development of a style which many composers of electroacoustic music of the recent past have termed as "idiomatic".

Most of the so-called idiomatic electroacoustic music style consists of long tracks of static, slow-moving sounds punctuated by occasional bursts of aperiodical ejaculations, and driven towards a climax of loud, amorphous masses of irritating sound. Infinite variations of this pitiful pattern constitute a great percentage of the present electroacoustic music repertoire. Not all composers, however, have assumed that the dogma of idiomaticity of electroacoustic music is the only possible serious alternative for this medium. To cite only a couple names among American composers, E. Blackwood (*Twelve Microtonal Etudes for Electronic Media*), and W. Carlos (*Beauty in The Beast*), have successfully used the electroacoustic medium in ways that contradict the supposed idiomaticity of electroacoustic music.

The achievements of these and other composers remind us that the line dividing the idiomatic and the non-idiomatic in music is always blurred, if not perhaps nonexistent. Who would maintain nowadays that Beethoven's writing for strings in his last quartets, Chopin's piano etudes, Wagner's vocal writing or Bartok's pianistic demands are not idiomatic? It is a matter of raising technical standards: either one has the sufficient knowledge and technique necessary to accomplish the performance of a given piece of music, or one does not have such technique, in which case, one must work in order to obtain the required technique.

Nevertheless, if electroacoustic music begins to take a more active role in the performance of real-time concert music, the quality of timbres used needs to be as outstanding as that of the instruments of the standard

orchestra - which is a yet distant goal. Control and a great capacity for nuance and expression need to be available in every electroacoustic instrument. Only when these conditions become a permanent reality at reasonable prices can we expect the flourishing of live performances of new concert music performed on electroacoustic instruments. On the other hand, a greater and more subtle problem lies hidden in the midst of any considerations about electroacoustically generated timbres.

When composers write for traditional instruments, the choice of instruments will determine the timbral output. The composer knows what to expect according to the timbral characteristics of the selected instruments. No standardization exists, however, for practical purposes, in the description of electronically-generated timbres. If a composer of electroacoustic music has a very specific timbre in mind, the only alternative left is to specify the particular algorithm, computer language, and hardware implementation, or the brand and model type of the instrument that was originally used to produce that exact timbre. This would not be such a great problem if it were not for the fact that manufacturers of small systems are constantly discontinuing the production of older models to substitute them for newer ones. Frequently, newer models will have a different design and therefore will not be able to produce the exact kind of timbres that the older ones were able to produce.

It is not uncommon that a manufacturer of electroacoustic instruments goes out of business, and a certain type of instrument disappears forever from the market. Not surprisingly, composers of electroacoustic music have tended to favor magnetic analogue tape - more recently digital tape, as both, the medium and the technique, where a unique timbre will remain forever even if the instrument used to produce it vanishes from the surface of the earth.

Composers of electroacoustic music need to specify the exact nature of the timbres to be used in a composition. This calls for a generalized, standard, practical method to notate in the score of a composition the physical nature of timbres. Even if a performer were limited to the use of certain instruments that cannot accurately recreate a described timbre, the

precision of the timbre's description would help to achieve the closest approximation. In turn, the performer would have to know how the described timbres relate to the design and possibilities of the employed instrument. We cannot stress too much the importance of a standardized timbral notation, for such a system is a necessary condition for the real permanence of musical works of art in which the nature of specifically demanded timbres constitutes an essential and inalienable condition for the existence of the works as such.

By "real permanence" we mean not the frozen permanence that a musical composition achieves when it is recorded on a analogue or digital device, but the *dynamic* permanence that an extremely precise and accurate notation confers on a piece of music. Dynamic permanence means, in this context, that a piece of music, no matter how complex or difficult, appears accurately notated, and that a trained musician can interpret the notation with exactness, and subsequently perform the piece.

Music endowed with dynamic permanence is susceptible of being performed by future generations of musicians trained in the tradition from which such music springs. This is the great achievement of an exact and standardized musical notation: faithful performance.

Contrary to the optimism of composers of tape music, we believe that music not endowed with dynamic permanence is already half-dead at the time it is born. Even among the computer music community, where tape music is a predominant form of musical output, a vocal minority raises questions once in a while concerning this issue. Gareth Loy, for example, in his essay "Composing with computers -a survey" (1989), writes: "...making recordings has become the principal creative outlet of most musicians. But once made, a recording is the same forever. If even "perfect" performances wear thin after many literal repetitions, lesser performances may quickly become unbearable." We may wonder here if this could not be the case with tape music in general, where the composition itself is its only and eternal "performance", if we may stretch the meaning of this term so far. Live performance is the life of music, and this is seen, among many other considerations, in the fact that music lovers take a great pleasure in evaluating not only the intrinsic qualities of compositions, but the abilities,

merit, and artistic capabilities of performers.

In particular, when it comes to the standard repertory, inveterate music lovers find much gratification in criticizing the execution of a well-known piece. There is no substitute for this experience; a piece is always new every time a performer plays it - not every time we turn the tape recorder on. In order to evaluate the merits of a particular performance of a piece, the piece must have a definitive identity; yet, it must leave room for the unpredictable character that a performance will stamp upon it. A piece that only exists as a recording is one hundred percent determined and offers no opportunity to enjoy the particular variations that make the difference between different performances and performers of the piece. A piece of aleatory music, or one heavily based on chance, has no definitive identity, prevents the pleasures of knowledge and identification, and totally rules out judging the fine merits of performance, since it lacks a standard ideal identity or a temporarily established one. We refer not to thoroughly composed pieces that have been composed by a random process or a process involving chance, but pieces in which the performance is accomplished by means of mostly random, impromptu decisions based on vague or gestural indications demanded by the composer. This type of musical farce has been responsible, in part, for the noticeable abhorrence that many music lovers, concert audiences, and even professional musicians generically feel for "contemporary music", whatever this expression may mean to them. These statements should not be construed as diminishing the artistic possibilities of musical improvisation nor the merits of many tape compositions. Their intention is to remark the inescapable and essential importance of live performance, and the danger of performance becoming a mockery.

A universal timbre notation would collaborate to free electroacoustic music from the straightjacket of tape composition, ensuring with this the dynamic permanence of new compositions for the medium, among which, we could expect compositions in expanded tunings.

Therefore, since composition with expanded tunings depends at present on the electroacoustic medium, it is reasonable to assume that expanded tunings will not become very popular or widespread until the

fundamental problems of electroacoustic music -greater and professional timbral quality and control, and a universal system of timbral notation - have been solved, or until acoustic instruments are capable of total, precise mathematical control of pitch by means of computer technologies.

Another enormous problem, as far as the popularization of alternative forms of tuning among composers is concerned, is the inertia of the pedagogical establishment. Music is rapidly evolving towards a stage in which the intercourse between performance and composition, and science, technology and history will demand an updated education for musicians. Not only composers, but also performers need to benefit from the updating. On one hand, we have seen a great and laudable concern, during the last twenty years, for achieving historical authenticity in the performance of music of the past. In general, conservatories and universities have begun to place a healthy emphasis on the relationship between history, research, and performance. This move towards objectivity, very much in accordance with the spirit of our times, has transformed the way we perform and listen to the music of the past; yet, on the other hand, the quest for objectivity has remained mainly confined to the humanities, and has not addressed the upcoming demands that science and technology present to "serious" music and musicians.

The perfect example is the aura of esotericism and practical uselessness that surrounds the topic of intonation systems, at least among the majority of composers and performers. This may be, in part, the result of the fact that a regrettable pedagogical neglect has reduced the possibilities of tuning and temperament to a form of theoretical curiosity, or at the most to a highly specialized scholarly topic connected with music history and the historically correct performance of Baroque and Renaissance music, or even with the more specialized field of ethnomusicological research of non-Western musical traditions. In any case, these specializations are not oriented towards composition. In order to form an at least a little bit objective idea of how much information an average student of music composition does have about the possibilities that intonation systems offer to his or her art, the present author has selected at random, from a university library, fifty catalogs or pamphlets describing the

curricula of two music schools in England, three in France, three in Austria, one in Canada and the rest in the United States of America. Not one of these fifty schools offered a class or seminar on tuning and applications.

After looking at several textbooks in acoustics for musicians, the author observed that these textbooks fail to convey, even remotely, the notion that a tuning scheme could be an essential and most determinant part of the composition process. Whenever the subject of "the musical scale" (usually in singular) is treated, these textbooks indulge in the idea that there is a natural scale, and that "equal temperament" (meaning twelve-tone-to-the-octave equal temperament) is a regrettable compromise that should offend any educated ear, but that the same educated ear should be content with the evils of equal temperament because the natural scale is not "practical". Some of these books engage in fruitless and ridiculous discussions about consonance and dissonance (connecting aesthetics with numerology), and most of them lack in precise and comprehensive mathematical discussions of the few temperaments they mention. These textbooks convey the same message to the unaware reader: "Thou shalt not doubt that there is one and only one natural scale" and "Thou shalt not doubt that equal temperament is its only practical representation." It is no surprise, then, that a young composer, if she or he has ever had a class in musical acoustics, may conclude that the whole subject of tuning is totally irrelevant. If it is true that most music students are not required to learn about tuning systems, and those who are observe the prejudices that traditionally appear in textbooks of acoustics for musicians, then we may in justice wonder how many composers are prepared to face the fact that computer technology has already begun to make viable the application of ideas that disrupt violently their comfortable habits and their traditional assumptions.

There are many encouraging signs, however, indicating that this situation is changing (however slowly) and will continue to change. One of the most conspicuous examples is the Royal Conservatory at the Hague, in the Netherlands. An informational pamphlet of the Royal Conservatory at the Hague (1989/90) tells us Of a new six-year undergraduate program in music called "Sonology". In this program, according to the pamphlet, the

following are required subjects:

- acoustics

- computer programming

- mathematics

- artificial intelligence

- digital sound synthesis

- interactive realtime composition

- programming of structural and formal process

- electro-instrumentation

- instrumentation/ analysis

- history of music and culture

- music sociology

- music psychology

- composition projects

- keyboard instrument

- solfeggio workshop

- signal processing

- theory of algorithms

- formal logic

- psycho-acoustics

- introduction to serial and electronic music

- analog studio techniques

- theory of 20th-Century music

- music psychology

- counterpoint

- experimental work

- introduction to new music analysis

- advanced instrumentation

- theoretical training (theory and harmony)

The program is aimed at musicians who want to "independently do research and to ... involve themselves in the field of electroacoustic and computer music" (Royal Conservatory at the Hague, 1989). Evidently, it would be inconceivable that this heavily academic program could be combined with the training requirements and number of practice hours that the career of a concert performer demands. However, the program is a landmark, and, in our opinion, an indicator of future developments in the area of music pedagogy.

In effect, the traditional curricula of music schools and conservatories

will have to be updated in order to give young generations of musicians a more realistic professional training in accordance with the advancements of related sciences and technologies. It is possible, however, that the musical pedagogical establishment refuses to acknowledge that these advancements actually bring a vast richness of possibilities to the future of serious music, or that even if it acknowledges this as being true, it remains aloof and unconcerned, waiting cautiously for some more tangible results in the form of a generalized practice outside and without the blessing of Academia. In any case, developments like those in the science of music perception, computer music and related technologies, and new composition and performance techniques - like the present theory of expanded tunings - demand a basic training including not only the traditional music subjects found in most conservatories' curricula, but also mathematics, psychoacoustic science, tuning theory, theory of sound synthesis, and computer literacy. These subjects should form part of the basic training of all musicians, composers and performers.

Several of the present author's friends in the area of performance have remarked to him that the natural character of some performers and people inclined to pure artistic pursuits shows a dislike for scientific or technical subjects and would find so much theory onerous and distracting. Whatever these remarks may show of intuition, or even if they only represented long-established habits (as they probably do), the fact that new instruments and techniques ask for an at least elementary scientific training is undeniable. In consequence, there is a strong dependency between changes in music pedagogy and the generalization and popularization of composition and performance in poorly-explored or unexplored forms of tuning.

The final blow to the possibility of an immediate widespreading of alternative tunings as the basis of new music composition is, however, a cultural obstacle that cannot be overcome as easily as the ones mentioned above. This is a difficult and controversial point, and we will not elaborate here upon it beyond the present paragraph. Let the reader consider, then, if he or she has any familiarity with concerts, recordings, compositions, and composers of current serious acoustical, computer and electroacoustic music, how the styles and philosophies behind so much of the current

compositional work and criticism point to the pervading assumption that rhythmic periodicity, tonal centerdness, and cohesively perceptual melodic-thematic work constitute a label of obsoleteness, lack of imagination and originality, a refusal to explore new possibilities, and so forth. The problem is that, as explained in the first chapters of this book, in order for our brains to perceive the richness and complicated conceptual topology of a tuning schema operating through a complex, dynamical network of hierarchically interwoven tonal structures, a rather clear system of tonal centers, and periodical rhythmic and/or melodic structures must prevail in the fabric of the music. In simpler words: if the music is serial-atonal, highly dissonant, lacking in rhythmic and thematic periodicity, or if it is random, or concrete, or the like, then the choice of a tuning schema brings no new possibilities to the music (for exactly the opposite reasons that it does for tonally and periodically oriented music [see Chaps. Two and Six]), and therefore, playing around with different tunings results totally superfluous. Expanded tunings must wait, so it seems, for the pendulum of the zeitgeist to turn back and initiate a new cultural cycle where artists and composers are less disturbed by the obsessions of originality and novelty, and more interested in subtlety and beauty.

Considering the possibilities of success for expanded tunings as a generalized compositional technique, two points of final relevance deserve to be stated. The first, we must repeat, is that, because expanded tunings are a mathematical and technical possibility, we realize that they will be explored by a number of composers sooner or later. It is also possible that some of the resulting compositions will be of great artistic standing. The second point is in a way a corollary of the first, and refers to the reasonable assumption that it is difficult to see composition with alternative tunings becoming a widespread musical practice unless a substantial group of well-known masterworks have consolidated, with their own musical merits, the idea of their usefulness.

Perhaps the best way to conclude this study is by citing the words of Igor Stravinsky in 1959. Robert Craft asks the following question: "Is any musical element still susceptible to radical exploitation and development?" Stravinsky answers: "Yes, pitch" (Stravinsky and Craft, 1960). The old

master continues:

> I even risk a prediction that pitch will comprise the main difference between the "music of the future" and our music, and I consider that the most important aspect of electronic music is that it can manufacture pitch. Our mid-twentieth-century situation, in regard to pitch, might perhaps be compared to that of the mid-sixteenth-century, when, after Willaert and others had proved the necessity of equal temperament, the great pitch experiments began - Zarlino's quarter-tone instrument, Vicentino's thirty-one-tones-to-the-octave archicembalo, and others. These instruments failed, of course, and the well-tempered clavier was established (though at least three hundred years before Bach), but our ears are more ready for such experiments now - mine are, at any rate.

REFERENCES

References to works on music are given in the standard reference style for the Humanities and Fine Arts. Works on the Psychology and Science of Music will be referred to according to the style commonly found in psychology books and journals.

I. Works on Music

Benjamin, Gerald. Julián Carrillo and "Sonido Trece". *American Institute for Musical Research Yearbook,* 3 (1967): 37-68.

Blackwood, Easley. *The Structure of Recognizable Diatonic Tunings.* Princeton, New Jersey: Princeton University Press, 1985.

Busoni, Ferrucio. *Sketch of a New Esthetic of Music.* New York: Schirmer, 1911.

Carlos, Wendy.	"Tuning: At the Crossroads". *Computer Music Journal,* 11 (January 1987): 29-43.
Carrillo, Julián.	*Sonido 13 - fundamento científico e histórico.* México: Julián Carrillo, 1948.
Forte, Allan	*The Structure of Atonal Music.* New Haven, Connecticut: Yale University Press, 1973.
Haba, Alois.	*Neue Harmonielehre des diatonischen, chromatischen, Viertel-Drittel-Sechstel-Zwölftel-Ton Systems.* Leipzig: Fr. Kestner und C. F. V. Siegel, 1927.
Meyer, Max.	"The Musician's Arithmetic". *University of Missouri Studies* , vol. 4 no. 1, 1929.
Moreno, Enrique.	"Introduction to An Expanded Theory of Tuning and Scales". Report presented to the College Honors Program, University of Kansas, 1987.
Nettl, Bruno.	*Music in Primitive Culture.* Cambridge, Massachusetts: Harvard University Press, 1956.
Overmeyer, Grace.	"Quarter-Tones and Less". *The American Mercury,* 12 (October 1927): 207-210.
Royal Conservatory at The Hague	Sonology and Music Registration. The Hague: Royal Conservatory at the Hague, 1989.
Russolo, Luigi.	*L'art des bruites - manifeste futuriste et autres textes*, ed. by Giovani Lista. Lausanne: Editions

L'Age d'Homme, 1975.

Sachs, Curt. *The Wellsprings of Music.* The Hague: Martinus Nyhofif, 1962.

Schaeffer, Pierre. *A la recherche d'une musique concrète.* Paris: Editions du Seuil, 1952.

———— *Traité des objects musicaux.* Paris: Editions du Seuil, 1966.

Stravinsky, Igor, & Craft, Robert *Memories and Commentaries.* NewYork: Doubleday & Co., Inc., 1960.

Yasser, Joseph. *A Theory of Evolving Tonality.* New York: American Library of Musicology, 1932.

Zuckerkandl, Victor. *The Sense of music.* Princeton: Princeton University Press, 1971.

II. Works on the Psychology of Music

Allen, D. Octave discriminability of musical and non-musical subjects. *Psychonomic Science*, 1967, F, 421-422.

Bachem, A. Note on Nev's review of the literature on absolute pitch. *Psychological Bulletin*, 1948, 45, 161-162.

Balzano, G. The pitch set as a level of description for studying musical pitch perception. In Manfred Clyne's (Ed.), *Music, Mind, and Brain.* New York: Plenum Press, 1982.

Bohlen, H.	13 Tonstufen in der Duodezeme. *Acoustica*, 1978, 39, 76-86.
Burns, E., & Ward, W. D.	Intervals, scales and tuning. In D. Deutsch (Ed.), *The Psychology of Music*. New York: Academic Press, 1982.
Deutsch, D.	The processing of pitch combinations. In D. Deutsch (Ed.), *The Psychology of Music*. NewYork: Academic Press, 1982.
Drobisch, M.	Über musikalsche Tonbestimmung und Temperatur. In *Abhandlungen der Koeniglich saechsischen Gesellschaft der Wissenschaften*. Leipzig, 1852. Vierter Band: Abhandlungen der mathematisch-physichen Klasse. Leipzig: S. Hirzel, August 1855, pp. 33-121.
Francès, R.	*La perception de la musique*. Paris: Vrin, 1958.
Gerson, A., & Goldstein, J. L.	Evidence for a general template in central optimal processing for pitch of complex tones. *Journal of the Acoustical Society of America*, 1978, 63, 498-510.
Houtsma, A. J. M.	Musical pitch of two-tone complexes and predictions by modern pitch theories. *Journal of the Acoustical Society of America*, 1978, 66, 87-99.
Loy, D. G.	Composing with computers - a survey. In Max V. Mathews and John R. Pierce (Eds.), *Current Directions in Computer Music*. Cambridge, Massachusetts: The MIT Press, 1989.

Lundin, R.W.   *An Objective Psychology of Music.* New York: Ronald Press, 1953.

Mathews, M. V., Pierce, J. R., et al.   Theoretical and experimental explorations of the Bohlen-Pierce scale. *Journal of the Acoustical Society of America*, 1988, 84, 1214-1222.

Pierce, J. R.   Attaining consonance in arbitrary scales. *Journal of the Acoustical Society of America*, 1966, 40, 249.

Risset, J.   Musical Acoustics. In E. C. Corterette, & M. D. Friedman (Eds.), *Handbook of Perception* (Volume IV), New York: Academic Press, 1978.

Roederer, J. G.   *Introduction to The Physics and Psychophysics of Music.* New York: Springer-Verlag, 1979.

Shepard, R. N.   Circularity in judgments of relative pitch. *Journal of the Acoustical Society of America*, 1964 36, 2346-2353

———   Approximation to uniform gradients of generalization by monotone transformations of scale. In D. I. Mostofsky (Ed.), *Stimulus Generalization.* Stanford, California: Stanford University Press, 1965.

Schubert, E.   Personal communication (at Stanford University, 1991).

Terhardt, E.   Pitch, consonance, and harmony. *Journal of the Acoustical Society of America*, 1974, 55, 1061-1069.

Thurlow, W.R.& Hercul, W. P.   Judged similarity in pitch of octave multiples. *Perception and Psychophysics*, 1977, 22, 177-182.

Zenati, A.   Le developpment genetique de la perception musicale. *Monographies francaises de psychologie* (No. 17). Centre National de La Recherche Scientifique, 1969.

APPENDIX I

MUSICAL EXAMPLES

(SCORES)

Example 1

AVE MARIA
for Soprano and Synthesizer
E. Moreno

Copyright © Enrique Moreno 1989

Example no.2: melody

Enrique Moreno

Example no.3: chorale

Enrique Moreno

Tuning: A-12
Initial Frequency: 52 Hz.
Name of First Key: C1
Position:

Example no.4: theme with alberti bass

Enrique Moreno

APPENDIX II

TABLES

Table 1

Initial Catalog of Tunings: Octave 5

Scale Deg.	HZ	Cts	TU	Scale Deg.	HZ	Cts	TU	Scale Deg.	HZ	Cts	TU
1	27.50	0.00	1,706.00	14	166.73	3,120.00	4,368.40	27	1,010.85	6,240.00	7,030.80
2	31.59	240.00	1,910.80	15	191.52	3,360.00	4,573.20	28	1,161.17	6,480.00	7,235.60
3	36.29	480.00	2,115.60	16	220.00	3,600.00	4,778.00	29	1,333.83	6,720.00	7,440.40
4	41.68	720.00	2,320.40	17	252.71	3,840.00	4,982.80	30	1,532.17	6,960.00	7,645.20
5	47.88	960.00	2,525.20	18	290.29	4,080.00	5,187.60	31	1,760.00	7,200.00	7,850.00
6	55.00	1,200.00	2,730.00	19	333.46	4,320.00	5,392.40	32	2,021.71	7,440.00	8,054.80
7	63.18	1,440.00	2,934.80	20	383.04	4,560.00	5,597.20	33	2,322.33	7,680.00	8,259.60
8	72.57	1,680.00	3,139.60	21	440.00	4,800.00	5,802.00	34	2,667.66	7,920.00	8,464.40
9	83.36	1,920.00	3,344.40	22	505.43	5,040.00	6,006.80	35	3,064.34	8,160.00	8,669.20
10	95.76	2,160.00	3,549.20	23	580.58	5,280.00	6,211.60	36	3,520.00	8,400.00	8,874.00
11	110.00	2,400.00	3,754.00	24	666.92	5,520.00	6,416.40	37	4,043.42	8,640.00	9,078.80
12	126.36	2,640.00	3,958.80	25	766.08	5,760.00	6,621.20				
13	145.15	2,880.00	4,163.60	26	880.00	6,000.00	6,826.00				

Initial Catalog of Tunings: Octave 6

Scale Deg.	HZ	Cts	TU	Scale Deg.	HZ	Cts	TU	Scale Deg.	HZ	Cts	TU
1	27.50	0.00	1,706.00	17	174.61	3,200.00	4,436.67	33	1,108.73	6,400.00	7,167.33
2	30.87	200.00	1,876.67	18	196.00	3,400.00	4,607.33	34	1,244.51	6,600.00	7,338.00
3	34.65	400.00	2,047.33	19	220.00	3,600.00	4,778.00	35	1,396.91	6,800.00	7,508.67
4	38.89	600.00	2,218.00	20	246.94	3,800.00	4,948.67	36	1,567.98	7,000.00	7,679.33
5	43.65	800.00	2,388.67	21	277.18	4,000.00	5,119.33	37	1,760.00	7,200.00	7,850.00
6	49.00	1,000.00	2,559.33	22	311.13	4,200.00	5,290.00	38	1,975.53	7,400.00	8,020.67
7	55.00	1,200.00	2,730.00	23	349.23	4,400.00	5,460.67	39	2,217.46	7,600.00	8,191.33
8	61.74	1,400.00	2,900.67	24	392.00	4,600.00	5,631.33	40	2,489.02	7,800.00	8,362.00
9	69.30	1,600.00	3,071.33	25	440.00	4,800.00	5,802.00	41	2,793.83	8,000.00	8,532.67
10	77.78	1,800.00	3,242.00	26	493.88	5,000.00	5,972.67	42	3,135.96	8,200.00	8,703.33
11	87.31	2,000.00	3,412.67	27	554.37	5,200.00	6,143.33	43	3,520.00	8,400.00	8,874.00
12	98.00	2,200.00	3,583.33	28	622.25	5,400.00	6,314.00	44	3,951.07	8,600.00	9,044.67
13	110.00	2,400.00	3,754.00	29	698.46	5,600.00	6,484.67	45	4,434.92	8,800.00	9,215.33
14	123.47	2,600.00	3,924.67	30	783.99	5,800.00	6,655.33				
15	138.59	2,800.00	4,095.33	31	880.00	6,000.00	6,826.00				
16	155.56	3,000.00	4,266.00	32	987.77	6,200.00	6,996.67				

Initial Catalog of Tunings: Octave 7

Scale Deg.	HZ	Cts	TU	Scale Deg.	HZ	Cts	TU	Scale Deg.	HZ	Cts	TU
1	27.50	0.00	1,706.00	19	163.46	3,085.71	4,339.14	37	971.60	6,171.43	6,972.29
2	30.36	171.43	1,852.29	20	180.47	3,257.14	4,485.43	38	1,072.73	6,342.86	7,118.57
3	33.52	342.86	1,998.57	21	199.26	3,428.57	4,631.71	39	1,184.39	6,514.29	7,264.86
4	37.01	514.29	2,144.86	22	220.00	3,600.00	4,778.00	40	1,307.67	6,685.71	7,411.14
5	40.86	685.71	2,291.14	23	242.90	3,771.43	4,924.29	41	1,443.79	6,857.14	7,557.43
6	45.12	857.14	2,437.43	24	268.18	3,942.86	5,070.57	42	1,594.07	7,028.57	7,703.71
7	49.81	1,028.57	2,583.71	25	296.10	4,114.29	5,216.86	43	1,760.00	7,200.00	7,850.00
8	55.00	1,200.00	2,730.00	26	326.92	4,285.71	5,363.14	44	1,943.20	7,371.43	7,996.29
9	60.72	1,371.43	2,876.29	27	360.95	4,457.14	5,509.43	45	2,145.46	7,542.86	8,142.57
10	67.05	1,542.86	3,022.57	28	398.52	4,628.57	5,655.71	46	2,368.78	7,714.29	8,288.86
11	74.02	1,714.29	3,168.86	29	440.00	4,800.00	5,802.00	47	2,615.35	7,885.71	8,435.14
12	81.73	1,885.71	3,315.14	30	485.80	4,971.43	5,948.29	48	2,887.58	8,057.14	8,581.43
13	90.24	2,057.14	3,461.43	31	536.37	5,142.86	6,094.57	49	3,188.15	8,228.57	8,727.71
14	99.63	2,228.57	3,607.71	32	592.20	5,314.29	6,240.86	50	3,520.00	8,400.00	8,874.00
15	110.00	2,400.00	3,754.00	33	653.84	5,485.71	6,387.14	51	3,886.40	8,571.43	9,020.29
16	121.45	2,571.43	3,900.29	34	721.90	5,657.14	6,533.43	52	4,290.93	8,742.86	9,166.57
17	134.09	2,742.86	4,046.57	35	797.04	5,828.57	6,679.71				
18	148.05	2,914.29	4,192.86	36	880.00	6,000.00	6,826.00				

Table 1 (continues)

Initial Catalog of Tunings : Octave 8

Scale Deg.	HZ	Cts	TU	Scale Deg.	HZ	Cts	TU	Scale Deg.	HZ	Cts	TU
1	27.50	0.00	1,706.00	22	169.64	3,150.00	4,394.00	43	1,046.50	6,300.00	7,082.00
2	29.99	150.00	1,834.00	23	185.00	3,300.00	4,522.00	44	1,141.22	6,450.00	7,210.00
3	32.70	300.00	1,962.00	24	201.74	3,450.00	4,650.00	45	1,244.51	6,600.00	7,338.00
4	35.66	450.00	2,090.00	25	220.00	3,600.00	4,778.00	46	1,357.15	6,750.00	7,466.00
5	38.89	600.00	2,218.00	26	239.91	3,750.00	4,906.00	47	1,479.98	6,900.00	7,594.00
6	42.41	750.00	2,346.00	27	261.63	3,900.00	5,034.00	48	1,613.93	7,050.00	7,722.00
7	46.25	900.00	2,474.00	28	285.30	4,050.00	5,162.00	49	1,760.00	7,200.00	7,850.00
8	50.44	1,050.00	2,602.00	29	311.13	4,200.00	5,290.00	50	1,919.29	7,350.00	7,978.00
9	55.00	1,200.00	2,730.00	30	339.29	4,350.00	5,418.00	51	2,093.00	7,500.00	8,106.00
10	59.98	1,350.00	2,858.00	31	369.99	4,500.00	5,546.00	52	2,282.44	7,650.00	8,234.00
11	65.41	1,500.00	2,986.00	32	403.48	4,650.00	5,674.00	53	2,489.02	7,800.00	8,362.00
12	71.33	1,650.00	3,114.00	33	440.00	4,800.00	5,802.00	54	2,714.29	7,950.00	8,490.00
13	77.78	1,800.00	3,242.00	34	479.82	4,950.00	5,930.00	55	2,959.96	8,100.00	8,618.00
14	84.82	1,950.00	3,370.00	35	523.25	5,100.00	6,058.00	56	3,227.85	8,250.00	8,746.00
15	92.50	2,100.00	3,498.00	36	570.61	5,250.00	6,186.00	57	3,520.00	8,400.00	8,874.00
16	100.87	2,250.00	3,626.00	37	622.25	5,400.00	6,314.00	58	3,838.59	8,550.00	9,002.00
17	110.00	2,400.00	3,754.00	38	678.57	5,550.00	6,442.00	59	4,186.01	8,700.00	9,130.00
18	119.96	2,550.00	3,882.00	39	739.99	5,700.00	6,570.00	60	4,564.88	8,850.00	9,258.00
19	130.81	2,700.00	4,010.00	40	806.96	5,850.00	6,698.00				
20	142.65	2,850.00	4,138.00	41	880.00	6,000.00	6,826.00				
21	155.56	3,000.00	4,266.00	42	959.65	6,150.00	6,954.00				

Initial Catalog of Tunings : Octave 9

Scale Deg.	HZ	Cts	TU	Scale Deg.	HZ	Cts	TU	Scale Deg.	HZ	Cts	TU
1	27.50	0.00	1,706.00	24	161.67	3,066.67	4,322.89	47	950.45	6,133.33	6,939.78
2	29.70	133.33	1,819.78	25	174.61	3,200.00	4,436.67	48	1,026.55	6,266.67	7,053.56
3	32.08	266.67	1,933.56	26	188.59	3,333.33	4,550.44	49	1,108.73	6,400.00	7,167.33
4	34.65	400.00	2,047.33	27	203.69	3,466.67	4,664.22	50	1,197.50	6,533.33	7,281.11
5	37.42	533.33	2,161.11	28	220.00	3,600.00	4,778.00	51	1,293.37	6,666.67	7,394.89
6	40.42	666.67	2,274.89	29	237.61	3,733.33	4,891.78	52	1,396.91	6,800.00	7,508.67
7	43.65	800.00	2,388.67	30	256.64	3,866.67	5,005.56	53	1,508.75	6,933.33	7,622.44
8	47.15	933.33	2,502.44	31	277.18	4,000.00	5,119.33	54	1,629.54	7,066.67	7,736.22
9	50.92	1,066.67	2,616.22	32	299.37	4,133.33	5,233.11	55	1,760.00	7,200.00	7,850.00
10	55.00	1,200.00	2,730.00	33	323.34	4,266.67	5,346.89	56	1,900.91	7,333.33	7,963.78
11	59.40	1,333.33	2,843.78	34	349.23	4,400.00	5,460.67	57	2,053.09	7,466.67	8,077.56
12	64.16	1,466.67	2,957.56	35	377.19	4,533.33	5,574.44	58	2,217.46	7,600.00	8,191.33
13	69.30	1,600.00	3,071.33	36	407.38	4,666.67	5,688.22	59	2,394.99	7,733.33	8,305.11
14	74.84	1,733.33	3,185.11	37	440.00	4,800.00	5,802.00	60	2,586.73	7,866.67	8,418.89
15	80.84	1,866.67	3,298.89	38	475.23	4,933.33	5,915.78	61	2,793.83	8,000.00	8,532.67
16	87.31	2,000.00	3,412.67	39	513.27	5,066.67	6,029.56	62	3,017.50	8,133.33	8,646.44
17	94.30	2,133.33	3,526.44	40	554.37	5,200.00	6,143.33	63	3,259.08	8,266.67	8,760.22
18	101.85	2,266.67	3,640.22	41	598.75	5,333.33	6,257.11	64	3,520.00	8,400.00	8,874.00
19	110.00	2,400.00	3,754.00	42	646.68	5,466.67	6,370.89	65	3,801.81	8,533.33	8,987.78
20	118.81	2,533.33	3,867.78	43	698.46	5,600.00	6,484.67	66	4,106.18	8,666.67	9,101.56
21	128.32	2,666.67	3,981.56	44	754.37	5,733.33	6,598.44	67	4,434.92	8,800.00	9,215.33
22	138.59	2,800.00	4,095.33	45	814.77	5,866.67	6,712.22				
23	149.69	2,933.33	4,209.11	46	880.00	6,000.00	6,826.00				

Table 1 (continues)

Initial Catalog of Tunings : Octave 10

Scale Deg.	HZ	Cts	TU	Scale Deg.	HZ	Cts	TU	Scale Deg.	HZ	Cts	TU
1	27.50	0.00	1,706.00	27	166.73	3,120.00	4,368.40	53	1,010.85	6,240.00	7,030.80
2	29.47	120.00	1,808.40	28	178.70	3,240.00	4,470.80	54	1,083.41	6,360.00	7,133.20
3	31.59	240.00	1,910.80	29	191.52	3,360.00	4,573.20	55	1,161.17	6,480.00	7,235.60
4	33.86	360.00	2,013.20	30	205.27	3,480.00	4,675.60	56	1,244.51	6,600.00	7,338.00
5	36.29	480.00	2,115.60	31	220.00	3,600.00	4,778.00	57	1,333.83	6,720.00	7,440.40
6	38.89	600.00	2,218.00	32	235.79	3,720.00	4,880.40	58	1,429.56	6,840.00	7,542.80
7	41.68	720.00	2,320.40	33	252.71	3,840.00	4,982.80	59	1,532.17	6,960.00	7,645.20
8	44.67	840.00	2,422.80	34	270.85	3,960.00	5,085.20	60	1,642.14	7,080.00	7,747.60
9	47.88	960.00	2,525.20	35	290.29	4,080.00	5,187.60	61	1,760.00	7,200.00	7,850.00
10	51.32	1,080.00	2,627.60	36	311.13	4,200.00	5,290.00	62	1,886.32	7,320.00	7,952.40
11	55.00	1,200.00	2,730.00	37	333.46	4,320.00	5,392.40	63	2,021.71	7,440.00	8,054.80
12	58.95	1,320.00	2,832.40	38	357.39	4,440.00	5,494.80	64	2,166.81	7,560.00	8,157.20
13	63.18	1,440.00	2,934.80	39	383.04	4,560.00	5,597.20	65	2,322.33	7,680.00	8,259.60
14	67.71	1,560.00	3,037.20	40	410.53	4,680.00	5,699.60	66	2,489.02	7,800.00	8,362.00
15	72.57	1,680.00	3,139.60	41	440.00	4,800.00	5,802.00	67	2,667.66	7,920.00	8,464.40
16	77.78	1,800.00	3,242.00	42	471.58	4,920.00	5,904.40	68	2,859.13	8,040.00	8,566.80
17	83.36	1,920.00	3,344.40	43	505.43	5,040.00	6,006.80	69	3,064.34	8,160.00	8,669.20
18	89.35	2,040.00	3,446.80	44	541.70	5,160.00	6,109.20	70	3,284.28	8,280.00	8,771.60
19	95.76	2,160.00	3,549.20	45	580.58	5,280.00	6,211.60	71	3,520.00	8,400.00	8,874.00
20	102.63	2,280.00	3,651.60	46	622.25	5,400.00	6,314.00	72	3,772.64	8,520.00	8,976.40
21	110.00	2,400.00	3,754.00	47	666.92	5,520.00	6,416.40	73	4,043.42	8,640.00	9,078.80
22	117.90	2,520.00	3,856.40	48	714.78	5,640.00	6,518.80	74	4,333.63	8,760.00	9,181.20
23	126.36	2,640.00	3,958.80	49	766.08	5,760.00	6,621.20	75	4,644.67	8,880.00	9,283.60
24	135.43	2,760.00	4,061.20	50	821.07	5,880.00	6,723.60				
25	145.15	2,880.00	4,163.60	51	880.00	6,000.00	6,826.00				
26	155.56	3,000.00	4,266.00	52	943.16	6,120.00	6,928.40				

Initial Catalog of Tunings : Octave 11

Scale Deg.	HZ	Cts	TU	Scale Deg.	HZ	Cts	TU	Scale Deg.	HZ	Cts	TU
1	27.50	0.00	1,706.00	29	160.54	3,054.55	4,312.55	57	937.24	6,109.09	6,919.09
2	29.29	109.09	1,799.09	30	170.98	3,163.64	4,405.64	58	998.20	6,218.18	7,012.18
3	31.19	218.18	1,892.18	31	182.11	3,272.73	4,498.73	59	1,063.12	6,327.27	7,105.27
4	33.22	327.27	1,985.27	32	193.95	3,381.82	4,591.82	60	1,132.27	6,436.36	7,198.36
5	35.38	436.36	2,078.36	33	206.56	3,490.91	4,684.91	61	1,205.91	6,545.45	7,291.45
6	37.68	545.45	2,171.45	34	220.00	3,600.00	4,778.00	62	1,284.34	6,654.55	7,384.55
7	40.14	654.55	2,264.55	35	234.31	3,709.09	4,871.09	63	1,367.88	6,763.64	7,477.64
8	42.75	763.64	2,357.64	36	249.55	3,818.18	4,964.18	64	1,456.85	6,872.73	7,570.73
9	45.53	872.73	2,450.73	37	265.78	3,927.27	5,057.27	65	1,551.60	6,981.82	7,663.82
10	48.49	981.82	2,543.82	38	283.07	4,036.36	5,150.36	66	1,652.52	7,090.91	7,756.91
11	51.64	1,090.91	2,636.91	39	301.48	4,145.45	5,243.45	67	1,760.00	7,200.00	7,850.00
12	55.00	1,200.00	2,730.00	40	321.09	4,254.55	5,336.55	68	1,874.47	7,309.09	7,943.09
13	58.58	1,309.09	2,823.09	41	341.97	4,363.64	5,429.64	69	1,996.39	7,418.18	8,036.18
14	62.39	1,418.18	2,916.18	42	364.21	4,472.73	5,522.73	70	2,126.24	7,527.27	8,129.27
15	66.44	1,527.27	3,009.27	43	387.90	4,581.82	5,615.82	71	2,264.53	7,636.36	8,222.36
16	70.77	1,636.36	3,102.36	44	413.13	4,690.91	5,708.91	72	2,411.82	7,745.45	8,315.45
17	75.37	1,745.45	3,195.45	45	440.00	4,800.00	5,802.00	73	2,568.68	7,854.55	8,408.55
18	80.27	1,854.55	3,288.55	46	468.62	4,909.09	5,895.09	74	2,735.76	7,963.64	8,501.64
19	85.49	1,963.64	3,381.64	47	499.10	5,018.18	5,988.18	75	2,913.69	8,072.73	8,594.73
20	91.05	2,072.73	3,474.73	48	531.56	5,127.27	6,081.27	76	3,103.20	8,181.82	8,687.82
21	96.98	2,181.82	3,567.82	49	566.13	5,236.36	6,174.36	77	3,305.04	8,290.91	8,780.91
22	103.28	2,290.91	3,660.91	50	602.95	5,345.45	6,267.45	78	3,520.00	8,400.00	8,874.00
23	110.00	2,400.00	3,754.00	51	642.17	5,454.55	6,360.55	79	3,748.94	8,509.09	8,967.09
24	117.15	2,509.09	3,847.09	52	683.94	5,563.64	6,453.64	80	3,992.78	8,618.18	9,060.18
25	124.77	2,618.18	3,940.18	53	728.42	5,672.73	6,546.73	81	4,252.47	8,727.27	9,153.27
26	132.89	2,727.27	4,033.27	54	775.80	5,781.82	6,639.82	82	4,529.06	8,836.36	9,246.36
27	141.53	2,836.36	4,126.36	55	826.26	5,890.91	6,732.91				
28	150.74	2,945.45	4,219.45	56	880.00	6,000.00	6,826.00				

Table 1 (continues)

Initial Catalog of Tunings : Octave 12

Scale Deg.	HZ	Cts	TU	Scale Deg.	HZ	Cts	TU	Scale Deg.	HZ	Cts	TU
1	27.50	0.00	1,706.00	31	155.56	3,000.00	4,266.00	61	880.00	6,000.00	6,826.00
2	29.14	100.00	1,791.33	32	164.81	3,100.00	4,351.33	62	932.33	6,100.00	6,911.33
3	30.87	200.00	1,876.67	33	174.61	3,200.00	4,436.67	63	987.77	6,200.00	6,996.67
4	32.70	300.00	1,962.00	34	185.00	3,300.00	4,522.00	64	1,046.50	6,300.00	7,082.00
5	34.65	400.00	2,047.33	35	196.00	3,400.00	4,607.33	65	1,108.73	6,400.00	7,167.33
6	36.71	500.00	2,132.67	36	207.65	3,500.00	4,692.67	66	1,174.66	6,500.00	7,252.67
7	38.89	600.00	2,218.00	37	220.00	3,600.00	4,778.00	67	1,244.51	6,600.00	7,338.00
8	41.20	700.00	2,303.33	38	233.08	3,700.00	4,863.33	68	1,318.51	6,700.00	7,423.33
9	43.65	800.00	2,388.67	39	246.94	3,800.00	4,948.67	69	1,396.91	6,800.00	7,508.67
10	46.25	900.00	2,474.00	40	261.63	3,900.00	5,034.00	70	1,479.98	6,900.00	7,594.00
11	49.00	1,000.00	2,559.33	41	277.18	4,000.00	5,119.33	71	1,567.98	7,000.00	7,679.33
12	51.91	1,100.00	2,644.67	42	293.66	4,100.00	5,204.67	72	1,661.22	7,100.00	7,764.67
13	55.00	1,200.00	2,730.00	43	311.13	4,200.00	5,290.00	73	1,760.00	7,200.00	7,850.00
14	58.27	1,300.00	2,815.33	44	329.63	4,300.00	5,375.33	74	1,864.66	7,300.00	7,935.33
15	61.74	1,400.00	2,900.67	45	349.23	4,400.00	5,460.67	75	1,975.53	7,400.00	8,020.67
16	65.41	1,500.00	2,986.00	46	369.99	4,500.00	5,546.00	76	2,093.00	7,500.00	8,106.00
17	69.30	1,600.00	3,071.33	47	392.00	4,600.00	5,631.33	77	2,217.46	7,600.00	8,191.33
18	73.42	1,700.00	3,156.67	48	415.30	4,700.00	5,716.67	78	2,349.32	7,700.00	8,276.67
19	77.78	1,800.00	3,242.00	49	440.00	4,800.00	5,802.00	79	2,489.02	7,800.00	8,362.00
20	82.41	1,900.00	3,327.33	50	466.16	4,900.00	5,887.33	80	2,637.02	7,900.00	8,447.33
21	87.31	2,000.00	3,412.67	51	493.88	5,000.00	5,972.67	81	2,793.83	8,000.00	8,532.67
22	92.50	2,100.00	3,498.00	52	523.25	5,100.00	6,058.00	82	2,959.96	8,100.00	8,618.00
23	98.00	2,200.00	3,583.33	53	554.37	5,200.00	6,143.33	83	3,135.96	8,200.00	8,703.33
24	103.83	2,300.00	3,668.67	54	587.33	5,300.00	6,228.67	84	3,322.44	8,300.00	8,788.67
25	110.00	2,400.00	3,754.00	55	622.25	5,400.00	6,314.00	85	3,520.00	8,400.00	8,874.00
26	116.54	2,500.00	3,839.33	56	659.26	5,500.00	6,399.33	86	3,729.31	8,500.00	8,959.33
27	123.47	2,600.00	3,924.67	57	698.46	5,600.00	6,484.67	87	3,951.07	8,600.00	9,044.67
28	130.81	2,700.00	4,010.00	58	739.99	5,700.00	6,570.00	88	4,186.01	8,700.00	9,130.00
29	138.59	2,800.00	4,095.33	59	783.99	5,800.00	6,655.33				
30	146.83	2,900.00	4,180.67	60	830.61	5,900.00	6,740.67				

Initial Catalog of Tunings : Octave 13

Scale Deg.	HZ	Cts	TU	Scale Deg.	HZ	Cts	TU	Scale Deg.	HZ	Cts	TU
1	27.50	0.00	1,706.00	31	136.15	2,769.23	4,069.08	61	674.07	5,538.46	6,432.15
2	29.01	92.31	1,784.77	32	143.61	2,861.54	4,147.85	62	710.98	5,630.77	6,510.92
3	30.59	184.62	1,863.54	33	151.47	2,953.85	4,226.62	63	749.92	5,723.08	6,589.69
4	32.27	276.92	1,942.31	34	159.77	3,046.15	4,305.38	64	790.99	5,815.38	6,668.46
5	34.04	369.23	2,021.08	35	168.52	3,138.46	4,384.15	65	834.31	5,907.69	6,747.23
6	35.90	461.54	2,099.85	36	177.75	3,230.77	4,462.92	66	880.00	6,000.00	6,826.00
7	37.87	553.85	2,178.62	37	187.48	3,323.08	4,541.69	67	928.19	6,092.31	6,904.77
8	39.94	646.15	2,257.38	38	197.75	3,415.38	4,620.46	68	979.03	6,184.62	6,983.54
9	42.13	738.46	2,336.15	39	208.58	3,507.69	4,699.23	69	1,032.65	6,276.92	7,062.31
10	44.44	830.77	2,414.92	40	220.00	3,600.00	4,778.00	70	1,089.20	6,369.23	7,141.08
11	46.87	923.08	2,493.69	41	232.05	3,692.31	4,856.77	71	1,148.85	6,461.54	7,219.85
12	49.44	1,015.38	2,572.46	42	244.76	3,784.62	4,935.54	72	1,211.77	6,553.85	7,298.62
13	52.14	1,107.69	2,651.23	43	258.16	3,876.92	5,014.31	73	1,278.13	6,646.15	7,377.38
14	55.00	1,200.00	2,730.00	44	272.30	3,969.23	5,093.08	74	1,348.13	6,738.46	7,456.15
15	58.01	1,292.31	2,808.77	45	287.21	4,061.54	5,171.85	75	1,421.96	6,830.77	7,534.92
16	61.19	1,384.62	2,887.54	46	302.94	4,153.85	5,250.62	76	1,499.84	6,923.08	7,613.69
17	64.54	1,476.92	2,966.31	47	319.53	4,246.15	5,329.38	77	1,581.98	7,015.38	7,692.46
18	68.07	1,569.23	3,045.08	48	337.03	4,338.46	5,408.15	78	1,668.62	7,107.69	7,771.23
19	71.80	1,661.54	3,123.85	49	355.49	4,430.77	5,486.92	79	1,760.00	7,200.00	7,850.00
20	75.74	1,753.85	3,202.62	50	374.96	4,523.08	5,565.69	80	1,856.39	7,292.31	7,928.77
21	79.88	1,846.15	3,281.38	51	395.49	4,615.38	5,644.46	81	1,958.06	7,384.62	8,007.54
22	84.26	1,938.46	3,360.15	52	417.15	4,707.69	5,723.23	82	2,065.29	7,476.92	8,086.31
23	88.87	2,030.77	3,438.92	53	440.00	4,800.00	5,802.00	83	2,178.40	7,569.23	8,165.08
24	93.74	2,123.08	3,517.69	54	464.10	4,892.31	5,880.77	84	2,297.70	7,661.54	8,243.85
25	98.87	2,215.38	3,596.46	55	489.51	4,984.62	5,959.54	85	2,423.54	7,753.85	8,322.62
26	104.29	2,307.69	3,675.23	56	516.32	5,076.92	6,038.31	86	2,556.26	7,846.15	8,401.38
27	110.00	2,400.00	3,754.00	57	544.60	5,169.23	6,117.08	87	2,696.26	7,938.46	8,480.15
28	116.02	2,492.31	3,832.77	58	574.43	5,261.54	6,195.85	88	2,843.92	8,030.77	8,558.92
29	122.38	2,584.62	3,911.54	59	605.88	5,353.85	6,274.62				
30	129.08	2,676.92	3,990.31	60	639.07	5,446.15	6,353.38				

Table 1 (continues)

Initial Catalog of Tunings : Octave 14

Scale Deg.	HZ	Cts	TU	Scale Deg.	HZ	Cts	TU	Scale Deg.	HZ	Cts	TU
1	27.50	0.00	1,706.00	31	121.45	2,571.43	3,900.29	61	536.37	5,142.86	6,094.57
2	28.90	85.71	1,779.14	32	127.61	2,657.14	3,973.43	62	563.59	5,228.57	6,167.71
3	30.36	171.43	1,852.29	33	134.09	2,742.86	4,046.57	63	592.20	5,314.29	6,240.86
4	31.90	257.14	1,925.43	34	140.90	2,828.57	4,119.71	64	622.25	5,400.00	6,314.00
5	33.52	342.86	1,998.57	35	148.05	2,914.29	4,192.86	65	653.84	5,485.71	6,387.14
6	35.22	428.57	2,071.71	36	155.56	3,000.00	4,266.00	66	687.02	5,571.43	6,460.29
7	37.01	514.29	2,144.86	37	163.46	3,085.71	4,339.14	67	721.90	5,657.14	6,533.43
8	38.89	600.00	2,218.00	38	171.76	3,171.43	4,412.29	68	758.54	5,742.86	6,606.57
9	40.86	685.71	2,291.14	39	180.47	3,257.14	4,485.43	69	797.04	5,828.57	6,679.71
10	42.94	771.43	2,364.29	40	189.63	3,342.86	4,558.57	70	837.49	5,914.29	6,752.86
11	45.12	857.14	2,437.43	41	199.26	3,428.57	4,631.71	71	880.00	6,000.00	6,826.00
12	47.41	942.86	2,510.57	42	209.37	3,514.29	4,704.86	72	924.67	6,085.71	6,899.14
13	49.81	1,028.57	2,583.71	43	220.00	3,600.00	4,778.00	73	971.60	6,171.43	6,972.29
14	52.34	1,114.29	2,656.86	44	231.17	3,685.71	4,851.14	74	1,020.91	6,257.14	7,045.43
15	55.00	1,200.00	2,730.00	45	242.90	3,771.43	4,924.29	75	1,072.73	6,342.86	7,118.57
16	57.79	1,285.71	2,803.14	46	255.23	3,857.14	4,997.43	76	1,127.18	6,428.57	7,191.71
17	60.72	1,371.43	2,876.29	47	268.18	3,942.86	5,070.57	77	1,184.39	6,514.29	7,264.86
18	63.81	1,457.14	2,949.43	48	281.80	4,028.57	5,143.71	78	1,244.51	6,600.00	7,338.00
19	67.05	1,542.86	3,022.57	49	296.10	4,114.29	5,216.86	79	1,307.67	6,685.71	7,411.14
20	70.45	1,628.57	3,095.71	50	311.13	4,200.00	5,290.00	80	1,374.05	6,771.43	7,484.29
21	74.02	1,714.29	3,168.86	51	326.92	4,285.71	5,363.14	81	1,443.79	6,857.14	7,557.43
22	77.78	1,800.00	3,242.00	52	343.51	4,371.43	5,436.29	82	1,517.07	6,942.86	7,630.57
23	81.73	1,885.71	3,315.14	53	360.95	4,457.14	5,509.43	83	1,594.07	7,028.57	7,703.71
24	85.88	1,971.43	3,388.29	54	379.27	4,542.86	5,582.57	84	1,674.98	7,114.29	7,776.86
25	90.24	2,057.14	3,461.43	55	398.52	4,628.57	5,655.71	85	1,760.00	7,200.00	7,850.00
26	94.82	2,142.86	3,534.57	56	418.75	4,714.29	5,728.86	86	1,849.33	7,285.71	7,923.14
27	99.63	2,228.57	3,607.71	57	440.00	4,800.00	5,802.00	87	1,943.20	7,371.43	7,996.29
28	104.69	2,314.29	3,680.86	58	462.33	4,885.71	5,875.14	88	2,041.83	7,457.14	8,069.43
29	110.00	2,400.00	3,754.00	59	485.80	4,971.43	5,948.29				
30	115.58	2,485.71	3,827.14	60	510.46	5,057.14	6,021.43				

Initial Catalog of Tunings : Octave 15

Scale Deg.	HZ	Cts	TU	Scale Deg.	HZ	Cts	TU	Scale Deg.	HZ	Cts	TU
1	27.50	0.00	1,706.00	31	110.00	2,400.00	3,754.00	61	440.00	4,800.00	5,802.00
2	28.80	80.00	1,774.27	32	115.20	2,480.00	3,822.27	62	460.81	4,880.00	5,870.27
3	30.16	160.00	1,842.53	33	120.65	2,560.00	3,890.53	63	482.60	4,960.00	5,938.53
4	31.59	240.00	1,910.80	34	126.36	2,640.00	3,958.80	64	505.43	5,040.00	6,006.80
5	33.08	320.00	1,979.07	35	132.33	2,720.00	4,027.07	65	529.33	5,120.00	6,075.07
6	34.65	400.00	2,047.33	36	138.59	2,800.00	4,095.33	66	554.37	5,200.00	6,143.33
7	36.29	480.00	2,115.60	37	145.15	2,880.00	4,163.60	67	580.58	5,280.00	6,211.60
8	38.00	560.00	2,183.87	38	152.01	2,960.00	4,231.87	68	608.04	5,360.00	6,279.87
9	39.80	640.00	2,252.13	39	159.20	3,040.00	4,300.13	69	636.80	5,440.00	6,348.13
10	41.68	720.00	2,320.40	40	166.73	3,120.00	4,368.40	70	666.92	5,520.00	6,416.40
11	43.65	800.00	2,388.67	41	174.61	3,200.00	4,436.67	71	698.46	5,600.00	6,484.67
12	45.72	880.00	2,456.93	42	182.87	3,280.00	4,504.93	72	731.49	5,680.00	6,552.93
13	47.88	960.00	2,525.20	43	191.52	3,360.00	4,573.20	73	766.08	5,760.00	6,621.20
14	50.14	1,040.00	2,593.47	44	200.58	3,440.00	4,641.47	74	802.32	5,840.00	6,689.47
15	52.52	1,120.00	2,661.73	45	210.07	3,520.00	4,709.73	75	840.26	5,920.00	6,757.73
16	55.00	1,200.00	2,730.00	46	220.00	3,600.00	4,778.00	76	880.00	6,000.00	6,826.00
17	57.60	1,280.00	2,798.27	47	230.40	3,680.00	4,846.27	77	921.62	6,080.00	6,894.27
18	60.33	1,360.00	2,866.53	48	241.30	3,760.00	4,914.53	78	965.21	6,160.00	6,962.53
19	63.18	1,440.00	2,934.80	49	252.71	3,840.00	4,982.80	79	1,010.85	6,240.00	7,030.80
20	66.17	1,520.00	3,003.07	50	264.67	3,920.00	5,051.07	80	1,058.66	6,320.00	7,099.07
21	69.30	1,600.00	3,071.33	51	277.18	4,000.00	5,119.33	81	1,108.73	6,400.00	7,167.33
22	72.57	1,680.00	3,139.60	52	290.29	4,080.00	5,187.60	82	1,161.17	6,480.00	7,235.60
23	76.01	1,760.00	3,207.87	53	304.02	4,160.00	5,255.87	83	1,216.08	6,560.00	7,303.87
24	79.60	1,840.00	3,276.13	54	318.40	4,240.00	5,324.13	84	1,273.60	6,640.00	7,372.13
25	83.36	1,920.00	3,344.40	55	333.46	4,320.00	5,392.40	85	1,333.83	6,720.00	7,440.40
26	87.31	2,000.00	3,412.67	56	349.23	4,400.00	5,460.67	86	1,396.91	6,800.00	7,508.67
27	91.44	2,080.00	3,480.93	57	365.74	4,480.00	5,528.93	87	1,462.98	6,880.00	7,576.93
28	95.76	2,160.00	3,549.20	58	383.04	4,560.00	5,597.20	88	1,532.17	6,960.00	7,645.20
29	100.29	2,240.00	3,617.47	59	401.16	4,640.00	5,665.47				
30	105.03	2,320.00	3,685.73	60	420.13	4,720.00	5,733.73				

Table 1 (continues)

Initial Catalog of Tunings : Octave 16

Scale Deg.	HZ	Cis	TU	Scale Deg.	HZ	Cis	TU	Scale Deg.	HZ	Cis	TU
1	27.50	0.00	1,706.00	31	100.87	2,250.00	3,626.00	61	369.99	4,500.00	5,546.00
2	28.72	75.00	1,770.00	32	105.34	2,325.00	3,690.00	62	386.38	4,575.00	5,610.00
3	29.99	150.00	1,834.00	33	110.00	2,400.00	3,754.00	63	403.48	4,650.00	5,674.00
4	31.32	225.00	1,898.00	34	114.87	2,475.00	3,818.00	64	421.35	4,725.00	5,738.00
5	32.70	300.00	1,962.00	35	119.96	2,550.00	3,882.00	65	440.00	4,800.00	5,802.00
6	34.15	375.00	2,026.00	36	125.27	2,625.00	3,946.00	66	459.48	4,875.00	5,866.00
7	35.66	450.00	2,090.00	37	130.81	2,700.00	4,010.00	67	479.82	4,950.00	5,930.00
8	37.24	525.00	2,154.00	38	136.60	2,775.00	4,074.00	68	501.07	5,025.00	5,994.00
9	38.89	600.00	2,218.00	39	142.65	2,850.00	4,138.00	69	523.25	5,100.00	6,058.00
10	40.61	675.00	2,282.00	40	148.97	2,925.00	4,202.00	70	546.42	5,175.00	6,122.00
11	42.41	750.00	2,346.00	41	155.56	3,000.00	4,266.00	71	570.61	5,250.00	6,186.00
12	44.29	825.00	2,410.00	42	162.45	3,075.00	4,330.00	72	595.87	5,325.00	6,250.00
13	46.25	900.00	2,474.00	43	169.64	3,150.00	4,394.00	73	622.25	5,400.00	6,314.00
14	48.30	975.00	2,538.00	44	177.15	3,225.00	4,458.00	74	649.80	5,475.00	6,378.00
15	50.44	1,050.00	2,602.00	45	185.00	3,300.00	4,522.00	75	678.57	5,550.00	6,442.00
16	52.67	1,125.00	2,666.00	46	193.19	3,375.00	4,586.00	76	708.62	5,625.00	6,506.00
17	55.00	1,200.00	2,730.00	47	201.74	3,450.00	4,650.00	77	739.99	5,700.00	6,570.00
18	57.44	1,275.00	2,794.00	48	210.67	3,525.00	4,714.00	78	772.75	5,775.00	6,634.00
19	59.98	1,350.00	2,858.00	49	220.00	3,600.00	4,778.00	79	806.96	5,850.00	6,698.00
20	62.63	1,425.00	2,922.00	50	229.74	3,675.00	4,842.00	80	842.69	5,925.00	6,762.00
21	65.41	1,500.00	2,986.00	51	239.91	3,750.00	4,906.00	81	880.00	6,000.00	6,826.00
22	68.30	1,575.00	3,050.00	52	250.53	3,825.00	4,970.00	82	918.96	6,075.00	6,890.00
23	71.33	1,650.00	3,114.00	53	261.63	3,900.00	5,034.00	83	959.65	6,150.00	6,954.00
24	74.48	1,725.00	3,178.00	54	273.21	3,975.00	5,098.00	84	1,002.13	6,225.00	7,018.00
25	77.78	1,800.00	3,242.00	55	285.30	4,050.00	5,162.00	85	1,046.50	6,300.00	7,082.00
26	81.23	1,875.00	3,306.00	56	297.94	4,125.00	5,226.00	86	1,092.83	6,375.00	7,146.00
27	84.82	1,950.00	3,370.00	57	311.13	4,200.00	5,290.00	87	1,141.22	6,450.00	7,210.00
28	88.58	2,025.00	3,434.00	58	324.90	4,275.00	5,354.00	88	1,191.74	6,525.00	7,274.00
29	92.50	2,100.00	3,498.00	59	339.29	4,350.00	5,418.00				
30	96.59	2,175.00	3,562.00	60	354.31	4,425.00	5,482.00				

Initial Catalog of Tunings : Octave 17

Scale Deg.	HZ	Cis	TU	Scale Deg.	HZ	Cis	TU	Scale Deg.	HZ	Cis	TU
1	27.50	0.00	1,706.00	31	93.45	2,117.65	3,513.06	61	317.53	4,235.29	5,320.12
2	28.64	70.59	1,766.24	32	97.34	2,188.24	3,573.29	62	330.75	4,305.88	5,380.35
3	29.84	141.18	1,826.47	33	101.39	2,258.82	3,633.53	63	344.51	4,376.47	5,440.59
4	31.08	211.76	1,886.71	34	105.61	2,329.41	3,693.76	64	358.85	4,447.06	5,500.82
5	32.37	282.35	1,946.94	35	110.00	2,400.00	3,754.00	65	373.79	4,517.65	5,561.06
6	33.72	352.94	2,007.18	36	114.58	2,470.59	3,814.24	66	389.34	4,588.24	5,621.29
7	35.12	423.53	2,067.41	37	119.35	2,541.18	3,874.47	67	405.54	4,658.82	5,681.53
8	36.58	494.12	2,127.65	38	124.31	2,611.76	3,934.71	68	422.42	4,729.41	5,741.76
9	38.11	564.71	2,187.88	39	129.49	2,682.35	3,994.94	69	440.00	4,800.00	5,802.00
10	39.69	635.29	2,248.12	40	134.87	2,752.94	4,055.18	70	458.31	4,870.59	5,862.24
11	41.34	705.88	2,308.35	41	140.49	2,823.53	4,115.41	71	477.38	4,941.18	5,922.47
12	43.06	776.47	2,368.59	42	146.33	2,894.12	4,175.65	72	497.25	5,011.76	5,982.71
13	44.86	847.06	2,428.82	43	152.42	2,964.71	4,235.88	73	517.94	5,082.35	6,042.94
14	46.72	917.65	2,489.06	44	158.77	3,035.29	4,296.12	74	539.50	5,152.94	6,103.18
15	48.67	988.24	2,549.29	45	165.37	3,105.88	4,356.35	75	561.95	5,223.53	6,163.41
16	50.69	1,058.82	2,609.53	46	172.26	3,176.47	4,416.59	76	585.34	5,294.12	6,223.65
17	52.80	1,129.41	2,669.76	47	179.43	3,247.06	4,476.82	77	609.70	5,364.71	6,283.88
18	55.00	1,200.00	2,730.00	48	186.89	3,317.65	4,537.06	78	635.07	5,435.29	6,344.12
19	57.29	1,270.59	2,790.24	49	194.67	3,388.24	4,597.29	79	661.50	5,505.88	6,404.35
20	59.67	1,341.18	2,850.47	50	202.77	3,458.82	4,657.53	80	689.03	5,576.47	6,464.59
21	62.16	1,411.76	2,910.71	51	211.21	3,529.41	4,717.76	81	717.70	5,647.06	6,524.82
22	64.74	1,482.35	2,970.94	52	220.00	3,600.00	4,778.00	82	747.57	5,717.65	6,585.06
23	67.44	1,552.94	3,031.18	53	229.16	3,670.59	4,838.24	83	778.68	5,788.24	6,645.29
24	70.24	1,623.53	3,091.41	54	238.69	3,741.18	4,898.47	84	811.09	5,858.82	6,705.53
25	73.17	1,694.12	3,151.65	55	248.63	3,811.76	4,958.71	85	844.84	5,929.41	6,765.76
26	76.21	1,764.71	3,211.88	56	258.97	3,882.35	5,018.94	86	880.00	6,000.00	6,826.00
27	79.38	1,835.29	3,272.12	57	269.75	3,952.94	5,079.18	87	916.62	6,070.59	6,886.24
28	82.69	1,905.88	3,332.35	58	280.98	4,023.53	5,139.41	88	954.77	6,141.18	6,946.47
29	86.13	1,976.47	3,392.59	59	292.67	4,094.12	5,199.65				
30	89.71	2,047.06	3,452.82	60	304.85	4,164.71	5,259.88				

Table 1 (continues)

Initial Catalog of Tunings : Octave 18

Scale Deg.	HZ	Cts	TU	Scale Deg.	HZ	Cts	TU	Scale Deg.	HZ	Cts	TU
1	27.50	0.00	1,706.00	31	87.31	2,000.00	3,412.67	61	277.18	4,000.00	5,119.33
2	28.58	66.67	1,762.89	32	90.73	2,066.67	3,469.56	62	288.06	4,066.67	5,176.22
3	29.70	133.33	1,819.78	33	94.30	2,133.33	3,526.44	63	299.37	4,133.33	5,233.11
4	30.87	200.00	1,876.67	34	98.00	2,200.00	3,583.33	64	311.13	4,200.00	5,290.00
5	32.08	266.67	1,933.56	35	101.85	2,266.67	3,640.22	65	323.34	4,266.67	5,346.89
6	33.34	333.33	1,990.44	36	105.84	2,333.33	3,697.11	66	336.04	4,333.33	5,403.78
7	34.65	400.00	2,047.33	37	110.00	2,400.00	3,754.00	67	349.23	4,400.00	5,460.67
8	36.01	466.67	2,104.22	38	114.32	2,466.67	3,810.89	68	362.94	4,466.67	5,517.56
9	37.42	533.33	2,161.11	39	118.81	2,533.33	3,867.78	69	377.19	4,533.33	5,574.44
10	38.89	600.00	2,218.00	40	123.47	2,600.00	3,924.67	70	392.00	4,600.00	5,631.33
11	40.42	666.67	2,274.89	41	128.32	2,666.67	3,981.56	71	407.38	4,666.67	5,688.22
12	42.00	733.33	2,331.78	42	133.36	2,733.33	4,038.44	72	423.38	4,733.33	5,745.11
13	43.65	800.00	2,388.67	43	138.59	2,800.00	4,095.33	73	440.00	4,800.00	5,802.00
14	45.37	866.67	2,445.56	44	144.03	2,866.67	4,152.22	74	457.27	4,866.67	5,858.89
15	47.15	933.33	2,502.44	45	149.69	2,933.33	4,209.11	75	475.23	4,933.33	5,915.78
16	49.00	1,000.00	2,559.33	46	155.56	3,000.00	4,266.00	76	493.88	5,000.00	5,972.67
17	50.92	1,066.67	2,616.22	47	161.67	3,066.67	4,322.89	77	513.27	5,066.67	6,029.56
18	52.92	1,133.33	2,673.11	48	168.02	3,133.33	4,379.78	78	533.42	5,133.33	6,086.44
19	55.00	1,200.00	2,730.00	49	174.61	3,200.00	4,436.67	79	554.37	5,200.00	6,143.33
20	57.16	1,266.67	2,786.89	50	181.47	3,266.67	4,493.56	80	576.13	5,266.67	6,200.22
21	59.40	1,333.33	2,843.78	51	188.59	3,333.33	4,550.44	81	598.75	5,333.33	6,257.11
22	61.74	1,400.00	2,900.67	52	196.00	3,400.00	4,607.33	82	622.25	5,400.00	6,314.00
23	64.16	1,466.67	2,957.56	53	203.69	3,466.67	4,664.22	83	646.68	5,466.67	6,370.89
24	66.68	1,533.33	3,014.44	54	211.69	3,533.33	4,721.11	84	672.07	5,533.33	6,427.78
25	69.30	1,600.00	3,071.33	55	220.00	3,600.00	4,778.00	85	698.46	5,600.00	6,484.67
26	72.02	1,666.67	3,128.22	56	228.64	3,666.67	4,834.89	86	725.88	5,666.67	6,541.56
27	74.84	1,733.33	3,185.11	57	237.61	3,733.33	4,891.78	87	754.37	5,733.33	6,598.44
28	77.78	1,800.00	3,242.00	58	246.94	3,800.00	4,948.67	88	783.99	5,800.00	6,655.33
29	80.84	1,866.67	3,298.89	59	256.64	3,866.67	5,005.56				
30	84.01	1,933.33	3,355.78	60	266.71	3,933.33	5,062.44				

Initial Catalog of Tunings : Octave 19

Scale Deg.	HZ	Cts	TU	Scale Deg.	HZ	Cts	TU	Scale Deg.	HZ	Cts	TU
1	27.50	0.00	1,706.00	31	82.16	1,894.74	3,322.84	61	245.44	3,789.47	4,939.68
2	28.52	63.16	1,759.89	32	85.21	1,957.89	3,376.74	62	254.56	3,852.63	4,993.58
3	29.58	126.32	1,813.79	33	88.38	2,021.05	3,430.63	63	264.02	3,915.79	5,047.47
4	30.68	189.47	1,867.68	34	91.66	2,084.21	3,484.53	64	273.83	3,978.95	5,101.37
5	31.82	252.63	1,921.58	35	95.06	2,147.37	3,538.42	65	284.01	4,042.11	5,155.26
6	33.00	315.79	1,975.47	36	98.60	2,210.53	3,592.32	66	294.56	4,105.26	5,209.16
7	34.23	378.95	2,029.37	37	102.26	2,273.68	3,646.21	67	305.50	4,168.42	5,263.05
8	35.50	442.11	2,083.26	38	106.06	2,336.84	3,700.11	68	316.85	4,231.58	5,316.95
9	36.82	505.26	2,137.16	39	110.00	2,400.00	3,754.00	69	328.63	4,294.74	5,370.84
10	38.19	568.42	2,191.05	40	114.09	2,463.16	3,807.89	70	340.84	4,357.89	5,424.74
11	39.61	631.58	2,244.95	41	118.33	2,526.32	3,861.79	71	353.50	4,421.05	5,478.63
12	41.08	694.74	2,298.84	42	122.72	2,589.47	3,915.68	72	366.64	4,484.21	5,532.53
13	42.60	757.89	2,352.74	43	127.28	2,652.63	3,969.58	73	380.26	4,547.37	5,586.42
14	44.19	821.05	2,406.63	44	132.01	2,715.79	4,023.47	74	394.39	4,610.53	5,640.32
15	45.83	884.21	2,460.53	45	136.92	2,778.95	4,077.37	75	409.04	4,673.68	5,694.21
16	47.53	947.37	2,514.42	46	142.00	2,842.11	4,131.26	76	424.24	4,736.84	5,748.11
17	49.30	1,010.53	2,568.32	47	147.28	2,905.26	4,185.16	77	440.00	4,800.00	5,802.00
18	51.13	1,073.68	2,622.21	48	152.75	2,968.42	4,239.05	78	456.35	4,863.16	5,855.89
19	53.03	1,136.84	2,676.11	49	158.43	3,031.58	4,292.95	79	473.30	4,926.32	5,909.79
20	55.00	1,200.00	2,730.00	50	164.31	3,094.74	4,346.84	80	490.89	4,989.47	5,963.68
21	57.04	1,263.16	2,783.89	51	170.42	3,157.89	4,400.74	81	509.13	5,052.63	6,017.58
22	59.16	1,326.32	2,837.79	52	176.75	3,221.05	4,454.63	82	528.05	5,115.79	6,071.47
23	61.36	1,389.47	2,891.68	53	183.32	3,284.21	4,508.53	83	547.66	5,178.95	6,125.37
24	63.64	1,452.63	2,945.58	54	190.13	3,347.37	4,562.42	84	568.01	5,242.11	6,179.26
25	66.01	1,515.79	2,999.47	55	197.19	3,410.53	4,616.32	85	589.12	5,305.26	6,233.16
26	68.46	1,578.95	3,053.37	56	204.52	3,473.68	4,670.21	86	611.01	5,368.42	6,287.05
27	71.00	1,642.11	3,107.26	57	212.12	3,536.84	4,724.11	87	633.71	5,431.58	6,340.95
28	73.64	1,705.26	3,161.16	58	220.00	3,600.00	4,778.00	88	657.25	5,494.74	6,394.84
29	76.38	1,768.42	3,215.05	59	228.17	3,663.16	4,831.89				
30	79.21	1,831.58	3,268.95	60	236.65	3,726.32	4,885.79				

143

144

Table 1 (continues)

Initial Catalog of Tunings : Octave 20

Scale Deg.	HZ	Cts	TU	Scale Deg.	HZ	Cts	TU	Scale Deg.	HZ	Cts	TU
1	27.50	0.00	1,706.00	31	77.78	1,800.00	3,242.00	61	220.00	3,600.00	4,778.00
2	28.47	60.00	1,757.20	32	80.52	1,860.00	3,293.20	62	227.76	3,660.00	4,829.20
3	29.47	120.00	1,808.40	33	83.36	1,920.00	3,344.40	63	235.79	3,720.00	4,880.40
4	30.51	180.00	1,859.60	34	86.30	1,980.00	3,395.60	64	244.11	3,780.00	4,931.60
5	31.59	240.00	1,910.80	35	89.35	2,040.00	3,446.80	65	252.71	3,840.00	4,982.80
6	32.70	300.00	1,962.00	36	92.50	2,100.00	3,498.00	66	261.63	3,900.00	5,034.00
7	33.86	360.00	2,013.20	37	95.76	2,160.00	3,549.20	67	270.85	3,960.00	5,085.20
8	35.05	420.00	2,064.40	38	99.14	2,220.00	3,600.40	68	280.40	4,020.00	5,136.40
9	36.29	480.00	2,115.60	39	102.63	2,280.00	3,651.60	69	290.29	4,080.00	5,187.60
10	37.57	540.00	2,166.80	40	106.25	2,340.00	3,702.80	70	300.53	4,140.00	5,238.80
11	38.89	600.00	2,218.00	41	110.00	2,400.00	3,754.00	71	311.13	4,200.00	5,290.00
12	40.26	660.00	2,269.20	42	113.88	2,460.00	3,805.20	72	322.10	4,260.00	5,341.20
13	41.68	720.00	2,320.40	43	117.90	2,520.00	3,856.40	73	333.46	4,320.00	5,392.40
14	43.15	780.00	2,371.60	44	122.05	2,580.00	3,907.60	74	345.22	4,380.00	5,443.60
15	44.67	840.00	2,422.80	45	126.36	2,640.00	3,958.80	75	357.39	4,440.00	5,494.80
16	46.25	900.00	2,474.00	46	130.81	2,700.00	4,010.00	76	369.99	4,500.00	5,546.00
17	47.88	960.00	2,525.20	47	135.43	2,760.00	4,061.20	77	383.04	4,560.00	5,597.20
18	49.57	1,020.00	2,576.40	48	140.20	2,820.00	4,112.40	78	396.55	4,620.00	5,648.40
19	51.32	1,080.00	2,627.60	49	145.15	2,880.00	4,163.60	79	410.53	4,680.00	5,699.60
20	53.13	1,140.00	2,678.80	50	150.26	2,940.00	4,214.80	80	425.01	4,740.00	5,750.80
21	55.00	1,200.00	2,730.00	51	155.56	3,000.00	4,266.00	81	440.00	4,800.00	5,802.00
22	56.94	1,260.00	2,781.20	52	161.05	3,060.00	4,317.20	82	455.52	4,860.00	5,853.20
23	58.95	1,320.00	2,832.40	53	166.73	3,120.00	4,368.40	83	471.58	4,920.00	5,904.40
24	61.03	1,380.00	2,883.60	54	172.61	3,180.00	4,419.60	84	488.21	4,980.00	5,955.60
25	63.18	1,440.00	2,934.80	55	178.70	3,240.00	4,470.80	85	505.43	5,040.00	6,006.80
26	65.41	1,500.00	2,986.00	56	185.00	3,300.00	4,522.00	86	523.25	5,100.00	6,058.00
27	67.71	1,560.00	3,037.20	57	191.52	3,360.00	4,573.20	87	541.70	5,160.00	6,109.20
28	70.10	1,620.00	3,088.40	58	198.28	3,420.00	4,624.40	88	560.81	5,220.00	6,160.40
29	72.57	1,680.00	3,139.60	59	205.27	3,480.00	4,675.60				
30	75.13	1,740.00	3,190.80	60	212.51	3,540.00	4,726.80				

Initial Catalog of Tunings : Octave 21

Scale Deg.	HZ	Cts	TU	Scale Deg.	HZ	Cts	TU	Scale Deg.	HZ	Cts	TU
1	27.50	0.00	1,706.00	31	74.02	1,714.29	3,168.86	61	199.26	3,428.57	4,631.71
2	28.42	57.14	1,754.76	32	76.51	1,771.43	3,217.62	62	205.95	3,485.71	4,680.48
3	29.38	114.29	1,803.52	33	79.08	1,828.57	3,266.38	63	212.86	3,542.86	4,729.24
4	30.36	171.43	1,852.29	34	81.73	1,885.71	3,315.14	64	220.00	3,600.00	4,778.00
5	31.38	228.57	1,901.05	35	84.47	1,942.86	3,363.90	65	227.38	3,657.14	4,826.76
6	32.43	285.71	1,949.81	36	87.31	2,000.00	3,412.67	66	235.01	3,714.29	4,875.52
7	33.52	342.86	1,998.57	37	90.24	2,057.14	3,461.43	67	242.90	3,771.43	4,924.29
8	34.65	400.00	2,047.33	38	93.27	2,114.29	3,510.19	68	251.05	3,828.57	4,973.05
9	35.81	457.14	2,096.10	39	96.39	2,171.43	3,558.95	69	259.48	3,885.71	5,021.81
10	37.01	514.29	2,144.86	40	99.63	2,228.57	3,607.71	70	268.18	3,942.86	5,070.57
11	38.25	571.43	2,193.62	41	102.97	2,285.71	3,656.48	71	277.18	4,000.00	5,119.33
12	39.54	628.57	2,242.38	42	106.43	2,342.86	3,705.24	72	286.48	4,057.14	5,168.10
13	40.86	685.71	2,291.14	43	110.00	2,400.00	3,754.00	73	296.10	4,114.29	5,216.86
14	42.24	742.86	2,339.90	44	113.69	2,457.14	3,802.76	74	306.03	4,171.43	5,265.62
15	43.65	800.00	2,388.67	45	117.51	2,514.29	3,851.52	75	316.30	4,228.57	5,314.38
16	45.12	857.14	2,437.43	46	121.45	2,571.43	3,900.29	76	326.92	4,285.71	5,363.14
17	46.63	914.29	2,486.19	47	125.53	2,628.57	3,949.05	77	337.89	4,342.86	5,411.90
18	48.20	971.43	2,534.95	48	129.74	2,685.71	3,997.81	78	349.23	4,400.00	5,460.67
19	49.81	1,028.57	2,583.71	49	134.09	2,742.86	4,046.57	79	360.95	4,457.14	5,509.43
20	51.49	1,085.71	2,632.48	50	138.59	2,800.00	4,095.33	80	373.06	4,514.29	5,558.19
21	53.21	1,142.86	2,681.24	51	143.24	2,857.14	4,144.10	81	385.58	4,571.43	5,606.95
22	55.00	1,200.00	2,730.00	52	148.05	2,914.29	4,192.86	82	398.52	4,628.57	5,655.71
23	56.85	1,257.14	2,778.76	53	153.02	2,971.43	4,241.62	83	411.89	4,685.71	5,704.48
24	58.75	1,314.29	2,827.52	54	158.15	3,028.57	4,290.38	84	425.71	4,742.86	5,753.24
25	60.72	1,371.43	2,876.29	55	163.46	3,085.71	4,339.14	85	440.00	4,800.00	5,802.00
26	62.76	1,428.57	2,925.05	56	168.94	3,142.86	4,387.90	86	454.77	4,857.14	5,850.76
27	64.87	1,485.71	2,973.81	57	174.61	3,200.00	4,436.67	87	470.03	4,914.29	5,899.52
28	67.05	1,542.86	3,022.57	58	180.47	3,257.14	4,485.43	88	485.80	4,971.43	5,948.29
29	69.30	1,600.00	3,071.33	59	186.53	3,314.29	4,534.19				
30	71.62	1,657.14	3,120.10	60	192.79	3,371.43	4,582.95				

Table 1 (continues)

Initial Catalog of Tunings : Octave 22

Scale Deg.	HZ	Cis	TU	Scale Deg.	HZ	Cis	TU	Scale Deg.	HZ	Cis	TU
1	27.50	0.00	1,706.00	31	70.77	1,636.36	3,102.36	61	182.11	3,272.73	4,498.73
2	28.38	54.55	1,752.55	32	73.03	1,690.91	3,148.91	62	187.93	3,327.27	4,545.27
3	29.29	109.09	1,799.09	33	75.37	1,745.45	3,195.45	63	193.95	3,381.82	4,591.82
4	30.23	163.64	1,845.64	34	77.78	1,800.00	3,242.00	64	200.16	3,436.36	4,638.36
5	31.19	218.18	1,892.18	35	80.27	1,854.55	3,288.55	65	206.56	3,490.91	4,684.91
6	32.19	272.73	1,938.73	36	82.84	1,909.09	3,335.09	66	213.18	3,545.45	4,731.45
7	33.22	327.27	1,985.27	37	85.49	1,963.64	3,381.64	67	220.00	3,600.00	4,778.00
8	34.29	381.82	2,031.82	38	88.23	2,018.18	3,428.18	68	227.04	3,654.55	4,824.55
9	35.38	436.36	2,078.36	39	91.05	2,072.73	3,474.73	69	234.31	3,709.09	4,871.09
10	36.52	490.91	2,124.91	40	93.97	2,127.27	3,521.27	70	241.81	3,763.64	4,917.64
11	37.68	545.45	2,171.45	41	96.98	2,181.82	3,567.82	71	249.55	3,818.18	4,964.18
12	38.89	600.00	2,218.00	42	100.08	2,236.36	3,614.36	72	257.54	3,872.73	5,010.73
13	40.14	654.55	2,264.55	43	103.28	2,290.91	3,660.91	73	265.78	3,927.27	5,057.27
14	41.42	709.09	2,311.09	44	106.59	2,345.45	3,707.45	74	274.29	3,981.82	5,103.82
15	42.75	763.64	2,357.64	45	110.00	2,400.00	3,754.00	75	283.07	4,036.36	5,150.36
16	44.11	818.18	2,404.18	46	113.52	2,454.55	3,800.55	76	292.13	4,090.91	5,196.91
17	45.53	872.73	2,450.73	47	117.15	2,509.09	3,847.09	77	301.48	4,145.45	5,243.45
18	46.98	927.27	2,497.27	48	120.90	2,563.64	3,893.64	78	311.13	4,200.00	5,290.00
19	48.49	981.82	2,543.82	49	124.77	2,618.18	3,940.18	79	321.09	4,254.55	5,336.55
20	50.04	1,036.36	2,590.36	50	128.77	2,672.73	3,986.73	80	331.36	4,309.09	5,383.09
21	51.64	1,090.91	2,636.91	51	132.89	2,727.27	4,033.27	81	341.97	4,363.64	5,429.64
22	53.29	1,145.45	2,683.45	52	137.14	2,781.82	4,079.82	82	352.92	4,418.18	5,476.18
23	55.00	1,200.00	2,730.00	53	141.53	2,836.36	4,126.36	83	364.21	4,472.73	5,522.73
24	56.76	1,254.55	2,776.55	54	146.06	2,890.91	4,172.91	84	375.87	4,527.27	5,569.27
25	58.58	1,309.09	2,823.09	55	150.74	2,945.45	4,219.45	85	387.90	4,581.82	5,615.82
26	60.45	1,363.64	2,869.64	56	155.56	3,000.00	4,266.00	86	400.32	4,636.36	5,662.36
27	62.39	1,418.18	2,916.18	57	160.54	3,054.55	4,312.55	87	413.13	4,690.91	5,708.91
28	64.38	1,472.73	2,962.73	58	165.68	3,109.09	4,359.09	88	426.35	4,745.45	5,755.45
29	66.44	1,527.27	3,009.27	59	170.98	3,163.64	4,405.64				
30	68.57	1,581.82	3,055.82	60	176.46	3,218.18	4,452.18				

Initial Catalog of Tunings : Octave 23

Scale Deg.	HZ	Cis	TU	Scale Deg.	HZ	Cis	TU	Scale Deg.	HZ	Cis	TU
1	27.50	0.00	1,706.00	31	67.92	1,565.22	3,041.65	61	167.74	3,130.43	4,377.30
2	28.34	52.17	1,750.52	32	70.00	1,617.39	3,086.17	62	172.87	3,182.61	4,421.83
3	29.21	104.35	1,795.04	33	72.14	1,669.57	3,130.70	63	178.16	3,234.78	4,466.35
4	30.10	156.52	1,839.57	34	74.34	1,721.74	3,175.22	64	183.61	3,286.96	4,510.87
5	31.02	208.70	1,884.09	35	76.62	1,773.91	3,219.74	65	189.23	3,339.13	4,555.39
6	31.97	260.87	1,928.61	36	78.96	1,826.09	3,264.26	66	195.02	3,391.30	4,599.91
7	32.95	313.04	1,973.13	37	81.38	1,878.26	3,308.78	67	200.98	3,443.48	4,644.43
8	33.96	365.22	2,017.65	38	83.87	1,930.43	3,353.30	68	207.13	3,495.65	4,688.96
9	35.00	417.39	2,062.17	39	86.43	1,982.61	3,397.83	69	213.47	3,547.83	4,733.48
10	36.07	469.57	2,106.70	40	89.08	2,034.78	3,442.35	70	220.00	3,600.00	4,778.00
11	37.17	521.74	2,151.22	41	91.80	2,086.96	3,486.87	71	226.73	3,652.17	4,822.52
12	38.31	573.91	2,195.74	42	94.61	2,139.13	3,531.39	72	233.67	3,704.35	4,867.04
13	39.48	626.09	2,240.26	43	97.51	2,191.30	3,575.91	73	240.82	3,756.52	4,911.57
14	40.69	678.26	2,284.78	44	100.49	2,243.48	3,620.43	74	248.19	3,808.70	4,956.09
15	41.93	730.43	2,329.30	45	103.57	2,295.65	3,664.96	75	255.78	3,860.87	5,000.61
16	43.22	782.61	2,373.83	46	106.73	2,347.83	3,709.48	76	263.60	3,913.04	5,045.13
17	44.54	834.78	2,418.35	47	110.00	2,400.00	3,754.00	77	271.67	3,965.22	5,089.65
18	45.90	886.96	2,462.87	48	113.37	2,452.17	3,798.52	78	279.98	4,017.39	5,134.17
19	47.31	939.13	2,507.39	49	116.83	2,504.35	3,843.04	79	288.55	4,069.57	5,178.70
20	48.75	991.30	2,551.91	50	120.41	2,556.52	3,887.57	80	297.38	4,121.74	5,223.22
21	50.25	1,043.48	2,596.43	51	124.09	2,608.70	3,932.09	81	306.47	4,173.91	5,267.74
22	51.78	1,095.65	2,640.96	52	127.89	2,660.87	3,976.61	82	315.85	4,226.09	5,312.26
23	53.37	1,147.83	2,685.48	53	131.80	2,713.04	4,021.13	83	325.51	4,278.26	5,356.78
24	55.00	1,200.00	2,730.00	54	135.83	2,765.22	4,065.65	84	335.47	4,330.43	5,401.30
25	56.68	1,252.17	2,774.52	55	139.99	2,817.39	4,110.17	85	345.74	4,382.61	5,445.83
26	58.42	1,304.35	2,819.04	56	144.27	2,869.57	4,154.70	86	356.32	4,434.78	5,490.35
27	60.20	1,356.52	2,863.57	57	148.69	2,921.74	4,199.22	87	367.22	4,486.96	5,534.87
28	62.05	1,408.70	2,908.09	58	153.24	2,973.91	4,243.74	88	378.45	4,539.13	5,579.39
29	63.94	1,460.87	2,952.61	59	157.93	3,026.09	4,288.26				
30	65.90	1,513.04	2,997.13	60	162.76	3,078.26	4,332.78				

Table 1 (continues)

Initial Catalog of Tunings : Octave 24

Scale Deg.	HZ	Cts	TU	Scale Deg.	HZ	Cts	TU	Scale Deg.	HZ	Cts	TU
1	27.50	0.00	1,706.00	31	65.41	1,500.00	2,986.00	61	155.56	3,000.00	4,266.00
2	28.31	50.00	1,748.67	32	67.32	1,550.00	3,028.67	62	160.12	3,050.00	4,308.67
3	29.14	100.00	1,791.33	33	69.30	1,600.00	3,071.33	63	164.81	3,100.00	4,351.33
4	29.99	150.00	1,834.00	34	71.33	1,650.00	3,114.00	64	169.64	3,150.00	4,394.00
5	30.87	200.00	1,876.67	35	73.42	1,700.00	3,156.67	65	174.61	3,200.00	4,436.67
6	31.77	250.00	1,919.33	36	75.57	1,750.00	3,199.33	66	179.73	3,250.00	4,479.33
7	32.70	300.00	1,962.00	37	77.78	1,800.00	3,242.00	67	185.00	3,300.00	4,522.00
8	33.66	350.00	2,004.67	38	80.06	1,850.00	3,284.67	68	190.42	3,350.00	4,564.67
9	34.65	400.00	2,047.33	39	82.41	1,900.00	3,327.33	69	196.00	3,400.00	4,607.33
10	35.66	450.00	2,090.00	40	84.82	1,950.00	3,370.00	70	201.74	3,450.00	4,650.00
11	36.71	500.00	2,132.67	41	87.31	2,000.00	3,412.67	71	207.65	3,500.00	4,692.67
12	37.78	550.00	2,175.33	42	89.87	2,050.00	3,455.33	72	213.74	3,550.00	4,735.33
13	38.89	600.00	2,218.00	43	92.50	2,100.00	3,498.00	73	220.00	3,600.00	4,778.00
14	40.03	650.00	2,260.67	44	95.21	2,150.00	3,540.67	74	226.45	3,650.00	4,820.67
15	41.20	700.00	2,303.33	45	98.00	2,200.00	3,583.33	75	233.08	3,700.00	4,863.33
16	42.41	750.00	2,346.00	46	100.87	2,250.00	3,626.00	76	239.91	3,750.00	4,906.00
17	43.65	800.00	2,388.67	47	103.83	2,300.00	3,668.67	77	246.94	3,800.00	4,948.67
18	44.93	850.00	2,431.33	48	106.87	2,350.00	3,711.33	78	254.18	3,850.00	4,991.33
19	46.25	900.00	2,474.00	49	110.00	2,400.00	3,754.00	79	261.63	3,900.00	5,034.00
20	47.60	950.00	2,516.67	50	113.22	2,450.00	3,796.67	80	269.29	3,950.00	5,076.67
21	49.00	1,000.00	2,559.33	51	116.54	2,500.00	3,839.33	81	277.18	4,000.00	5,119.33
22	50.44	1,050.00	2,602.00	52	119.96	2,550.00	3,882.00	82	285.30	4,050.00	5,162.00
23	51.91	1,100.00	2,644.67	53	123.47	2,600.00	3,924.67	83	293.66	4,100.00	5,204.67
24	53.43	1,150.00	2,687.33	54	127.09	2,650.00	3,967.33	84	302.27	4,150.00	5,247.33
25	55.00	1,200.00	2,730.00	55	130.81	2,700.00	4,010.00	85	311.13	4,200.00	5,290.00
26	56.61	1,250.00	2,772.67	56	134.65	2,750.00	4,052.67	86	320.24	4,250.00	5,332.67
27	58.27	1,300.00	2,815.33	57	138.59	2,800.00	4,095.33	87	329.63	4,300.00	5,375.33
28	59.98	1,350.00	2,858.00	58	142.65	2,850.00	4,138.00	88	339.29	4,350.00	5,418.00
29	61.74	1,400.00	2,900.67	59	146.83	2,900.00	4,180.67				
30	63.54	1,450.00	2,943.33	60	151.13	2,950.00	4,223.33				

Initial Catalog of Tunings : A-8

Scale Deg.	HZ	Cts	TU	Scale Deg.	HZ	Cts	TU	Scale Deg.	HZ	Cts	TU
1	27.50	0.00	1,706.00	14	163.93	3,090.69	4,343.38	27	977.18	6,181.37	6,980.75
2	31.55	237.75	1,908.88	15	188.06	3,328.43	4,546.25	28	1,121.03	6,419.12	7,183.63
3	36.19	475.49	2,111.75	16	215.74	3,566.18	4,749.13	29	1,286.05	6,656.86	7,386.50
4	41.52	713.24	2,314.63	17	247.50	3,803.92	4,952.00	30	1,475.36	6,894.61	7,589.38
5	47.63	950.98	2,517.50	18	283.93	4,041.67	5,154.88	31	1,692.53	7,132.35	7,792.25
6	54.64	1,188.73	2,720.38	19	325.73	4,279.41	5,357.75	32	1,941.68	7,370.10	7,995.13
7	62.69	1,426.47	2,923.25	20	373.68	4,517.16	5,560.63	33	2,227.50	7,607.84	8,198.00
8	71.91	1,664.22	3,126.13	21	428.68	4,754.90	5,763.50	34	2,555.39	7,845.59	8,400.88
9	82.50	1,901.96	3,329.00	22	491.79	4,992.65	5,966.38	35	2,931.55	8,083.33	8,603.75
10	94.64	2,139.71	3,531.88	23	564.18	5,230.39	6,169.25	36	3,363.09	8,321.08	8,806.63
11	108.58	2,377.45	3,734.75	24	647.23	5,468.14	6,372.13	37	3,858.14	8,558.82	9,009.50
12	124.56	2,615.20	3,937.63	25	742.50	5,705.88	6,575.00				
13	142.89	2,852.94	4,140.50	26	851.80	5,943.63	6,777.88				

Initial Catalog of Tunings : A-9

Scale Deg.	HZ	Cts	TU	Scale Deg.	HZ	Cts	TU	Scale Deg.	HZ	Cts	TU
1	27.50	0.00	1,706.00	16	171.61	3,169.93	4,411.00	31	1,070.87	6,339.87	7,116.00
2	31.07	211.33	1,886.33	17	193.89	3,381.26	4,591.33	32	1,209.90	6,551.20	7,296.33
3	35.10	422.66	2,066.67	18	219.06	3,592.59	4,771.67	33	1,366.99	6,762.52	7,476.67
4	39.66	633.99	2,247.00	19	247.50	3,803.92	4,952.00	34	1,544.46	6,973.85	7,657.00
5	44.81	845.32	2,427.33	20	279.63	4,015.25	5,132.33	35	1,744.98	7,185.18	7,837.33
6	50.63	1,056.64	2,607.67	21	315.94	4,226.58	5,312.67	36	1,971.53	7,396.51	8,017.67
7	57.20	1,267.97	2,788.00	22	356.96	4,437.91	5,493.00	37	2,227.50	7,607.84	8,198.00
8	64.63	1,479.30	2,968.33	23	403.30	4,649.24	5,673.33	38	2,516.70	7,819.17	8,378.33
9	73.02	1,690.63	3,148.67	24	455.66	4,860.56	5,853.67	39	2,843.44	8,030.50	8,558.67
10	82.50	1,901.96	3,329.00	25	514.82	5,071.89	6,034.00	40	3,212.61	8,241.83	8,739.00
11	93.21	2,113.29	3,509.33	26	581.66	5,283.22	6,214.33	41	3,629.71	8,453.16	8,919.33
12	105.31	2,324.62	3,689.67	27	657.18	5,494.55	6,394.67	42	4,100.96	8,664.48	9,099.67
13	118.99	2,535.95	3,870.00	28	742.50	5,705.88	6,575.00				
14	134.43	2,747.28	4,050.33	29	838.90	5,917.21	6,755.33				
15	151.89	2,958.60	4,230.67	30	947.81	6,128.54	6,935.67				

147

Table 1 (continues)

Initial Catalog of Tunings : A-10

Scale Deg.	HZ	Cts	TU	Scale Deg.	HZ	Cts	TU	Scale Deg.	HZ	Cts	TU
1	27.50	0.00	1,706.00	18	178.01	3,233.33	4,465.10	35	1,152.25	6,466.66	7,224.20
2	30.69	190.20	1,868.30	19	198.68	3,423.53	4,627.40	36	1,286.05	6,656.86	7,386.50
3	34.26	380.39	2,030.60	20	221.75	3,613.72	4,789.70	37	1,435.39	6,847.06	7,548.80
4	38.24	570.59	2,192.90	21	247.50	3,803.92	4,952.00	38	1,602.07	7,037.25	7,711.10
5	42.68	760.78	2,355.20	22	276.24	3,994.12	5,114.30	39	1,788.11	7,227.45	7,873.40
6	47.63	950.98	2,517.50	23	308.32	4,184.31	5,276.60	40	1,995.75	7,417.64	8,035.70
7	53.16	1,141.18	2,679.80	24	344.12	4,374.51	5,438.90	41	2,227.50	7,607.84	8,198.00
8	59.34	1,331.37	2,842.10	25	384.08	4,564.70	5,601.20	42	2,486.16	7,798.04	8,360.30
9	66.23	1,521.57	3,004.40	26	428.68	4,754.90	5,763.50	43	2,774.87	7,988.23	8,522.60
10	73.92	1,711.76	3,166.70	27	478.46	4,945.10	5,925.80	44	3,097.09	8,178.43	8,684.90
11	82.50	1,901.96	3,329.00	28	534.02	5,135.29	6,088.10	45	3,456.74	8,368.62	8,847.20
12	92.08	2,092.16	3,491.30	29	596.04	5,325.49	6,250.40	46	3,858.14	8,558.82	9,009.50
13	102.77	2,282.35	3,653.60	30	665.25	5,515.68	6,412.70	47	4,306.16	8,749.02	9,171.80
14	114.71	2,472.55	3,815.90	31	742.50	5,705.88	6,575.00				
15	128.03	2,662.74	3,978.20	32	828.72	5,896.08	6,737.30				
16	142.89	2,852.94	4,140.50	33	924.96	6,086.27	6,899.60				
17	159.49	3,043.14	4,302.80	34	1,032.36	6,276.47	7,061.90				

Initial Catalog of Tunings : A-11

Scale Deg.	HZ	Cts	TU	Scale Deg.	HZ	Cts	TU	Scale Deg.	HZ	Cts	TU
1	27.50	0.00	1,706.00	19	165.99	3,112.30	4,361.82	37	1,001.89	6,224.60	7,017.64
2	30.39	172.91	1,853.55	20	183.42	3,285.20	4,509.36	38	1,107.12	6,397.50	7,165.18
3	33.58	345.81	2,001.09	21	202.69	3,458.11	4,656.91	39	1,223.40	6,570.41	7,312.73
4	37.11	518.72	2,148.64	22	223.98	3,631.01	4,804.45	40	1,351.90	6,743.31	7,460.27
5	41.00	691.62	2,296.18	23	247.50	3,803.92	4,952.00	41	1,493.89	6,916.22	7,607.82
6	45.31	864.53	2,443.73	24	273.50	3,976.83	5,099.55	42	1,650.80	7,089.12	7,755.36
7	50.07	1,037.43	2,591.27	25	302.22	4,149.73	5,247.09	43	1,824.18	7,262.03	7,902.91
8	55.33	1,210.34	2,738.82	26	333.96	4,322.64	5,394.64	44	2,015.78	7,434.93	8,050.45
9	61.14	1,383.24	2,886.36	27	369.04	4,495.54	5,542.18	45	2,227.50	7,607.84	8,198.00
10	67.56	1,556.15	3,033.91	28	407.80	4,668.45	5,689.73	46	2,461.46	7,780.75	8,345.55
11	74.66	1,729.05	3,181.45	29	450.63	4,841.35	5,837.27	47	2,719.99	7,953.65	8,493.09
12	82.50	1,901.96	3,329.00	30	497.96	5,014.26	5,984.82	48	3,005.67	8,126.56	8,640.64
13	91.17	2,074.87	3,476.55	31	550.27	5,187.16	6,132.36	49	3,321.36	8,299.46	8,788.18
14	100.74	2,247.77	3,624.09	32	608.06	5,360.07	6,279.91	50	3,670.21	8,472.37	8,935.73
15	111.32	2,420.68	3,771.64	33	671.93	5,532.97	6,427.45	51	4,055.70	8,645.27	9,083.27
16	123.01	2,593.58	3,919.18	34	742.50	5,705.88	6,575.00	52	4,481.67	8,818.18	9,230.82
17	135.93	2,766.49	4,066.73	35	820.49	5,878.79	6,722.55				
18	150.21	2,939.39	4,214.27	36	906.66	6,051.69	6,870.09				

Initial Catalog of Tunings : A-12

Scale Deg.	HZ	Cts	TU	Scale Deg.	HZ	Cts	TU	Scale Deg.	HZ	Cts	TU
1	27.50	0.00	1,706.00	21	171.61	3,169.93	4,411.00	41	1,070.87	6,339.87	7,116.00
2	30.14	158.50	1,841.25	22	188.06	3,328.43	4,546.25	42	1,173.54	6,498.36	7,251.25
3	33.03	316.99	1,976.50	23	206.09	3,486.93	4,681.50	43	1,286.05	6,656.86	7,386.50
4	36.19	475.49	2,111.75	24	225.85	3,645.42	4,816.75	44	1,409.34	6,815.36	7,521.75
5	39.66	633.99	2,247.00	25	247.50	3,803.92	4,952.00	45	1,544.46	6,973.85	7,657.00
6	43.46	792.48	2,382.25	26	271.23	3,962.42	5,087.25	46	1,692.53	7,132.35	7,792.25
7	47.63	950.98	2,517.50	27	297.23	4,120.91	5,222.50	47	1,854.80	7,290.85	7,927.50
8	52.20	1,109.48	2,652.75	28	325.73	4,279.41	5,357.75	48	2,032.63	7,449.34	8,062.75
9	57.20	1,267.97	2,788.00	29	356.96	4,437.91	5,493.00	49	2,227.50	7,607.84	8,198.00
10	62.69	1,426.47	2,923.25	30	391.18	4,596.40	5,628.25	50	2,441.06	7,766.34	8,333.25
11	68.70	1,584.97	3,058.50	31	428.68	4,754.90	5,763.50	51	2,675.09	7,924.83	8,468.50
12	75.28	1,743.46	3,193.75	32	469.78	4,913.40	5,898.75	52	2,931.55	8,083.33	8,603.75
13	82.50	1,901.96	3,329.00	33	514.82	5,071.89	6,034.00	53	3,212.61	8,241.83	8,739.00
14	90.41	2,060.46	3,464.25	34	564.18	5,230.39	6,169.25	54	3,520.61	8,400.32	8,874.25
15	99.08	2,218.95	3,599.50	35	618.27	5,388.89	6,304.50	55	3,858.14	8,558.82	9,009.50
16	108.58	2,377.45	3,734.75	36	677.54	5,547.38	6,439.75	56	4,228.03	8,717.32	9,144.75
17	118.99	2,535.95	3,870.00	37	742.50	5,705.88	6,575.00				
18	130.39	2,694.44	4,005.25	38	813.69	5,864.38	6,710.25				
19	142.89	2,852.94	4,140.50	39	891.70	6,022.87	6,845.50				
20	156.59	3,011.44	4,275.75	40	977.18	6,181.37	6,980.75				

Table 1 (continues)

Initial Catalog of Tunings : A-13

Scale Deg.	HZ	Cts	TU	Scale Deg.	HZ	Cts	TU	Scale Deg.	HZ	Cts	TU
1	27.50	0.00	1,706.00	22	162.21	3,072.40	4,327.77	43	956.76	6,144.79	6,949.54
2	29.93	146.30	1,830.85	23	176.51	3,218.70	4,452.62	44	1,041.13	6,291.10	7,074.38
3	32.56	292.61	1,955.69	24	192.07	3,365.01	4,577.46	45	1,132.93	6,437.40	7,199.23
4	35.44	438.91	2,080.54	25	209.01	3,511.31	4,702.31	46	1,232.84	6,583.71	7,324.08
5	38.56	585.22	2,205.38	26	227.44	3,657.62	4,827.15	47	1,341.55	6,730.01	7,448.92
6	41.96	731.52	2,330.23	27	247.50	3,803.92	4,952.00	48	1,459.85	6,876.32	7,573.77
7	45.66	877.83	2,455.08	28	269.33	3,950.22	5,076.85	49	1,588.59	7,022.62	7,698.62
8	49.69	1,024.13	2,579.92	29	293.07	4,096.53	5,201.69	50	1,728.67	7,168.93	7,823.46
9	54.07	1,170.44	2,704.77	30	318.92	4,242.83	5,326.54	51	1,881.11	7,315.23	7,948.31
10	58.84	1,316.74	2,829.62	31	347.04	4,389.14	5,451.38	52	2,046.99	7,461.54	8,073.15
11	64.02	1,463.05	2,954.46	32	377.64	4,535.44	5,576.23	53	2,227.50	7,607.84	8,198.00
12	69.67	1,609.35	3,079.31	33	410.95	4,681.75	5,701.08	54	2,423.93	7,754.14	8,322.85
13	75.81	1,755.66	3,204.15	34	447.18	4,828.05	5,825.92	55	2,637.67	7,900.45	8,447.69
14	82.50	1,901.96	3,329.00	35	486.62	4,974.36	5,950.77	56	2,870.27	8,046.75	8,572.54
15	89.78	2,048.26	3,453.85	36	529.53	5,120.66	6,075.62	57	3,123.38	8,193.06	8,697.38
16	97.69	2,194.57	3,578.69	37	576.22	5,266.97	6,200.46	58	3,398.80	8,339.36	8,822.23
17	106.31	2,340.87	3,703.54	38	627.04	5,413.27	6,325.31	59	3,698.52	8,485.67	8,947.08
18	115.68	2,487.18	3,828.38	39	682.33	5,559.58	6,450.15	60	4,024.66	8,631.97	9,071.92
19	125.88	2,633.48	3,953.23	40	742.50	5,705.88	6,575.00	61	4,379.56	8,778.28	9,196.77
20	136.98	2,779.79	4,078.08	41	807.98	5,852.18	6,699.85				
21	149.06	2,926.09	4,202.92	42	879.22	5,998.49	6,824.69				

Initial Catalog of Tunings : A-14

Scale Deg.	HZ	Cts	TU	Scale Deg.	HZ	Cts	TU	Scale Deg.	HZ	Cts	TU
1	27.50	0.00	1,706.00	24	167.18	3,124.65	4,372.36	47	1,016.29	6,249.30	7,038.71
2	29.74	135.85	1,821.93	25	180.82	3,260.50	4,488.29	48	1,099.25	6,385.15	7,154.64
3	32.17	271.71	1,937.86	26	195.58	3,396.36	4,604.21	49	1,188.99	6,521.01	7,270.57
4	34.80	407.56	2,053.79	27	211.55	3,532.21	4,720.14	50	1,286.05	6,656.86	7,386.50
5	37.64	543.42	2,169.71	28	228.82	3,668.07	4,836.07	51	1,391.03	6,792.71	7,502.43
6	40.71	679.27	2,285.64	29	247.50	3,803.92	4,952.00	52	1,504.59	6,928.57	7,618.36
7	44.04	815.13	2,401.57	30	267.70	3,939.77	5,067.93	53	1,627.41	7,064.42	7,734.29
8	47.63	950.98	2,517.50	31	289.56	4,075.63	5,183.86	54	1,760.26	7,200.28	7,850.21
9	51.52	1,086.83	2,633.43	32	313.20	4,211.48	5,299.79	55	1,903.96	7,336.13	7,966.14
10	55.73	1,222.69	2,749.36	33	338.76	4,347.34	5,415.71	56	2,059.39	7,471.99	8,082.07
11	60.27	1,358.54	2,865.29	34	366.42	4,483.19	5,531.64	57	2,227.50	7,607.84	8,198.00
12	65.19	1,494.40	2,981.21	35	396.33	4,619.05	5,647.57	58	2,409.34	7,743.69	8,313.93
13	70.52	1,630.25	3,097.14	36	428.68	4,754.90	5,763.50	59	2,606.02	7,879.55	8,429.86
14	76.27	1,766.11	3,213.07	37	463.68	4,890.75	5,879.43	60	2,818.76	8,015.40	8,545.79
15	82.50	1,901.96	3,329.00	38	501.53	5,026.61	5,995.36	61	3,048.86	8,151.26	8,661.71
16	89.23	2,037.81	3,444.93	39	542.47	5,162.46	6,111.29	62	3,297.75	8,287.11	8,777.64
17	96.52	2,173.67	3,560.86	40	586.75	5,298.32	6,227.21	63	3,566.96	8,422.97	8,893.57
18	104.40	2,309.52	3,676.79	41	634.65	5,434.17	6,343.14	64	3,858.14	8,558.82	9,009.50
19	112.92	2,445.38	3,792.71	42	686.46	5,570.03	6,459.07	65	4,173.10	8,694.67	9,125.43
20	122.14	2,581.23	3,908.64	43	742.50	5,705.88	6,575.00	66	4,513.76	8,830.53	9,241.36
21	132.11	2,717.09	4,024.57	44	803.11	5,841.73	6,690.93				
22	142.89	2,852.94	4,140.50	45	868.67	5,977.59	6,806.86				
23	154.56	2,988.79	4,256.43	46	939.59	6,113.44	6,922.79				

149

Table 1 (continues)

Initial Catalog of Tunings : A-15

Scale Deg.	HZ	Cts	TU	Scale Deg.	HZ	Cts	TU	Scale Deg.	HZ	Cts	TU
1	27.50	0.00	1,706.00	26	171.61	3,169.93	4,411.00	51	1,070.87	6,339.87	7,116.00
2	29.59	126.80	1,814.20	27	184.65	3,296.73	4,519.20	52	1,152.25	6,466.66	7,224.20
3	31.84	253.59	1,922.40	28	198.68	3,423.53	4,627.40	53	1,239.80	6,593.46	7,332.40
4	34.26	380.39	2,030.60	29	213.78	3,550.33	4,735.60	54	1,334.02	6,720.26	7,440.60
5	36.86	507.19	2,138.80	30	230.02	3,677.12	4,843.80	55	1,435.39	6,847.06	7,548.80
6	39.66	633.99	2,247.00	31	247.50	3,803.92	4,952.00	56	1,544.46	6,973.85	7,657.00
7	42.68	760.78	2,355.20	32	266.31	3,930.72	5,060.20	57	1,661.83	7,100.65	7,765.20
8	45.92	887.58	2,463.40	33	286.54	4,057.51	5,168.40	58	1,788.11	7,227.45	7,873.40
9	49.41	1,014.38	2,571.60	34	308.32	4,184.31	5,276.60	59	1,923.98	7,354.25	7,981.60
10	53.16	1,141.18	2,679.80	35	331.75	4,311.11	5,384.80	60	2,070.19	7,481.04	8,089.80
11	57.20	1,267.97	2,788.00	36	356.96	4,437.91	5,493.00	61	2,227.50	7,607.84	8,198.00
12	61.55	1,394.77	2,896.20	37	384.08	4,564.70	5,601.20	62	2,396.77	7,734.64	8,306.20
13	66.23	1,521.57	3,004.40	38	413.27	4,691.50	5,709.40	63	2,578.90	7,861.43	8,414.40
14	71.26	1,648.37	3,112.60	39	444.67	4,818.30	5,817.60	64	2,774.87	7,988.23	8,522.60
15	76.67	1,775.16	3,220.80	40	478.46	4,945.10	5,925.80	65	2,985.73	8,115.03	8,630.80
16	82.50	1,901.96	3,329.00	41	514.82	5,071.89	6,034.00	66	3,212.61	8,241.83	8,739.00
17	88.77	2,028.76	3,437.20	42	553.94	5,198.69	6,142.20	67	3,456.74	8,368.62	8,847.20
18	95.51	2,155.55	3,545.40	43	596.04	5,325.49	6,250.40	68	3,719.41	8,495.42	8,955.40
19	102.77	2,282.35	3,653.60	44	641.33	5,452.29	6,358.60	69	4,002.05	8,622.22	9,063.60
20	110.58	2,409.15	3,761.80	45	690.06	5,579.08	6,466.80	70	4,306.16	8,749.02	9,171.80
21	118.99	2,535.95	3,870.00	46	742.50	5,705.88	6,575.00	71	4,633.39	8,875.81	9,280.00
22	128.03	2,662.74	3,978.20	47	798.92	5,832.68	6,683.20				
23	137.76	2,789.54	4,086.40	48	859.63	5,959.47	6,791.40				
24	148.22	2,916.34	4,194.60	49	924.96	6,086.27	6,899.60				
25	159.49	3,043.14	4,302.80	50	995.24	6,213.07	7,007.80				

Initial Catalog of Tunings : A-16

Scale Deg.	HZ	Cts	TU	Scale Deg.	HZ	Cts	TU	Scale Deg.	HZ	Cts	TU
1	27.50	0.00	1,706.00	27	163.93	3,090.69	4,343.38	53	977.18	6,181.37	6,980.75
2	29.45	118.87	1,807.44	28	175.58	3,209.56	4,444.81	54	1,046.64	6,300.24	7,082.19
3	31.55	237.75	1,908.88	29	188.06	3,328.43	4,546.25	55	1,121.03	6,419.12	7,183.63
4	33.79	356.62	2,010.31	30	201.43	3,447.30	4,647.69	56	1,200.71	6,537.99	7,285.06
5	36.19	475.49	2,111.75	31	215.74	3,566.18	4,749.13	57	1,286.05	6,656.86	7,386.50
6	38.76	594.36	2,213.19	32	231.08	3,685.05	4,850.56	58	1,377.45	6,775.73	7,487.94
7	41.52	713.24	2,314.63	33	247.50	3,803.92	4,952.00	59	1,475.36	6,894.61	7,589.38
8	44.47	832.11	2,416.06	34	265.09	3,922.79	5,053.44	60	1,580.22	7,013.48	7,690.81
9	47.63	950.98	2,517.50	35	283.93	4,041.67	5,154.88	61	1,692.53	7,132.35	7,792.25
10	51.02	1,069.85	2,618.94	36	304.11	4,160.54	5,256.31	62	1,812.83	7,251.22	7,893.69
11	54.64	1,188.73	2,720.38	37	325.73	4,279.41	5,357.75	63	1,941.68	7,370.10	7,995.13
12	58.53	1,307.60	2,821.81	38	348.88	4,398.28	5,459.19	64	2,079.69	7,488.97	8,096.56
13	62.69	1,426.47	2,923.25	39	373.68	4,517.16	5,560.63	65	2,227.50	7,607.84	8,198.00
14	67.14	1,545.34	3,024.69	40	400.24	4,636.03	5,662.06	66	2,385.82	7,726.71	8,299.44
15	71.91	1,664.22	3,126.13	41	428.68	4,754.90	5,763.50	67	2,555.39	7,845.59	8,400.88
16	77.03	1,783.09	3,227.56	42	459.15	4,873.77	5,864.94	68	2,737.02	7,964.46	8,502.31
17	82.50	1,901.96	3,329.00	43	491.79	4,992.65	5,966.38	69	2,931.55	8,083.33	8,603.75
18	88.36	2,020.83	3,430.44	44	526.74	5,111.52	6,067.81	70	3,139.92	8,202.20	8,705.19
19	94.64	2,139.71	3,531.88	45	564.18	5,230.39	6,169.25	71	3,363.09	8,321.08	8,806.63
20	101.37	2,258.58	3,633.31	46	604.28	5,349.26	6,270.69	72	3,602.12	8,439.95	8,908.06
21	108.58	2,377.45	3,734.75	47	647.23	5,468.14	6,372.13	73	3,858.14	8,558.82	9,009.50
22	116.29	2,496.32	3,836.19	48	693.23	5,587.01	6,473.56	74	4,132.36	8,677.69	9,110.94
23	124.56	2,615.20	3,937.63	49	742.50	5,705.88	6,575.00	75	4,426.07	8,796.57	9,212.38
24	133.41	2,734.07	4,039.06	50	795.27	5,824.75	6,676.44				
25	142.89	2,852.94	4,140.50	51	851.80	5,943.63	6,777.88				
26	153.05	2,971.81	4,241.94	52	912.34	6,062.50	6,879.31				

150

Table 1 (continues)

Initial Catalog of Tunings : A-17

Scale Deg.	HZ	Cts	TU	Scale Deg.	HZ	Cts	TU	Scale Deg.	HZ	Cts	TU
1	27.50	0.00	1,706.00	29	167.95	3,132.64	4,379.18	57	1,025.71	6,265.28	7,052.35
2	29.34	111.88	1,801.47	30	179.16	3,244.52	4,474.65	58	1,094.19	6,377.16	7,147.82
3	31.29	223.76	1,896.94	31	191.12	3,356.40	4,570.12	59	1,167.23	6,489.04	7,243.29
4	33.38	335.64	1,992.41	32	203.88	3,468.28	4,665.59	60	1,245.16	6,600.92	7,338.76
5	35.61	447.52	2,087.88	33	217.49	3,580.16	4,761.06	61	1,328.28	6,712.80	7,434.24
6	37.99	559.40	2,183.35	34	232.01	3,692.04	4,856.53	62	1,416.95	6,824.68	7,529.71
7	40.53	671.28	2,278.82	35	247.50	3,803.92	4,952.00	63	1,511.55	6,936.56	7,625.18
8	43.23	783.16	2,374.29	36	264.02	3,915.80	5,047.47	64	1,612.46	7,048.44	7,720.65
9	46.12	895.04	2,469.76	37	281.65	4,027.68	5,142.94	65	1,720.10	7,160.32	7,816.12
10	49.20	1,006.92	2,565.24	38	300.45	4,139.56	5,238.41	66	1,834.93	7,272.20	7,911.59
11	52.48	1,118.80	2,660.71	39	320.51	4,251.44	5,333.88	67	1,957.43	7,384.08	8,007.06
12	55.98	1,230.68	2,756.18	40	341.90	4,363.32	5,429.35	68	2,088.10	7,495.96	8,102.53
13	59.72	1,342.56	2,851.65	41	364.73	4,475.20	5,524.82	69	2,227.50	7,607.84	8,198.00
14	63.71	1,454.44	2,947.12	42	389.08	4,587.08	5,620.29	70	2,376.20	7,719.72	8,293.47
15	67.96	1,566.32	3,042.59	43	415.05	4,698.96	5,715.76	71	2,534.83	7,831.60	8,388.94
16	72.50	1,678.20	3,138.06	44	442.76	4,810.84	5,811.24	72	2,704.06	7,943.48	8,484.41
17	77.34	1,790.08	3,233.53	45	472.32	4,922.72	5,906.71	73	2,884.57	8,055.36	8,579.88
18	82.50	1,901.96	3,329.00	46	503.85	5,034.60	6,002.18	74	3,077.14	8,167.24	8,675.35
19	88.01	2,013.84	3,424.47	47	537.49	5,146.48	6,097.65	75	3,282.57	8,279.12	8,770.82
20	93.88	2,125.72	3,519.94	48	573.37	5,258.36	6,193.12	76	3,501.70	8,391.00	8,866.29
21	100.15	2,237.60	3,615.41	49	611.64	5,370.24	6,288.59	77	3,735.47	8,502.88	8,961.76
22	106.84	2,349.48	3,710.88	50	652.48	5,482.12	6,384.06	78	3,984.84	8,614.76	9,057.24
23	113.97	2,461.36	3,806.35	51	696.03	5,594.00	6,479.53	79	4,250.86	8,726.64	9,152.71
24	121.58	2,573.24	3,901.82	52	742.50	5,705.88	6,575.00	80	4,534.64	8,838.52	9,248.18
25	129.69	2,685.12	3,997.29	53	792.07	5,817.76	6,670.47				
26	138.35	2,797.00	4,092.76	54	844.94	5,929.64	6,765.94				
27	147.59	2,908.88	4,188.24	55	901.35	6,041.52	6,861.41				
28	157.44	3,020.76	4,283.71	56	961.52	6,153.40	6,956.88				

Initial Catalog of Tunings : A-18

Scale Deg.	HZ	Cts	TU	Scale Deg.	HZ	Cts	TU	Scale Deg.	HZ	Cts	TU
1	27.50	0.00	1,706.00	30	161.45	3,064.27	4,320.83	59	947.81	6,128.54	6,935.67
2	29.23	105.66	1,796.17	31	171.61	3,169.93	4,411.00	60	1,007.47	6,234.20	7,025.83
3	31.07	211.33	1,886.33	32	182.41	3,275.60	4,501.17	61	1,070.87	6,339.87	7,116.00
4	33.03	316.99	1,976.50	33	193.89	3,381.26	4,591.33	62	1,138.27	6,445.53	7,206.17
5	35.10	422.66	2,066.67	34	206.09	3,486.93	4,681.50	63	1,209.90	6,551.20	7,296.33
6	37.31	528.32	2,156.83	35	219.06	3,592.59	4,771.67	64	1,286.05	6,656.86	7,386.50
7	39.66	633.99	2,247.00	36	232.85	3,698.26	4,861.83	65	1,366.99	6,762.52	7,476.67
8	42.16	739.65	2,337.17	37	247.50	3,803.92	4,952.00	66	1,453.02	6,868.19	7,566.83
9	44.81	845.32	2,427.33	38	263.08	3,909.58	5,042.17	67	1,544.46	6,973.85	7,657.00
10	47.63	950.98	2,517.50	39	279.63	4,015.25	5,132.33	68	1,641.66	7,079.52	7,747.17
11	50.63	1,056.64	2,607.67	40	297.23	4,120.91	5,222.50	69	1,744.98	7,185.18	7,837.33
12	53.82	1,162.31	2,697.83	41	315.94	4,226.58	5,312.67	70	1,854.80	7,290.85	7,927.50
13	57.20	1,267.97	2,788.00	42	335.82	4,332.24	5,402.83	71	1,971.53	7,396.51	8,017.67
14	60.80	1,373.64	2,878.17	43	356.96	4,437.91	5,493.00	72	2,095.61	7,502.18	8,107.83
15	64.63	1,479.30	2,968.33	44	379.42	4,543.57	5,583.17	73	2,227.50	7,607.84	8,198.00
16	68.70	1,584.97	3,058.50	45	403.30	4,649.24	5,673.33	74	2,367.69	7,713.50	8,288.17
17	73.02	1,690.63	3,148.67	46	428.68	4,754.90	5,763.50	75	2,516.70	7,819.17	8,378.33
18	77.62	1,796.30	3,238.83	47	455.66	4,860.56	5,853.67	76	2,675.09	7,924.83	8,468.50
19	82.50	1,901.96	3,329.00	48	484.34	4,966.23	5,943.83	77	2,843.44	8,030.50	8,558.67
20	87.69	2,007.62	3,419.17	49	514.82	5,071.89	6,034.00	78	3,022.40	8,136.16	8,648.83
21	93.21	2,113.29	3,509.33	50	547.22	5,177.56	6,124.17	79	3,212.61	8,241.83	8,739.00
22	99.08	2,218.95	3,599.50	51	581.66	5,283.22	6,214.33	80	3,414.80	8,347.49	8,829.17
23	105.31	2,324.62	3,689.67	52	618.27	5,388.89	6,304.50	81	3,629.71	8,453.16	8,919.33
24	111.94	2,430.28	3,779.83	53	657.18	5,494.55	6,394.67	82	3,858.14	8,558.82	9,009.50
25	118.99	2,535.95	3,870.00	54	698.54	5,600.22	6,484.83	83	4,100.96	8,664.48	9,099.67
26	126.47	2,641.61	3,960.17	55	742.50	5,705.88	6,575.00	84	4,359.05	8,770.15	9,189.83
27	134.43	2,747.28	4,050.33	56	789.23	5,811.54	6,665.17	85	4,633.39	8,875.81	9,280.00
28	142.89	2,852.94	4,140.50	57	838.90	5,917.21	6,755.33				
29	151.89	2,958.60	4,230.67	58	891.70	6,022.87	6,845.50				

151

Table 1 (continues)

Initial Catalog of Tunings : A-19

Scale Deg.	HZ	Cts	TU	Scale Deg.	HZ	Cts	TU	Scale Deg.	HZ	Cts	TU
1	27.50	0.00	1,706.00	31	155.84	3,003.09	4,268.63	61	883.14	6,006.19	6,831.26
2	29.14	100.10	1,791.42	32	165.12	3,103.20	4,354.05	62	935.71	6,106.29	6,916.68
3	30.87	200.21	1,876.84	33	174.95	3,203.30	4,439.47	63	991.41	6,206.40	7,002.11
4	32.71	300.31	1,962.26	34	185.36	3,303.40	4,524.89	64	1,050.43	6,306.50	7,087.53
5	34.66	400.41	2,047.68	35	196.39	3,403.51	4,610.32	65	1,112.96	6,406.60	7,172.95
6	36.72	500.52	2,133.11	36	208.08	3,503.61	4,695.74	66	1,179.21	6,506.71	7,258.37
7	38.90	600.62	2,218.53	37	220.47	3,603.71	4,781.16	67	1,249.40	6,606.81	7,343.79
8	41.22	700.72	2,303.95	38	233.60	3,703.82	4,866.58	68	1,323.77	6,706.91	7,429.21
9	43.67	800.83	2,389.37	39	247.50	3,803.92	4,952.00	69	1,402.57	6,807.01	7,514.63
10	46.27	900.93	2,474.79	40	262.23	3,904.02	5,037.42	70	1,486.06	6,907.12	7,600.05
11	49.03	1,001.03	2,560.21	41	277.84	4,004.13	5,122.84	71	1,574.52	7,007.22	7,685.47
12	51.95	1,101.13	2,645.63	42	294.38	4,104.23	5,208.26	72	1,668.24	7,107.32	7,770.89
13	55.04	1,201.24	2,731.05	43	311.90	4,204.33	5,293.68	73	1,767.55	7,207.43	7,856.32
14	58.32	1,301.34	2,816.47	44	330.47	4,304.44	5,379.11	74	1,872.76	7,307.53	7,941.74
15	61.79	1,401.44	2,901.89	45	350.14	4,404.54	5,464.53	75	1,984.24	7,407.63	8,027.16
16	65.46	1,501.55	2,987.32	46	370.99	4,504.64	5,549.95	76	2,102.36	7,507.74	8,112.58
17	69.36	1,601.65	3,072.74	47	393.07	4,604.75	5,635.37	77	2,227.50	7,607.84	8,198.00
18	73.49	1,701.75	3,158.16	48	416.47	4,704.85	5,720.79	78	2,360.09	7,707.94	8,283.42
19	77.87	1,801.86	3,243.58	49	441.26	4,804.95	5,806.21	79	2,500.58	7,808.05	8,368.84
20	82.50	1,901.96	3,329.00	50	467.52	4,905.05	5,891.63	80	2,649.43	7,908.15	8,454.26
21	87.41	2,002.06	3,414.42	51	495.35	5,005.16	5,977.05	81	2,807.14	8,008.25	8,539.68
22	92.61	2,102.17	3,499.84	52	524.84	5,105.26	6,062.47	82	2,974.24	8,108.36	8,625.11
23	98.13	2,202.27	3,585.26	53	556.08	5,205.36	6,147.89	83	3,151.28	8,208.46	8,710.53
24	103.97	2,302.37	3,670.68	54	589.18	5,305.47	6,233.32	84	3,338.87	8,308.56	8,795.95
25	110.16	2,402.48	3,756.11	55	624.25	5,405.57	6,318.74	85	3,537.62	8,408.67	8,881.37
26	116.71	2,502.58	3,841.53	56	661.41	5,505.67	6,404.16	86	3,748.20	8,508.77	8,966.79
27	123.66	2,602.68	3,926.95	57	700.79	5,605.78	6,489.58	87	3,971.31	8,608.87	9,052.21
28	131.02	2,702.79	4,012.37	58	742.50	5,705.88	6,575.00	88	4,207.71	8,708.97	9,137.63
29	138.82	2,802.89	4,097.79	59	786.70	5,805.98	6,660.42				
30	147.09	2,902.99	4,183.21	60	833.53	5,906.09	6,745.84				

Initial Catalog of Tunings : A-20

Scale Deg.	HZ	Cts	TU	Scale Deg.	HZ	Cts	TU	Scale Deg.	HZ	Cts	TU
1	27.50	0.00	1,706.00	31	142.89	2,852.94	4,140.50	61	742.50	5,705.88	6,575.00
2	29.05	95.10	1,787.15	32	150.96	2,948.04	4,221.65	62	784.43	5,800.98	6,656.15
3	30.69	190.20	1,868.30	33	159.49	3,043.14	4,302.80	63	828.72	5,896.08	6,737.30
4	32.43	285.29	1,949.45	34	168.49	3,138.23	4,383.95	64	875.52	5,991.17	6,818.45
5	34.26	380.39	2,030.60	35	178.01	3,233.33	4,465.10	65	924.96	6,086.27	6,899.60
6	36.19	475.49	2,111.75	36	188.06	3,328.43	4,546.25	66	977.18	6,181.37	6,980.75
7	38.24	570.59	2,192.90	37	198.68	3,423.53	4,627.40	67	1,032.36	6,276.47	7,061.90
8	40.39	665.69	2,274.05	38	209.90	3,518.63	4,708.55	68	1,090.66	6,371.57	7,143.05
9	42.68	760.78	2,355.20	39	221.75	3,613.72	4,789.70	69	1,152.25	6,466.66	7,224.20
10	45.09	855.88	2,436.35	40	234.27	3,708.82	4,870.85	70	1,217.31	6,561.76	7,305.35
11	47.63	950.98	2,517.50	41	247.50	3,803.92	4,952.00	71	1,286.05	6,656.86	7,386.50
12	50.32	1,046.08	2,598.65	42	261.48	3,899.02	5,033.15	72	1,358.67	6,751.96	7,467.65
13	53.16	1,141.18	2,679.80	43	276.24	3,994.12	5,114.30	73	1,435.39	6,847.06	7,548.80
14	56.16	1,236.27	2,760.95	44	291.84	4,089.21	5,195.45	74	1,516.44	6,942.15	7,629.95
15	59.34	1,331.37	2,842.10	45	308.32	4,184.31	5,276.60	75	1,602.07	7,037.25	7,711.10
16	62.69	1,426.47	2,923.25	46	325.73	4,279.41	5,357.75	76	1,692.53	7,132.35	7,792.25
17	66.23	1,521.57	3,004.40	47	344.12	4,374.51	5,438.90	77	1,788.11	7,227.45	7,873.40
18	69.97	1,616.67	3,085.55	48	363.55	4,469.61	5,520.05	78	1,889.08	7,322.55	7,954.55
19	73.92	1,711.76	3,166.70	49	384.08	4,564.70	5,601.20	79	1,995.75	7,417.64	8,035.70
20	78.09	1,806.86	3,247.85	50	405.77	4,659.80	5,682.35	80	2,108.44	7,512.74	8,116.85
21	82.50	1,901.96	3,329.00	51	428.68	4,754.90	5,763.50	81	2,227.50	7,607.84	8,198.00
22	87.16	1,997.06	3,410.15	52	452.89	4,850.00	5,844.65	82	2,353.28	7,702.94	8,279.15
23	92.08	2,092.16	3,491.30	53	478.46	4,945.10	5,925.80	83	2,486.16	7,798.04	8,360.30
24	97.28	2,187.25	3,572.45	54	505.48	5,040.19	6,006.95	84	2,626.55	7,893.13	8,441.45
25	102.77	2,282.35	3,653.60	55	534.02	5,135.29	6,088.10	85	2,774.87	7,988.23	8,522.60
26	108.58	2,377.45	3,734.75	56	564.18	5,230.39	6,169.25	86	2,931.55	8,083.33	8,603.75
27	114.71	2,472.55	3,815.90	57	596.04	5,325.49	6,250.40	87	3,097.09	8,178.43	8,684.90
28	121.18	2,567.65	3,897.05	58	629.69	5,420.59	6,331.55	88	3,271.98	8,273.53	8,766.05
29	128.03	2,662.74	3,978.20	59	665.25	5,515.68	6,412.70				
30	135.26	2,757.84	4,059.35	60	702.81	5,610.78	6,493.85				

Table 1 (continues)

Initial Catalog of Tunings : A-21

Scale Deg.	HZ	Cts	TU	Scale Deg.	HZ	Cts	TU	Scale Deg.	HZ	Cts	TU
1	27.50	0.00	1,706.00	31	132.11	2,717.09	4,024.57	61	634.65	5,434.17	6,343.14
2	28.98	90.57	1,783.29	32	139.20	2,807.66	4,101.86	62	668.74	5,524.74	6,420.43
3	30.53	181.14	1,860.57	33	146.68	2,898.22	4,179.14	63	704.65	5,615.31	6,497.71
4	32.17	271.71	1,937.86	34	154.56	2,988.79	4,256.43	64	742.50	5,705.88	6,575.00
5	33.90	362.28	2,015.14	35	162.86	3,079.36	4,333.71	65	782.38	5,796.45	6,652.29
6	35.72	452.85	2,092.43	36	171.61	3,169.93	4,411.00	66	824.40	5,887.02	6,729.57
7	37.64	543.42	2,169.71	37	180.82	3,260.50	4,488.29	67	868.67	5,977.59	6,806.86
8	39.66	633.99	2,247.00	38	190.54	3,351.07	4,565.57	68	915.33	6,068.16	6,884.14
9	41.79	724.56	2,324.29	39	200.77	3,441.64	4,642.86	69	964.49	6,158.73	6,961.43
10	44.04	815.13	2,401.57	40	211.55	3,532.21	4,720.14	70	1,016.29	6,249.30	7,038.71
11	46.40	905.70	2,478.86	41	222.91	3,622.78	4,797.43	71	1,070.87	6,339.87	7,116.00
12	48.89	996.26	2,556.14	42	234.88	3,713.35	4,874.71	72	1,128.38	6,430.44	7,193.29
13	51.52	1,086.83	2,633.43	43	247.50	3,803.92	4,952.00	73	1,188.99	6,521.01	7,270.57
14	54.29	1,177.40	2,710.71	44	260.79	3,894.49	5,029.29	74	1,252.84	6,611.58	7,347.86
15	57.20	1,267.97	2,788.00	45	274.80	3,985.06	5,106.57	75	1,320.13	6,702.14	7,425.14
16	60.27	1,358.54	2,865.29	46	289.56	4,075.63	5,183.86	76	1,391.03	6,792.71	7,502.43
17	63.51	1,449.11	2,942.57	47	305.11	4,166.20	5,261.14	77	1,465.74	6,883.28	7,579.71
18	66.92	1,539.68	3,019.86	48	321.50	4,256.77	5,338.43	78	1,544.46	6,973.85	7,657.00
19	70.52	1,630.25	3,097.14	49	338.76	4,347.34	5,415.71	79	1,627.41	7,064.42	7,734.29
20	74.30	1,720.82	3,174.43	50	356.96	4,437.91	5,493.00	80	1,714.82	7,154.99	7,811.57
21	78.29	1,811.39	3,251.71	51	376.13	4,528.48	5,570.29	81	1,806.91	7,245.56	7,888.86
22	82.50	1,901.96	3,329.00	52	396.33	4,619.05	5,647.57	82	1,903.96	7,336.13	7,966.14
23	86.93	1,992.53	3,406.29	53	417.61	4,709.62	5,724.86	83	2,006.22	7,426.70	8,043.43
24	91.60	2,083.10	3,483.57	54	440.04	4,800.18	5,802.14	84	2,113.96	7,517.27	8,120.71
25	96.52	2,173.67	3,560.86	55	463.68	4,890.75	5,879.43	85	2,227.50	7,607.84	8,198.00
26	101.70	2,264.24	3,638.14	56	488.58	4,981.32	5,956.71	86	2,347.13	7,698.41	8,275.29
27	107.17	2,354.81	3,715.43	57	514.82	5,071.89	6,034.00	87	2,473.19	7,788.98	8,352.57
28	112.92	2,445.38	3,792.71	58	542.47	5,162.46	6,111.29	88	2,606.02	7,879.55	8,429.86
29	118.99	2,535.95	3,870.00	59	571.61	5,253.03	6,188.57				
30	125.38	2,626.52	3,947.29	60	602.30	5,343.60	6,265.86				

Initial Catalog of Tunings : A-22

Scale Deg.	HZ	Cts	TU	Scale Deg.	HZ	Cts	TU	Scale Deg.	HZ	Cts	TU
1	27.50	0.00	1,706.00	31	123.01	2,593.58	3,919.18	61	550.27	5,187.16	6,132.36
2	28.91	86.45	1,779.77	32	129.31	2,680.03	3,992.95	62	578.44	5,273.62	6,206.14
3	30.39	172.91	1,853.55	33	135.93	2,766.49	4,066.73	63	608.06	5,360.07	6,279.91
4	31.94	259.36	1,927.32	34	142.89	2,852.94	4,140.50	64	639.20	5,446.52	6,353.68
5	33.58	345.81	2,001.09	35	150.21	2,939.39	4,214.27	65	671.93	5,532.97	6,427.45
6	35.30	432.26	2,074.86	36	157.90	3,025.85	4,288.05	66	706.33	5,619.43	6,501.23
7	37.11	518.72	2,148.64	37	165.99	3,112.30	4,361.82	67	742.50	5,705.88	6,575.00
8	39.01	605.17	2,222.41	38	174.49	3,198.75	4,435.59	68	780.52	5,792.33	6,648.77
9	41.00	691.62	2,296.18	39	183.42	3,285.20	4,509.36	69	820.49	5,878.79	6,722.55
10	43.10	778.07	2,369.95	40	192.81	3,371.66	4,583.14	70	862.50	5,965.24	6,796.32
11	45.31	864.53	2,443.73	41	202.69	3,458.11	4,656.91	71	906.66	6,051.69	6,870.09
12	47.63	950.98	2,517.50	42	213.07	3,544.56	4,730.68	72	953.09	6,138.14	6,943.86
13	50.07	1,037.43	2,591.27	43	223.98	3,631.01	4,804.45	73	1,001.89	6,224.60	7,017.64
14	52.63	1,123.89	2,665.05	44	235.44	3,717.47	4,878.23	74	1,053.19	6,311.05	7,091.41
15	55.33	1,210.34	2,738.82	45	247.50	3,803.92	4,952.00	75	1,107.12	6,397.50	7,165.18
16	58.16	1,296.79	2,812.59	46	260.17	3,890.37	5,025.77	76	1,163.81	6,483.95	7,238.95
17	61.14	1,383.24	2,886.36	47	273.50	3,976.83	5,099.55	77	1,223.40	6,570.41	7,312.73
18	64.27	1,469.70	2,960.14	48	287.50	4,063.28	5,173.32	78	1,286.05	6,656.86	7,386.50
19	67.56	1,556.15	3,033.91	49	302.22	4,149.73	5,247.09	79	1,351.90	6,743.31	7,460.27
20	71.02	1,642.60	3,107.68	50	317.70	4,236.18	5,320.86	80	1,421.12	6,829.77	7,534.05
21	74.66	1,729.05	3,181.45	51	333.96	4,322.64	5,394.64	81	1,493.89	6,916.22	7,607.82
22	78.48	1,815.51	3,255.23	52	351.06	4,409.09	5,468.41	82	1,570.39	7,002.67	7,681.59
23	82.50	1,901.96	3,329.00	53	369.04	4,495.54	5,542.18	83	1,650.80	7,089.12	7,755.36
24	86.72	1,988.41	3,402.77	54	387.94	4,581.99	5,615.95	84	1,735.33	7,175.58	7,829.14
25	91.17	2,074.87	3,476.55	55	407.80	4,668.45	5,689.73	85	1,824.18	7,262.03	7,902.91
26	95.83	2,161.32	3,550.32	56	428.68	4,754.90	5,763.50	86	1,917.59	7,348.48	7,976.68
27	100.74	2,247.77	3,624.09	57	450.63	4,841.35	5,837.27	87	2,015.78	7,434.93	8,050.45
28	105.90	2,334.22	3,697.86	58	473.71	4,927.81	5,911.05	88	2,119.00	7,521.39	8,124.23
29	111.32	2,420.68	3,771.64	59	497.96	5,014.26	5,984.82				
30	117.02	2,507.13	3,845.41	60	523.46	5,100.71	6,058.59				

Table 1 (continues)

Initial Catalog of Tunings : A-23

Scale Deg.	HZ	Cts	TU	Scale Deg.	HZ	Cts	TU	Scale Deg.	HZ	Cts	TU
1	27.50	0.00	1,706.00	31	115.26	2,480.82	3,822.96	61	483.06	4,961.63	5,939.91
2	28.85	82.69	1,776.57	32	120.90	2,563.51	3,893.52	62	506.69	5,044.33	6,010.48
3	30.26	165.39	1,847.13	33	126.81	2,646.21	3,964.09	63	531.48	5,127.02	6,081.04
4	31.74	248.08	1,917.70	34	133.01	2,728.90	4,034.65	64	557.48	5,209.72	6,151.61
5	33.29	330.78	1,988.26	35	139.52	2,811.59	4,105.22	65	584.76	5,292.41	6,222.17
6	34.92	413.47	2,058.83	36	146.35	2,894.29	4,175.78	66	613.36	5,375.10	6,292.74
7	36.63	496.16	2,129.39	37	153.51	2,976.98	4,246.35	67	643.37	5,457.80	6,363.30
8	38.42	578.86	2,199.96	38	161.02	3,059.67	4,316.91	68	674.85	5,540.49	6,433.87
9	40.30	661.55	2,270.52	39	168.90	3,142.37	4,387.48	69	707.87	5,623.19	6,504.43
10	42.27	744.25	2,341.09	40	177.16	3,225.06	4,458.04	70	742.50	5,705.88	6,575.00
11	44.34	826.94	2,411.65	41	185.83	3,307.76	4,528.61	71	778.83	5,788.57	6,645.57
12	46.51	909.63	2,482.22	42	194.92	3,390.45	4,599.17	72	816.93	5,871.27	6,716.13
13	48.78	992.33	2,552.78	43	204.45	3,473.14	4,669.74	73	856.90	5,953.96	6,786.70
14	51.17	1,075.02	2,623.35	44	214.46	3,555.84	4,740.30	74	898.82	6,036.66	6,857.26
15	53.67	1,157.71	2,693.91	45	224.95	3,638.53	4,810.87	75	942.80	6,119.35	6,927.83
16	56.30	1,240.41	2,764.48	46	235.96	3,721.23	4,881.43	76	988.92	6,202.04	6,998.39
17	59.05	1,323.10	2,835.04	47	247.50	3,803.92	4,952.00	77	1,037.31	6,284.74	7,068.96
18	61.94	1,405.80	2,905.61	48	259.61	3,886.61	5,022.57	78	1,088.06	6,367.43	7,139.52
19	64.97	1,488.49	2,976.17	49	272.31	3,969.31	5,093.13	79	1,141.29	6,450.13	7,210.09
20	68.15	1,571.18	3,046.74	50	285.63	4,052.00	5,163.70	80	1,197.13	6,532.82	7,280.65
21	71.49	1,653.88	3,117.30	51	299.61	4,134.70	5,234.26	81	1,255.70	6,615.51	7,351.22
22	74.98	1,736.57	3,187.87	52	314.27	4,217.39	5,304.83	82	1,317.13	6,698.21	7,421.78
23	78.65	1,819.27	3,258.43	53	329.64	4,300.08	5,375.39	83	1,381.57	6,780.90	7,492.35
24	82.50	1,901.96	3,329.00	54	345.77	4,382.78	5,445.96	84	1,449.17	6,863.59	7,562.91
25	86.54	1,984.65	3,399.57	55	362.69	4,465.47	5,516.52	85	1,520.07	6,946.29	7,633.48
26	90.77	2,067.35	3,470.13	56	380.43	4,548.17	5,587.09	86	1,594.44	7,028.98	7,704.04
27	95.21	2,150.04	3,540.70	57	399.04	4,630.86	5,657.65	87	1,672.44	7,111.68	7,774.61
28	99.87	2,232.74	3,611.26	58	418.57	4,713.55	5,728.22	88	1,754.27	7,194.37	7,845.17
29	104.76	2,315.43	3,681.83	59	439.04	4,796.25	5,798.78				
30	109.88	2,398.12	3,752.39	60	460.52	4,878.94	5,869.35				

Initial Catalog of Tunings : A-24

Scale Deg.	HZ	Cts	TU	Scale Deg.	HZ	Cts	TU	Scale Deg.	HZ	Cts	TU
1	27.50	0.00	1,706.00	31	108.58	2,377.45	3,734.75	61	428.68	4,754.90	5,763.50
2	28.79	79.25	1,773.63	32	113.66	2,456.70	3,802.38	62	448.76	4,834.15	5,831.13
3	30.14	158.50	1,841.25	33	118.99	2,535.95	3,870.00	63	469.78	4,913.40	5,898.75
4	31.55	237.75	1,908.88	34	124.56	2,615.20	3,937.63	64	491.79	4,992.65	5,966.38
5	33.03	316.99	1,976.50	35	130.39	2,694.44	4,005.25	65	514.82	5,071.89	6,034.00
6	34.57	396.24	2,044.13	36	136.50	2,773.69	4,072.88	66	538.93	5,151.14	6,101.63
7	36.19	475.49	2,111.75	37	142.89	2,852.94	4,140.50	67	564.18	5,230.39	6,169.25
8	37.89	554.74	2,179.38	38	149.59	2,932.19	4,208.13	68	590.60	5,309.64	6,236.88
9	39.66	633.99	2,247.00	39	156.59	3,011.44	4,275.75	69	618.27	5,388.89	6,304.50
10	41.52	713.24	2,314.63	40	163.93	3,090.69	4,343.38	70	647.23	5,468.14	6,372.13
11	43.46	792.48	2,382.25	41	171.61	3,169.93	4,411.00	71	677.54	5,547.38	6,439.75
12	45.50	871.73	2,449.88	42	179.64	3,249.18	4,478.63	72	709.28	5,626.63	6,507.38
13	47.63	950.98	2,517.50	43	188.06	3,328.43	4,546.25	73	742.50	5,705.88	6,575.00
14	49.86	1,030.23	2,585.13	44	196.87	3,407.68	4,613.88	74	777.28	5,785.13	6,642.63
15	52.20	1,109.48	2,652.75	45	206.09	3,486.93	4,681.50	75	813.69	5,864.38	6,710.25
16	54.64	1,188.73	2,720.38	46	215.74	3,566.18	4,749.13	76	851.80	5,943.63	6,777.88
17	57.20	1,267.97	2,788.00	47	225.85	3,645.42	4,816.75	77	891.70	6,022.87	6,845.50
18	59.88	1,347.22	2,855.63	48	236.43	3,724.67	4,884.38	78	933.46	6,102.12	6,913.13
19	62.69	1,426.47	2,923.25	49	247.50	3,803.92	4,952.00	79	977.18	6,181.37	6,980.75
20	65.62	1,505.72	2,990.88	50	259.09	3,883.17	5,019.63	80	1,022.96	6,260.62	7,048.38
21	68.70	1,584.97	3,058.50	51	271.23	3,962.42	5,087.25	81	1,070.87	6,339.87	7,116.00
22	71.91	1,664.22	3,126.13	52	283.93	4,041.67	5,154.88	82	1,121.03	6,419.12	7,183.63
23	75.28	1,743.46	3,193.75	53	297.23	4,120.91	5,222.50	83	1,173.54	6,498.36	7,251.25
24	78.81	1,822.71	3,261.38	54	311.15	4,200.16	5,290.13	84	1,228.51	6,577.61	7,318.88
25	82.50	1,901.96	3,329.00	55	325.73	4,279.41	5,357.75	85	1,286.05	6,656.86	7,386.50
26	86.36	1,981.21	3,396.63	56	340.99	4,358.66	5,425.38	86	1,346.29	6,736.11	7,454.13
27	90.41	2,060.46	3,464.25	57	356.96	4,437.91	5,493.00	87	1,409.34	6,815.36	7,521.75
28	94.64	2,139.71	3,531.88	58	373.68	4,517.16	5,560.63	88	1,475.36	6,894.61	7,589.38
29	99.08	2,218.95	3,599.50	59	391.18	4,596.40	5,628.25				
30	103.72	2,298.20	3,667.13	60	409.50	4,675.65	5,695.88				

Table 1 (continues)

Initial Catalog of Tunings : A-25

Scale Deg.	HZ	Cts	TU	Scale Deg.	HZ	Cts	TU	Scale Deg.	HZ	Cts	TU
1	27.50	0.00	1,706.00	31	102.77	2,282.35	3,653.60	61	384.08	4,564.70	5,601.20
2	28.74	76.08	1,770.92	32	107.39	2,358.43	3,718.52	62	401.34	4,640.78	5,666.12
3	30.03	152.16	1,835.84	33	112.21	2,434.51	3,783.44	63	419.37	4,716.86	5,731.04
4	31.38	228.24	1,900.76	34	117.26	2,510.59	3,848.36	64	438.21	4,792.94	5,795.96
5	32.78	304.31	1,965.68	35	122.52	2,586.67	3,913.28	65	457.89	4,869.02	5,860.88
6	34.26	380.39	2,030.60	36	128.03	2,662.74	3,978.20	66	478.46	4,945.10	5,925.80
7	35.80	456.47	2,095.52	37	133.78	2,738.82	4,043.12	67	499.96	5,021.17	5,990.72
8	37.40	532.55	2,160.44	38	139.79	2,814.90	4,108.04	68	522.42	5,097.25	6,055.64
9	39.09	608.63	2,225.36	39	146.07	2,890.98	4,172.96	69	545.89	5,173.33	6,120.56
10	40.84	684.71	2,290.28	40	152.63	2,967.06	4,237.88	70	570.41	5,249.41	6,185.48
11	42.68	760.78	2,355.20	41	159.49	3,043.14	4,302.80	71	596.04	5,325.49	6,250.40
12	44.59	836.86	2,420.12	42	166.65	3,119.21	4,367.72	72	622.81	5,401.57	6,315.32
13	46.60	912.94	2,485.04	43	174.14	3,195.29	4,432.64	73	650.79	5,477.64	6,380.24
14	48.69	989.02	2,549.96	44	181.96	3,271.37	4,497.56	74	680.03	5,553.72	6,445.16
15	50.88	1,065.10	2,614.88	45	190.14	3,347.45	4,562.48	75	710.58	5,629.80	6,510.08
16	53.16	1,141.18	2,679.80	46	198.68	3,423.53	4,627.40	76	742.50	5,705.88	6,575.00
17	55.55	1,217.25	2,744.72	47	207.60	3,499.61	4,692.32	77	775.86	5,781.96	6,639.92
18	58.05	1,293.33	2,809.64	48	216.93	3,575.68	4,757.24	78	810.71	5,858.04	6,704.84
19	60.65	1,369.41	2,874.56	49	226.68	3,651.76	4,822.16	79	847.13	5,934.12	6,769.76
20	63.38	1,445.49	2,939.48	50	236.86	3,727.84	4,887.08	80	885.19	6,010.19	6,834.68
21	66.23	1,521.57	3,004.40	51	247.50	3,803.92	4,952.00	81	924.96	6,086.27	6,899.60
22	69.20	1,597.65	3,069.32	52	258.62	3,880.00	5,016.92	82	966.51	6,162.35	6,964.52
23	72.31	1,673.72	3,134.24	53	270.24	3,956.08	5,081.84	83	1,009.93	6,238.43	7,029.44
24	75.56	1,749.80	3,199.16	54	282.38	4,032.16	5,146.76	84	1,055.30	6,314.51	7,094.36
25	78.95	1,825.88	3,264.08	55	295.06	4,108.23	5,211.68	85	1,102.71	6,390.59	7,159.28
26	82.50	1,901.96	3,329.00	56	308.32	4,184.31	5,276.60	86	1,152.25	6,466.66	7,224.20
27	86.21	1,978.04	3,393.92	57	322.17	4,260.39	5,341.52	87	1,204.01	6,542.74	7,289.12
28	90.08	2,054.12	3,458.84	58	336.64	4,336.47	5,406.44	88	1,258.10	6,618.82	7,354.04
29	94.13	2,130.20	3,523.76	59	351.77	4,412.55	5,471.36				
30	98.35	2,206.27	3,588.68	60	367.57	4,488.63	5,536.28				

Initial Catalog of Tunings : A-26

Scale Deg.	HZ	Cts	TU	Scale Deg.	HZ	Cts	TU	Scale Deg.	HZ	Cts	TU
1	27.50	0.00	1,706.00	31	97.69	2,194.57	3,578.69	61	347.04	4,389.14	5,451.38
2	28.69	73.15	1,768.42	32	101.91	2,267.72	3,641.12	62	362.02	4,462.29	5,513.81
3	29.93	146.30	1,830.85	33	106.31	2,340.87	3,703.54	63	377.64	4,535.44	5,576.23
4	31.22	219.46	1,893.27	34	110.89	2,414.03	3,765.96	64	393.94	4,608.60	5,638.65
5	32.56	292.61	1,955.69	35	115.68	2,487.18	3,828.38	65	410.95	4,681.75	5,701.08
6	33.97	365.76	2,018.12	36	120.67	2,560.33	3,890.81	66	428.68	4,754.90	5,763.50
7	35.44	438.91	2,080.54	37	125.88	2,633.48	3,953.23	67	447.18	4,828.05	5,825.92
8	36.96	512.07	2,142.96	38	131.31	2,706.64	4,015.65	68	466.48	4,901.20	5,888.35
9	38.56	585.22	2,205.38	39	136.98	2,779.79	4,078.08	69	486.62	4,974.36	5,950.77
10	40.22	658.37	2,267.81	40	142.89	2,852.94	4,140.50	70	507.62	5,047.51	6,013.19
11	41.96	731.52	2,330.23	41	149.06	2,926.09	4,202.92	71	529.53	5,120.66	6,075.62
12	43.77	804.68	2,392.65	42	155.49	2,999.24	4,265.35	72	552.38	5,193.81	6,138.04
13	45.66	877.83	2,455.08	43	162.21	3,072.40	4,327.77	73	576.22	5,266.97	6,200.46
14	47.63	950.98	2,517.50	44	169.21	3,145.55	4,390.19	74	601.09	5,340.12	6,262.88
15	49.69	1,024.13	2,579.92	45	176.51	3,218.70	4,452.62	75	627.04	5,413.27	6,325.31
16	51.83	1,097.28	2,642.35	46	184.13	3,291.85	4,515.04	76	654.10	5,486.42	6,387.73
17	54.07	1,170.44	2,704.77	47	192.07	3,365.01	4,577.46	77	682.33	5,559.58	6,450.15
18	56.40	1,243.59	2,767.19	48	200.36	3,438.16	4,639.88	78	711.78	5,632.73	6,512.58
19	58.84	1,316.74	2,829.62	49	209.01	3,511.31	4,702.31	79	742.50	5,705.88	6,575.00
20	61.38	1,389.89	2,892.04	50	218.03	3,584.46	4,764.73	80	774.55	5,779.03	6,637.42
21	64.02	1,463.05	2,954.46	51	227.44	3,657.62	4,827.15	81	807.98	5,852.18	6,699.85
22	66.79	1,536.20	3,016.88	52	237.26	3,730.77	4,889.58	82	842.85	5,925.34	6,762.27
23	69.67	1,609.35	3,079.31	53	247.50	3,803.92	4,952.00	83	879.22	5,998.49	6,824.69
24	72.68	1,682.50	3,141.73	54	258.18	3,877.07	5,014.42	84	917.17	6,071.64	6,887.12
25	75.81	1,755.66	3,204.15	55	269.33	3,950.22	5,076.85	85	956.76	6,144.79	6,949.54
26	79.09	1,828.81	3,266.58	56	280.95	4,023.38	5,139.27	86	998.05	6,217.95	7,011.96
27	82.50	1,901.96	3,329.00	57	293.07	4,096.53	5,201.69	87	1,041.13	6,291.10	7,074.38
28	86.06	1,975.11	3,391.42	58	305.72	4,169.68	5,264.12	88	1,086.06	6,364.25	7,136.81
29	89.78	2,048.26	3,453.85	59	318.92	4,242.83	5,326.54				
30	93.65	2,121.42	3,516.27	60	332.68	4,315.99	5,388.96				

Table 1 (continues)

Initial Catalog of Tunings : A-27

Scale Deg.	HZ	Cts	TU	Scale Deg.	HZ	Cts	TU	Scale Deg.	HZ	Cts	TU
1	27.50	0.00	1,706.00	31	93.21	2,113.29	3,509.33	61	315.94	4,226.58	5,312.67
2	28.64	70.44	1,766.11	32	97.08	2,183.73	3,569.44	62	329.06	4,297.02	5,372.78
3	29.83	140.89	1,826.22	33	101.11	2,254.17	3,629.56	63	342.72	4,367.46	5,432.89
4	31.07	211.33	1,886.33	34	105.31	2,324.62	3,689.67	64	356.96	4,437.91	5,493.00
5	32.36	281.77	1,946.44	35	109.69	2,395.06	3,749.78	65	371.78	4,508.35	5,553.11
6	33.70	352.21	2,006.56	36	114.24	2,465.50	3,809.89	66	387.22	4,578.79	5,613.22
7	35.10	422.66	2,066.67	37	118.99	2,535.95	3,870.00	67	403.30	4,649.24	5,673.33
8	36.56	493.10	2,126.78	38	123.93	2,606.39	3,930.11	68	420.05	4,719.68	5,733.44
9	38.08	563.54	2,186.89	39	129.07	2,676.83	3,990.22	69	437.49	4,790.12	5,793.56
10	39.66	633.99	2,247.00	40	134.43	2,747.28	4,050.33	70	455.66	4,860.56	5,853.67
11	41.31	704.43	2,307.11	41	140.02	2,817.72	4,110.44	71	474.58	4,931.01	5,913.78
12	43.02	774.87	2,367.22	42	145.83	2,888.16	4,170.56	72	494.29	5,001.45	5,973.89
13	44.81	845.32	2,427.33	43	151.89	2,958.60	4,230.67	73	514.82	5,071.89	6,034.00
14	46.67	915.76	2,487.44	44	158.19	3,029.05	4,290.78	74	536.20	5,142.34	6,094.11
15	48.61	986.20	2,547.56	45	164.76	3,099.49	4,350.89	75	558.47	5,212.78	6,154.22
16	50.63	1,056.64	2,607.67	46	171.61	3,169.93	4,411.00	76	581.66	5,283.22	6,214.33
17	52.73	1,127.09	2,667.78	47	178.73	3,240.38	4,471.11	77	605.82	5,353.67	6,274.44
18	54.92	1,197.53	2,727.89	48	186.16	3,310.82	4,531.22	78	630.97	5,424.11	6,334.56
19	57.20	1,267.97	2,788.00	49	193.89	3,381.26	4,591.33	79	657.18	5,494.55	6,394.67
20	59.58	1,338.42	2,848.11	50	201.94	3,451.71	4,651.44	80	684.47	5,564.99	6,454.78
21	62.05	1,408.86	2,908.22	51	210.32	3,522.15	4,711.56	81	712.89	5,635.44	6,514.89
22	64.63	1,479.30	2,968.33	52	219.06	3,592.59	4,771.67	82	742.50	5,705.88	6,575.00
23	67.31	1,549.75	3,028.44	53	228.16	3,663.03	4,831.78	83	773.33	5,776.32	6,635.11
24	70.11	1,620.19	3,088.56	54	237.63	3,733.48	4,891.89	84	805.45	5,846.77	6,695.22
25	73.02	1,690.63	3,148.67	55	247.50	3,803.92	4,952.00	85	838.90	5,917.21	6,755.33
26	76.05	1,761.07	3,208.78	56	257.78	3,874.36	5,012.11	86	873.74	5,987.65	6,815.44
27	79.21	1,831.52	3,268.89	57	268.48	3,944.81	5,072.22	87	910.02	6,058.09	6,875.56
28	82.50	1,901.96	3,329.00	58	279.63	4,015.25	5,132.33	88	947.81	6,128.54	6,935.67
29	85.93	1,972.40	3,389.11	59	291.25	4,085.69	5,192.44				
30	89.49	2,042.85	3,449.22	60	303.34	4,156.13	5,252.56				

Initial Catalog of Tunings : B-12

Scale Deg.	HZ	Cts	TU	Scale Deg.	HZ	Cts	TU	Scale Deg.	HZ	Cts	TU
1	27.50	0.00	1,706.00	15	179.80	3,250.70	4,479.92	29	1,175.61	6,501.39	7,253.85
2	31.45	232.19	1,904.14	16	205.61	3,482.89	4,678.06	30	1,344.34	6,733.58	7,451.99
3	35.96	464.39	2,102.28	17	235.12	3,715.08	4,876.20	31	1,537.30	6,965.78	7,650.12
4	41.12	696.58	2,300.41	18	268.87	3,947.27	5,074.34	32	1,757.94	7,197.97	7,848.26
5	47.02	928.77	2,498.55	19	307.46	4,179.47	5,272.47	33	2,010.26	7,430.16	8,046.40
6	53.77	1,160.96	2,696.69	20	351.59	4,411.66	5,470.61	34	2,298.79	7,662.35	8,244.54
7	61.49	1,393.16	2,894.82	21	402.05	4,643.85	5,668.75	35	2,628.74	7,894.55	8,442.67
8	70.32	1,625.35	3,092.96	22	459.76	4,876.04	5,866.89	36	3,006.04	8,126.74	8,640.81
9	80.41	1,857.54	3,291.10	23	525.75	5,108.24	6,065.02	37	3,437.50	8,358.93	8,838.95
10	91.95	2,089.73	3,489.24	24	601.21	5,340.43	6,263.16	38	3,930.88	8,591.12	9,037.09
11	105.15	2,321.93	3,687.37	25	687.50	5,572.62	6,461.30				
12	120.24	2,554.12	3,885.51	26	786.18	5,804.81	6,659.44				
13	137.50	2,786.31	4,083.65	27	899.02	6,037.01	6,857.57				
14	157.24	3,018.50	4,281.79	28	1,028.05	6,269.20	7,055.71				

Initial Catalog of Tunings : B-13

Scale Deg.	HZ	Cts	TU	Scale Deg.	HZ	Cts	TU	Scale Deg.	HZ	Cts	TU
1	27.50	0.00	1,706.00	16	176.13	3,214.97	4,449.44	31	1,128.08	6,429.95	7,192.88
2	31.12	214.33	1,888.90	17	199.34	3,429.30	4,632.34	32	1,276.75	6,644.28	7,375.78
3	35.23	428.66	2,071.79	18	225.62	3,643.64	4,815.23	33	1,445.02	6,858.61	7,558.68
4	39.87	642.99	2,254.69	19	255.35	3,857.97	4,998.13	34	1,635.46	7,072.94	7,741.57
5	45.12	857.33	2,437.58	20	289.00	4,072.30	5,181.03	35	1,851.01	7,287.27	7,924.47
6	51.07	1,071.66	2,620.48	21	327.09	4,286.63	5,363.92	36	2,094.96	7,501.60	8,107.37
7	57.80	1,285.99	2,803.38	22	370.20	4,500.96	5,546.82	37	2,371.06	7,715.94	8,290.26
8	65.42	1,500.32	2,986.27	23	418.99	4,715.29	5,729.72	38	2,683.54	7,930.27	8,473.16
9	74.04	1,714.65	3,169.17	24	474.21	4,929.63	5,912.61	39	3,037.22	8,144.60	8,656.05
10	83.80	1,928.98	3,352.07	25	536.71	5,143.96	6,095.51	40	3,437.50	8,358.93	8,838.95
11	94.84	2,143.32	3,534.96	26	607.44	5,358.29	6,278.40	41	3,890.54	8,573.26	9,021.85
12	107.34	2,357.65	3,717.86	27	687.50	5,572.62	6,461.30	42	4,403.28	8,787.59	9,204.74
13	121.49	2,571.98	3,900.75	28	778.11	5,786.95	6,644.20				
14	137.50	2,786.31	4,083.65	29	880.66	6,001.28	6,827.09				
15	155.62	3,000.64	4,266.55	30	996.72	6,215.61	7,009.99				

155

Table 1 (continues)

Initial Catalog of Tunings : B-14

Scale Deg.	HZ	Cts	TU	Scale Deg.	HZ	Cts	TU	Scale Deg.	HZ	Cts	TU
1	27.50	0.00	1,706.00	17	173.04	3,184.35	4,423.31	33	1,088.88	6,368.71	7,140.63
2	30.85	199.02	1,875.83	18	194.13	3,383.38	4,593.15	34	1,221.53	6,567.73	7,310.46
3	34.61	398.04	2,045.66	19	217.78	3,582.40	4,762.98	35	1,370.35	6,766.75	7,480.29
4	38.83	597.07	2,215.50	20	244.31	3,781.42	4,932.81	36	1,537.30	6,965.78	7,650.12
5	43.56	796.09	2,385.33	21	274.07	3,980.44	5,102.64	37	1,724.58	7,164.80	7,819.96
6	48.86	995.11	2,555.16	22	307.46	4,179.47	5,272.48	38	1,934.69	7,363.82	7,989.79
7	54.81	1,194.13	2,724.99	23	344.92	4,378.49	5,442.31	39	2,170.39	7,562.84	8,159.62
8	61.49	1,393.16	2,894.83	24	386.94	4,577.51	5,612.14	40	2,434.80	7,761.86	8,329.45
9	68.98	1,592.18	3,064.66	25	434.08	4,776.53	5,781.97	41	2,731.43	7,960.89	8,499.29
10	77.39	1,791.20	3,234.49	26	486.96	4,975.55	5,951.80	42	3,064.19	8,159.91	8,669.12
11	86.82	1,990.22	3,404.32	27	546.29	5,174.58	6,121.64	43	3,437.50	8,358.93	8,838.95
12	97.39	2,189.24	3,574.15	28	612.84	5,373.60	6,291.47	44	3,856.29	8,557.95	9,008.78
13	109.26	2,388.27	3,743.99	29	687.50	5,572.62	6,461.30	45	4,326.09	8,756.97	9,178.61
14	122.57	2,587.29	3,913.82	30	771.26	5,771.64	6,631.13				
15	137.50	2,786.31	4,083.65	31	865.22	5,970.66	6,800.96				
16	154.25	2,985.33	4,253.48	32	970.63	6,169.69	6,970.80				

Initial Catalog of Tunings : B-15

Scale Deg.	HZ	Cts	TU	Scale Deg.	HZ	Cts	TU	Scale Deg.	HZ	Cts	TU
1	27.50	0.00	1,706.00	18	170.41	3,157.82	4,400.67	35	1,056.00	6,315.64	7,095.34
2	30.61	185.75	1,864.51	19	189.71	3,343.57	4,559.18	36	1,175.61	6,501.39	7,253.85
3	34.08	371.51	2,023.02	20	211.20	3,529.33	4,717.69	37	1,308.76	6,687.14	7,412.36
4	37.94	557.26	2,181.53	21	235.12	3,715.08	4,876.20	38	1,457.00	6,872.90	7,570.87
5	42.24	743.02	2,340.04	22	261.75	3,900.83	5,034.71	39	1,622.02	7,058.65	7,729.38
6	47.02	928.77	2,498.55	23	291.40	4,086.59	5,193.22	40	1,805.74	7,244.41	7,887.89
7	52.35	1,114.52	2,657.06	24	324.40	4,272.34	5,351.73	41	2,010.26	7,430.16	8,046.40
8	58.28	1,300.28	2,815.57	25	361.15	4,458.10	5,510.24	42	2,237.95	7,615.91	8,204.91
9	64.88	1,486.03	2,974.08	26	402.05	4,643.85	5,668.75	43	2,491.43	7,801.67	8,363.42
10	72.23	1,671.79	3,132.59	27	447.59	4,829.60	5,827.26	44	2,773.62	7,987.42	8,521.93
11	80.41	1,857.54	3,291.10	28	498.29	5,015.36	5,985.77	45	3,087.77	8,173.18	8,680.44
12	89.52	2,043.29	3,449.61	29	554.72	5,201.11	6,144.28	46	3,437.50	8,358.93	8,838.95
13	99.66	2,229.05	3,608.12	30	617.55	5,386.87	6,302.79	47	3,826.84	8,544.68	8,997.46
14	110.94	2,414.80	3,766.63	31	687.50	5,572.62	6,461.30	48	4,260.29	8,730.44	9,155.97
15	123.51	2,600.56	3,925.14	32	765.37	5,758.37	6,619.81				
16	137.50	2,786.31	4,083.65	33	852.06	5,944.13	6,778.32				
17	153.07	2,972.06	4,242.16	34	948.56	6,129.88	6,936.83				

Initial Catalog of Tunings : B-16

Scale Deg.	HZ	Cts	TU	Scale Deg.	HZ	Cts	TU	Scale Deg.	HZ	Cts	TU
1	27.50	0.00	1,706.00	19	168.14	3,134.60	4,380.86	37	1,028.05	6,269.20	7,055.71
2	30.41	174.14	1,854.60	20	185.93	3,308.74	4,529.46	38	1,136.84	6,443.34	7,204.32
3	33.63	348.29	2,003.21	21	205.61	3,482.89	4,678.06	39	1,257.15	6,617.49	7,352.92
4	37.19	522.43	2,151.81	22	227.37	3,657.03	4,826.67	40	1,390.18	6,791.63	7,501.52
5	41.12	696.58	2,300.41	23	251.43	3,831.18	4,975.27	41	1,537.30	6,965.78	7,650.12
6	45.47	870.72	2,449.02	24	278.04	4,005.32	5,123.87	42	1,699.98	7,139.92	7,798.73
7	50.29	1,044.87	2,597.62	25	307.46	4,179.47	5,272.47	43	1,879.87	7,314.06	7,947.33
8	55.61	1,219.01	2,746.22	26	340.00	4,353.61	5,421.08	44	2,078.81	7,488.21	8,095.93
9	61.49	1,393.16	2,894.83	27	375.97	4,527.75	5,569.68	45	2,298.79	7,662.35	8,244.54
10	68.00	1,567.30	3,043.43	28	415.76	4,701.90	5,718.28	46	2,542.06	7,836.50	8,393.14
11	75.19	1,741.44	3,192.03	29	459.76	4,876.04	5,866.89	47	2,811.07	8,010.64	8,541.74
12	83.15	1,915.59	3,340.63	30	508.41	5,050.19	6,015.49	48	3,108.54	8,184.79	8,690.35
13	91.95	2,089.73	3,489.24	31	562.21	5,224.33	6,164.09	49	3,437.50	8,358.93	8,838.95
14	101.68	2,263.88	3,637.84	32	621.71	5,398.48	6,312.70	50	3,801.27	8,533.07	8,987.55
15	112.44	2,438.02	3,786.44	33	687.50	5,572.62	6,461.30	51	4,203.53	8,707.22	9,136.16
16	124.34	2,612.17	3,935.05	34	760.25	5,746.76	6,609.90				
17	137.50	2,786.31	4,083.65	35	840.71	5,920.91	6,758.51				
18	152.05	2,960.45	4,232.25	36	929.67	6,095.05	6,907.11				

157

Table 1 (continues)

Initial Catalog of Tunings : B-17

Scale Deg.	HZ	Cts	TU	Scale Deg.	HZ	Cts	TU	Scale Deg.	HZ	Cts	TU
1	27.50	0.00	1,706.00	20	166.16	3,114.11	4,363.37	39	1,004.01	6,228.22	7,020.75
2	30.23	163.90	1,845.86	21	182.66	3,278.01	4,503.24	40	1,103.70	6,392.12	7,160.61
3	33.23	327.80	1,985.72	22	200.80	3,441.91	4,643.10	41	1,213.30	6,556.02	7,300.47
4	36.53	491.70	2,125.59	23	220.74	3,605.81	4,782.96	42	1,333.78	6,719.92	7,440.33
5	40.16	655.60	2,265.45	24	242.66	3,769.71	4,922.82	43	1,466.22	6,883.82	7,580.19
6	44.15	819.50	2,405.31	25	266.76	3,933.61	5,062.68	44	1,611.82	7,047.73	7,720.06
7	48.53	983.40	2,545.17	26	293.24	4,097.51	5,202.54	45	1,771.87	7,211.63	7,859.92
8	53.35	1,147.30	2,685.03	27	322.36	4,261.42	5,342.41	46	1,947.81	7,375.53	7,999.78
9	58.65	1,311.20	2,824.89	28	354.37	4,425.32	5,482.27	47	2,141.23	7,539.43	8,139.64
10	64.47	1,475.11	2,964.76	29	389.56	4,589.22	5,622.13	48	2,353.85	7,703.33	8,279.50
11	70.87	1,639.01	3,104.62	30	428.25	4,753.12	5,761.99	49	2,587.59	7,867.23	8,419.36
12	77.91	1,802.91	3,244.48	31	470.77	4,917.02	5,901.85	50	2,844.53	8,031.13	8,559.23
13	85.65	1,966.81	3,384.34	32	517.52	5,080.92	6,041.71	51	3,126.99	8,195.03	8,699.09
14	94.15	2,130.71	3,524.20	33	568.91	5,244.82	6,181.58	52	3,437.50	8,358.93	8,838.95
15	103.50	2,294.61	3,664.06	34	625.40	5,408.72	6,321.44	53	3,778.84	8,522.83	8,978.81
16	113.78	2,458.51	3,803.93	35	687.50	5,572.62	6,461.30	54	4,154.08	8,686.73	9,118.67
17	125.08	2,622.41	3,943.79	36	755.77	5,736.52	6,601.16				
18	137.50	2,786.31	4,083.65	37	830.82	5,900.42	6,741.02				
19	151.15	2,950.21	4,223.51	38	913.31	6,064.32	6,880.89				

Initial Catalog of Tunings : B-18

Scale Deg.	HZ	Cts	TU	Scale Deg.	HZ	Cts	TU	Scale Deg.	HZ	Cts	TU
1	27.50	0.00	1,706.00	21	164.42	3,095.90	4,347.83	41	983.10	6,191.80	6,989.67
2	30.07	154.80	1,838.09	22	179.80	3,250.70	4,479.93	42	1,075.06	6,346.60	7,121.76
3	32.88	309.59	1,970.18	23	196.62	3,405.49	4,612.02	43	1,175.61	6,501.39	7,253.85
4	35.96	464.39	2,102.28	24	215.01	3,560.29	4,744.11	44	1,285.57	6,656.19	7,385.94
5	39.32	619.18	2,234.37	25	235.12	3,715.08	4,876.20	45	1,405.81	6,810.98	7,518.03
6	43.00	773.98	2,366.46	26	257.11	3,869.88	5,008.29	46	1,537.30	6,965.78	7,650.12
7	47.02	928.77	2,498.55	27	281.16	4,024.67	5,140.38	47	1,681.08	7,120.57	7,782.22
8	51.42	1,083.57	2,630.64	28	307.46	4,179.47	5,272.47	48	1,838.32	7,275.37	7,914.31
9	56.23	1,238.36	2,762.73	29	336.22	4,334.26	5,404.57	49	2,010.26	7,430.16	8,046.40
10	61.49	1,393.16	2,894.83	30	367.66	4,489.06	5,536.66	50	2,198.29	7,584.96	8,178.49
11	67.24	1,547.95	3,026.92	31	402.05	4,643.85	5,668.75	51	2,403.90	7,739.75	8,310.58
12	73.53	1,702.75	3,159.01	32	439.66	4,798.65	5,800.84	52	2,628.74	7,894.55	8,442.67
13	80.41	1,857.54	3,291.10	33	480.78	4,953.44	5,932.93	53	2,874.61	8,049.34	8,574.77
14	87.93	2,012.34	3,423.19	34	525.75	5,108.24	6,065.02	54	3,143.48	8,204.14	8,706.86
15	96.16	2,167.13	3,555.28	35	574.92	5,263.03	6,197.12	55	3,437.50	8,358.93	8,838.95
16	105.15	2,321.93	3,687.38	36	628.70	5,417.83	6,329.21	56	3,759.02	8,513.73	8,971.04
17	114.98	2,476.72	3,819.47	37	687.50	5,572.62	6,461.30	57	4,110.61	8,668.52	9,103.13
18	125.74	2,631.52	3,951.56	38	751.80	5,727.42	6,593.39	58	4,495.08	8,823.32	9,235.22
19	137.50	2,786.31	4,083.65	39	822.12	5,882.21	6,725.48				
20	150.36	2,941.11	4,215.74	40	899.02	6,037.01	6,857.57				

Initial Catalog of Tunings : B-19

Scale Deg.	HZ	Cts	TU	Scale Deg.	HZ	Cts	TU	Scale Deg.	HZ	Cts	TU
1	27.50	0.00	1,706.00	22	162.88	3,079.61	4,333.93	43	964.77	6,159.21	6,961.86
2	29.93	146.65	1,831.14	23	177.28	3,226.25	4,459.07	44	1,050.06	6,305.86	7,087.00
3	32.58	293.30	1,956.28	24	192.95	3,372.90	4,584.21	45	1,142.88	6,452.51	7,212.14
4	35.46	439.94	2,081.42	25	210.01	3,519.55	4,709.35	46	1,243.91	6,599.16	7,337.28
5	38.59	586.59	2,206.56	26	228.58	3,666.20	4,834.49	47	1,353.87	6,745.80	7,462.42
6	42.00	733.24	2,331.70	27	248.78	3,812.85	4,959.63	48	1,473.55	6,892.45	7,587.56
7	45.72	879.89	2,456.84	28	270.77	3,959.49	5,084.77	49	1,603.81	7,039.10	7,712.69
8	49.76	1,026.54	2,581.98	29	294.71	4,106.14	5,209.91	50	1,745.58	7,185.75	7,837.83
9	54.15	1,173.18	2,707.12	30	320.76	4,252.79	5,335.04	51	1,899.89	7,332.39	7,962.97
10	58.94	1,319.83	2,832.26	31	349.12	4,399.44	5,460.18	52	2,067.83	7,479.04	8,088.11
11	64.15	1,466.48	2,957.39	32	379.98	4,546.08	5,585.32	53	2,250.63	7,625.69	8,213.25
12	69.82	1,613.13	3,082.53	33	413.57	4,692.73	5,710.46	54	2,449.58	7,772.34	8,338.39
13	76.00	1,759.77	3,207.67	34	450.13	4,839.38	5,835.60	55	2,666.12	7,918.99	8,463.53
14	82.71	1,906.42	3,332.81	35	489.92	4,986.03	5,960.74	56	2,901.80	8,065.63	8,588.67
15	90.03	2,053.07	3,457.95	36	533.22	5,132.68	6,085.88	57	3,158.31	8,212.28	8,713.81
16	97.98	2,199.72	3,583.09	37	580.36	5,279.32	6,211.02	58	3,437.50	8,358.93	8,838.95
17	106.64	2,346.37	3,708.23	38	631.66	5,425.97	6,336.16	59	3,741.37	8,505.58	8,964.09
18	116.07	2,493.01	3,833.37	39	687.50	5,572.62	6,461.30	60	4,072.10	8,652.23	9,089.23
19	126.33	2,639.66	3,958.51	40	748.27	5,719.27	6,586.44	61	4,432.07	8,798.87	9,214.37
20	137.50	2,786.31	4,083.65	41	814.42	5,865.92	6,711.58				
21	149.65	2,932.96	4,208.79	42	886.41	6,012.56	6,836.72				

Table 1 (continues)

Initial Catalog of Tunings : B-20

Scale Deg.	HZ	Cts	TU	Scale Deg.	HZ	Cts	TU	Scale Deg.	HZ	Cts	TU
1	27.50	0.00	1,706.00	23	161.51	3,064.94	4,321.42	45	948.56	6,129.88	6,936.83
2	29.80	139.32	1,824.88	24	175.04	3,204.26	4,440.30	46	1,028.05	6,269.20	7,055.71
3	32.30	278.63	1,943.77	25	189.71	3,343.57	4,559.18	47	1,114.20	6,408.51	7,174.59
4	35.01	417.95	2,062.65	26	205.61	3,482.89	4,678.06	48	1,207.57	6,547.83	7,293.48
5	37.94	557.26	2,181.53	27	222.84	3,622.20	4,796.95	49	1,308.76	6,687.14	7,412.36
6	41.12	696.58	2,300.41	28	241.51	3,761.52	4,915.83	50	1,418.43	6,826.46	7,531.24
7	44.57	835.89	2,419.30	29	261.75	3,900.83	5,034.71	51	1,537.30	6,965.78	7,650.12
8	48.30	975.21	2,538.18	30	283.69	4,040.15	5,153.59	52	1,666.12	7,105.09	7,769.01
9	52.35	1,114.52	2,657.06	31	307.46	4,179.47	5,272.48	53	1,805.74	7,244.41	7,887.89
10	56.74	1,253.84	2,775.94	32	333.22	4,318.78	5,391.36	54	1,957.06	7,383.72	8,006.77
11	61.49	1,393.16	2,894.83	33	361.15	4,458.10	5,510.24	55	2,121.05	7,523.04	8,125.65
12	66.64	1,532.47	3,013.71	34	391.41	4,597.41	5,629.12	56	2,298.79	7,662.35	8,244.54
13	72.23	1,671.79	3,132.59	35	424.21	4,736.73	5,748.01	57	2,491.43	7,801.67	8,363.42
14	78.28	1,811.10	3,251.47	36	459.76	4,876.04	5,866.89	58	2,700.21	7,940.98	8,482.30
15	84.84	1,950.42	3,370.36	37	498.29	5,015.36	5,985.77	59	2,926.48	8,080.30	8,601.18
16	91.95	2,089.73	3,489.24	38	540.04	5,154.67	6,104.65	60	3,171.72	8,219.61	8,720.07
17	99.66	2,229.05	3,608.12	39	585.30	5,293.99	6,223.53	61	3,437.50	8,358.93	8,838.95
18	108.01	2,368.36	3,727.00	40	634.34	5,433.30	6,342.42	62	3,725.56	8,498.25	8,957.83
19	117.06	2,507.68	3,845.89	41	687.50	5,572.62	6,461.30	63	4,037.75	8,637.56	9,076.71
20	126.87	2,646.99	3,964.77	42	745.11	5,711.94	6,580.18	64	4,376.11	8,776.88	9,195.60
21	137.50	2,786.31	4,083.65	43	807.55	5,851.25	6,699.06				
22	149.02	2,925.63	4,202.53	44	875.22	5,990.57	6,817.95				

Initial Catalog of Tunings : B-21

Scale Deg.	HZ	Cts	TU	Scale Deg.	HZ	Cts	TU	Scale Deg.	HZ	Cts	TU
1	27.50	0.00	1,706.00	24	160.28	3,051.67	4,310.09	47	934.14	6,103.35	6,914.19
2	29.69	132.68	1,819.22	25	173.04	3,184.35	4,423.31	48	1,008.54	6,236.03	7,027.41
3	32.06	265.36	1,932.44	26	186.83	3,317.04	4,536.54	49	1,088.88	6,368.71	7,140.63
4	34.61	398.04	2,045.66	27	201.71	3,449.72	4,649.76	50	1,175.61	6,501.39	7,253.85
5	37.37	530.73	2,158.89	28	217.78	3,582.40	4,762.98	51	1,269.25	6,634.07	7,367.07
6	40.34	663.41	2,272.11	29	235.12	3,715.08	4,876.20	52	1,370.35	6,766.75	7,480.29
7	43.56	796.09	2,385.33	30	253.85	3,847.76	4,989.42	53	1,479.50	6,899.43	7,593.51
8	47.02	928.77	2,498.55	31	274.07	3,980.44	5,102.64	54	1,597.35	7,032.12	7,706.74
9	50.77	1,061.45	2,611.77	32	295.90	4,113.12	5,215.86	55	1,724.58	7,164.80	7,819.96
10	54.81	1,194.13	2,724.99	33	319.47	4,245.81	5,329.09	56	1,861.95	7,297.48	7,933.18
11	59.18	1,326.81	2,838.21	34	344.92	4,378.49	5,442.31	57	2,010.26	7,430.16	8,046.40
12	63.89	1,459.50	2,951.44	35	372.39	4,511.17	5,555.53	58	2,170.39	7,562.84	8,159.62
13	68.98	1,592.18	3,064.66	36	402.05	4,643.85	5,668.75	59	2,343.26	7,695.52	8,272.84
14	74.48	1,724.86	3,177.88	37	434.08	4,776.53	5,781.97	60	2,529.91	7,828.20	8,386.06
15	80.41	1,857.54	3,291.10	38	468.65	4,909.21	5,895.19	61	2,731.43	7,960.89	8,499.29
16	86.82	1,990.22	3,404.32	39	505.98	5,041.89	6,008.41	62	2,949.00	8,093.57	8,612.51
17	93.73	2,122.90	3,517.54	40	546.29	5,174.58	6,121.64	63	3,183.89	8,226.25	8,725.73
18	101.20	2,255.58	3,630.76	41	589.80	5,307.26	6,234.86	64	3,437.50	8,358.93	8,838.95
19	109.26	2,388.27	3,743.99	42	636.78	5,439.94	6,348.08	65	3,711.31	8,491.61	8,952.17
20	117.96	2,520.95	3,857.21	43	687.50	5,572.62	6,461.30	66	4,006.93	8,624.29	9,065.39
21	127.36	2,653.63	3,970.43	44	742.26	5,705.30	6,574.52	67	4,326.09	8,756.97	9,178.61
22	137.50	2,786.31	4,083.65	45	801.39	5,837.98	6,687.74				
23	148.45	2,918.99	4,196.87	46	865.22	5,970.66	6,800.96				

Table 1 (continues)

Initial Catalog of Tunings : B-22

Scale Deg.	HZ	Cts	TU	Scale Deg.	HZ	Cts	TU	Scale Deg.	HZ	Cts	TU
1	27.50	0.00	1,706.00	26	171.24	3,166.26	4,407.87	51	1,066.35	6,332.52	7,109.75
2	29.59	126.65	1,814.08	27	184.24	3,292.91	4,515.95	52	1,147.29	6,459.17	7,217.82
3	31.83	253.30	1,922.15	28	198.23	3,419.56	4,624.02	53	1,234.37	6,585.82	7,325.90
4	34.25	379.95	2,030.23	29	213.27	3,546.21	4,732.10	54	1,328.05	6,712.47	7,433.97
5	36.85	506.60	2,138.30	30	229.46	3,672.86	4,840.17	55	1,428.85	6,839.12	7,542.05
6	39.65	633.25	2,246.38	31	246.87	3,799.51	4,948.25	56	1,537.30	6,965.78	7,650.12
7	42.65	759.90	2,354.45	32	265.61	3,926.16	5,056.32	57	1,653.98	7,092.43	7,758.20
8	45.89	886.55	2,462.53	33	285.77	4,052.81	5,164.40	58	1,779.51	7,219.08	7,866.27
9	49.37	1,013.20	2,570.60	34	307.46	4,179.47	5,272.47	59	1,914.57	7,345.73	7,974.35
10	53.12	1,139.85	2,678.67	35	330.80	4,306.12	5,380.55	60	2,059.89	7,472.38	8,082.42
11	57.15	1,266.50	2,786.75	36	355.90	4,432.77	5,488.62	61	2,216.23	7,599.03	8,190.50
12	61.49	1,393.16	2,894.82	37	382.91	4,559.42	5,596.70	62	2,384.44	7,725.68	8,298.57
13	66.16	1,519.81	3,002.90	38	411.98	4,686.07	5,704.77	63	2,565.41	7,852.33	8,406.65
14	71.18	1,646.46	3,110.97	39	443.25	4,812.72	5,812.85	64	2,760.12	7,978.98	8,514.72
15	76.58	1,773.11	3,219.05	40	476.89	4,939.37	5,920.92	65	2,969.61	8,105.63	8,622.80
16	82.40	1,899.76	3,327.12	41	513.08	5,066.02	6,029.00	66	3,195.00	8,232.28	8,730.87
17	88.65	2,026.41	3,435.20	42	552.02	5,192.67	6,137.07	67	3,437.50	8,358.93	8,838.95
18	95.38	2,153.06	3,543.27	43	593.92	5,319.32	6,245.15	68	3,698.40	8,485.58	8,947.02
19	102.62	2,279.71	3,651.35	44	639.00	5,445.97	6,353.22	69	3,979.11	8,612.23	9,055.10
20	110.40	2,406.36	3,759.42	45	687.50	5,572.62	6,461.30	70	4,281.11	8,738.88	9,163.17
21	118.78	2,533.01	3,867.50	46	739.68	5,699.27	6,569.37	71	4,606.04	8,865.53	9,271.25
22	127.80	2,659.66	3,975.57	47	795.82	5,825.92	6,677.45				
23	137.50	2,786.31	4,083.65	48	856.22	5,952.57	6,785.52				
24	147.94	2,912.96	4,191.72	49	921.21	6,079.22	6,893.60				
25	159.16	3,039.61	4,299.80	50	991.13	6,205.87	7,001.67				

Initial Catalog of Tunings : B-23

Scale Deg.	HZ	Cts	TU	Scale Deg.	HZ	Cts	TU	Scale Deg.	HZ	Cts	TU
1	27.50	0.00	1,706.00	27	169.62	3,149.74	4,393.78	53	1,046.20	6,299.48	7,081.56
2	29.49	121.14	1,809.38	28	181.91	3,270.89	4,497.15	54	1,122.03	6,420.63	7,184.93
3	31.63	242.29	1,912.75	29	195.10	3,392.03	4,600.53	55	1,203.35	6,541.77	7,288.31
4	33.92	363.43	2,016.13	30	209.24	3,513.17	4,703.91	56	1,290.57	6,662.92	7,391.68
5	36.38	484.58	2,119.50	31	224.41	3,634.32	4,807.28	57	1,384.12	6,784.06	7,495.06
6	39.02	605.72	2,222.88	32	240.67	3,755.46	4,910.66	58	1,484.44	6,905.20	7,598.44
7	41.85	726.86	2,326.26	33	258.11	3,876.61	5,014.03	59	1,592.04	7,026.35	7,701.81
8	44.88	848.01	2,429.63	34	276.82	3,997.75	5,117.41	60	1,707.43	7,147.49	7,805.19
9	48.13	969.15	2,533.01	35	296.89	4,118.89	5,220.79	61	1,831.19	7,268.63	7,908.57
10	51.62	1,090.30	2,636.38	36	318.41	4,240.04	5,324.16	62	1,963.92	7,389.78	8,011.94
11	55.36	1,211.44	2,739.76	37	341.49	4,361.18	5,427.54	63	2,106.26	7,510.92	8,115.32
12	59.38	1,332.58	2,843.14	38	366.24	4,482.32	5,530.92	64	2,258.93	7,632.07	8,218.69
13	63.68	1,453.73	2,946.51	39	392.78	4,603.47	5,634.29	65	2,422.66	7,753.21	8,322.07
14	68.30	1,574.87	3,049.89	40	421.25	4,724.61	5,737.67	66	2,598.26	7,874.35	8,425.45
15	73.25	1,696.01	3,153.27	41	451.79	4,845.76	5,841.04	67	2,786.59	7,995.50	8,528.82
16	78.56	1,817.16	3,256.64	42	484.53	4,966.90	5,944.42	68	2,988.57	8,116.64	8,632.20
17	84.25	1,938.30	3,360.02	43	519.65	5,088.04	6,047.80	69	3,205.18	8,237.79	8,735.57
18	90.36	2,059.45	3,463.39	44	557.32	5,209.19	6,151.17	70	3,437.50	8,358.93	8,838.95
19	96.91	2,180.59	3,566.77	45	597.71	5,330.33	6,254.55	71	3,686.66	8,480.07	8,942.33
20	103.93	2,301.73	3,670.15	46	641.04	5,451.48	6,357.92	72	3,953.87	8,601.22	9,045.70
21	111.46	2,422.88	3,773.52	47	687.50	5,572.62	6,461.30	73	4,240.46	8,722.36	9,149.08
22	119.54	2,544.02	3,876.90	48	737.33	5,693.76	6,564.68	74	4,547.81	8,843.51	9,252.45
23	128.21	2,665.17	3,980.27	49	790.77	5,814.91	6,668.05				
24	137.50	2,786.31	4,083.65	50	848.09	5,936.05	6,771.43				
25	147.47	2,907.45	4,187.03	51	909.56	6,057.20	6,874.80				
26	158.15	3,028.60	4,290.40	52	975.49	6,178.34	6,978.18				

Table 1 (continues)

Initial Catalog of Tunings : B-24

Scale Deg.	HZ	Cts	TU	Scale Deg.	HZ	Cts	TU	Scale Deg.	HZ	Cts	TU
1	27.50	0.00	1,706.00	28	168.14	3,134.60	4,380.86	55	1,028.05	6,269.20	7,055.71
2	29.41	116.10	1,805.07	29	179.80	3,250.70	4,479.93	56	1,099.36	6,385.29	7,154.78
3	31.45	232.19	1,904.14	30	192.27	3,366.79	4,578.99	57	1,175.61	6,501.39	7,253.85
4	33.63	348.29	2,003.21	31	205.61	3,482.89	4,678.06	58	1,257.15	6,617.49	7,352.92
5	35.96	464.39	2,102.28	32	219.87	3,598.98	4,777.13	59	1,344.34	6,733.58	7,451.99
6	38.45	580.48	2,201.34	33	235.12	3,715.08	4,876.20	60	1,437.59	6,849.68	7,551.06
7	41.12	696.58	2,300.41	34	251.43	3,831.18	4,975.27	61	1,537.30	6,965.78	7,650.13
8	43.97	812.67	2,399.48	35	268.87	3,947.27	5,074.34	62	1,643.92	7,081.87	7,749.19
9	47.02	928.77	2,498.55	36	287.52	4,063.37	5,173.41	63	1,757.94	7,197.97	7,848.26
10	50.29	1,044.87	2,597.62	37	307.46	4,179.47	5,272.48	64	1,879.87	7,314.06	7,947.33
11	53.77	1,160.96	2,696.69	38	328.78	4,295.56	5,371.54	65	2,010.26	7,430.16	8,046.40
12	57.50	1,277.06	2,795.76	39	351.59	4,411.66	5,470.61	66	2,149.69	7,546.26	8,145.47
13	61.49	1,393.16	2,894.82	40	375.97	4,527.75	5,569.68	67	2,298.79	7,662.35	8,244.54
14	65.76	1,509.25	2,993.89	41	402.05	4,643.85	5,668.75	68	2,458.24	7,778.45	8,343.61
15	70.32	1,625.35	3,092.96	42	429.94	4,759.95	5,767.82	69	2,628.74	7,894.55	8,442.68
16	75.19	1,741.44	3,192.03	43	459.76	4,876.04	5,866.89	70	2,811.07	8,010.64	8,541.74
17	80.41	1,857.54	3,291.10	44	491.65	4,992.14	5,965.96	71	3,006.04	8,126.74	8,640.81
18	85.99	1,973.64	3,390.17	45	525.75	5,108.24	6,065.03	72	3,214.54	8,242.83	8,739.88
19	91.95	2,089.73	3,489.24	46	562.21	5,224.33	6,164.09	73	3,437.50	8,358.93	8,838.95
20	98.33	2,205.83	3,588.31	47	601.21	5,340.43	6,263.16	74	3,675.92	8,475.03	8,938.02
21	105.15	2,321.93	3,687.37	48	642.91	5,456.52	6,362.23	75	3,930.88	8,591.12	9,037.09
22	112.44	2,438.02	3,786.44	49	687.50	5,572.62	6,461.30	76	4,203.53	8,707.22	9,136.16
23	120.24	2,554.12	3,885.51	50	735.18	5,688.72	6,560.37	77	4,495.08	8,823.32	9,235.23
24	128.58	2,670.21	3,984.58	51	786.18	5,804.81	6,659.44				
25	137.50	2,786.31	4,083.65	52	840.71	5,920.91	6,758.51				
26	147.04	2,902.41	4,182.72	53	899.02	6,037.01	6,857.58				
27	157.24	3,018.50	4,281.79	54	961.37	6,153.10	6,956.64				

Initial Catalog of Tunings : B-25

Scale Deg.	HZ	Cts	TU	Scale Deg.	HZ	Cts	TU	Scale Deg.	HZ	Cts	TU
1	27.50	0.00	1,706.00	29	166.79	3,120.67	4,368.97	57	1,011.64	6,241.33	7,031.94
2	29.33	111.45	1,801.11	30	177.88	3,232.12	4,464.07	58	1,078.91	6,352.79	7,127.04
3	31.28	222.90	1,896.21	31	189.71	3,343.57	4,559.18	59	1,150.65	6,464.24	7,222.15
4	33.36	334.36	1,991.32	32	202.33	3,455.02	4,654.29	60	1,227.16	6,575.69	7,317.25
5	35.58	445.81	2,086.42	33	215.78	3,566.48	4,749.39	61	1,308.76	6,687.14	7,412.36
6	37.94	557.26	2,181.53	34	230.13	3,677.93	4,844.50	62	1,395.79	6,798.60	7,507.47
7	40.47	668.71	2,276.64	35	245.43	3,789.38	4,939.60	63	1,488.60	6,910.05	7,602.57
8	43.16	780.17	2,371.74	36	261.75	3,900.83	5,034.71	64	1,587.59	7,021.50	7,697.68
9	46.03	891.62	2,466.85	37	279.16	4,012.29	5,129.82	65	1,693.15	7,132.95	7,792.78
10	49.09	1,003.07	2,561.95	38	297.72	4,123.74	5,224.92	66	1,805.74	7,244.41	7,887.89
11	52.35	1,114.52	2,657.06	39	317.52	4,235.19	5,320.03	67	1,925.81	7,355.86	7,983.00
12	55.83	1,225.98	2,752.17	40	338.63	4,346.64	5,415.13	68	2,053.87	7,467.31	8,078.10
13	59.54	1,337.43	2,847.27	41	361.15	4,458.10	5,510.24	69	2,190.44	7,578.76	8,173.21
14	63.50	1,448.88	2,942.38	42	385.16	4,569.55	5,605.35	70	2,336.09	7,690.22	8,268.31
15	67.73	1,560.33	3,037.48	43	410.77	4,681.00	5,700.45	71	2,491.43	7,801.67	8,363.42
16	72.23	1,671.79	3,132.59	44	438.09	4,792.45	5,795.56	72	2,657.10	7,913.12	8,458.53
17	77.03	1,783.24	3,227.70	45	467.22	4,903.91	5,890.66	73	2,833.78	8,024.57	8,553.63
18	82.15	1,894.69	3,322.80	46	498.29	5,015.36	5,985.77	74	3,022.21	8,136.03	8,648.74
19	87.62	2,006.14	3,417.91	47	531.42	5,126.81	6,080.88	75	3,223.18	8,247.48	8,743.84
20	93.44	2,117.60	3,513.01	48	566.76	5,238.26	6,175.98	76	3,437.50	8,358.93	8,838.95
21	99.66	2,229.05	3,608.12	49	604.44	5,349.72	6,271.09	77	3,666.08	8,470.38	8,934.06
22	106.28	2,340.50	3,703.23	50	644.64	5,461.17	6,366.19	78	3,909.85	8,581.83	9,029.16
23	113.35	2,451.95	3,798.33	51	687.50	5,572.62	6,461.30	79	4,169.84	8,693.29	9,124.27
24	120.89	2,563.41	3,893.44	52	733.22	5,684.07	6,556.41	80	4,447.11	8,804.74	9,219.37
25	128.93	2,674.86	3,988.54	53	781.97	5,795.52	6,651.51				
26	137.50	2,786.31	4,083.65	54	833.97	5,906.98	6,746.62				
27	146.64	2,897.76	4,178.76	55	889.42	6,018.43	6,841.72				
28	156.39	3,009.21	4,273.86	56	948.56	6,129.88	6,936.83				

161

Table 1 (continues)

Initial Catalog of Tunings : B-26

Scale Deg.	HZ	Cts	TU	Scale Deg.	HZ	Cts	TU	Scale Deg.	HZ	Cts	TU
1	27.50	0.00	1,706.00	30	163.56	3,107.81	4,357.99	59	996.72	6,215.61	7,009.99
2	29.26	107.17	1,797.45	31	176.13	3,214.97	4,449.44	60	1,060.37	6,322.78	7,101.44
3	31.12	214.33	1,888.90	32	187.38	3,322.14	4,540.89	61	1,128.08	6,429.95	7,192.88
4	33.11	321.50	1,980.34	33	199.34	3,429.30	4,632.34	62	1,200.12	6,537.11	7,284.33
5	35.23	428.66	2,071.79	34	212.07	3,536.47	4,723.79	63	1,276.75	6,644.28	7,375.78
6	37.48	535.83	2,163.24	35	225.62	3,643.64	4,815.23	64	1,358.28	6,751.44	7,467.23
7	39.87	642.99	2,254.69	36	240.02	3,750.80	4,906.68	65	1,445.02	6,858.61	7,558.68
8	42.41	750.16	2,346.14	37	255.35	3,857.97	4,998.13	66	1,537.30	6,965.78	7,650.12
9	45.12	857.33	2,437.58	38	271.66	3,965.13	5,089.58	67	1,635.46	7,072.94	7,741.57
10	48.00	964.49	2,529.03	39	289.00	4,072.30	5,181.03	68	1,739.90	7,180.11	7,833.02
11	51.07	1,071.66	2,620.48	40	307.46	4,179.47	5,272.47	69	1,851.01	7,287.27	7,924.47
12	54.33	1,178.82	2,711.93	41	327.09	4,286.63	5,363.92	70	1,969.21	7,394.44	8,015.92
13	57.80	1,285.99	2,803.38	42	347.98	4,393.80	5,455.37	71	2,094.96	7,501.60	8,107.37
14	61.49	1,393.16	2,894.82	43	370.20	4,500.96	5,546.82	72	2,228.74	7,608.77	8,198.81
15	65.42	1,500.32	2,986.27	44	393.84	4,608.13	5,638.27	73	2,371.06	7,715.94	8,290.26
16	69.60	1,607.49	3,077.72	45	418.99	4,715.29	5,729.72	74	2,522.47	7,823.10	8,381.71
17	74.04	1,714.65	3,169.17	46	445.75	4,822.46	5,821.16	75	2,683.54	7,930.27	8,473.16
18	78.77	1,821.82	3,260.62	47	474.21	4,929.63	5,912.61	76	2,854.91	8,037.43	8,564.61
19	83.80	1,928.98	3,352.07	48	504.49	5,036.79	6,004.06	77	3,037.22	8,144.60	8,656.05
20	89.15	2,036.15	3,443.51	49	536.71	5,143.96	6,095.51	78	3,231.17	8,251.76	8,747.50
21	94.84	2,143.32	3,534.96	50	570.98	5,251.12	6,186.96	79	3,437.50	8,358.93	8,838.95
22	100.90	2,250.48	3,626.41	51	607.44	5,358.29	6,278.40	80	3,657.01	8,466.10	8,930.40
23	107.34	2,357.65	3,717.86	52	646.23	5,465.45	6,369.85	81	3,890.54	8,573.26	9,021.85
24	114.20	2,464.81	3,809.31	53	687.50	5,572.62	6,461.30	82	4,138.98	8,680.43	9,113.29
25	121.49	2,571.98	3,900.75	54	731.40	5,679.79	6,552.75	83	4,403.28	8,787.59	9,204.74
26	129.25	2,679.14	3,992.20	55	778.11	5,786.95	6,644.20	84	4,684.47	8,894.76	9,296.19
27	137.50	2,786.31	4,083.65	56	827.80	5,894.12	6,735.64				
28	146.28	2,893.48	4,175.10	57	880.66	6,001.28	6,827.09				
29	155.62	3,000.64	4,266.55	58	936.89	6,108.45	6,918.54				

Initial Catalog of Tunings : B-27

Scale Deg.	HZ	Cts	TU	Scale Deg.	HZ	Cts	TU	Scale Deg.	HZ	Cts	TU
1	27.50	0.00	1,706.00	31	164.42	3,095.90	4,347.83	61	983.10	6,191.80	6,989.67
2	29.19	103.20	1,794.06	32	174.52	3,199.10	4,435.89	62	1,043.49	6,295.00	7,077.73
3	30.98	206.39	1,882.12	33	185.24	3,302.29	4,523.96	63	1,107.58	6,398.19	7,165.79
4	32.88	309.59	1,970.18	34	196.62	3,405.49	4,612.02	64	1,175.61	6,501.39	7,253.85
5	34.90	412.79	2,058.24	35	208.70	3,508.69	4,700.08	65	1,247.82	6,604.59	7,341.91
6	37.05	515.98	2,146.31	36	221.52	3,611.88	4,788.14	66	1,324.46	6,707.78	7,429.97
7	39.32	619.18	2,234.37	37	235.12	3,715.08	4,876.20	67	1,405.81	6,810.98	7,518.03
8	41.74	722.38	2,322.43	38	249.56	3,818.28	4,964.26	68	1,492.15	6,914.18	7,606.09
9	44.30	825.57	2,410.49	39	264.89	3,921.47	5,052.32	69	1,583.80	7,017.37	7,694.16
10	47.02	928.77	2,498.55	40	281.16	4,024.67	5,140.38	70	1,681.08	7,120.57	7,782.22
11	49.91	1,031.97	2,586.61	41	298.43	4,127.87	5,228.44	71	1,784.34	7,223.77	7,870.28
12	52.98	1,135.16	2,674.67	42	316.76	4,231.06	5,316.51	72	1,893.93	7,326.96	7,958.34
13	56.23	1,238.36	2,762.73	43	336.22	4,334.26	5,404.57	73	2,010.26	7,430.16	8,046.40
14	59.69	1,341.56	2,850.79	44	356.87	4,437.46	5,492.63	74	2,133.74	7,533.36	8,134.46
15	63.35	1,444.75	2,938.86	45	378.79	4,540.65	5,580.69	75	2,264.79	7,636.55	8,222.52
16	67.24	1,547.95	3,026.92	46	402.05	4,643.85	5,668.75	76	2,403.90	7,739.75	8,310.58
17	71.37	1,651.15	3,114.98	47	426.75	4,747.05	5,756.81	77	2,551.55	7,842.95	8,398.64
18	75.76	1,754.34	3,203.04	48	452.96	4,850.24	5,844.87	78	2,708.27	7,946.14	8,486.71
19	80.41	1,857.54	3,291.10	49	480.78	4,953.44	5,932.93	79	2,874.61	8,049.34	8,574.77
20	85.35	1,960.74	3,379.16	50	510.31	5,056.64	6,020.99	80	3,051.18	8,152.54	8,662.83
21	90.59	2,063.93	3,467.22	51	541.65	5,159.83	6,109.06	81	3,238.58	8,255.73	8,750.89
22	96.16	2,167.13	3,555.28	52	574.92	5,263.03	6,197.12	82	3,437.50	8,358.93	8,838.95
23	102.06	2,270.33	3,643.34	53	610.24	5,366.23	6,285.18	83	3,648.64	8,462.13	8,927.01
24	108.33	2,373.52	3,731.41	54	647.72	5,469.42	6,373.24	84	3,872.74	8,565.32	9,015.07
25	114.98	2,476.72	3,819.47	55	687.50	5,572.62	6,461.30	85	4,110.61	8,668.52	9,103.13
26	122.05	2,579.92	3,907.53	56	729.73	5,675.82	6,549.36	86	4,363.09	8,771.72	9,191.19
27	129.54	2,683.11	3,995.59	57	774.55	5,779.01	6,637.42	87	4,631.07	8,874.91	9,279.26
28	137.50	2,786.31	4,083.65	58	822.12	5,882.21	6,725.48	88	4,915.52	8,978.11	9,367.32
29	145.95	2,889.51	4,171.71	59	872.62	5,985.41	6,813.54				
30	154.91	2,992.70	4,259.77	60	926.21	6,088.60	6,901.61				

Table 1 (continues)

Initial Catalog of Tunings : B-28

Scale Deg.	HZ	Cts	TU	Scale Deg.	HZ	Cts	TU	Scale Deg.	HZ	Cts	TU
1	27.50	0.00	1,706.00	31	154.25	2,985.33	4,253.48	61	865.22	5,970.66	6,800.96
2	29.13	99.51	1,790.92	32	163.38	3,084.84	4,338.40	62	916.41	6,070.18	6,885.88
3	30.85	199.02	1,875.83	33	173.04	3,184.35	4,423.31	63	970.63	6,169.69	6,970.80
4	32.68	298.53	1,960.75	34	183.28	3,283.87	4,508.23	64	1,028.05	6,269.20	7,055.71
5	34.61	398.04	2,045.66	35	194.13	3,383.38	4,593.15	65	1,088.88	6,368.71	7,140.63
6	36.66	497.56	2,130.58	36	205.61	3,482.89	4,678.06	66	1,153.30	6,468.22	7,225.54
7	38.83	597.07	2,215.50	37	217.78	3,582.40	4,762.98	67	1,221.53	6,567.73	7,310.46
8	41.12	696.58	2,300.41	38	230.66	3,681.91	4,847.89	68	1,293.80	6,667.24	7,395.38
9	43.56	796.09	2,385.33	39	244.31	3,781.42	4,932.81	69	1,370.35	6,766.75	7,480.29
10	46.13	895.60	2,470.24	40	258.76	3,880.93	5,017.73	70	1,451.42	6,866.26	7,565.21
11	48.86	995.11	2,555.16	41	274.07	3,980.44	5,102.64	71	1,537.30	6,965.78	7,650.13
12	51.75	1,094.62	2,640.08	42	290.28	4,079.95	5,187.56	72	1,628.25	7,065.29	7,735.04
13	54.81	1,194.13	2,724.99	43	307.46	4,179.47	5,272.48	73	1,724.58	7,164.80	7,819.96
14	58.06	1,293.64	2,809.91	44	325.65	4,278.98	5,357.39	74	1,826.62	7,264.31	7,904.87
15	61.49	1,393.16	2,894.82	45	344.92	4,378.49	5,442.31	75	1,934.69	7,363.82	7,989.79
16	65.13	1,492.67	2,979.74	46	365.32	4,478.00	5,527.22	76	2,049.15	7,463.33	8,074.71
17	68.98	1,592.18	3,064.66	47	386.94	4,577.51	5,612.14	77	2,170.39	7,562.84	8,159.62
18	73.06	1,691.69	3,149.57	48	409.83	4,677.02	5,697.06	78	2,298.79	7,662.35	8,244.54
19	77.39	1,791.20	3,234.49	49	434.08	4,776.53	5,781.97	79	2,434.80	7,761.86	8,329.45
20	81.97	1,890.71	3,319.41	50	459.76	4,876.04	5,866.89	80	2,578.85	7,861.37	8,414.37
21	86.82	1,990.22	3,404.32	51	486.96	4,975.55	5,951.80	81	2,731.43	7,960.89	8,499.29
22	91.95	2,089.73	3,489.24	52	515.77	5,075.06	6,036.72	82	2,893.03	8,060.40	8,584.20
23	97.39	2,189.24	3,574.15	53	546.29	5,174.58	6,121.64	83	3,064.19	8,159.91	8,669.12
24	103.15	2,288.75	3,659.07	54	578.61	5,274.09	6,206.55	84	3,245.48	8,259.42	8,754.03
25	109.26	2,388.27	3,743.99	55	612.84	5,373.60	6,291.47	85	3,437.50	8,358.93	8,838.95
26	115.72	2,487.78	3,828.90	56	649.10	5,473.11	6,376.38	86	3,640.88	8,458.44	8,923.87
27	122.57	2,587.29	3,913.82	57	687.50	5,572.62	6,461.30	87	3,856.29	8,557.95	9,008.78
28	129.82	2,686.80	3,998.73	58	728.18	5,672.13	6,546.22	88	4,084.44	8,657.46	9,093.70
29	137.50	2,786.31	4,083.65	59	771.26	5,771.64	6,631.13				
30	145.64	2,885.82	4,168.57	60	816.89	5,871.15	6,716.05				

Initial Catalog of Tunings : B-29

Scale Deg.	HZ	Cts	TU	Scale Deg.	HZ	Cts	TU	Scale Deg.	HZ	Cts	TU
1	27.50	0.00	1,706.00	31	145.35	2,882.39	4,165.64	61	768.21	5,764.78	6,625.28
2	29.07	96.08	1,787.99	32	153.64	2,978.47	4,247.63	62	812.04	5,860.86	6,707.29
3	30.73	192.16	1,869.98	33	162.41	3,074.55	4,329.61	63	858.39	5,956.94	6,789.25
4	32.48	288.24	1,951.96	34	171.68	3,170.63	4,411.60	64	907.37	6,053.02	6,871.24
5	34.34	384.32	2,033.95	35	181.47	3,266.71	4,493.59	65	959.15	6,149.10	6,953.23
6	36.29	480.40	2,115.94	36	191.83	3,362.79	4,575.58	66	1,013.89	6,245.18	7,035.22
7	38.37	576.48	2,197.93	37	202.78	3,458.87	4,657.57	67	1,071.75	6,341.26	7,117.20
8	40.56	672.56	2,279.92	38	214.35	3,554.95	4,739.55	68	1,132.91	6,437.34	7,199.19
9	42.87	768.64	2,361.90	39	226.58	3,651.03	4,821.54	69	1,197.56	6,533.42	7,281.18
10	45.32	864.72	2,443.89	40	239.51	3,747.11	4,903.53	70	1,265.90	6,629.50	7,363.17
11	47.90	960.80	2,525.88	41	253.18	3,843.19	4,985.52	71	1,338.14	6,725.58	7,445.16
12	50.64	1,056.88	2,607.87	42	267.63	3,939.27	5,067.51	72	1,414.50	6,821.66	7,527.14
13	53.53	1,152.96	2,689.86	43	282.90	4,035.35	5,149.49	73	1,495.22	6,917.74	7,609.13
14	56.58	1,249.04	2,771.84	44	299.04	4,131.43	5,231.48	74	1,580.55	7,013.81	7,691.12
15	59.81	1,345.12	2,853.83	45	316.11	4,227.50	5,313.47	75	1,670.75	7,109.89	7,773.11
16	63.22	1,441.19	2,935.82	46	334.15	4,323.58	5,395.46	76	1,766.09	7,205.97	7,855.09
17	66.83	1,537.27	3,017.81	47	353.22	4,419.66	5,477.44	77	1,866.88	7,302.05	7,937.08
18	70.64	1,633.35	3,099.79	48	373.38	4,515.74	5,559.43	78	1,973.42	7,398.13	8,019.07
19	74.68	1,729.43	3,181.78	49	394.68	4,611.82	5,641.42	79	2,086.03	7,494.21	8,101.06
20	78.94	1,825.51	3,263.77	50	417.21	4,707.90	5,723.41	80	2,205.08	7,590.29	8,183.05
21	83.44	1,921.59	3,345.76	51	441.02	4,803.98	5,805.40	81	2,330.91	7,686.37	8,265.03
22	88.20	2,017.67	3,427.75	52	466.18	4,900.06	5,887.38	82	2,463.93	7,782.45	8,347.02
23	93.24	2,113.75	3,509.73	53	492.79	4,996.14	5,969.37	83	2,604.54	7,878.53	8,429.01
24	98.56	2,209.83	3,591.72	54	520.91	5,092.22	6,051.36	84	2,753.17	7,974.61	8,511.00
25	104.18	2,305.91	3,673.71	55	550.63	5,188.30	6,133.35	85	2,910.28	8,070.69	8,592.99
26	110.13	2,401.99	3,755.70	56	582.06	5,284.38	6,215.34	86	3,076.37	8,166.77	8,674.97
27	116.41	2,498.07	3,837.69	57	615.27	5,380.46	6,297.32	87	3,251.92	8,262.85	8,756.96
28	123.05	2,594.15	3,919.67	58	650.38	5,476.54	6,379.31	88	3,437.50	8,358.93	8,838.95
29	130.08	2,690.23	4,001.66	59	687.50	5,572.62	6,461.30				
30	137.50	2,786.31	4,083.65	60	726.73	5,668.70	6,543.29				

Table 1 (continues)

Initial Catalog of Tunings : B-30

Scale Deg.	HZ	Cts	TU	Scale Deg.	HZ	Cts	TU	Scale Deg.	HZ	Cts	TU
1	27.50	0.00	1,706.00	31	137.50	2,786.31	4,083.65	61	687.50	5,572.62	6,461.30
2	29.02	92.88	1,785.26	32	145.08	2,879.19	4,162.91	62	725.39	5,665.50	6,540.56
3	30.61	185.75	1,864.51	33	153.07	2,972.06	4,242.16	63	765.37	5,758.37	6,619.81
4	32.30	278.63	1,943.77	34	161.51	3,064.94	4,321.42	64	807.55	5,851.25	6,699.07
5	34.08	371.51	2,023.02	35	170.41	3,157.82	4,400.67	65	852.06	5,944.13	6,778.32
6	35.96	464.39	2,102.28	36	179.80	3,250.70	4,479.93	66	899.02	6,037.01	6,857.58
7	37.94	557.26	2,181.53	37	189.71	3,343.57	4,559.18	67	948.56	6,129.88	6,936.83
8	40.03	650.14	2,260.79	38	200.17	3,436.45	4,638.44	68	1,000.84	6,222.76	7,016.09
9	42.24	743.02	2,340.04	39	211.20	3,529.33	4,717.69	69	1,056.00	6,315.64	7,095.34
10	44.57	835.89	2,419.30	40	222.84	3,622.20	4,796.95	70	1,114.20	6,408.51	7,174.60
11	47.02	928.77	2,498.55	41	235.12	3,715.08	4,876.20	71	1,175.61	6,501.39	7,253.85
12	49.62	1,021.65	2,577.81	42	248.08	3,807.96	4,955.46	72	1,240.40	6,594.27	7,333.11
13	52.35	1,114.52	2,657.06	43	261.75	3,900.83	5,034.71	73	1,308.76	6,687.14	7,412.36
14	55.24	1,207.40	2,736.32	44	276.18	3,993.71	5,113.97	74	1,380.89	6,780.02	7,491.62
15	58.28	1,300.28	2,815.57	45	291.40	4,086.59	5,193.22	75	1,457.00	6,872.90	7,570.87
16	61.49	1,393.16	2,894.83	46	307.46	4,179.47	5,272.48	76	1,537.30	6,965.78	7,650.13
17	64.88	1,486.03	2,974.08	47	324.40	4,272.34	5,351.73	77	1,622.02	7,058.65	7,729.38
18	68.46	1,578.91	3,053.34	48	342.28	4,365.22	5,430.99	78	1,711.42	7,151.53	7,808.64
19	72.23	1,671.79	3,132.59	49	361.15	4,458.10	5,510.24	79	1,805.74	7,244.41	7,887.89
20	76.21	1,764.66	3,211.85	50	381.05	4,550.97	5,589.50	80	1,905.26	7,337.28	7,967.15
21	80.41	1,857.54	3,291.10	51	402.05	4,643.85	5,668.75	81	2,010.26	7,430.16	8,046.40
22	84.84	1,950.42	3,370.36	52	424.21	4,736.73	5,748.01	82	2,121.05	7,523.04	8,125.66
23	89.52	2,043.29	3,449.61	53	447.59	4,829.60	5,827.26	83	2,237.95	7,615.91	8,204.91
24	94.45	2,136.17	3,528.87	54	472.26	4,922.48	5,906.52	84	2,361.29	7,708.79	8,284.17
25	99.66	2,229.05	3,608.12	55	498.29	5,015.36	5,985.77	85	2,491.43	7,801.67	8,363.42
26	105.15	2,321.93	3,687.38	56	525.75	5,108.24	6,065.03	86	2,628.74	7,894.55	8,442.68
27	110.94	2,414.80	3,766.63	57	554.72	5,201.11	6,144.28	87	2,773.62	7,987.42	8,521.93
28	117.06	2,507.68	3,845.89	58	585.30	5,293.99	6,223.54	88	2,926.48	8,080.30	8,601.19
29	123.51	2,600.56	3,925.14	59	617.55	5,386.87	6,302.79				
30	130.32	2,693.43	4,004.40	60	651.59	5,479.74	6,382.05				

Initial Catalog of Tunings : B-31

Scale Deg.	HZ	Cts	TU	Scale Deg.	HZ	Cts	TU	Scale Deg.	HZ	Cts	TU
1	27.50	0.00	1,706.00	31	130.54	2,696.45	4,006.95	61	619.69	5,392.86	6,307.90
2	28.97	89.88	1,782.70	32	137.50	2,786.31	4,083.65	62	652.72	5,482.74	6,384.60
3	30.51	179.76	1,859.40	33	144.83	2,876.19	4,160.35	63	687.50	5,572.62	6,461.30
4	32.13	269.64	1,936.10	34	152.54	2,966.07	4,237.05	64	724.14	5,662.50	6,538.00
5	33.85	359.52	2,012.79	35	160.67	3,055.95	4,313.75	65	762.72	5,752.38	6,614.70
6	35.65	449.40	2,089.49	36	169.24	3,145.83	4,390.44	66	803.37	5,842.26	6,691.40
7	37.55	539.29	2,166.19	37	178.25	3,235.71	4,467.14	67	846.18	5,932.14	6,768.09
8	39.55	629.17	2,242.89	38	187.75	3,325.60	4,543.84	68	891.27	6,022.02	6,844.79
9	41.66	719.05	2,319.59	39	197.76	3,415.48	4,620.54	69	938.77	6,111.91	6,921.49
10	43.88	808.93	2,396.29	40	208.30	3,505.36	4,697.24	70	988.79	6,201.79	6,998.19
11	46.22	898.81	2,472.98	41	219.40	3,595.24	4,773.94	71	1,041.48	6,291.67	7,074.89
12	48.68	988.69	2,549.68	42	231.09	3,685.12	4,850.63	72	1,096.98	6,381.55	7,151.59
13	51.27	1,078.57	2,626.38	43	243.40	3,775.00	4,927.33	73	1,155.44	6,471.43	7,228.28
14	54.01	1,168.45	2,703.08	44	256.37	3,864.88	5,004.03	74	1,217.01	6,561.31	7,304.98
15	56.88	1,258.33	2,779.78	45	270.03	3,954.76	5,080.73	75	1,281.86	6,651.19	7,381.68
16	59.92	1,348.21	2,856.48	46	284.42	4,044.64	5,157.43	76	1,350.17	6,741.07	7,458.38
17	63.11	1,438.10	2,933.17	47	299.58	4,134.52	5,234.13	77	1,422.12	6,830.95	7,535.08
18	66.47	1,527.98	3,009.87	48	315.55	4,224.41	5,310.82	78	1,497.90	6,920.83	7,611.78
19	70.01	1,617.86	3,086.57	49	332.36	4,314.29	5,387.52	79	1,577.73	7,010.72	7,688.47
20	73.75	1,707.74	3,163.27	50	350.07	4,404.17	5,464.22	80	1,661.80	7,100.60	7,765.17
21	77.67	1,797.62	3,239.97	51	368.73	4,494.05	5,540.92	81	1,750.36	7,190.48	7,841.87
22	81.81	1,887.50	3,316.67	52	388.37	4,583.93	5,617.62	82	1,843.63	7,280.36	7,918.57
23	86.17	1,977.38	3,393.36	53	409.07	4,673.81	5,694.32	83	1,941.87	7,370.24	7,995.27
24	90.77	2,067.26	3,470.06	54	430.87	4,763.69	5,771.01	84	2,045.35	7,460.12	8,071.97
25	95.60	2,157.14	3,546.76	55	453.83	4,853.57	5,847.71	85	2,154.35	7,550.00	8,148.66
26	100.70	2,247.02	3,623.46	56	478.01	4,943.45	5,924.41	86	2,269.15	7,639.88	8,225.36
27	106.06	2,336.91	3,700.16	57	503.49	5,033.33	6,001.11	87	2,390.07	7,729.76	8,302.06
28	111.72	2,426.79	3,776.86	58	530.32	5,123.22	6,077.81	88	2,517.43	7,819.64	8,378.76
29	117.67	2,516.67	3,853.55	59	558.58	5,213.10	6,154.51				
30	123.94	2,606.55	3,930.25	60	588.34	5,302.98	6,231.20				

Table 1 (continues)

Initial Catalog of Tunings : C-12

Scale Deg.	HZ	Cts	TU	Scale Deg.	HZ	Cts	TU	Scale Deg.	HZ	Cts	TU
1	27.50	0.00	1,706.00	13	165.00	3,101.96	4,353.00	25	990.00	6,203.92	7,000.00
2	31.93	258.50	1,926.58	14	191.57	3,360.46	4,573.58	26	1,149.43	6,462.42	7,220.58
3	37.07	516.99	2,147.17	15	222.42	3,618.95	4,794.17	27	1,334.53	6,720.91	7,441.17
4	43.04	775.49	2,367.75	16	258.24	3,877.45	5,014.75	28	1,549.43	6,979.41	7,661.75
5	49.97	1,033.99	2,588.33	17	299.82	4,135.95	5,235.33	29	1,798.95	7,237.91	7,882.33
6	58.02	1,292.48	2,808.92	18	348.11	4,394.44	5,455.92	30	2,088.65	7,496.40	8,102.92
7	67.36	1,550.98	3,029.50	19	404.17	4,652.94	5,676.50	31	2,424.99	7,754.90	8,323.50
8	78.21	1,809.48	3,250.08	20	469.25	4,911.44	5,897.08	32	2,815.51	8,013.40	8,544.08
9	90.80	2,067.97	3,470.67	21	544.82	5,169.93	6,117.67	33	3,268.91	8,271.89	8,764.67
10	105.43	2,326.47	3,691.25	22	632.55	5,428.43	6,338.25	34	3,795.32	8,530.39	8,985.25
11	122.40	2,584.97	3,911.83	23	734.42	5,686.93	6,558.83				
12	142.11	2,843.46	4,132.42	24	852.69	5,945.42	6,779.42				

Initial Catalog of Tunings : C-13

Scale Deg.	HZ	Cts	TU	Scale Deg.	HZ	Cts	TU	Scale Deg.	HZ	Cts	TU
1	27.50	0.00	1,706.00	14	165.00	3,101.96	4,353.00	27	990.00	6,203.92	7,000.00
2	31.56	238.61	1,909.62	15	189.38	3,340.57	4,556.62	28	1,136.30	6,442.53	7,203.62
3	36.23	477.22	2,113.23	16	217.37	3,579.18	4,760.23	29	1,304.22	6,681.14	7,407.23
4	41.58	715.84	2,316.85	17	249.49	3,817.80	4,963.85	30	1,496.95	6,919.76	7,610.85
5	47.73	954.45	2,520.46	18	286.36	4,056.41	5,167.46	31	1,718.17	7,158.37	7,814.46
6	54.78	1,193.06	2,724.08	19	328.68	4,295.02	5,371.08	32	1,972.08	7,396.98	8,018.08
7	62.88	1,431.67	2,927.69	20	377.25	4,533.63	5,574.69	33	2,263.51	7,635.59	8,221.69
8	72.17	1,670.29	3,131.31	21	433.00	4,772.25	5,778.31	34	2,598.00	7,874.21	8,425.31
9	82.83	1,908.90	3,334.92	22	496.99	5,010.86	5,981.92	35	2,981.93	8,112.82	8,628.92
10	95.07	2,147.51	3,538.54	23	570.43	5,249.47	6,185.54	36	3,422.59	8,351.43	8,832.54
11	109.12	2,386.12	3,742.15	24	654.73	5,488.08	6,389.15	37	3,928.38	8,590.04	9,036.15
12	125.25	2,624.74	3,945.77	25	751.48	5,726.70	6,592.77				
13	143.76	2,863.35	4,149.38	26	862.54	5,965.31	6,796.38				

Initial Catalog of Tunings : C-14

Scale Deg.	HZ	Cts	TU	Scale Deg.	HZ	Cts	TU	Scale Deg.	HZ	Cts	TU
1	27.50	0.00	1,706.00	15	165.00	3,101.96	4,353.00	29	990.00	6,203.92	7,000.00
2	31.25	221.57	1,895.07	16	187.53	3,323.53	4,542.07	30	1,125.17	6,425.49	7,189.07
3	35.52	443.14	2,084.14	17	213.13	3,545.10	4,731.14	31	1,278.79	6,647.06	7,378.14
4	40.37	664.71	2,273.21	18	242.23	3,766.67	4,920.21	32	1,453.39	6,868.63	7,567.21
5	45.88	886.27	2,462.29	19	275.30	3,988.23	5,109.29	33	1,651.83	7,090.19	7,756.29
6	52.15	1,107.84	2,651.36	20	312.89	4,209.80	5,298.36	34	1,877.35	7,311.76	7,945.36
7	59.27	1,329.41	2,840.43	21	355.61	4,431.37	5,487.43	35	2,133.68	7,533.33	8,134.43
8	67.36	1,550.98	3,029.50	22	404.17	4,652.94	5,676.50	36	2,424.99	7,754.90	8,323.50
9	76.56	1,772.55	3,218.57	23	459.35	4,874.51	5,865.57	37	2,756.09	7,976.47	8,512.57
10	87.01	1,994.12	3,407.64	24	522.06	5,096.08	6,054.64	38	3,132.39	8,198.04	8,701.64
11	98.89	2,215.69	3,596.71	25	593.34	5,317.65	6,243.71	39	3,560.06	8,419.61	8,890.71
12	112.39	2,437.25	3,785.79	26	674.35	5,539.21	6,432.79	40	4,046.13	8,641.17	9,079.79
13	127.74	2,658.82	3,974.86	27	766.43	5,760.78	6,621.86				
14	145.18	2,880.39	4,163.93	28	871.07	5,982.35	6,810.93				

Initial Catalog of Tunings : C-15

Scale Deg.	HZ	Cts	TU	Scale Deg.	HZ	Cts	TU	Scale Deg.	HZ	Cts	TU
1	27.50	0.00	1,706.00	16	165.00	3,101.96	4,353.00	31	990.00	6,203.92	7,000.00
2	30.99	206.80	1,882.47	17	185.93	3,308.76	4,529.47	32	1,115.61	6,410.72	7,176.47
3	34.92	413.59	2,058.93	18	209.53	3,515.55	4,705.93	33	1,257.15	6,617.51	7,352.93
4	39.35	620.39	2,235.40	19	236.11	3,722.35	4,882.40	34	1,416.66	6,824.31	7,529.40
5	44.34	827.19	2,411.87	20	266.07	3,929.15	5,058.87	35	1,596.40	7,031.11	7,705.87
6	49.97	1,033.99	2,588.33	21	299.82	4,135.95	5,235.33	36	1,798.95	7,237.91	7,882.33
7	56.31	1,240.78	2,764.80	22	337.87	4,342.74	5,411.80	37	2,027.20	7,444.70	8,058.80
8	63.46	1,447.58	2,941.27	23	380.73	4,549.54	5,588.27	38	2,284.40	7,651.50	8,235.27
9	71.51	1,654.38	3,117.73	24	429.04	4,756.34	5,764.73	39	2,574.24	7,858.30	8,411.73
10	80.58	1,861.18	3,294.20	25	483.48	4,963.14	5,941.20	40	2,900.85	8,065.10	8,588.20
11	90.80	2,067.97	3,470.67	26	544.82	5,169.93	6,117.67	41	3,268.91	8,271.89	8,764.67
12	102.32	2,274.77	3,647.13	27	613.94	5,376.73	6,294.13	42	3,683.66	8,478.69	8,941.13
13	115.31	2,481.57	3,823.60	28	691.84	5,583.53	6,470.60	43	4,151.03	8,685.49	9,117.60
14	129.94	2,688.37	4,000.07	29	779.62	5,790.33	6,647.07				
15	146.42	2,895.16	4,176.53	30	878.53	5,997.12	6,823.53				

Table 1 (continues)

Initial Catalog of Tunings : C-16

Scale Deg.	HZ	Cts	TU	Scale Deg.	HZ	Cts	TU	Scale Deg.	HZ	Cts	TU
1	27.50	0.00	1,706.00	17	165.00	3,101.96	4,353.00	33	990.00	6,203.92	7,000.00
2	30.76	193.87	1,871.44	18	184.55	3,295.83	4,518.44	34	1,107.31	6,397.79	7,165.44
3	34.40	387.75	2,036.88	19	206.42	3,489.71	4,683.88	35	1,238.52	6,591.67	7,330.88
4	38.48	581.62	2,202.31	20	230.88	3,683.58	4,849.31	36	1,385.28	6,785.54	7,496.31
5	43.04	775.49	2,367.75	21	258.24	3,877.45	5,014.75	37	1,549.43	6,979.41	7,661.75
6	48.14	969.36	2,533.19	22	288.84	4,071.32	5,180.19	38	1,733.04	7,173.28	7,827.19
7	53.84	1,163.24	2,698.63	23	323.07	4,265.20	5,345.63	39	1,938.39	7,367.16	7,992.63
8	60.22	1,357.11	2,864.06	24	361.35	4,459.07	5,511.06	40	2,168.09	7,561.03	8,158.06
9	67.36	1,550.98	3,029.50	25	404.17	4,652.94	5,676.50	41	2,424.99	7,754.90	8,323.50
10	75.34	1,744.85	3,194.94	26	452.06	4,846.81	5,841.94	42	2,712.35	7,948.77	8,488.94
11	84.27	1,938.73	3,360.38	27	505.62	5,040.69	6,007.38	43	3,033.75	8,142.65	8,654.38
12	94.26	2,132.60	3,525.81	28	565.54	5,234.56	6,172.81	44	3,393.24	8,336.52	8,819.81
13	105.43	2,326.47	3,691.25	29	632.55	5,428.43	6,338.25	45	3,795.32	8,530.39	8,985.25
14	117.92	2,520.34	3,856.69	30	707.51	5,622.30	6,503.69	46	4,245.05	8,724.26	9,150.69
15	131.89	2,714.22	4,022.13	31	791.35	5,816.18	6,669.13				
16	147.52	2,908.09	4,187.56	32	885.12	6,010.05	6,834.56				

Initial Catalog of Tunings : C-17

Scale Deg.	HZ	Cts	TU	Scale Deg.	HZ	Cts	TU	Scale Deg.	HZ	Cts	TU
1	27.50	0.00	1,706.00	18	165.00	3,101.96	4,353.00	35	990.00	6,203.92	7,000.00
2	30.56	182.47	1,861.71	19	183.34	3,284.43	4,508.71	36	1,100.04	6,386.39	7,155.71
3	33.95	364.94	2,017.41	20	203.72	3,466.90	4,664.41	37	1,222.31	6,568.86	7,311.41
4	37.73	547.40	2,173.12	21	226.36	3,649.36	4,820.12	38	1,358.18	6,751.32	7,467.12
5	41.92	729.87	2,328.82	22	251.52	3,831.83	4,975.82	39	1,509.14	6,933.79	7,622.82
6	46.58	912.34	2,484.53	23	279.48	4,014.30	5,131.53	40	1,676.88	7,116.26	7,778.53
7	51.76	1,094.81	2,640.24	24	310.55	4,196.77	5,287.24	41	1,863.27	7,298.73	7,934.24
8	57.51	1,277.28	2,795.94	25	345.06	4,379.24	5,442.94	42	2,070.38	7,481.20	8,089.94
9	63.90	1,459.75	2,951.65	26	383.42	4,561.71	5,598.65	43	2,300.51	7,663.67	8,245.65
10	71.01	1,642.21	3,107.35	27	426.04	4,744.17	5,754.35	44	2,556.22	7,846.13	8,401.35
11	78.90	1,824.68	3,263.06	28	473.39	4,926.64	5,910.06	45	2,840.35	8,028.60	8,557.06
12	87.67	2,007.15	3,418.76	29	526.01	5,109.11	6,065.76	46	3,156.06	8,211.07	8,712.76
13	97.41	2,189.62	3,574.47	30	584.48	5,291.58	6,221.47	47	3,506.86	8,393.54	8,868.47
14	108.24	2,372.09	3,730.18	31	649.44	5,474.05	6,377.18	48	3,896.66	8,576.01	9,024.18
15	120.27	2,554.56	3,885.88	32	721.63	5,656.52	6,532.88	49	4,329.78	8,758.48	9,179.88
16	133.64	2,737.02	4,041.59	33	801.84	5,838.98	6,688.59				
17	148.49	2,919.49	4,197.29	34	890.97	6,021.45	6,844.29				

Initial Catalog of Tunings : C-18

Scale Deg.	HZ	Cts	TU	Scale Deg.	HZ	Cts	TU	Scale Deg.	HZ	Cts	TU
1	27.50	0.00	1,706.00	19	165.00	3,101.96	4,353.00	37	990.00	6,203.92	7,000.00
2	30.38	172.33	1,853.06	20	182.27	3,274.29	4,500.06	38	1,093.62	6,376.25	7,147.06
3	33.56	344.66	2,000.11	21	201.35	3,446.62	4,647.11	39	1,208.08	6,548.58	7,294.11
4	37.07	516.99	2,147.17	22	222.42	3,618.95	4,794.17	40	1,334.53	6,720.91	7,441.17
5	40.95	689.32	2,294.22	23	245.70	3,791.28	4,941.22	41	1,474.20	6,893.24	7,588.22
6	45.24	861.66	2,441.28	24	271.42	3,963.62	5,088.28	42	1,628.50	7,065.58	7,735.28
7	49.97	1,033.99	2,588.33	25	299.82	4,135.95	5,235.33	43	1,798.95	7,237.91	7,882.33
8	55.20	1,206.32	2,735.39	26	331.21	4,308.28	5,382.39	44	1,987.24	7,410.24	8,029.39
9	60.98	1,378.65	2,882.44	27	365.87	4,480.61	5,529.44	45	2,195.23	7,582.57	8,176.44
10	67.36	1,550.98	3,029.50	28	404.17	4,652.94	5,676.50	46	2,424.99	7,754.90	8,323.50
11	74.41	1,723.31	3,176.56	29	446.47	4,825.27	5,823.56	47	2,678.81	7,927.23	8,470.56
12	82.20	1,895.64	3,323.61	30	493.20	4,997.60	5,970.61	48	2,959.18	8,099.56	8,617.61
13	90.80	2,067.97	3,470.67	31	544.82	5,169.93	6,117.67	49	3,268.91	8,271.89	8,764.67
14	100.31	2,240.30	3,617.72	32	601.84	5,342.26	6,264.72	50	3,611.05	8,444.22	8,911.72
15	110.81	2,412.64	3,764.78	33	664.83	5,514.60	6,411.78	51	3,989.00	8,616.56	9,058.78
16	122.40	2,584.97	3,911.83	34	734.42	5,686.93	6,558.83	52	4,406.51	8,788.89	9,205.83
17	135.21	2,757.30	4,058.89	35	811.29	5,859.26	6,705.89				
18	149.37	2,929.63	4,205.94	36	896.20	6,031.59	6,852.94				

166

Table 1 (continues)

Initial Catalog of Tunings : C-19

Scale Deg.	HZ	Cts	TU	Scale Deg.	HZ	Cts	TU	Scale Deg.	HZ	Cts	TU
1	27.50	0.00	1,706.00	20	165.00	3,101.96	4,353.00	39	990.00	6,203.92	7,000.00
2	30.22	163.26	1,845.32	21	181.32	3,265.22	4,492.32	40	1,087.90	6,367.18	7,139.32
3	33.21	326.52	1,984.63	22	199.25	3,428.48	4,631.63	41	1,195.49	6,530.44	7,278.63
4	36.49	489.78	2,123.95	23	218.95	3,591.74	4,770.95	42	1,313.72	6,693.70	7,417.95
5	40.10	653.04	2,263.26	24	240.61	3,755.00	4,910.26	43	1,443.63	6,856.96	7,557.26
6	44.07	816.31	2,402.58	25	264.40	3,918.27	5,049.58	44	1,586.40	7,020.23	7,696.58
7	48.42	979.57	2,541.89	26	290.55	4,081.53	5,188.89	45	1,743.28	7,183.49	7,835.89
8	53.21	1,142.83	2,681.21	27	319.28	4,244.79	5,328.21	46	1,915.68	7,346.75	7,975.21
9	58.48	1,306.09	2,820.53	28	350.85	4,408.05	5,467.53	47	2,105.12	7,510.01	8,114.53
10	64.26	1,469.35	2,959.84	29	385.55	4,571.31	5,606.84	48	2,313.31	7,673.27	8,253.84
11	70.61	1,632.61	3,099.16	30	423.68	4,734.57	5,746.16	49	2,542.08	7,836.53	8,393.16
12	77.60	1,795.87	3,238.47	31	465.58	4,897.83	5,885.47	50	2,793.47	7,999.79	8,532.47
13	85.27	1,959.13	3,377.79	32	511.62	5,061.09	6,024.79	51	3,069.72	8,163.05	8,671.79
14	93.70	2,122.39	3,517.11	33	562.22	5,224.35	6,164.11	52	3,373.30	8,326.31	8,811.11
15	102.97	2,285.65	3,656.42	34	617.82	5,387.61	6,303.42	53	3,706.89	8,489.57	8,950.42
16	113.15	2,448.92	3,795.74	35	678.91	5,550.88	6,442.74	54	4,073.48	8,652.84	9,089.74
17	124.34	2,612.18	3,935.05	36	746.05	5,714.14	6,582.05	55	4,476.31	8,816.10	9,229.05
18	136.64	2,775.44	4,074.37	37	819.83	5,877.40	6,721.37				
19	150.15	2,938.70	4,213.68	38	900.91	6,040.66	6,860.68				

Initial Catalog of Tunings : C-20

Scale Deg.	HZ	Cts	TU	Scale Deg.	HZ	Cts	TU	Scale Deg.	HZ	Cts	TU
1	27.50	0.00	1,706.00	21	165.00	3,101.96	4,353.00	41	990.00	6,203.92	7,000.00
2	30.08	155.10	1,838.35	22	180.46	3,257.06	4,485.35	42	1,082.79	6,359.02	7,132.35
3	32.90	310.20	1,970.70	23	197.38	3,412.16	4,617.70	43	1,184.27	6,514.12	7,264.70
4	35.98	465.29	2,103.05	24	215.88	3,567.25	4,750.05	44	1,295.26	6,669.21	7,397.05
5	39.35	620.39	2,235.40	25	236.11	3,722.35	4,882.40	45	1,416.66	6,824.31	7,529.40
6	43.04	775.49	2,367.75	26	258.24	3,877.45	5,014.75	46	1,549.43	6,979.41	7,661.75
7	47.07	930.59	2,500.10	27	282.44	4,032.55	5,147.10	47	1,694.65	7,134.51	7,794.10
8	51.49	1,085.69	2,632.45	28	308.91	4,187.65	5,279.45	48	1,853.48	7,289.61	7,926.45
9	56.31	1,240.78	2,764.80	29	337.87	4,342.74	5,411.80	49	2,027.20	7,444.70	8,058.80
10	61.59	1,395.88	2,897.15	30	369.53	4,497.84	5,544.15	50	2,217.19	7,599.80	8,191.15
11	67.36	1,550.98	3,029.50	31	404.17	4,652.94	5,676.50	51	2,424.99	7,754.90	8,323.50
12	73.67	1,706.08	3,161.85	32	442.05	4,808.04	5,808.85	52	2,652.27	7,910.00	8,455.85
13	80.58	1,861.18	3,294.20	33	483.48	4,963.14	5,941.20	53	2,900.85	8,065.10	8,588.20
14	88.13	2,016.27	3,426.55	34	528.79	5,118.23	6,073.55	54	3,172.73	8,220.19	8,720.55
15	96.39	2,171.37	3,558.90	35	578.35	5,273.33	6,205.90	55	3,470.09	8,375.29	8,852.90
16	105.43	2,326.47	3,691.25	36	632.55	5,428.43	6,338.25	56	3,795.32	8,530.39	8,985.25
17	115.31	2,481.57	3,823.60	37	691.84	5,583.53	6,470.60	57	4,151.03	8,685.49	9,117.60
18	126.11	2,636.67	3,955.95	38	756.68	5,738.63	6,602.95	58	4,540.08	8,840.59	9,249.95
19	137.93	2,791.76	4,088.30	39	827.60	5,893.72	6,735.30				
20	150.86	2,946.86	4,220.65	40	905.16	6,048.82	6,867.65				

Initial Catalog of Tunings : C-21

Scale Deg.	HZ	Cts	TU	Scale Deg.	HZ	Cts	TU	Scale Deg.	HZ	Cts	TU
1	27.50	0.00	1,706.00	22	165.00	3,101.96	4,353.00	43	990.00	6,203.92	7,000.00
2	29.95	147.71	1,832.05	23	179.70	3,249.67	4,479.05	44	1,078.18	6,351.63	7,126.05
3	32.62	295.42	1,958.10	24	195.70	3,397.38	4,605.10	45	1,174.21	6,499.34	7,252.10
4	35.52	443.14	2,084.14	25	213.13	3,545.10	4,731.14	46	1,278.79	6,647.06	7,378.14
5	38.69	590.85	2,210.19	26	232.12	3,692.81	4,857.19	47	1,392.69	6,794.77	7,504.19
6	42.13	738.56	2,336.24	27	252.79	3,840.52	4,983.24	48	1,516.73	6,942.48	7,630.24
7	45.88	886.27	2,462.29	28	275.30	3,988.23	5,109.29	49	1,651.83	7,090.19	7,756.29
8	49.97	1,033.99	2,588.33	29	299.82	4,135.95	5,235.33	50	1,798.95	7,237.91	7,882.33
9	54.42	1,181.70	2,714.38	30	326.53	4,283.66	5,361.38	51	1,959.18	7,385.62	8,008.38
10	59.27	1,329.41	2,840.43	31	355.61	4,431.37	5,487.43	52	2,133.68	7,533.33	8,134.43
11	64.55	1,477.12	2,966.48	32	387.29	4,579.08	5,613.48	53	2,323.72	7,681.04	8,260.48
12	70.30	1,624.84	3,092.52	33	421.78	4,726.80	5,739.52	54	2,530.69	7,828.76	8,386.52
13	76.56	1,772.55	3,218.57	34	459.35	4,874.51	5,865.57	55	2,756.09	7,976.47	8,512.57
14	83.38	1,920.26	3,344.62	35	500.26	5,022.22	5,991.62	56	3,001.57	8,124.18	8,638.62
15	90.80	2,067.97	3,470.67	36	544.82	5,169.93	6,117.67	57	3,268.91	8,271.89	8,764.67
16	98.89	2,215.69	3,596.71	37	593.34	5,317.65	6,243.71	58	3,560.06	8,419.61	8,890.71
17	107.70	2,363.40	3,722.76	38	646.19	5,465.36	6,369.76	59	3,877.15	8,567.32	9,016.76
18	117.29	2,511.11	3,848.81	39	703.75	5,613.07	6,495.81	60	4,222.48	8,715.03	9,142.81
19	127.74	2,658.82	3,974.86	40	766.43	5,760.78	6,621.86				
20	139.12	2,806.54	4,100.90	41	834.69	5,908.50	6,747.90				
21	151.51	2,954.25	4,226.95	42	909.03	6,056.21	6,873.95				

Table 1 (continues)

Initial Catalog of Tunings : C-22

Scale Deg.	HZ	Cts	TU	Scale Deg.	HZ	Cts	TU	Scale Deg.	HZ	Cts	TU
1	27.50	0.00	1,706.00	23	165.00	3,101.96	4,353.00	45	990.00	6,203.92	7,000.00
2	29.83	141.00	1,826.32	24	179.00	3,242.96	4,473.32	46	1,074.00	6,344.92	7,120.32
3	32.36	282.00	1,946.64	25	194.19	3,383.96	4,593.64	47	1,165.13	6,485.92	7,240.64
4	35.11	422.99	2,066.95	26	210.67	3,524.95	4,713.95	48	1,264.00	6,626.91	7,360.95
5	38.09	563.99	2,187.27	27	228.54	3,665.95	4,834.27	49	1,371.25	6,767.91	7,481.27
6	41.32	704.99	2,307.59	28	247.93	3,806.95	4,954.59	50	1,487.61	6,908.91	7,601.59
7	44.83	845.99	2,427.91	29	268.97	3,947.95	5,074.91	51	1,613.83	7,049.91	7,721.91
8	48.63	986.99	2,548.23	30	291.79	4,088.95	5,195.23	52	1,750.77	7,190.91	7,842.23
9	52.76	1,127.99	2,668.55	31	316.55	4,229.95	5,315.55	53	1,899.33	7,331.91	7,962.55
10	57.24	1,268.98	2,788.86	32	343.41	4,370.94	5,435.86	54	2,060.49	7,472.90	8,082.86
11	62.09	1,409.98	2,909.18	33	372.55	4,511.94	5,556.18	55	2,235.32	7,613.90	8,203.18
12	67.36	1,550.98	3,029.50	34	404.17	4,652.94	5,676.50	56	2,424.99	7,754.90	8,323.50
13	73.08	1,691.98	3,149.82	35	438.46	4,793.94	5,796.82	57	2,630.76	7,895.90	8,443.82
14	79.28	1,832.98	3,270.14	36	475.66	4,934.94	5,917.14	58	2,853.99	8,036.90	8,564.14
15	86.00	1,973.97	3,390.45	37	516.03	5,075.93	6,037.45	59	3,096.15	8,177.89	8,684.45
16	93.30	2,114.97	3,510.77	38	559.81	5,216.93	6,157.77	60	3,358.87	8,318.89	8,804.77
17	101.22	2,255.97	3,631.09	39	607.31	5,357.93	6,278.09	61	3,643.87	8,459.89	8,925.09
18	109.81	2,396.97	3,751.41	40	658.84	5,498.93	6,398.41	62	3,953.06	8,600.89	9,045.41
19	119.12	2,537.97	3,871.73	41	714.75	5,639.93	6,518.73	63	4,288.49	8,741.89	9,165.73
20	129.23	2,678.97	3,992.05	42	775.40	5,780.93	6,639.05				
21	140.20	2,819.96	4,112.36	43	841.19	5,921.92	6,759.36				
22	152.09	2,960.96	4,232.68	44	912.57	6,062.92	6,879.68				

Initial Catalog of Tunings : C-23

Scale Deg.	HZ	Cts	TU	Scale Deg.	HZ	Cts	TU	Scale Deg.	HZ	Cts	TU
1	27.50	0.00	1,706.00	24	165.00	3,101.96	4,353.00	47	990.00	6,203.92	7,000.00
2	29.73	134.87	1,821.09	25	178.37	3,236.83	4,468.09	48	1,070.21	6,338.79	7,115.09
3	32.14	269.74	1,936.17	26	192.82	3,371.70	4,583.17	49	1,156.91	6,473.66	7,230.17
4	34.74	404.60	2,051.26	27	208.44	3,506.56	4,698.26	50	1,250.64	6,608.52	7,345.26
5	37.55	539.47	2,166.35	28	225.33	3,641.43	4,813.35	51	1,351.97	6,743.39	7,460.35
6	40.60	674.34	2,281.43	29	243.58	3,776.30	4,928.43	52	1,461.50	6,878.26	7,575.43
7	43.89	809.21	2,396.52	30	263.32	3,911.17	5,043.52	53	1,579.91	7,013.13	7,690.52
8	47.44	944.07	2,511.61	31	284.65	4,046.03	5,158.61	54	1,707.91	7,147.99	7,805.61
9	51.29	1,078.94	2,626.70	32	307.71	4,180.90	5,273.70	55	1,846.28	7,282.86	7,920.70
10	55.44	1,213.81	2,741.78	33	332.64	4,315.77	5,388.78	56	1,995.86	7,417.73	8,035.78
11	59.93	1,348.68	2,856.87	34	359.59	4,450.64	5,503.87	57	2,157.55	7,552.60	8,150.87
12	64.79	1,483.55	2,971.96	35	388.73	4,585.51	5,618.96	58	2,332.35	7,687.47	8,265.96
13	70.04	1,618.41	3,087.04	36	420.22	4,720.37	5,734.04	59	2,521.32	7,822.33	8,381.04
14	75.71	1,753.28	3,202.13	37	454.26	4,855.24	5,849.13	60	2,725.59	7,957.20	8,496.13
15	81.84	1,888.15	3,317.22	38	491.07	4,990.11	5,964.22	61	2,946.41	8,092.07	8,611.22
16	88.48	2,023.02	3,432.30	39	530.85	5,124.98	6,079.30	62	3,185.12	8,226.94	8,726.30
17	95.64	2,157.89	3,547.39	40	573.86	5,259.85	6,194.39	63	3,443.16	8,361.81	8,841.39
18	103.39	2,292.75	3,662.48	41	620.35	5,394.71	6,309.48	64	3,722.12	8,496.67	8,956.48
19	111.77	2,427.62	3,777.57	42	670.61	5,529.58	6,424.57	65	4,023.68	8,631.54	9,071.57
20	120.82	2,562.49	3,892.65	43	724.94	5,664.45	6,539.65	66	4,349.66	8,766.41	9,186.65
21	130.61	2,697.36	4,007.74	44	783.68	5,799.32	6,654.74				
22	141.19	2,832.22	4,122.83	45	847.17	5,934.18	6,769.83				
23	152.63	2,967.09	4,237.91	46	915.80	6,069.05	6,884.91				

168

Table 1 (continues)

Initial Catalog of Tunings : C-24

Scale Deg.	HZ	Cts	TU	Scale Deg.	HZ	Cts	TU	Scale Deg.	HZ	Cts	TU
1	27.50	0.00	1,706.00	25	165.00	3,101.96	4,353.00	49	990.00	6,203.92	7,000.00
2	29.63	129.25	1,816.29	26	177.79	3,231.21	4,463.29	50	1,066.74	6,333.17	7,110.29
3	31.93	258.50	1,926.58	27	191.57	3,360.46	4,573.58	51	1,149.43	6,462.42	7,220.58
4	34.40	387.75	2,036.88	28	206.42	3,489.71	4,683.88	52	1,238.52	6,591.67	7,330.88
5	37.07	516.99	2,147.17	29	222.42	3,618.95	4,794.17	53	1,334.53	6,720.91	7,441.17
6	39.94	646.24	2,257.46	30	239.66	3,748.20	4,904.46	54	1,437.97	6,850.16	7,551.46
7	43.04	775.49	2,367.75	31	258.24	3,877.45	5,014.75	55	1,549.43	6,979.41	7,661.75
8	46.38	904.74	2,478.04	32	278.26	4,006.70	5,125.04	56	1,669.54	7,108.66	7,772.04
9	49.97	1,033.99	2,588.33	33	299.82	4,135.95	5,235.33	57	1,798.95	7,237.91	7,882.33
10	53.84	1,163.24	2,698.63	34	323.07	4,265.20	5,345.63	58	1,938.39	7,367.16	7,992.63
11	58.02	1,292.48	2,808.92	35	348.11	4,394.44	5,455.92	59	2,088.65	7,496.40	8,102.92
12	62.52	1,421.73	2,919.21	36	375.09	4,523.69	5,566.21	60	2,250.55	7,625.65	8,213.21
13	67.36	1,550.98	3,029.50	37	404.17	4,652.94	5,676.50	61	2,424.99	7,754.90	8,323.50
14	72.58	1,680.23	3,139.79	38	435.49	4,782.19	5,786.79	62	2,612.97	7,884.15	8,433.79
15	78.21	1,809.48	3,250.08	39	469.25	4,911.44	5,897.08	63	2,815.51	8,013.40	8,544.08
16	84.27	1,938.73	3,360.37	40	505.62	5,040.69	6,007.38	64	3,033.75	8,142.65	8,654.38
17	90.80	2,067.97	3,470.67	41	544.82	5,169.93	6,117.67	65	3,268.91	8,271.89	8,764.67
18	97.84	2,197.22	3,580.96	42	587.05	5,299.18	6,227.96	66	3,522.29	8,401.14	8,874.96
19	105.43	2,326.47	3,691.25	43	632.55	5,428.43	6,338.25	67	3,795.32	8,530.39	8,985.25
20	113.60	2,455.72	3,801.54	44	681.59	5,557.68	6,448.54	68	4,089.51	8,659.64	9,095.54
21	122.40	2,584.97	3,911.83	45	734.42	5,686.93	6,558.83	69	4,406.51	8,788.89	9,205.83
22	131.89	2,714.22	4,022.12	46	791.35	5,816.18	6,669.13				
23	142.11	2,843.46	4,132.42	47	852.69	5,945.42	6,779.42				
24	153.13	2,972.71	4,242.71	48	918.78	6,074.67	6,889.71				

Initial Catalog of Tunings : C-25

Scale Deg.	HZ	Cts	TU	Scale Deg.	HZ	Cts	TU	Scale Deg.	HZ	Cts	TU
1	27.50	0.00	1,706.00	26	165.00	3,101.96	4,353.00	51	990.00	6,203.92	7,000.00
2	29.54	124.08	1,811.88	27	177.26	3,226.04	4,458.88	52	1,063.56	6,328.00	7,105.88
3	31.74	248.16	1,917.76	28	190.43	3,350.12	4,564.76	53	1,142.58	6,452.08	7,211.76
4	34.10	372.24	2,023.64	29	204.58	3,474.20	4,670.64	54	1,227.48	6,576.16	7,317.64
5	36.63	496.31	2,129.52	30	219.78	3,598.27	4,776.52	55	1,318.68	6,700.23	7,423.52
6	39.35	620.39	2,235.40	31	236.11	3,722.35	4,882.40	56	1,416.66	6,824.31	7,529.40
7	42.28	744.47	2,341.28	32	253.65	3,846.43	4,988.28	57	1,521.92	6,948.39	7,635.28
8	45.42	868.55	2,447.16	33	272.50	3,970.51	5,094.16	58	1,635.00	7,072.47	7,741.16
9	48.79	992.63	2,553.04	34	292.75	4,094.59	5,200.04	59	1,756.48	7,196.55	7,847.04
10	52.42	1,116.71	2,658.92	35	314.50	4,218.67	5,305.92	60	1,886.99	7,320.63	7,952.92
11	56.31	1,240.78	2,764.80	36	337.87	4,342.74	5,411.80	61	2,027.20	7,444.70	8,058.80
12	60.49	1,364.86	2,870.68	37	362.97	4,466.82	5,517.68	62	2,177.82	7,568.78	8,164.68
13	64.99	1,488.94	2,976.56	38	389.94	4,590.90	5,623.56	63	2,339.63	7,692.86	8,270.56
14	69.82	1,613.02	3,082.44	39	418.91	4,714.98	5,729.44	64	2,513.47	7,816.94	8,376.44
15	75.01	1,737.10	3,188.32	40	450.04	4,839.06	5,835.32	65	2,700.22	7,941.02	8,482.32
16	80.58	1,861.18	3,294.20	41	483.48	4,963.14	5,941.20	66	2,900.85	8,065.10	8,588.20
17	86.57	1,985.25	3,400.08	42	519.40	5,087.21	6,047.08	67	3,116.39	8,189.17	8,694.08
18	93.00	2,109.33	3,505.96	43	557.99	5,211.29	6,152.96	68	3,347.94	8,313.25	8,799.96
19	99.91	2,233.41	3,611.84	44	599.45	5,335.37	6,258.84	69	3,596.70	8,437.33	8,905.84
20	107.33	2,357.49	3,717.72	45	643.99	5,459.45	6,364.72	70	3,863.94	8,561.41	9,011.72
21	115.31	2,481.57	3,823.60	46	691.84	5,583.53	6,470.60	71	4,151.03	8,685.49	9,117.60
22	123.87	2,605.65	3,929.48	47	743.24	5,707.61	6,576.48	72	4,459.46	8,809.57	9,223.48
23	133.08	2,729.72	4,035.36	48	798.47	5,831.68	6,682.36				
24	142.97	2,853.80	4,141.24	49	857.79	5,955.76	6,788.24				
25	153.59	2,977.88	4,247.12	50	921.53	6,079.84	6,894.12				

Table 1 (continues)

Initial Catalog of Tunings : C-26

Scale Deg.	HZ	Cts	TU	Scale Deg.	HZ	Cts	TU	Scale Deg.	HZ	Cts	TU
1	27.50	0.00	1,706.00	27	165.00	3,101.96	4,353.00	53	990.00	6,203.92	7,000.00
2	29.46	119.31	1,807.81	28	176.77	3,221.27	4,454.81	54	1,060.63	6,323.23	7,101.81
3	31.56	238.61	1,909.62	29	189.38	3,340.57	4,556.62	55	1,136.30	6,442.53	7,203.62
4	33.82	357.92	2,011.42	30	202.89	3,459.88	4,658.42	56	1,217.37	6,561.84	7,305.42
5	36.23	477.22	2,113.23	31	217.37	3,579.18	4,760.23	57	1,304.22	6,681.14	7,407.23
6	38.81	596.53	2,215.04	32	232.88	3,698.49	4,862.04	58	1,397.27	6,800.45	7,509.04
7	41.58	715.84	2,316.85	33	249.49	3,817.80	4,963.85	59	1,496.95	6,919.76	7,610.85
8	44.55	835.14	2,418.65	34	267.29	3,937.10	5,065.65	60	1,603.75	7,039.06	7,712.65
9	47.73	954.45	2,520.46	35	286.36	4,056.41	5,167.46	61	1,718.17	7,158.37	7,814.46
10	51.13	1,073.76	2,622.27	36	306.79	4,175.72	5,269.27	62	1,840.75	7,277.68	7,916.27
11	54.78	1,193.06	2,724.08	37	328.68	4,295.02	5,371.08	63	1,972.08	7,396.98	8,018.08
12	58.69	1,312.37	2,825.88	38	352.13	4,414.33	5,472.88	64	2,112.77	7,516.29	8,119.88
13	62.88	1,431.67	2,927.69	39	377.25	4,533.63	5,574.69	65	2,263.51	7,635.59	8,221.69
14	67.36	1,550.98	3,029.50	40	404.17	4,652.94	5,676.50	66	2,424.99	7,754.90	8,323.50
15	72.17	1,670.29	3,131.31	41	433.00	4,772.25	5,778.31	67	2,598.00	7,874.21	8,425.31
16	77.32	1,789.59	3,233.12	42	463.89	4,891.55	5,880.12	68	2,783.36	7,993.51	8,527.12
17	82.83	1,908.90	3,334.92	43	496.99	5,010.86	5,981.92	69	2,981.93	8,112.82	8,628.92
18	88.74	2,028.20	3,436.73	44	532.45	5,130.16	6,083.73	70	3,194.67	8,232.12	8,730.73
19	95.07	2,147.51	3,538.54	45	570.43	5,249.47	6,185.54	71	3,422.59	8,351.43	8,832.54
20	101.85	2,266.82	3,640.35	46	611.13	5,368.78	6,287.35	72	3,666.77	8,470.74	8,934.35
21	109.12	2,386.12	3,742.15	47	654.73	5,488.08	6,389.15	73	3,928.38	8,590.04	9,036.15
22	116.91	2,505.43	3,843.96	48	701.44	5,607.39	6,490.96	74	4,208.64	8,709.35	9,137.96
23	125.25	2,624.74	3,945.77	49	751.48	5,726.70	6,592.77	75	4,508.90	8,828.66	9,239.77
24	134.18	2,744.04	4,047.58	50	805.10	5,846.00	6,694.58				
25	143.76	2,863.35	4,149.38	51	862.54	5,965.31	6,796.38				
26	154.01	2,982.65	4,251.19	52	924.07	6,084.61	6,898.19				

Initial Catalog of Tunings : C-27

Scale Deg.	HZ	Cts	TU	Scale Deg.	HZ	Cts	TU	Scale Deg.	HZ	Cts	TU
1	27.50	0.00	1,706.00	28	165.00	3,101.96	4,353.00	55	990.00	6,203.92	7,000.00
2	29.39	114.89	1,804.04	29	176.32	3,216.85	4,451.04	56	1,057.93	6,318.81	7,098.04
3	31.40	229.77	1,902.07	30	188.42	3,331.73	4,549.07	57	1,130.51	6,433.69	7,196.07
4	33.56	344.66	2,000.11	31	201.35	3,446.62	4,647.11	58	1,208.08	6,548.58	7,294.11
5	35.86	459.55	2,098.15	32	215.16	3,561.51	4,745.15	59	1,290.97	6,663.47	7,392.15
6	38.32	574.44	2,196.19	33	229.92	3,676.40	4,843.19	60	1,379.55	6,778.36	7,490.19
7	40.95	689.32	2,294.22	34	245.70	3,791.28	4,941.22	61	1,474.20	6,893.24	7,588.22
8	43.76	804.21	2,392.26	35	262.56	3,906.17	5,039.26	62	1,575.35	7,008.13	7,686.26
9	46.76	919.10	2,490.30	36	280.57	4,021.06	5,137.30	63	1,683.44	7,123.02	7,784.30
10	49.97	1,033.99	2,588.33	37	299.82	4,135.95	5,235.33	64	1,798.95	7,237.91	7,882.33
11	53.40	1,148.87	2,686.37	38	320.40	4,250.83	5,333.37	65	1,922.38	7,352.79	7,980.37
12	57.06	1,263.76	2,784.41	39	342.38	4,365.72	5,431.41	66	2,054.28	7,467.68	8,078.41
13	60.98	1,378.65	2,882.44	40	365.87	4,480.61	5,529.44	67	2,195.23	7,582.57	8,176.44
14	65.16	1,493.54	2,980.48	41	390.98	4,595.50	5,627.48	68	2,345.85	7,697.46	8,274.48
15	69.63	1,608.42	3,078.52	42	417.80	4,710.38	5,725.52	69	2,506.81	7,812.34	8,372.52
16	74.41	1,723.31	3,176.56	43	446.47	4,825.27	5,823.56	70	2,678.81	7,927.23	8,470.56
17	79.52	1,838.20	3,274.59	44	477.10	4,940.16	5,921.59	71	2,862.61	8,042.12	8,568.59
18	84.97	1,953.09	3,372.63	45	509.84	5,055.05	6,019.63	72	3,059.02	8,157.01	8,666.63
19	90.80	2,067.97	3,470.67	46	544.82	5,169.93	6,117.67	73	3,268.91	8,271.89	8,764.67
20	97.03	2,182.86	3,568.70	47	582.20	5,284.82	6,215.70	74	3,493.20	8,386.78	8,862.70
21	103.69	2,297.75	3,666.74	48	622.15	5,399.71	6,313.74	75	3,732.88	8,501.67	8,960.74
22	110.81	2,412.64	3,764.78	49	664.83	5,514.60	6,411.78	76	3,989.00	8,616.56	9,058.78
23	118.41	2,527.52	3,862.81	50	710.45	5,629.48	6,509.81	77	4,262.70	8,731.44	9,156.81
24	126.53	2,642.41	3,960.85	51	759.20	5,744.37	6,607.85	78	4,555.17	8,846.33	9,254.85
25	135.21	2,757.30	4,058.89	52	811.29	5,859.26	6,705.89				
26	144.49	2,872.19	4,156.93	53	866.95	5,974.15	6,803.93				
27	154.41	2,987.07	4,254.96	54	926.43	6,089.03	6,901.96				

Table 1 (continues)

Initial Catalog of Tunings : C-28

Scale Deg.	HZ	Cts	TU	Scale Deg.	HZ	Cts	TU	Scale Deg.	HZ	Cts	TU
1	27.50	0.00	1,706.00	29	165.00	3,101.96	4,353.00	57	990.00	6,203.92	7,000.00
2	29.32	110.78	1,800.54	30	175.90	3,212.74	4,447.54	58	1,055.42	6,314.70	7,094.54
3	31.25	221.57	1,895.07	31	187.53	3,323.53	4,542.07	59	1,125.17	6,425.49	7,189.07
4	33.32	332.35	1,989.61	32	199.92	3,434.31	4,636.61	60	1,199.52	6,536.27	7,283.61
5	35.52	443.14	2,084.14	33	213.13	3,545.10	4,731.14	61	1,278.79	6,647.06	7,378.14
6	37.87	553.92	2,178.68	34	227.22	3,655.88	4,825.68	62	1,363.30	6,757.84	7,472.68
7	40.37	664.71	2,273.21	35	242.23	3,766.67	4,920.21	63	1,453.39	6,868.63	7,567.21
8	43.04	775.49	2,367.75	36	258.24	3,877.45	5,014.75	64	1,549.43	6,979.41	7,661.75
9	45.88	886.27	2,462.29	37	275.30	3,988.23	5,109.29	65	1,651.83	7,090.19	7,756.29
10	48.92	997.06	2,556.82	38	293.50	4,099.02	5,203.82	66	1,760.98	7,200.98	7,850.82
11	52.15	1,107.84	2,651.36	39	312.89	4,209.80	5,298.36	67	1,877.35	7,311.76	7,945.36
12	55.59	1,218.63	2,745.89	40	333.57	4,320.59	5,392.89	68	2,001.42	7,422.55	8,039.89
13	59.27	1,329.41	2,840.43	41	355.61	4,431.37	5,487.43	69	2,133.68	7,533.33	8,134.43
14	63.19	1,440.20	2,934.96	42	379.11	4,542.16	5,581.96	70	2,274.68	7,644.12	8,228.96
15	67.36	1,550.98	3,029.50	43	404.17	4,652.94	5,676.50	71	2,424.99	7,754.90	8,323.50
16	71.81	1,661.76	3,124.04	44	430.87	4,763.72	5,771.04	72	2,585.25	7,865.68	8,418.04
17	76.56	1,772.55	3,218.57	45	459.35	4,874.51	5,865.57	73	2,756.09	7,976.47	8,512.57
18	81.62	1,883.33	3,313.11	46	489.70	4,985.29	5,960.11	74	2,938.22	8,087.25	8,607.11
19	87.01	1,994.12	3,407.64	47	522.06	5,096.08	6,054.64	75	3,132.39	8,198.04	8,701.64
20	92.76	2,104.90	3,502.18	48	556.56	5,206.86	6,149.18	76	3,339.38	8,308.82	8,796.18
21	98.89	2,215.69	3,596.71	49	593.34	5,317.65	6,243.71	77	3,560.06	8,419.61	8,890.71
22	105.43	2,326.47	3,691.25	50	632.55	5,428.43	6,338.25	78	3,795.32	8,530.39	8,985.25
23	112.39	2,437.25	3,785.79	51	674.35	5,539.21	6,432.79	79	4,046.13	8,641.17	9,079.79
24	119.82	2,548.04	3,880.32	52	718.92	5,650.00	6,527.32	80	4,313.51	8,751.96	9,174.32
25	127.74	2,658.82	3,974.86	53	766.43	5,760.78	6,621.86	81	4,598.56	8,862.74	9,268.86
26	136.18	2,769.61	4,069.39	54	817.07	5,871.57	6,716.39				
27	145.18	2,880.39	4,163.93	55	871.07	5,982.35	6,810.93				
28	154.77	2,991.18	4,258.46	56	928.63	6,093.14	6,905.46				

Initial Catalog of Tunings : C-29

Scale Deg.	HZ	Cts	TU	Scale Deg.	HZ	Cts	TU	Scale Deg.	HZ	Cts	TU
1	27.50	0.00	1,706.00	30	165.00	3,101.96	4,353.00	59	990.00	6,203.92	7,000.00
2	29.25	106.96	1,797.28	31	175.52	3,208.92	4,444.28	60	1,053.10	6,310.88	7,091.28
3	31.12	213.93	1,888.55	32	186.70	3,315.89	4,535.55	61	1,120.21	6,417.85	7,182.55
4	33.10	320.89	1,979.83	33	198.60	3,422.85	4,626.83	62	1,191.61	6,524.81	7,273.83
5	35.21	427.86	2,071.10	34	211.26	3,529.82	4,718.10	63	1,267.55	6,631.78	7,365.10
6	37.45	534.82	2,162.38	35	224.72	3,636.78	4,809.38	64	1,348.34	6,738.74	7,456.38
7	39.84	641.78	2,253.66	36	239.05	3,743.74	4,900.66	65	1,434.27	6,845.70	7,547.66
8	42.38	748.75	2,344.93	37	254.28	3,850.71	4,991.93	66	1,525.68	6,952.67	7,638.93
9	45.08	855.71	2,436.21	38	270.49	3,957.67	5,083.21	67	1,622.92	7,059.63	7,730.21
10	47.95	962.68	2,527.48	39	287.73	4,064.64	5,174.48	68	1,726.36	7,166.60	7,821.48
11	51.01	1,069.64	2,618.76	40	306.06	4,171.60	5,265.76	69	1,836.38	7,273.56	7,912.76
12	54.26	1,176.61	2,710.03	41	325.57	4,278.57	5,357.03	70	1,953.42	7,380.53	8,004.03
13	57.72	1,283.57	2,801.31	42	346.32	4,385.53	5,448.31	71	2,077.92	7,487.49	8,095.31
14	61.40	1,390.53	2,892.59	43	368.39	4,492.49	5,539.59	72	2,210.35	7,594.45	8,186.59
15	65.31	1,497.50	2,983.86	44	391.87	4,599.46	5,630.86	73	2,351.23	7,701.42	8,277.86
16	69.47	1,604.46	3,075.14	45	416.85	4,706.42	5,722.14	74	2,501.08	7,808.38	8,369.14
17	73.90	1,711.43	3,166.41	46	443.41	4,813.39	5,813.41	75	2,660.48	7,915.35	8,460.41
18	78.61	1,818.39	3,257.69	47	471.67	4,920.35	5,904.69	76	2,830.04	8,022.31	8,551.69
19	83.62	1,925.35	3,348.97	48	501.73	5,027.31	5,995.97	77	3,010.41	8,129.27	8,642.97
20	88.95	2,032.32	3,440.24	49	533.71	5,134.28	6,087.24	78	3,202.27	8,236.24	8,734.24
21	94.62	2,139.28	3,531.52	50	567.73	5,241.24	6,178.52	79	3,406.37	8,343.20	8,825.52
22	100.65	2,246.25	3,622.79	51	603.91	5,348.21	6,269.79	80	3,623.46	8,450.17	8,916.79
23	107.07	2,353.21	3,714.07	52	642.40	5,455.17	6,361.07	81	3,854.40	8,557.13	9,008.07
24	113.89	2,460.18	3,805.34	53	683.34	5,562.14	6,452.34	82	4,100.05	8,664.10	9,099.34
25	121.15	2,567.14	3,896.62	54	726.89	5,669.10	6,543.62	83	4,361.37	8,771.06	9,190.62
26	128.87	2,674.10	3,987.90	55	773.22	5,776.06	6,634.90	84	4,639.33	8,878.02	9,281.90
27	137.08	2,781.07	4,079.17	56	822.50	5,883.03	6,726.17				
28	145.82	2,888.03	4,170.45	57	874.92	5,989.99	6,817.45				
29	155.11	2,995.00	4,261.72	58	930.68	6,096.96	6,908.72				

Table 1 (continues)

Initial Catalog of Tunings : C-30

Scale Deg.	HZ	Cts	TU	Scale Deg.	HZ	Cts	TU	Scale Deg.	HZ	Cts	TU
1	27.50	0.00	1,706.00	31	165.00	3,101.96	4,353.00	61	990.00	6,203.92	7,000.00
2	29.19	103.40	1,794.23	32	175.15	3,205.36	4,441.23	62	1,050.93	6,307.32	7,088.23
3	30.99	206.80	1,882.47	33	185.93	3,308.76	4,529.47	63	1,115.61	6,410.72	7,176.47
4	32.90	310.20	1,970.70	34	197.38	3,412.16	4,617.70	64	1,184.27	6,514.12	7,264.70
5	34.92	413.59	2,058.93	35	209.53	3,515.55	4,705.93	65	1,257.15	6,617.51	7,352.93
6	37.07	516.99	2,147.17	36	222.42	3,618.95	4,794.17	66	1,334.53	6,720.91	7,441.17
7	39.35	620.39	2,235.40	37	236.11	3,722.35	4,882.40	67	1,416.66	6,824.31	7,529.40
8	41.77	723.79	2,323.63	38	250.64	3,825.75	4,970.63	68	1,503.85	6,927.71	7,617.63
9	44.34	827.19	2,411.87	39	266.07	3,929.15	5,058.87	69	1,596.40	7,031.11	7,705.87
10	47.07	930.59	2,500.10	40	282.44	4,032.55	5,147.10	70	1,694.65	7,134.51	7,794.10
11	49.97	1,033.99	2,588.33	41	299.82	4,135.95	5,235.33	71	1,798.95	7,237.91	7,882.33
12	53.05	1,137.39	2,676.57	42	318.28	4,239.35	5,323.57	72	1,909.67	7,341.31	7,970.57
13	56.31	1,240.78	2,764.80	43	337.87	4,342.74	5,411.80	73	2,027.20	7,444.70	8,058.80
14	59.78	1,344.18	2,853.03	44	358.66	4,446.14	5,500.03	74	2,151.96	7,548.10	8,147.03
15	63.46	1,447.58	2,941.27	45	380.73	4,549.54	5,588.27	75	2,284.40	7,651.50	8,235.27
16	67.36	1,550.98	3,029.50	46	404.17	4,652.94	5,676.50	76	2,424.99	7,754.90	8,323.50
17	71.51	1,654.38	3,117.73	47	429.04	4,756.34	5,764.73	77	2,574.24	7,858.30	8,411.73
18	75.91	1,757.78	3,205.97	48	455.45	4,859.74	5,852.97	78	2,732.67	7,961.70	8,499.97
19	80.58	1,861.18	3,294.20	49	483.48	4,963.14	5,941.20	79	2,900.85	8,065.10	8,588.20
20	85.54	1,964.57	3,382.43	50	513.23	5,066.53	6,029.43	80	3,079.39	8,168.49	8,676.43
21	90.80	2,067.97	3,470.67	51	544.82	5,169.93	6,117.67	81	3,268.91	8,271.89	8,764.67
22	96.39	2,171.37	3,558.90	52	578.35	5,273.33	6,205.90	82	3,470.09	8,375.29	8,852.90
23	102.32	2,274.77	3,647.13	53	613.94	5,376.73	6,294.13	83	3,683.66	8,478.69	8,941.13
24	108.62	2,378.17	3,735.37	54	651.73	5,480.13	6,382.37	84	3,910.37	8,582.09	9,029.37
25	115.31	2,481.57	3,823.60	55	691.84	5,583.53	6,470.60	85	4,151.03	8,685.49	9,117.60
26	122.40	2,584.97	3,911.83	56	734.42	5,686.93	6,558.83	86	4,406.51	8,788.89	9,205.83
27	129.94	2,688.37	4,000.07	57	779.62	5,790.33	6,647.07	87	4,677.71	8,892.29	9,294.07
28	137.93	2,791.76	4,088.30	58	827.60	5,893.72	6,735.30	88	4,965.60	8,995.68	9,382.30
29	146.42	2,895.16	4,176.53	59	878.53	5,997.12	6,823.53				
30	155.43	2,998.56	4,264.73	60	932.60	6,100.52	6,911.77				

Initial Catalog of Tunings : C-31

Scale Deg.	HZ	Cts	TU	Scale Deg.	HZ	Cts	TU	Scale Deg.	HZ	Cts	TU
1	27.50	0.00	1,706.00	31	155.73	3,001.90	4,267.61	61	881.93	6,003.79	6,829.23
2	29.14	100.06	1,791.39	32	165.00	3,101.96	4,353.00	62	934.40	6,103.86	6,914.61
3	30.87	200.13	1,876.77	33	174.82	3,202.02	4,438.39	63	990.00	6,203.92	7,000.00
4	32.71	300.19	1,962.16	34	185.22	3,302.09	4,523.77	64	1,048.91	6,303.98	7,085.39
5	34.65	400.25	2,047.55	35	196.24	3,402.15	4,609.16	65	1,111.32	6,404.05	7,170.77
6	36.71	500.32	2,132.94	36	207.92	3,502.21	4,694.55	66	1,177.44	6,504.11	7,256.16
7	38.90	600.38	2,218.32	37	220.29	3,602.28	4,779.94	67	1,247.50	6,604.17	7,341.55
8	41.21	700.44	2,303.71	38	233.40	3,702.34	4,865.32	68	1,321.73	6,704.24	7,426.94
9	43.67	800.51	2,389.10	39	247.28	3,802.40	4,950.71	69	1,400.38	6,804.30	7,512.32
10	46.26	900.57	2,474.48	40	262.00	3,902.47	5,036.10	70	1,483.70	6,904.36	7,597.71
11	49.02	1,000.63	2,559.87	41	277.59	4,002.53	5,121.48	71	1,571.99	7,004.43	7,683.10
12	51.93	1,100.70	2,645.26	42	294.10	4,102.59	5,206.87	72	1,665.52	7,104.49	7,768.48
13	55.02	1,200.76	2,730.65	43	311.60	4,202.66	5,292.26	73	1,764.62	7,204.55	7,853.87
14	58.30	1,300.82	2,816.03	44	330.14	4,302.72	5,377.65	74	1,869.62	7,304.62	7,939.26
15	61.77	1,400.89	2,901.42	45	349.79	4,402.78	5,463.03	75	1,980.87	7,404.68	8,024.65
16	65.44	1,500.95	2,986.81	46	370.60	4,502.85	5,548.42	76	2,098.73	7,504.74	8,110.03
17	69.34	1,601.01	3,072.19	47	392.65	4,602.91	5,633.81	77	2,223.61	7,604.81	8,195.42
18	73.46	1,701.07	3,157.58	48	416.02	4,702.97	5,719.19	78	2,355.92	7,704.87	8,280.81
19	77.83	1,801.14	3,242.97	49	440.77	4,803.03	5,804.58	79	2,496.10	7,804.93	8,366.19
20	82.46	1,901.20	3,328.35	50	467.00	4,903.10	5,889.97	80	2,644.62	7,904.99	8,451.58
21	87.37	2,001.26	3,413.74	51	494.78	5,003.16	5,975.35	81	2,801.98	8,005.06	8,536.97
22	92.57	2,101.33	3,499.13	52	524.22	5,103.22	6,060.74	82	2,968.70	8,105.12	8,622.35
23	98.08	2,201.39	3,584.52	53	555.42	5,203.29	6,146.13	83	3,145.34	8,205.18	8,707.74
24	103.91	2,301.45	3,669.90	54	588.46	5,303.35	6,231.52	84	3,332.50	8,305.25	8,793.13
25	110.10	2,401.52	3,755.29	55	623.48	5,403.41	6,316.90	85	3,530.79	8,405.31	8,878.52
26	116.65	2,501.58	3,840.68	56	660.58	5,503.48	6,402.29	86	3,740.88	8,505.37	8,963.90
27	123.59	2,601.64	3,926.06	57	699.88	5,603.54	6,487.68	87	3,963.46	8,605.44	9,049.29
28	130.94	2,701.71	4,011.45	58	741.53	5,703.60	6,573.06	88	4,199.30	8,705.50	9,134.68
29	138.73	2,801.77	4,096.84	59	785.65	5,803.67	6,658.45				
30	146.99	2,901.83	4,182.23	60	832.40	5,903.73	6,743.84				

171

172

Table 1 (continues)

Initial Catalog of Tunings : C-32

Scale Deg.	HZ	Cts	TU	Scale Deg.	HZ	Cts	TU	Scale Deg.	HZ	Cts	TU
1	27.50	0.00	1,706.00	31	147.52	2,908.09	4,187.56	61	791.35	5,816.18	6,669.13
2	29.08	96.94	1,788.72	32	156.02	3,005.02	4,270.28	62	836.92	5,913.11	6,751.84
3	30.76	193.87	1,871.44	33	165.00	3,101.96	4,353.00	63	885.12	6,010.05	6,834.56
4	32.53	290.81	1,954.16	34	174.50	3,198.90	4,435.72	64	936.09	6,106.98	6,917.28
5	34.40	387.75	2,036.88	35	184.55	3,295.83	4,518.44	65	990.00	6,203.92	7,000.00
6	36.38	484.68	2,119.59	36	195.18	3,392.77	4,601.16	66	1,047.01	6,300.86	7,082.72
7	38.48	581.62	2,202.31	37	206.42	3,489.71	4,683.88	67	1,107.31	6,397.79	7,165.44
8	40.70	678.55	2,285.03	38	218.31	3,586.64	4,766.59	68	1,171.08	6,494.73	7,248.16
9	43.04	775.49	2,367.75	39	230.88	3,683.58	4,849.31	69	1,238.52	6,591.67	7,330.88
10	45.52	872.43	2,450.47	40	244.18	3,780.51	4,932.03	70	1,309.85	6,688.60	7,413.59
11	48.14	969.36	2,533.19	41	258.24	3,877.45	5,014.75	71	1,385.28	6,785.54	7,496.31
12	50.91	1,066.30	2,615.91	42	273.11	3,974.39	5,097.47	72	1,465.06	6,882.47	7,579.03
13	53.84	1,163.24	2,698.63	43	288.84	4,071.32	5,180.19	73	1,549.43	6,979.41	7,661.75
14	56.95	1,260.17	2,781.34	44	305.47	4,168.26	5,262.91	74	1,638.67	7,076.35	7,744.47
15	60.22	1,357.11	2,864.06	45	323.07	4,265.20	5,345.63	75	1,733.04	7,173.28	7,827.19
16	63.69	1,454.04	2,946.78	46	341.67	4,362.13	5,428.34	76	1,832.84	7,270.22	7,909.91
17	67.36	1,550.98	3,029.50	47	361.35	4,459.07	5,511.06	77	1,938.39	7,367.16	7,992.63
18	71.24	1,647.92	3,112.22	48	382.16	4,556.00	5,593.78	78	2,050.02	7,464.09	8,075.34
19	75.34	1,744.85	3,194.94	49	404.17	4,652.94	5,676.50	79	2,168.09	7,561.03	8,158.06
20	79.68	1,841.79	3,277.66	50	427.44	4,749.88	5,759.22	80	2,292.94	7,657.96	8,240.78
21	84.27	1,938.73	3,360.38	51	452.06	4,846.81	5,841.94	81	2,424.99	7,754.90	8,323.50
22	89.12	2,035.66	3,443.09	52	478.09	4,943.75	5,924.66	82	2,564.65	7,851.84	8,406.22
23	94.26	2,132.60	3,525.81	53	505.62	5,040.69	6,007.38	83	2,712.35	7,948.77	8,488.94
24	99.68	2,229.53	3,608.53	54	534.74	5,137.62	6,090.09	84	2,868.55	8,045.71	8,571.66
25	105.43	2,326.47	3,691.25	55	565.54	5,234.56	6,172.81	85	3,033.75	8,142.65	8,654.38
26	111.50	2,423.41	3,773.97	56	598.11	5,331.49	6,255.53	86	3,208.46	8,239.58	8,737.09
27	117.92	2,520.34	3,856.69	57	632.55	5,428.43	6,338.25	87	3,393.24	8,336.52	8,819.81
28	124.71	2,617.28	3,939.41	58	668.98	5,525.37	6,420.97	88	3,588.65	8,433.45	8,902.53
29	131.89	2,714.22	4,022.13	59	707.51	5,622.30	6,503.69				
30	139.49	2,811.15	4,104.84	60	748.25	5,719.24	6,586.41				

Initial Catalog of Tunings : C-33

Scale Deg.	HZ	Cts	TU	Scale Deg.	HZ	Cts	TU	Scale Deg.	HZ	Cts	TU
1	27.50	0.00	1,706.00	31	140.20	2,819.96	4,112.36	61	714.75	5,639.93	6,518.73
2	29.03	94.00	1,786.21	32	148.02	2,913.96	4,192.58	62	754.63	5,733.93	6,598.94
3	30.65	188.00	1,866.42	33	156.28	3,007.96	4,272.79	63	796.73	5,827.92	6,679.15
4	32.36	282.00	1,946.64	34	165.00	3,101.96	4,353.00	64	841.19	5,921.92	6,759.36
5	34.17	376.00	2,026.85	35	174.21	3,195.96	4,433.21	65	888.13	6,015.92	6,839.58
6	36.08	469.99	2,107.06	36	183.93	3,289.96	4,513.42	66	937.68	6,109.92	6,919.79
7	38.09	563.99	2,187.27	37	194.19	3,383.96	4,593.64	67	990.00	6,203.92	7,000.00
8	40.22	657.99	2,267.48	38	205.02	3,477.96	4,673.85	68	1,045.24	6,297.92	7,080.21
9	42.46	751.99	2,347.70	39	216.46	3,571.95	4,754.06	69	1,103.56	6,391.92	7,160.42
10	44.83	845.99	2,427.91	40	228.54	3,665.95	4,834.27	70	1,165.13	6,485.92	7,240.64
11	47.33	939.99	2,508.12	41	241.29	3,759.95	4,914.48	71	1,230.15	6,579.92	7,320.85
12	49.97	1,033.99	2,588.33	42	254.76	3,853.95	4,994.70	72	1,298.78	6,673.91	7,401.06
13	52.76	1,127.99	2,668.55	43	268.97	3,947.95	5,074.91	73	1,371.25	6,767.91	7,481.27
14	55.70	1,221.98	2,748.76	44	283.98	4,041.95	5,155.12	74	1,447.76	6,861.91	7,561.48
15	58.81	1,315.98	2,828.97	45	299.82	4,135.95	5,235.33	75	1,528.54	6,955.91	7,641.70
16	62.09	1,409.98	2,909.18	46	316.55	4,229.95	5,315.55	76	1,613.83	7,049.91	7,721.91
17	65.56	1,503.98	2,989.39	47	334.22	4,323.94	5,395.76	77	1,703.88	7,143.91	7,802.12
18	69.21	1,597.98	3,069.61	48	352.87	4,417.94	5,475.97	78	1,798.95	7,237.91	7,882.33
19	73.08	1,691.98	3,149.82	49	372.55	4,511.94	5,556.18	79	1,899.33	7,331.91	7,962.55
20	77.15	1,785.98	3,230.03	50	393.34	4,605.94	5,636.39	80	2,005.30	7,425.90	8,042.76
21	81.46	1,879.98	3,310.24	51	415.29	4,699.94	5,716.61	81	2,117.19	7,519.90	8,122.97
22	86.00	1,973.97	3,390.45	52	438.46	4,793.94	5,796.82	82	2,235.32	7,613.90	8,203.18
23	90.80	2,067.97	3,470.67	53	462.92	4,887.94	5,877.03	83	2,360.05	7,707.90	8,283.39
24	95.87	2,161.97	3,550.88	54	488.75	4,981.94	5,957.24	84	2,491.73	7,801.90	8,363.61
25	101.22	2,255.97	3,631.09	55	516.03	5,075.93	6,037.45	85	2,630.76	7,895.90	8,443.82
26	106.87	2,349.97	3,711.30	56	544.82	5,169.93	6,117.67	86	2,777.55	7,989.90	8,524.03
27	112.83	2,443.97	3,791.52	57	575.22	5,263.93	6,197.88	87	2,932.53	8,083.90	8,604.24
28	119.12	2,537.97	3,871.73	58	607.31	5,357.93	6,278.09	88	3,096.15	8,177.89	8,684.45
29	125.77	2,631.97	3,951.94	59	641.20	5,451.93	6,358.30				
30	132.79	2,725.96	4,032.15	60	676.98	5,545.93	6,438.52				

Table 1 (continues)

Initial Catalog of Tunings : C-34

Scale Deg.	HZ	Cts	TU	Scale Deg.	HZ	Cts	TU	Scale Deg.	HZ	Cts	TU
1	27.50	0.00	1,706.00	31	133.64	2,737.02	4,041.59	61	649.44	5,474.05	6,377.18
2	28.99	91.23	1,783.85	32	140.87	2,828.26	4,119.44	62	684.59	5,565.28	6,455.03
3	30.56	182.47	1,861.71	33	148.49	2,919.49	4,197.29	63	721.63	5,656.52	6,532.88
4	32.21	273.70	1,939.56	34	156.53	3,010.73	4,275.15	64	760.68	5,747.75	6,610.74
5	33.95	364.94	2,017.41	35	165.00	3,101.96	4,353.00	65	801.84	5,838.98	6,688.59
6	35.79	456.17	2,095.26	36	173.93	3,193.19	4,430.85	66	845.23	5,930.22	6,766.44
7	37.73	547.40	2,173.12	37	183.34	3,284.43	4,508.71	67	890.97	6,021.45	6,844.29
8	39.77	638.64	2,250.97	38	193.26	3,375.66	4,586.56	68	939.18	6,112.69	6,922.15
9	41.92	729.87	2,328.82	39	203.72	3,466.90	4,664.41	69	990.00	6,203.92	7,000.00
10	44.19	821.11	2,406.68	40	214.74	3,558.13	4,742.26	70	1,043.57	6,295.15	7,077.85
11	46.58	912.34	2,484.53	41	226.36	3,649.36	4,820.12	71	1,100.04	6,386.39	7,155.71
12	49.10	1,003.58	2,562.38	42	238.61	3,740.60	4,897.97	72	1,159.57	6,477.62	7,233.56
13	51.76	1,094.81	2,640.24	43	251.52	3,831.83	4,975.82	73	1,222.31	6,568.86	7,311.41
14	54.56	1,186.04	2,718.09	44	265.13	3,923.07	5,053.68	74	1,288.45	6,660.09	7,389.26
15	57.51	1,277.28	2,795.94	45	279.48	4,014.30	5,131.53	75	1,358.18	6,751.32	7,467.12
16	60.62	1,368.51	2,873.79	46	294.60	4,105.54	5,209.38	76	1,431.67	6,842.56	7,544.97
17	63.90	1,459.75	2,951.65	47	310.55	4,196.77	5,287.24	77	1,509.14	6,933.79	7,622.82
18	67.36	1,550.98	3,029.50	48	327.35	4,288.00	5,365.09	78	1,590.80	7,025.03	7,700.68
19	71.01	1,642.21	3,107.35	49	345.06	4,379.24	5,442.94	79	1,676.88	7,116.26	7,778.53
20	74.85	1,733.45	3,185.21	50	363.74	4,470.47	5,520.79	80	1,767.62	7,207.50	7,856.38
21	78.90	1,824.68	3,263.06	51	383.42	4,561.71	5,598.65	81	1,863.27	7,298.73	7,934.24
22	83.17	1,915.92	3,340.91	52	404.17	4,652.94	5,676.50	82	1,964.10	7,389.96	8,012.09
23	87.67	2,007.15	3,418.76	53	426.04	4,744.17	5,754.35	83	2,070.38	7,481.20	8,089.94
24	92.41	2,098.38	3,496.62	54	449.09	4,835.41	5,832.21	84	2,182.41	7,572.43	8,167.79
25	97.41	2,189.62	3,574.47	55	473.39	4,926.64	5,910.06	85	2,300.51	7,663.67	8,245.65
26	102.68	2,280.85	3,652.32	56	499.01	5,017.88	5,987.91	86	2,424.99	7,754.90	8,323.50
27	108.24	2,372.09	3,730.18	57	526.01	5,109.11	6,065.76	87	2,556.22	7,846.13	8,401.35
28	114.10	2,463.32	3,808.03	58	554.47	5,200.34	6,143.62	88	2,694.54	7,937.37	8,479.21
29	120.27	2,554.56	3,885.88	59	584.48	5,291.58	6,221.47				
30	126.78	2,645.79	3,963.74	60	616.10	5,382.81	6,299.32				

Initial Catalog of Tunings : C-35

Scale Deg.	HZ	Cts	TU	Scale Deg.	HZ	Cts	TU	Scale Deg.	HZ	Cts	TU
1	27.50	0.00	1,706.00	31	127.74	2,658.82	3,974.86	61	593.34	5,317.65	6,243.71
2	28.94	88.63	1,781.63	32	134.45	2,747.45	4,050.49	62	624.51	5,406.27	6,319.34
3	30.46	177.25	1,857.26	33	141.51	2,836.08	4,126.11	63	657.31	5,494.90	6,394.97
4	32.07	265.88	1,932.89	34	148.94	2,924.71	4,201.74	64	691.84	5,583.53	6,470.60
5	33.75	354.51	2,008.51	35	156.77	3,013.33	4,277.37	65	728.18	5,672.16	6,546.23
6	35.52	443.14	2,084.14	36	165.00	3,101.96	4,353.00	66	766.43	5,760.78	6,621.86
7	37.39	531.76	2,159.77	37	173.67	3,190.59	4,428.63	67	806.68	5,849.41	6,697.49
8	39.35	620.39	2,235.40	38	182.79	3,279.21	4,504.26	68	849.06	5,938.04	6,773.11
9	41.42	709.02	2,311.03	39	192.39	3,367.84	4,579.89	69	893.65	6,026.67	6,848.74
10	43.59	797.65	2,386.66	40	202.50	3,456.47	4,655.51	70	940.59	6,115.29	6,924.37
11	45.88	886.27	2,462.29	41	213.13	3,545.10	4,731.14	71	990.00	6,203.92	7,000.00
12	48.29	974.90	2,537.91	42	224.33	3,633.72	4,806.77	72	1,042.00	6,292.55	7,075.63
13	50.83	1,063.53	2,613.54	43	236.11	3,722.35	4,882.40	73	1,096.73	6,381.17	7,151.26
14	53.50	1,152.16	2,689.17	44	248.51	3,810.98	4,958.03	74	1,154.34	6,469.80	7,226.89
15	56.31	1,240.78	2,764.80	45	261.57	3,899.61	5,033.66	75	1,214.97	6,558.43	7,302.51
16	59.27	1,329.41	2,840.43	46	275.30	3,988.23	5,109.29	76	1,278.79	6,647.06	7,378.14
17	62.38	1,418.04	2,916.06	47	289.76	4,076.86	5,184.91	77	1,345.96	6,735.68	7,453.77
18	65.66	1,506.67	2,991.69	48	304.99	4,165.49	5,260.54	78	1,416.66	6,824.31	7,529.40
19	69.11	1,595.29	3,067.31	49	321.00	4,254.12	5,336.17	79	1,491.07	6,912.94	7,605.03
20	72.74	1,683.92	3,142.94	50	337.87	4,342.74	5,411.80	80	1,569.39	7,001.57	7,680.66
21	76.56	1,772.55	3,218.57	51	355.61	4,431.37	5,487.43	81	1,651.83	7,090.19	7,756.29
22	80.58	1,861.18	3,294.20	52	374.29	4,520.00	5,563.06	82	1,738.59	7,178.82	7,831.91
23	84.81	1,949.80	3,369.83	53	393.95	4,608.63	5,638.69	83	1,829.91	7,267.45	7,907.54
24	89.27	2,038.43	3,445.46	54	414.64	4,697.25	5,714.31	84	1,926.03	7,356.08	7,983.17
25	93.96	2,127.06	3,521.09	55	436.42	4,785.88	5,789.94	85	2,027.20	7,444.70	8,058.80
26	98.89	2,215.69	3,596.71	56	459.35	4,874.51	5,865.57	86	2,133.68	7,533.33	8,134.43
27	104.08	2,304.31	3,672.34	57	483.48	4,963.14	5,941.20	87	2,245.75	7,621.96	8,210.06
28	109.55	2,392.94	3,747.97	58	508.87	5,051.76	6,016.83	88	2,363.71	7,710.59	8,285.69
29	115.31	2,481.57	3,823.60	59	535.60	5,140.39	6,092.46				
30	121.36	2,570.20	3,899.23	60	563.73	5,229.02	6,168.09				

174

Table 1 (continues)

Initial Catalog of Tunings : C-36

Scale Deg.	HZ	Cts	TU	Scale Deg.	HZ	Cts	TU	Scale Deg.	HZ	Cts	TU
1	27.50	0.00	1,706.00	31	122.40	2,584.97	3,911.83	61	544.82	5,169.93	6,117.67
2	28.90	86.17	1,779.53	32	128.65	2,671.13	3,985.36	62	572.62	5,256.10	6,191.19
3	30.38	172.33	1,853.06	33	135.21	2,757.30	4,058.89	63	601.84	5,342.26	6,264.72
4	31.93	258.50	1,926.58	34	142.11	2,843.46	4,132.42	64	632.55	5,428.43	6,338.25
5	33.56	344.66	2,000.11	35	149.37	2,929.63	4,205.94	65	664.83	5,514.60	6,411.78
6	35.27	430.83	2,073.64	36	156.99	3,015.79	4,279.47	66	698.76	5,600.76	6,485.31
7	37.07	516.99	2,147.17	37	165.00	3,101.96	4,353.00	67	734.42	5,686.93	6,558.83
8	38.96	603.16	2,220.69	38	173.42	3,188.13	4,426.53	68	771.90	5,773.09	6,632.36
9	40.95	689.32	2,294.22	39	182.27	3,274.29	4,500.06	69	811.29	5,859.26	6,705.89
10	43.04	775.49	2,367.75	40	191.57	3,360.46	4,573.58	70	852.69	5,945.42	6,779.42
11	45.24	861.66	2,441.28	41	201.35	3,446.62	4,647.11	71	896.20	6,031.59	6,852.94
12	47.54	947.82	2,514.81	42	211.62	3,532.79	4,720.64	72	941.93	6,117.75	6,926.47
13	49.97	1,033.99	2,588.33	43	222.42	3,618.95	4,794.17	73	990.00	6,203.92	7,000.00
14	52.52	1,120.15	2,661.86	44	233.77	3,705.12	4,867.69	74	1,040.52	6,290.09	7,073.53
15	55.20	1,206.32	2,735.39	45	245.70	3,791.28	4,941.22	75	1,093.62	6,376.25	7,147.06
16	58.02	1,292.48	2,808.92	46	258.24	3,877.45	5,014.75	76	1,149.43	6,462.42	7,220.58
17	60.98	1,378.65	2,882.44	47	271.42	3,963.62	5,088.28	77	1,208.08	6,548.58	7,294.11
18	64.09	1,464.81	2,955.97	48	285.27	4,049.78	5,161.81	78	1,269.73	6,634.75	7,367.64
19	67.36	1,550.98	3,029.50	49	299.82	4,135.95	5,235.33	79	1,334.53	6,720.91	7,441.17
20	70.80	1,637.15	3,103.03	50	315.13	4,222.11	5,308.86	80	1,402.63	6,807.08	7,514.69
21	74.41	1,723.31	3,176.56	51	331.21	4,308.28	5,382.39	81	1,474.20	6,893.24	7,588.22
22	78.21	1,809.48	3,250.08	52	348.11	4,394.44	5,455.92	82	1,549.43	6,979.41	7,661.75
23	82.20	1,895.64	3,323.61	53	365.87	4,480.61	5,529.44	83	1,628.50	7,065.58	7,735.28
24	86.39	1,981.81	3,397.14	54	384.54	4,566.77	5,602.97	84	1,711.61	7,151.74	7,808.81
25	90.80	2,067.97	3,470.67	55	404.17	4,652.94	5,676.50	85	1,798.95	7,237.91	7,882.33
26	95.44	2,154.14	3,544.19	56	424.79	4,739.11	5,750.03	86	1,890.75	7,324.07	7,955.86
27	100.31	2,240.30	3,617.72	57	446.47	4,825.27	5,823.56	87	1,987.24	7,410.24	8,029.39
28	105.43	2,326.47	3,691.25	58	469.25	4,911.44	5,897.08	88	2,088.65	7,496.40	8,102.92
29	110.81	2,412.64	3,764.78	59	493.20	4,997.60	5,970.61				
30	116.46	2,498.80	3,838.31	60	518.37	5,083.77	6,044.14				

Initial Catalog of Tunings : C-37

Scale Deg.	HZ	Cts	TU	Scale Deg.	HZ	Cts	TU	Scale Deg.	HZ	Cts	TU
1	27.50	0.00	1,706.00	31	117.56	2,515.10	3,852.22	61	502.57	5,030.21	5,998.43
2	28.86	83.84	1,777.54	32	123.39	2,598.94	3,923.76	62	527.51	5,114.04	6,069.97
3	30.30	167.67	1,849.08	33	129.52	2,682.78	3,995.30	63	553.68	5,197.88	6,141.51
4	31.80	251.51	1,920.62	34	135.94	2,766.61	4,066.84	64	581.16	5,281.72	6,213.05
5	33.38	335.35	1,992.16	35	142.69	2,850.45	4,138.38	65	609.99	5,365.55	6,284.59
6	35.03	419.18	2,063.70	36	149.77	2,934.29	4,209.92	66	640.26	5,449.39	6,356.14
7	36.77	503.02	2,135.24	37	157.20	3,018.12	4,281.46	67	672.03	5,533.23	6,427.68
8	38.60	586.86	2,206.78	38	165.00	3,101.96	4,353.00	68	705.37	5,617.06	6,499.22
9	40.51	670.69	2,278.32	39	173.19	3,185.80	4,424.54	69	740.37	5,700.90	6,570.76
10	42.52	754.53	2,349.86	40	181.78	3,269.63	4,496.08	70	777.10	5,784.74	6,642.30
11	44.63	838.37	2,421.41	41	190.80	3,353.47	4,567.62	71	815.66	5,868.57	6,713.84
12	46.85	922.20	2,492.95	42	200.27	3,437.31	4,639.16	72	856.13	5,952.41	6,785.38
13	49.17	1,006.04	2,564.49	43	210.20	3,521.14	4,710.70	73	898.61	6,036.25	6,856.92
14	51.61	1,089.88	2,636.03	44	220.63	3,604.98	4,782.24	74	943.20	6,120.08	6,928.46
15	54.17	1,173.71	2,707.57	45	231.58	3,688.82	4,853.78	75	990.00	6,203.92	7,000.00
16	56.86	1,257.55	2,779.11	46	243.07	3,772.65	4,925.32	76	1,039.12	6,287.76	7,071.54
17	59.68	1,341.39	2,850.65	47	255.13	3,856.49	4,996.86	77	1,090.68	6,371.59	7,143.08
18	62.64	1,425.22	2,922.19	48	267.79	3,940.33	5,068.41	78	1,144.80	6,455.43	7,214.62
19	65.75	1,509.06	2,993.73	49	281.08	4,024.16	5,139.95	79	1,201.60	6,539.27	7,286.16
20	69.01	1,592.90	3,065.27	50	295.02	4,108.00	5,211.49	80	1,261.22	6,623.10	7,357.70
21	72.44	1,676.74	3,136.81	51	309.66	4,191.84	5,283.03	81	1,323.80	6,706.94	7,429.24
22	76.03	1,760.57	3,208.35	52	325.03	4,275.67	5,354.57	82	1,389.48	6,790.78	7,500.78
23	79.80	1,844.41	3,279.89	53	341.15	4,359.51	5,426.11	83	1,458.43	6,874.61	7,572.32
24	83.76	1,928.25	3,351.43	54	358.08	4,443.35	5,497.65	84	1,530.79	6,958.45	7,643.86
25	87.92	2,012.08	3,422.97	55	375.85	4,527.18	5,569.19	85	1,606.74	7,042.29	7,715.41
26	92.28	2,095.92	3,494.51	56	394.50	4,611.02	5,640.73	86	1,686.47	7,126.12	7,786.95
27	96.86	2,179.76	3,566.05	57	414.07	4,694.86	5,712.27	87	1,770.14	7,209.96	7,858.49
28	101.67	2,263.59	3,637.59	58	434.62	4,778.70	5,783.81	88	1,857.97	7,293.80	7,930.03
29	106.71	2,347.43	3,709.14	59	456.18	4,862.53	5,855.35				
30	112.00	2,431.27	3,780.68	60	478.82	4,946.37	5,926.89				

175

Table 1 (continues)

Initial Catalog of Tunings : C-38

Scale Deg.	HZ	Cts	TU	Scale Deg.	HZ	Cts	TU	Scale Deg.	HZ	Cts	TU
1	27.50	0.00	1,706.00	31	113.15	2,448.92	3,795.74	61	465.58	4,897.83	5,885.47
2	28.83	81.63	1,775.66	32	118.62	2,530.55	3,865.39	62	488.06	4,979.46	5,955.13
3	30.22	163.26	1,845.32	33	124.34	2,612.18	3,935.05	63	511.62	5,061.09	6,024.79
4	31.68	244.89	1,914.97	34	130.35	2,693.81	4,004.71	64	536.32	5,142.72	6,094.45
5	33.21	326.52	1,984.63	35	136.64	2,775.44	4,074.37	65	562.22	5,224.35	6,164.11
6	34.81	408.15	2,054.29	36	143.24	2,857.07	4,144.03	66	589.36	5,305.98	6,233.76
7	36.49	489.78	2,123.95	37	150.15	2,938.70	4,213.68	67	617.82	5,387.61	6,303.42
8	38.25	571.41	2,193.61	38	157.40	3,020.33	4,283.34	68	647.64	5,469.25	6,373.08
9	40.10	653.04	2,263.26	39	165.00	3,101.96	4,353.00	69	678.91	5,550.88	6,442.74
10	42.04	734.67	2,332.92	40	172.97	3,183.59	4,422.66	70	711.69	5,632.51	6,512.39
11	44.07	816.31	2,402.58	41	181.32	3,265.22	4,492.32	71	746.05	5,714.14	6,582.05
12	46.19	897.94	2,472.24	42	190.07	3,346.85	4,561.97	72	782.07	5,795.77	6,651.71
13	48.42	979.57	2,541.89	43	199.25	3,428.48	4,631.63	73	819.83	5,877.40	6,721.37
14	50.76	1,061.20	2,611.55	44	208.87	3,510.11	4,701.29	74	859.41	5,959.03	6,791.03
15	53.21	1,142.83	2,681.21	45	218.95	3,591.74	4,770.95	75	900.91	6,040.66	6,860.68
16	55.78	1,224.46	2,750.87	46	229.52	3,673.37	4,840.61	76	944.40	6,122.29	6,930.34
17	58.48	1,306.09	2,820.53	47	240.61	3,755.00	4,910.26	77	990.00	6,203.92	7,000.00
18	61.30	1,387.72	2,890.18	48	252.22	3,836.63	4,979.92	78	1,037.80	6,285.55	7,069.66
19	64.26	1,469.35	2,959.84	49	264.40	3,918.27	5,049.58	79	1,087.90	6,367.18	7,139.32
20	67.36	1,550.98	3,029.50	50	277.16	3,999.90	5,119.24	80	1,140.43	6,448.81	7,208.97
21	70.61	1,632.61	3,099.16	51	290.55	4,081.53	5,188.89	81	1,195.49	6,530.44	7,278.63
22	74.02	1,714.24	3,168.82	52	304.57	4,163.16	5,258.55	82	1,253.21	6,612.07	7,348.29
23	77.60	1,795.87	3,238.47	53	319.28	4,244.79	5,328.21	83	1,313.72	6,693.70	7,417.95
24	81.34	1,877.50	3,308.13	54	334.69	4,326.42	5,397.87	84	1,377.14	6,775.33	7,487.61
25	85.27	1,959.13	3,377.79	55	350.85	4,408.05	5,467.53	85	1,443.63	6,856.96	7,557.26
26	89.39	2,040.76	3,447.45	56	367.79	4,489.68	5,537.18	86	1,513.33	6,938.59	7,626.92
27	93.70	2,122.39	3,517.11	57	385.55	4,571.31	5,606.84	87	1,586.40	7,020.23	7,696.58
28	98.23	2,204.02	3,586.76	58	404.17	4,652.94	5,676.50	88	1,662.99	7,101.86	7,766.24
29	102.97	2,285.65	3,656.42	59	423.68	4,734.57	5,746.16				
30	107.94	2,367.29	3,726.08	60	444.13	4,816.20	5,815.82				

Initial Catalog of Tunings : C-39

Scale Deg.	HZ	Cts	TU	Scale Deg.	HZ	Cts	TU	Scale Deg.	HZ	Cts	TU
1	27.50	0.00	1,706.00	31	109.12	2,386.12	3,742.15	61	433.00	4,772.25	5,778.31
2	28.79	79.54	1,773.87	32	114.25	2,465.66	3,810.03	62	453.36	4,851.78	5,846.18
3	30.15	159.07	1,841.74	33	119.62	2,545.20	3,877.90	63	474.67	4,931.32	5,914.05
4	31.56	238.61	1,909.62	34	125.25	2,624.74	3,945.77	64	496.99	5,010.86	5,981.92
5	33.05	318.15	1,977.49	35	131.14	2,704.27	4,013.64	65	520.35	5,090.40	6,049.79
6	34.60	397.69	2,045.36	36	137.30	2,783.81	4,081.51	66	544.82	5,169.93	6,117.67
7	36.23	477.22	2,113.23	37	143.76	2,863.35	4,149.38	67	570.43	5,249.47	6,185.54
8	37.93	556.76	2,181.10	38	150.51	2,942.89	4,217.26	68	597.25	5,329.01	6,253.41
9	39.71	636.30	2,248.97	39	157.59	3,022.42	4,285.13	69	625.33	5,408.55	6,321.28
10	41.58	715.84	2,316.85	40	165.00	3,101.96	4,353.00	70	654.73	5,488.08	6,389.15
11	43.54	795.37	2,384.72	41	172.76	3,181.50	4,420.87	71	685.51	5,567.62	6,457.03
12	45.58	874.91	2,452.59	42	180.88	3,261.03	4,488.74	72	717.74	5,647.16	6,524.90
13	47.73	954.45	2,520.46	43	189.38	3,340.57	4,556.62	73	751.48	5,726.70	6,592.77
14	49.97	1,033.99	2,588.33	44	198.29	3,420.11	4,624.49	74	786.81	5,806.23	6,660.64
15	52.32	1,113.52	2,656.21	45	207.61	3,499.65	4,692.36	75	823.81	5,885.77	6,728.51
16	54.78	1,193.06	2,724.08	46	217.37	3,579.18	4,760.23	76	862.54	5,965.31	6,796.38
17	57.36	1,272.60	2,791.95	47	227.59	3,658.72	4,828.10	77	903.09	6,044.85	6,864.26
18	60.05	1,352.14	2,859.82	48	238.29	3,738.26	4,895.97	78	945.55	6,124.38	6,932.13
19	62.88	1,431.67	2,927.69	49	249.49	3,817.80	4,963.85	79	990.00	6,203.92	7,000.00
20	65.83	1,511.21	2,995.56	50	261.22	3,897.33	5,031.72	80	1,036.54	6,283.46	7,067.87
21	68.93	1,590.75	3,063.44	51	273.50	3,976.87	5,099.59	81	1,085.28	6,362.99	7,135.74
22	72.17	1,670.29	3,131.31	52	286.36	4,056.41	5,167.46	82	1,136.30	6,442.53	7,203.62
23	75.56	1,749.82	3,199.18	53	299.82	4,135.95	5,235.33	83	1,189.72	6,522.07	7,271.49
24	79.11	1,829.36	3,267.05	54	313.92	4,215.48	5,303.21	84	1,245.66	6,601.61	7,339.36
25	82.83	1,908.90	3,334.92	55	328.68	4,295.02	5,371.08	85	1,304.22	6,681.14	7,407.23
26	86.73	1,988.44	3,402.79	56	344.13	4,374.56	5,438.95	86	1,365.54	6,760.68	7,475.10
27	90.80	2,067.97	3,470.67	57	360.31	4,454.10	5,506.82	87	1,429.74	6,840.22	7,542.97
28	95.07	2,147.51	3,538.54	58	377.25	4,533.63	5,574.69	88	1,496.95	6,919.76	7,610.85
29	99.54	2,227.05	3,606.41	59	394.99	4,613.17	5,642.56				
30	104.22	2,306.59	3,674.28	60	413.56	4,692.71	5,710.44				

Table 1 (continues)

Initial Catalog of Tunings: C-40

Scale Deg.	HZ	Cts	TU	Scale Deg.	HZ	Cts	TU	Scale Deg.	HZ	Cts	TU
1	27.50	0.00	1,706.00	31	105.43	2,326.47	3,691.25	61	404.17	4,652.94	5,676.50
2	28.76	77.55	1,772.18	32	110.26	2,404.02	3,757.43	62	422.68	4,730.49	5,742.68
3	30.08	155.10	1,838.35	33	115.31	2,481.57	3,823.60	63	442.05	4,808.04	5,808.85
4	31.46	232.65	1,904.53	34	120.59	2,559.12	3,889.78	64	462.30	4,885.59	5,875.03
5	32.90	310.20	1,970.70	35	126.11	2,636.67	3,955.95	65	483.48	4,963.14	5,941.20
6	34.40	387.75	2,036.88	36	131.89	2,714.22	4,022.13	66	505.62	5,040.69	6,007.38
7	35.98	465.29	2,103.05	37	137.93	2,791.76	4,088.30	67	528.79	5,118.23	6,073.55
8	37.63	542.84	2,169.23	38	144.25	2,869.31	4,154.48	68	553.01	5,195.78	6,139.73
9	39.35	620.39	2,235.40	39	150.86	2,946.86	4,220.65	69	578.35	5,273.33	6,205.90
10	41.15	697.94	2,301.58	40	157.77	3,024.41	4,286.83	70	604.84	5,350.88	6,272.08
11	43.04	775.49	2,367.75	41	165.00	3,101.96	4,353.00	71	632.55	5,428.43	6,338.25
12	45.01	853.04	2,433.93	42	172.56	3,179.51	4,419.18	72	661.53	5,505.98	6,404.43
13	47.07	930.59	2,500.10	43	180.46	3,257.06	4,485.35	73	691.84	5,583.53	6,470.60
14	49.23	1,008.14	2,566.28	44	188.73	3,334.61	4,551.53	74	723.53	5,661.08	6,536.78
15	51.49	1,085.69	2,632.45	45	197.38	3,412.16	4,617.70	75	756.68	5,738.63	6,602.95
16	53.84	1,163.24	2,698.63	46	206.42	3,489.71	4,683.88	76	791.35	5,816.18	6,669.13
17	56.31	1,240.78	2,764.80	47	215.88	3,567.25	4,750.05	77	827.60	5,893.72	6,735.30
18	58.89	1,318.33	2,830.98	48	225.77	3,644.80	4,816.23	78	865.51	5,971.27	6,801.48
19	61.59	1,395.88	2,897.15	49	236.11	3,722.35	4,882.40	79	905.16	6,048.82	6,867.65
20	64.41	1,473.43	2,963.33	50	246.93	3,799.90	4,948.58	80	946.63	6,126.37	6,933.83
21	67.36	1,550.98	3,029.50	51	258.24	3,877.45	5,014.75	81	990.00	6,203.92	7,000.00
22	70.45	1,628.53	3,095.68	52	270.07	3,955.00	5,080.93	82	1,035.35	6,281.47	7,066.18
23	73.67	1,706.08	3,161.85	53	282.44	4,032.55	5,147.10	83	1,082.79	6,359.02	7,132.35
24	77.05	1,783.63	3,228.03	54	295.38	4,110.10	5,213.28	84	1,132.39	6,436.57	7,198.53
25	80.58	1,861.18	3,294.20	55	308.91	4,187.65	5,279.45	85	1,184.27	6,514.12	7,264.70
26	84.27	1,938.73	3,360.38	56	323.07	4,265.20	5,345.63	86	1,238.52	6,591.67	7,330.88
27	88.13	2,016.27	3,426.55	57	337.87	4,342.74	5,411.80	87	1,295.26	6,669.21	7,397.05
28	92.17	2,093.82	3,492.73	58	353.34	4,420.29	5,477.98	88	1,354.60	6,746.76	7,463.23
29	96.39	2,171.37	3,558.90	59	369.53	4,497.84	5,544.15				
30	100.81	2,248.92	3,625.08	60	386.46	4,575.39	5,610.33				

Initial Catalog of Tunings: D-12

Scale Deg.	HZ	Cts	TU	Scale Deg.	HZ	Cts	TU	Scale Deg.	HZ	Cts	TU
1	27.50	0.00	1,706.00	13	192.50	3,368.83	4,580.73	25	1,347.50	6,737.66	7,455.46
2	32.34	280.74	1,945.56	14	226.39	3,649.57	4,820.29	26	1,584.72	7,018.40	7,695.02
3	38.03	561.47	2,185.12	15	266.24	3,930.30	5,059.85	27	1,863.71	7,299.13	7,934.58
4	44.73	842.21	2,424.68	16	313.12	4,211.04	5,299.41	28	2,191.81	7,579.87	8,174.14
5	52.61	1,122.94	2,664.24	17	368.24	4,491.77	5,538.97	29	2,577.67	7,860.60	8,413.70
6	61.87	1,403.68	2,903.80	18	433.07	4,772.51	5,778.53	30	3,031.47	8,141.34	8,653.26
7	72.76	1,684.42	3,143.37	19	509.31	5,053.25	6,018.09	31	3,565.15	8,422.08	8,892.82
8	85.57	1,965.15	3,382.93	20	598.97	5,333.98	6,257.66	32	4,192.79	8,702.81	9,132.39
9	100.63	2,245.89	3,622.49	21	704.42	5,614.72	6,497.22	33			
10	118.35	2,526.62	3,862.05	22	828.43	5,895.45	6,736.78				
11	139.18	2,807.36	4,101.61	23	974.27	6,176.19	6,976.34				
12	163.68	3,088.09	4,341.17	24	1,145.79	6,456.92	7,215.90				

Initial Catalog of Tunings: D-13

Scale Deg.	HZ	Cts	TU	Scale Deg.	HZ	Cts	TU	Scale Deg.	HZ	Cts	TU
1	27.50	0.00	1,706.00	13	165.74	3,109.69	4,359.60	25	998.88	6,219.38	7,013.19
2	31.94	259.14	1,927.13	14	192.50	3,368.83	4,580.73	26	1,160.17	6,478.52	7,234.33
3	37.10	518.28	2,148.27	15	223.58	3,627.97	4,801.86	27	1,347.50	6,737.66	7,455.46
4	43.09	777.42	2,369.40	16	259.68	3,887.11	5,023.00	28	1,565.08	6,996.80	7,676.59
5	50.05	1,036.56	2,590.53	17	301.62	4,146.25	5,244.13	29	1,817.79	7,255.94	7,897.73
6	58.13	1,295.70	2,811.67	18	350.32	4,405.39	5,465.26	30	2,111.31	7,515.08	8,118.86
7	67.51	1,554.84	3,032.80	19	406.88	4,664.53	5,686.40	31	2,452.22	7,774.22	8,339.99
8	78.41	1,813.99	3,253.93	20	472.58	4,923.67	5,907.53	32	2,848.17	8,033.36	8,561.13
9	91.07	2,073.13	3,475.06	21	548.89	5,182.82	6,128.66	33	3,308.06	8,292.50	8,782.26
10	105.78	2,332.27	3,696.20	22	637.52	5,441.96	6,349.79	34	3,842.21	8,551.65	9,003.39
11	122.86	2,591.41	3,917.33	23	740.45	5,701.10	6,570.93				
12	142.70	2,850.55	4,138.46	24	860.02	5,960.24	6,792.06				

177

Table 1 (continues)

Initial Catalog of Tunings : D-14

Scale Deg.	HZ	Cts	TU	Scale Deg.	HZ	Cts	TU	Scale Deg.	HZ	Cts	TU
1	27.50	0.00	1,706.00	14	167.52	3,128.20	4,375.39	27	1,020.47	6,256.40	7,044.78
2	31.60	240.63	1,911.34	15	192.50	3,368.83	4,580.73	28	1,172.64	6,497.03	7,250.12
3	36.31	481.26	2,116.68	16	221.20	3,609.46	4,786.07	29	1,347.50	6,737.66	7,455.46
4	41.73	721.89	2,322.01	17	254.19	3,850.09	4,991.41	30	1,548.43	6,978.29	7,660.80
5	47.95	962.52	2,527.35	18	292.09	4,090.72	5,196.74	31	1,779.33	7,218.92	7,866.14
6	55.10	1,203.15	2,732.69	19	335.65	4,331.35	5,402.08	32	2,044.66	7,459.55	8,071.47
7	63.32	1,443.78	2,938.03	20	385.70	4,571.98	5,607.42	33	2,349.55	7,700.18	8,276.81
8	72.76	1,684.42	3,143.36	21	443.22	4,812.61	5,812.76	34	2,699.91	7,940.81	8,482.15
9	83.61	1,925.05	3,348.70	22	509.31	5,053.25	6,018.10	35	3,102.51	8,181.44	8,687.49
10	96.07	2,165.68	3,554.04	23	585.25	5,293.88	6,223.43	36	3,565.15	8,422.08	8,892.83
11	110.40	2,406.31	3,759.38	24	672.52	5,534.51	6,428.77	37	4,096.77	8,662.71	9,098.16
12	126.86	2,646.94	3,964.72	25	772.81	5,775.14	6,634.11				
13	145.78	2,887.57	4,170.05	26	888.05	6,015.77	6,839.45				

Initial Catalog of Tunings : D-15

Scale Deg.	HZ	Cts	TU	Scale Deg.	HZ	Cts	TU	Scale Deg.	HZ	Cts	TU
1	27.50	0.00	1,706.00	15	169.08	3,144.24	4,389.08	29	1,039.56	6,288.48	7,072.16
2	31.31	224.59	1,897.65	16	192.50	3,368.83	4,580.73	30	1,183.56	6,513.07	7,263.81
3	35.65	449.18	2,089.30	17	219.16	3,593.42	4,772.38	31	1,347.50	6,737.66	7,455.46
4	40.58	673.77	2,280.95	18	249.52	3,818.01	4,964.03	32	1,534.15	6,962.25	7,647.11
5	46.21	898.35	2,472.59	19	284.09	4,042.60	5,155.68	33	1,746.66	7,186.84	7,838.76
6	52.61	1,122.94	2,664.24	20	323.44	4,267.18	5,347.32	34	1,988.60	7,411.43	8,030.41
7	59.89	1,347.53	2,855.89	21	368.24	4,491.77	5,538.97	35	2,264.06	7,636.01	8,222.05
8	68.19	1,572.12	3,047.54	22	419.25	4,716.36	5,730.62	36	2,577.67	7,860.60	8,413.70
9	77.63	1,796.71	3,239.19	23	477.32	4,940.95	5,922.27	37	2,934.73	8,085.19	8,605.35
10	88.39	2,021.30	3,430.84	24	543.44	5,165.54	6,113.92	38	3,341.24	8,309.78	8,797.00
11	100.63	2,245.89	3,622.49	25	618.71	5,390.13	6,305.57	39	3,804.06	8,534.37	8,988.65
12	114.57	2,470.48	3,814.14	26	704.42	5,614.72	6,497.22	40	4,330.99	8,758.96	9,180.30
13	130.44	2,695.06	4,005.78	27	801.99	5,839.31	6,688.87				
14	148.51	2,919.65	4,197.43	28	913.08	6,063.89	6,880.51				

Initial Catalog of Tunings : D-16

Scale Deg.	HZ	Cts	TU	Scale Deg.	HZ	Cts	TU	Scale Deg.	HZ	Cts	TU
1	27.50	0.00	1,706.00	16	170.46	3,158.28	4,401.05	31	1,056.55	6,316.55	7,096.12
2	31.06	210.55	1,885.67	17	192.50	3,368.83	4,580.73	32	1,193.19	6,527.11	7,275.79
3	35.07	421.10	2,065.34	18	217.39	3,579.38	4,760.40	33	1,347.50	6,737.66	7,455.46
4	39.61	631.66	2,245.01	19	245.51	3,789.93	4,940.07	34	1,521.76	6,948.21	7,635.13
5	44.73	842.21	2,424.68	20	277.26	4,000.49	5,119.74	35	1,718.57	7,158.76	7,814.80
6	50.52	1,052.76	2,604.35	21	313.12	4,211.04	5,299.41	36	1,940.82	7,369.32	7,994.47
7	57.05	1,263.31	2,784.02	22	353.61	4,421.59	5,479.08	37	2,191.81	7,579.87	8,174.14
8	64.43	1,473.86	2,963.69	23	399.34	4,632.14	5,658.75	38	2,475.27	7,790.42	8,353.81
9	72.76	1,684.42	3,143.36	24	450.98	4,842.69	5,838.42	39	2,795.38	8,000.97	8,533.48
10	82.17	1,894.97	3,323.04	25	509.31	5,053.25	6,018.09	40	3,156.89	8,211.52	8,713.15
11	92.79	2,105.52	3,502.71	26	575.17	5,263.80	6,197.77	41	3,565.15	8,422.08	8,892.82
12	104.79	2,316.07	3,682.38	27	649.56	5,474.35	6,377.44	42	4,026.21	8,632.63	9,072.50
13	118.35	2,526.62	3,862.05	28	733.56	5,684.90	6,557.11				
14	133.65	2,737.17	4,041.72	29	828.43	5,895.45	6,736.78				
15	150.94	2,947.73	4,221.39	30	935.56	6,106.00	6,916.45				

178

Table 1 (continues)

Initial Catalog of Tunings : D-17

Scale Deg.	HZ	Cts	TU	Scale Deg.	HZ	Cts	TU	Scale Deg.	HZ	Cts	TU
1	27.50	0.00	1,706.00	17	171.68	3,170.66	4,411.63	33	1,071.78	6,341.33	7,117.26
2	30.84	198.17	1,875.10	18	192.50	3,368.83	4,580.73	34	1,201.76	6,539.49	7,286.36
3	34.57	396.33	2,044.20	19	215.85	3,567.00	4,749.83	35	1,347.50	6,737.66	7,455.46
4	38.77	594.50	2,213.31	20	242.02	3,765.16	4,918.93	36	1,510.92	6,935.83	7,624.56
5	43.47	792.67	2,382.41	21	271.37	3,963.33	5,088.04	37	1,694.15	7,133.99	7,793.66
6	48.74	990.83	2,551.51	22	304.28	4,161.50	5,257.14	38	1,899.61	7,332.16	7,962.77
7	54.65	1,189.00	2,720.61	23	341.18	4,359.66	5,426.24	39	2,129.98	7,530.33	8,131.87
8	61.28	1,387.17	2,889.71	24	382.56	4,557.83	5,595.34	40	2,388.29	7,728.49	8,300.97
9	68.71	1,585.33	3,058.81	25	428.96	4,756.00	5,764.44	41	2,677.93	7,926.66	8,470.07
10	77.04	1,783.50	3,227.92	26	480.98	4,954.16	5,933.54	42	3,002.69	8,124.83	8,639.17
11	86.39	1,981.66	3,397.02	27	539.31	5,152.33	6,102.65	43	3,366.84	8,322.99	8,808.27
12	96.86	2,179.83	3,566.12	28	604.71	5,350.49	6,271.75	44	3,775.14	8,521.16	8,977.38
13	108.61	2,378.00	3,735.22	29	678.05	5,548.66	6,440.85	45	4,232.97	8,719.32	9,146.48
14	121.78	2,576.16	3,904.32	30	760.27	5,746.83	6,609.95				
15	136.55	2,774.33	4,073.42	31	852.48	5,944.99	6,779.05				
16	153.11	2,972.50	4,242.53	32	955.86	6,143.16	6,948.15				

Initial Catalog of Tunings : D-18

Scale Deg.	HZ	Cts	TU	Scale Deg.	HZ	Cts	TU	Scale Deg.	HZ	Cts	TU
1	27.50	0.00	1,706.00	18	172.77	3,181.67	4,421.02	35	1,085.50	6,363.35	7,136.05
2	30.64	187.16	1,865.71	19	192.50	3,368.83	4,580.73	36	1,209.42	6,550.50	7,295.75
3	34.14	374.31	2,025.41	20	214.48	3,555.99	4,740.44	37	1,347.50	6,737.66	7,455.46
4	38.03	561.47	2,185.12	21	238.96	3,743.14	4,900.14	38	1,501.34	6,924.82	7,615.17
5	42.38	748.63	2,344.83	22	266.24	3,930.30	5,059.85	39	1,672.74	7,111.97	7,774.87
6	47.22	935.79	2,504.54	23	296.64	4,117.46	5,219.56	40	1,863.71	7,299.13	7,934.58
7	52.61	1,122.94	2,664.24	24	330.51	4,304.62	5,379.27	41	2,076.48	7,486.29	8,094.29
8	58.61	1,310.10	2,823.95	25	368.24	4,491.77	5,538.97	42	2,313.55	7,673.45	8,254.00
9	65.30	1,497.26	2,983.66	26	410.28	4,678.93	5,698.68	43	2,577.67	7,860.60	8,413.70
10	72.76	1,684.42	3,143.37	27	457.12	4,866.09	5,858.39	44	2,871.96	8,047.76	8,573.41
11	81.06	1,871.57	3,303.07	28	509.31	5,053.25	6,018.10	45	3,199.84	8,234.92	8,733.12
12	90.32	2,058.73	3,462.78	29	567.45	5,240.40	6,177.80	46	3,565.15	8,422.08	8,892.83
13	100.63	2,245.89	3,622.49	30	632.24	5,427.56	6,337.51	47	3,972.17	8,609.23	9,052.53
14	112.12	2,433.04	3,782.19	31	704.42	5,614.72	6,497.22	48	4,425.66	8,796.39	9,212.24
15	124.92	2,620.20	3,941.90	32	784.84	5,801.87	6,656.92				
16	139.18	2,807.36	4,101.61	33	874.44	5,989.03	6,816.63				
17	155.07	2,994.52	4,261.32	34	974.27	6,176.19	6,976.34				

Initial Catalog of Tunings : D-19

Scale Deg.	HZ	Cts	TU	Scale Deg.	HZ	Cts	TU	Scale Deg.	HZ	Cts	TU
1	27.50	0.00	1,706.00	19	173.76	3,191.52	4,429.43	37	1,097.92	6,383.05	7,152.86
2	30.47	177.31	1,857.30	20	192.50	3,368.83	4,580.73	38	1,216.33	6,560.35	7,304.16
3	33.75	354.61	2,008.60	21	213.26	3,546.14	4,732.03	39	1,347.50	6,737.66	7,455.46
4	37.39	531.92	2,159.90	22	236.26	3,723.44	4,883.33	40	1,492.82	6,914.97	7,606.76
5	41.42	709.23	2,311.21	23	261.74	3,900.75	5,034.63	41	1,653.81	7,092.27	7,758.06
6	45.89	886.53	2,462.51	24	289.97	4,078.06	5,185.94	42	1,832.17	7,269.58	7,909.36
7	50.84	1,063.84	2,613.81	25	321.24	4,255.36	5,337.24	43	2,029.76	7,446.89	8,060.67
8	56.32	1,241.15	2,765.11	26	355.88	4,432.67	5,488.54	44	2,248.66	7,624.19	8,211.97
9	62.40	1,418.45	2,916.41	27	394.26	4,609.98	5,639.84	45	2,491.16	7,801.50	8,363.27
10	69.13	1,595.76	3,067.71	28	436.78	4,787.28	5,791.14	46	2,759.82	7,978.81	8,514.57
11	76.58	1,773.07	3,219.02	29	483.88	4,964.59	5,942.44	47	3,057.45	8,156.11	8,665.87
12	84.84	1,950.38	3,370.32	30	536.07	5,141.90	6,093.75	48	3,387.18	8,333.42	8,817.17
13	93.99	2,127.68	3,521.62	31	593.88	5,319.21	6,245.05	49	3,752.47	8,510.73	8,968.48
14	104.13	2,304.99	3,672.92	32	657.93	5,496.51	6,396.35	50	4,157.15	8,688.04	9,119.78
15	115.36	2,482.30	3,824.22	33	728.88	5,673.82	6,547.65				
16	127.80	2,659.60	3,975.52	34	807.49	5,851.13	6,698.95				
17	141.58	2,836.91	4,126.83	35	894.57	6,028.43	6,850.25				
18	156.85	3,014.22	4,278.13	36	991.04	6,205.74	7,001.56				

Table 1 (continues)

Initial Catalog of Tunings : D-20

Scale Deg.	HZ	Cts	TU	Scale Deg.	HZ	Cts	TU	Scale Deg.	HZ	Cts	TU
1	27.50	0.00	1,706.00	20	174.63	3,200.39	4,436.99	39	1,109.22	6,400.78	7,167.99
2	30.31	168.44	1,849.74	21	192.50	3,368.83	4,580.73	40	1,222.57	6,569.22	7,311.72
3	33.41	336.88	1,993.47	22	212.17	3,537.27	4,724.47	41	1,347.50	6,737.66	7,455.46
4	36.82	505.32	2,137.21	23	233.85	3,705.71	4,868.20	42	1,485.20	6,906.10	7,599.20
5	40.58	673.77	2,280.95	24	257.75	3,874.15	5,011.94	43	1,636.96	7,074.54	7,742.93
6	44.73	842.21	2,424.68	25	284.09	4,042.60	5,155.68	44	1,804.24	7,242.98	7,886.67
7	49.30	1,010.65	2,568.42	26	313.12	4,211.04	5,299.41	45	1,988.60	7,411.43	8,030.41
8	54.34	1,179.09	2,712.16	27	345.11	4,379.48	5,443.15	46	2,191.81	7,579.87	8,174.14
9	59.89	1,347.53	2,855.89	28	380.38	4,547.92	5,586.89	47	2,415.78	7,748.31	8,317.88
10	66.01	1,515.97	2,999.63	29	419.25	4,716.36	5,730.62	48	2,662.64	7,916.75	8,461.62
11	72.76	1,684.42	3,143.37	30	462.09	4,884.80	5,874.36	49	2,934.73	8,085.19	8,605.35
12	80.19	1,852.86	3,287.10	31	509.31	5,053.25	6,018.10	50	3,234.62	8,253.63	8,749.09
13	88.39	2,021.30	3,430.84	32	561.35	5,221.69	6,161.83	51	3,565.15	8,422.08	8,892.82
14	97.42	2,189.74	3,574.57	33	618.71	5,390.13	6,305.57	52	3,929.46	8,590.52	9,036.56
15	107.37	2,358.18	3,718.31	34	681.94	5,558.57	6,449.30	53	4,330.99	8,758.96	9,180.30
16	118.35	2,526.62	3,862.05	35	751.62	5,727.01	6,593.04				
17	130.44	2,695.06	4,005.78	36	828.43	5,895.45	6,736.78				
18	143.77	2,863.51	4,149.52	37	913.08	6,063.89	6,880.51				
19	158.46	3,031.95	4,293.26	38	1,006.38	6,232.34	7,024.25				

Initial Catalog of Tunings : D-21

Scale Deg.	HZ	Cts	TU	Scale Deg.	HZ	Cts	TU	Scale Deg.	HZ	Cts	TU
1	27.50	0.00	1,706.00	21	175.46	3,208.41	4,443.84	41	1,119.55	6,416.82	7,181.68
2	30.17	160.42	1,842.89	22	192.50	3,368.83	4,580.73	42	1,228.25	6,577.24	7,318.57
3	33.10	320.84	1,979.78	23	211.19	3,529.25	4,717.62	43	1,347.50	6,737.66	7,455.46
4	36.31	481.26	2,116.68	24	231.69	3,689.67	4,854.51	44	1,478.33	6,898.08	7,592.35
5	39.84	641.68	2,253.57	25	254.19	3,850.09	4,991.41	45	1,621.86	7,058.50	7,729.24
6	43.71	802.10	2,390.46	26	278.87	4,010.51	5,128.30	46	1,779.33	7,218.92	7,866.14
7	47.95	962.52	2,527.35	27	305.95	4,170.93	5,265.19	47	1,952.09	7,379.34	8,003.03
8	52.61	1,122.94	2,664.24	28	335.65	4,331.35	5,402.08	48	2,141.62	7,539.76	8,139.92
9	57.71	1,283.36	2,801.14	29	368.24	4,491.77	5,538.97	49	2,349.55	7,700.18	8,276.81
10	63.32	1,443.78	2,938.03	30	403.99	4,652.19	5,675.87	50	2,577.67	7,860.60	8,413.70
11	69.46	1,604.20	3,074.92	31	443.22	4,812.61	5,812.76	51	2,827.94	8,021.02	8,550.60
12	76.21	1,764.63	3,211.81	32	486.25	4,973.03	5,949.65	52	3,102.51	8,181.44	8,687.49
13	83.61	1,925.05	3,348.70	33	533.46	5,133.46	6,086.54	53	3,403.74	8,341.86	8,824.38
14	91.73	2,085.47	3,485.59	34	585.25	5,293.88	6,223.43	54	3,734.21	8,502.29	8,961.27
15	100.63	2,245.89	3,622.49	35	642.08	5,454.30	6,360.32	55	4,096.77	8,662.71	9,098.16
16	110.40	2,406.31	3,759.38	36	704.42	5,614.72	6,497.22	56	4,494.53	8,823.13	9,235.05
17	121.12	2,566.73	3,896.27	37	772.81	5,775.14	6,634.11				
18	132.88	2,727.15	4,033.16	38	847.84	5,935.56	6,771.00				
19	145.78	2,887.57	4,170.05	39	930.16	6,095.98	6,907.89				
20	159.94	3,047.99	4,306.95	40	1,020.47	6,256.40	7,044.78				

Initial Catalog of Tunings : D-22

Scale Deg.	HZ	Cts	TU	Scale Deg.	HZ	Cts	TU	Scale Deg.	HZ	Cts	TU
1	27.50	0.00	1,706.00	21	161.29	3,062.57	4,319.39	41	945.96	6,125.15	6,932.78
2	30.04	153.13	1,836.67	22	176.20	3,215.70	4,450.06	42	1,033.45	6,278.27	7,063.45
3	32.82	306.26	1,967.34	23	192.50	3,368.83	4,580.73	43	1,129.02	6,431.40	7,194.12
4	35.86	459.39	2,098.01	24	210.30	3,521.96	4,711.40	44	1,233.43	6,584.53	7,324.79
5	39.17	612.51	2,228.68	25	229.75	3,675.09	4,842.07	45	1,347.50	6,737.66	7,455.46
6	42.80	765.64	2,359.35	26	251.00	3,828.22	4,972.74	46	1,472.12	6,890.79	7,586.13
7	46.75	918.77	2,490.02	27	274.21	3,981.34	5,103.41	47	1,608.26	7,043.92	7,716.80
8	51.08	1,071.90	2,620.69	28	299.57	4,134.47	5,234.08	48	1,756.99	7,197.05	7,847.47
9	55.80	1,225.03	2,751.36	29	327.27	4,287.60	5,364.75	49	1,919.48	7,350.17	7,978.14
10	60.96	1,378.16	2,882.03	30	357.54	4,440.73	5,495.42	50	2,096.99	7,503.30	8,108.81
11	66.60	1,531.29	3,012.70	31	390.61	4,593.86	5,626.09	51	2,290.92	7,656.43	8,239.48
12	72.76	1,684.42	3,143.37	32	426.73	4,746.99	5,756.76	52	2,502.79	7,809.56	8,370.15
13	79.49	1,837.54	3,274.03	33	466.19	4,900.12	5,887.43	53	2,734.24	7,962.69	8,500.82
14	86.84	1,990.67	3,404.70	34	509.31	5,053.25	6,018.10	54	2,987.11	8,115.82	8,631.49
15	94.87	2,143.80	3,535.37	35	556.41	5,206.37	6,148.76	55	3,263.35	8,268.95	8,762.16
16	103.64	2,296.93	3,666.04	36	607.86	5,359.50	6,279.43	56	3,565.15	8,422.08	8,892.83
17	113.23	2,450.06	3,796.71	37	664.08	5,512.63	6,410.10	57	3,894.86	8,575.20	9,023.49
18	123.70	2,603.19	3,927.38	38	725.49	5,665.76	6,540.77	58	4,255.05	8,728.33	9,154.16
19	135.14	2,756.32	4,058.05	39	792.59	5,818.89	6,671.44				
20	147.64	2,909.44	4,188.72	40	865.89	5,972.02	6,802.11				

Table 1 (continues)

Initial Catalog of Tunings : D-23

Scale Deg.	HZ	Cts	TU	Scale Deg.	HZ	Cts	TU	Scale Deg.	HZ	Cts	TU
1	27.50	0.00	1,706.00	22	162.53	3,075.89	4,330.75	43	960.63	6,131.78	6,955.51
2	29.93	146.47	1,830.99	23	176.88	3,222.36	4,455.74	44	1,045.44	6,298.25	7,080.50
3	32.57	292.94	1,955.98	24	192.50	3,368.83	4,580.73	45	1,137.74	6,444.72	7,205.48
4	35.45	439.41	2,080.96	25	209.50	3,515.30	4,705.72	46	1,238.18	6,591.19	7,330.47
5	38.58	585.88	2,205.95	26	227.99	3,661.77	4,830.71	47	1,347.50	6,737.66	7,455.46
6	41.98	732.35	2,330.94	27	248.12	3,808.24	4,955.69	48	1,466.47	6,884.13	7,580.45
7	45.69	878.83	2,455.93	28	270.03	3,954.71	5,080.68	49	1,595.94	7,030.60	7,705.44
8	49.72	1,025.30	2,580.92	29	293.86	4,101.18	5,205.67	50	1,736.84	7,177.07	7,830.42
9	54.11	1,171.77	2,705.91	30	319.81	4,247.66	5,330.66	51	1,890.18	7,323.54	7,955.41
10	58.89	1,318.24	2,830.89	31	348.04	4,394.13	5,455.65	52	2,057.05	7,470.01	8,080.40
11	64.09	1,464.71	2,955.88	32	378.77	4,540.60	5,580.64	53	2,238.67	7,616.49	8,205.39
12	69.74	1,611.18	3,080.87	33	412.21	4,687.07	5,705.62	54	2,436.31	7,762.96	8,330.38
13	75.90	1,757.65	3,205.86	34	448.61	4,833.54	5,830.61	55	2,651.40	7,909.43	8,455.37
14	82.60	1,904.12	3,330.85	35	488.21	4,980.01	5,955.60	56	2,885.49	8,055.90	8,580.35
15	89.90	2,050.59	3,455.84	36	531.31	5,126.48	6,080.59	57	3,140.24	8,202.37	8,705.34
16	97.83	2,197.06	3,580.82	37	578.22	5,272.95	6,205.58	58	3,417.48	8,348.84	8,830.33
17	106.47	2,343.53	3,705.81	38	629.27	5,419.42	6,330.57	59	3,719.20	8,495.31	8,955.32
18	115.87	2,490.00	3,830.80	39	684.83	5,565.89	6,455.55	60	4,047.56	8,641.78	9,080.31
19	126.10	2,636.48	3,955.79	40	745.29	5,712.36	6,580.54	61	4,404.90	8,788.25	9,205.30
20	137.23	2,782.95	4,080.78	41	811.09	5,858.83	6,705.53				
21	149.35	2,929.42	4,205.77	42	882.70	6,005.31	6,830.52				

Initial Catalog of Tunings : D-24

Scale Deg.	HZ	Cts	TU	Scale Deg.	HZ	Cts	TU	Scale Deg.	HZ	Cts	TU
1	27.50	0.00	1,706.00	23	163.68	3,088.09	4,341.17	45	974.27	6,176.19	6,976.34
2	29.82	140.37	1,825.78	24	177.51	3,228.46	4,460.95	46	1,056.55	6,316.56	7,096.12
3	32.34	280.74	1,945.56	25	192.50	3,368.83	4,580.73	47	1,145.79	6,456.92	7,215.90
4	35.07	421.10	2,065.34	26	208.76	3,509.20	4,700.51	48	1,242.56	6,597.29	7,335.68
5	38.03	561.47	2,185.12	27	226.39	3,649.57	4,820.29	49	1,347.50	6,737.66	7,455.46
6	41.25	701.84	2,304.90	28	245.51	3,789.93	4,940.07	50	1,461.31	6,878.03	7,575.24
7	44.73	842.21	2,424.68	29	266.24	3,930.30	5,059.85	51	1,584.72	7,018.40	7,695.02
8	48.51	982.58	2,544.46	30	288.73	4,070.67	5,179.63	52	1,718.57	7,158.76	7,814.80
9	52.61	1,122.94	2,664.24	31	313.12	4,211.04	5,299.41	53	1,863.71	7,299.13	7,934.58
10	57.05	1,263.31	2,784.02	32	339.56	4,351.41	5,419.19	54	2,021.11	7,439.50	8,054.36
11	61.87	1,403.68	2,903.80	33	368.24	4,491.77	5,538.97	55	2,191.81	7,579.87	8,174.14
12	67.09	1,544.05	3,023.58	34	399.34	4,632.14	5,658.75	56	2,376.93	7,720.24	8,293.92
13	72.76	1,684.42	3,143.36	35	433.07	4,772.51	5,778.53	57	2,577.67	7,860.60	8,413.70
14	78.90	1,824.78	3,263.15	36	469.64	4,912.88	5,898.31	58	2,795.38	8,000.97	8,533.48
15	85.57	1,965.15	3,382.93	37	509.31	5,053.25	6,018.09	59	3,031.47	8,141.34	8,653.26
16	92.79	2,105.52	3,502.71	38	552.32	5,193.61	6,137.88	60	3,287.50	8,281.71	8,773.04
17	100.63	2,245.88	3,622.49	39	598.97	5,333.98	6,257.66	61	3,565.15	8,422.08	8,892.82
18	109.13	2,386.25	3,742.27	40	649.56	5,474.35	6,377.44	62	3,866.25	8,562.44	9,012.61
19	118.35	2,526.62	3,862.05	41	704.42	5,614.72	6,497.22	63	4,192.79	8,702.81	9,132.39
20	128.34	2,666.99	3,981.83	42	763.91	5,755.08	6,617.00	64	4,546.90	8,843.18	9,252.17
21	139.18	2,807.36	4,101.61	43	828.43	5,895.45	6,736.78				
22	150.94	2,947.73	4,221.39	44	898.39	6,035.82	6,856.56				

181

Table 1 (continues)

Initial Catalog of Tunings : D-25

Scale Deg.	HZ	Cts	TU	Scale Deg.	HZ	Cts	TU	Scale Deg.	HZ	Cts	TU
1	27.50	0.00	1,706.00	24	164.75	3,099.32	4,350.75	47	986.99	6,198.65	6,995.50
2	29.73	134.75	1,820.99	25	178.08	3,234.08	4,465.74	48	1,066.88	6,333.40	7,110.49
3	32.13	269.51	1,935.98	26	192.50	3,368.83	4,580.73	49	1,153.24	6,468.15	7,225.48
4	34.73	404.26	2,050.97	27	208.08	3,503.58	4,695.72	50	1,246.59	6,602.91	7,340.47
5	37.54	539.01	2,165.96	28	224.93	3,638.34	4,810.71	51	1,347.50	6,737.66	7,455.46
6	40.58	673.77	2,280.95	29	243.13	3,773.09	4,925.70	52	1,456.57	6,872.41	7,570.45
7	43.87	808.52	2,395.94	30	262.81	3,907.84	5,040.69	53	1,574.48	7,007.17	7,685.44
8	47.42	943.27	2,510.92	31	284.09	4,042.60	5,155.68	54	1,701.93	7,141.92	7,800.43
9	51.26	1,078.03	2,625.91	32	307.08	4,177.35	5,270.67	55	1,839.69	7,276.67	7,915.42
10	55.41	1,212.78	2,740.90	33	331.94	4,312.10	5,385.65	56	1,988.60	7,411.43	8,030.41
11	59.89	1,347.53	2,855.89	34	358.81	4,446.86	5,500.64	57	2,149.57	7,546.18	8,145.40
12	64.74	1,482.29	2,970.88	35	387.85	4,581.61	5,615.63	58	2,323.57	7,680.93	8,260.38
13	69.98	1,617.04	3,085.87	36	419.25	4,716.36	5,730.62	59	2,511.66	7,815.69	8,375.37
14	75.65	1,751.79	3,200.86	37	453.18	4,851.12	5,845.61	60	2,714.96	7,950.44	8,490.36
15	81.77	1,886.54	3,315.85	38	489.87	4,985.87	5,960.60	61	2,934.73	8,085.19	8,605.35
16	88.39	2,021.30	3,430.84	39	529.52	5,120.62	6,075.59	62	3,172.28	8,219.95	8,720.34
17	95.54	2,156.05	3,545.83	40	572.38	5,255.37	6,190.58	63	3,429.07	8,354.70	8,835.33
18	103.28	2,290.80	3,660.82	41	618.71	5,390.13	6,305.57	64	3,706.63	8,489.45	8,950.32
19	111.64	2,425.56	3,775.81	42	668.80	5,524.88	6,420.56	65	4,006.67	8,624.20	9,065.31
20	120.67	2,560.31	3,890.79	43	722.93	5,659.63	6,535.55	66	4,330.99	8,758.96	9,180.30
21	130.44	2,695.06	4,005.78	44	781.45	5,794.39	6,650.54				
22	141.00	2,829.82	4,120.77	45	844.71	5,929.14	6,765.52				
23	152.41	2,964.57	4,235.76	46	913.08	6,063.89	6,880.51				

Initial Catalog of Tunings : D-26

Scale Deg.	HZ	Cts	TU	Scale Deg.	HZ	Cts	TU	Scale Deg.	HZ	Cts	TU
1	27.50	0.00	1,706.00	25	165.74	3,109.69	4,359.60	49	998.88	6,219.38	7,013.19
2	29.64	129.57	1,816.57	26	178.62	3,239.26	4,470.16	50	1,076.51	6,348.95	7,123.76
3	31.94	259.14	1,927.13	27	192.50	3,368.83	4,580.73	51	1,160.17	6,478.52	7,234.33
4	34.42	388.71	2,037.70	28	207.46	3,498.40	4,691.30	52	1,250.33	6,608.09	7,344.89
5	37.10	518.28	2,148.27	29	223.58	3,627.97	4,801.86	53	1,347.50	6,737.66	7,455.46
6	39.98	647.85	2,258.83	30	240.96	3,757.54	4,912.43	54	1,452.22	6,867.23	7,566.03
7	43.09	777.42	2,369.40	31	259.68	3,887.11	5,023.00	55	1,565.08	6,996.80	7,676.59
8	46.44	906.99	2,479.97	32	279.87	4,016.68	5,133.56	56	1,686.71	7,126.37	7,787.16
9	50.05	1,036.56	2,590.53	33	301.62	4,146.25	5,244.13	57	1,817.79	7,255.94	7,897.73
10	53.93	1,166.13	2,701.10	34	325.06	4,275.82	5,354.70	58	1,959.06	7,385.51	8,008.29
11	58.13	1,295.70	2,811.67	35	350.32	4,405.39	5,465.26	59	2,111.31	7,515.08	8,118.86
12	62.64	1,425.27	2,922.23	36	377.54	4,534.96	5,575.83	60	2,275.39	7,644.65	8,229.43
13	67.51	1,554.84	3,032.80	37	406.88	4,664.53	5,686.40	61	2,452.22	7,774.22	8,339.99
14	72.76	1,684.42	3,143.37	38	438.50	4,794.10	5,796.96	62	2,642.79	7,903.79	8,450.56
15	78.41	1,813.99	3,253.93	39	472.58	4,923.67	5,907.53	63	2,848.17	8,033.36	8,561.13
16	84.51	1,943.56	3,364.50	40	509.31	5,053.25	6,018.10	64	3,069.52	8,162.93	8,671.69
17	91.07	2,073.13	3,475.06	41	548.89	5,182.82	6,128.66	65	3,308.06	8,292.50	8,782.26
18	98.15	2,202.70	3,585.63	42	591.54	5,312.39	6,239.23	66	3,565.15	8,422.08	8,892.83
19	105.78	2,332.27	3,696.20	43	637.52	5,441.96	6,349.79	67	3,842.21	8,551.65	9,003.39
20	114.00	2,461.84	3,806.76	44	687.06	5,571.53	6,460.36	68	4,140.81	8,681.22	9,113.96
21	122.86	2,591.41	3,917.33	45	740.45	5,701.10	6,570.93	69	4,462.61	8,810.79	9,224.52
22	132.41	2,720.98	4,027.90	46	798.00	5,830.67	6,681.49				
23	142.70	2,850.55	4,138.46	47	860.02	5,960.24	6,792.06				
24	153.79	2,980.12	4,249.03	48	926.85	6,089.81	6,902.63				

Table 1 (continues)

Initial Catalog of Tunings : D-27

Scale Deg.	HZ	Cts	TU	Scale Deg.	HZ	Cts	TU	Scale Deg.	HZ	Cts	TU
1	27.50	0.00	1,706.00	26	166.66	3,119.29	4,367.79	51	1,010.02	6,238.57	7,029.57
2	29.56	124.77	1,812.47	27	179.11	3,244.06	4,474.26	52	1,085.50	6,363.35	7,136.05
3	31.76	249.54	1,918.94	28	192.50	3,368.83	4,580.73	53	1,166.62	6,488.12	7,242.52
4	34.14	374.31	2,025.41	29	206.89	3,493.60	4,687.20	54	1,253.80	6,612.89	7,348.99
5	36.69	499.09	2,131.89	30	222.35	3,618.37	4,793.67	55	1,347.50	6,737.66	7,455.46
6	39.43	623.86	2,238.36	31	238.96	3,743.14	4,900.14	56	1,448.20	6,862.43	7,561.93
7	42.38	748.63	2,344.83	32	256.82	3,867.92	5,006.62	57	1,556.43	6,987.20	7,668.40
8	45.54	873.40	2,451.30	33	276.01	3,992.69	5,113.09	58	1,672.74	7,111.97	7,774.87
9	48.95	998.17	2,557.77	34	296.64	4,117.46	5,219.56	59	1,797.75	7,236.75	7,881.35
10	52.61	1,122.94	2,664.24	35	318.81	4,242.23	5,326.03	60	1,932.09	7,361.52	7,987.82
11	56.54	1,247.71	2,770.71	36	342.63	4,367.00	5,432.50	61	2,076.48	7,486.29	8,094.29
12	60.76	1,372.49	2,877.19	37	368.24	4,491.77	5,538.97	62	2,231.66	7,611.06	8,200.76
13	65.30	1,497.26	2,983.66	38	395.76	4,616.54	5,645.44	63	2,398.44	7,735.83	8,307.23
14	70.18	1,622.03	3,090.13	39	425.33	4,741.32	5,751.92	64	2,577.67	7,860.60	8,413.70
15	75.43	1,746.80	3,196.60	40	457.12	4,866.09	5,858.39	65	2,770.31	7,985.37	8,520.17
16	81.06	1,871.57	3,303.07	41	491.28	4,990.86	5,964.86	66	2,977.34	8,110.15	8,626.65
17	87.12	1,996.34	3,409.54	42	527.99	5,115.63	6,071.33	67	3,199.84	8,234.92	8,733.12
18	93.63	2,121.12	3,516.02	43	567.45	5,240.40	6,177.80	68	3,438.97	8,359.69	8,839.59
19	100.63	2,245.89	3,622.49	44	609.86	5,365.17	6,284.27	69	3,695.96	8,484.46	8,946.06
20	108.15	2,370.66	3,728.96	45	655.43	5,489.95	6,390.75	70	3,972.17	8,609.23	9,052.53
21	116.23	2,495.43	3,835.43	46	704.42	5,614.72	6,497.22	71	4,269.01	8,734.00	9,159.00
22	124.92	2,620.20	3,941.90	47	757.06	5,739.49	6,603.69	72	4,588.04	8,858.78	9,265.48
23	134.26	2,744.97	4,048.37	48	813.63	5,864.26	6,710.16				
24	144.29	2,869.74	4,154.84	49	874.44	5,989.03	6,816.63				
25	155.07	2,994.52	4,261.32	50	939.79	6,113.80	6,923.10				

Initial Catalog of Tunings : D-28

Scale Deg.	HZ	Cts	TU	Scale Deg.	HZ	Cts	TU	Scale Deg.	HZ	Cts	TU
1	27.50	0.00	1,706.00	27	167.52	3,128.20	4,375.39	53	1,020.47	6,256.40	7,044.76
2	29.48	120.32	1,808.67	28	179.58	3,248.51	4,478.06	54	1,093.91	6,376.71	7,147.45
3	31.60	240.63	1,911.34	29	192.50	3,368.83	4,580.73	55	1,172.64	6,497.03	7,250.12
4	33.87	360.95	2,014.01	30	206.35	3,489.15	4,683.40	56	1,257.03	6,617.34	7,352.79
5	36.31	481.26	2,116.68	31	221.20	3,609.46	4,786.07	57	1,347.50	6,737.66	7,455.46
6	38.93	601.58	2,219.34	32	237.12	3,729.78	4,888.74	58	1,444.48	6,857.98	7,558.13
7	41.73	721.89	2,322.01	33	254.19	3,850.09	4,991.41	59	1,548.43	6,978.29	7,660.80
8	44.73	842.21	2,424.68	34	272.48	3,970.41	5,094.07	60	1,659.87	7,098.61	7,763.47
9	47.95	962.52	2,527.35	35	292.09	4,090.72	5,196.74	61	1,779.33	7,218.92	7,866.14
10	51.40	1,082.84	2,630.02	36	313.12	4,211.04	5,299.41	62	1,907.39	7,339.24	7,968.80
11	55.10	1,203.15	2,732.69	37	335.65	4,331.35	5,402.08	63	2,044.66	7,459.55	8,071.47
12	59.07	1,323.47	2,835.36	38	359.81	4,451.67	5,504.75	64	2,191.81	7,579.87	8,174.14
13	63.32	1,443.78	2,938.03	39	385.70	4,571.98	5,607.42	65	2,349.55	7,700.18	8,276.81
14	67.87	1,564.10	3,040.70	40	413.46	4,692.30	5,710.09	66	2,518.65	7,820.50	8,379.48
15	72.76	1,684.42	3,143.37	41	443.22	4,812.61	5,812.76	67	2,699.91	7,940.81	8,482.15
16	77.99	1,804.73	3,246.03	42	475.11	4,932.93	5,915.43	68	2,894.22	8,061.13	8,584.82
17	83.61	1,925.05	3,348.70	43	509.31	5,053.25	6,018.09	69	3,102.51	8,181.44	8,687.49
18	89.62	2,045.36	3,451.37	44	545.96	5,173.56	6,120.76	70	3,325.80	8,301.76	8,790.16
19	96.07	2,165.68	3,554.04	45	585.25	5,293.88	6,223.43	71	3,565.15	8,422.08	8,892.82
20	102.99	2,285.99	3,656.71	46	627.37	5,414.19	6,326.10	72	3,821.73	8,542.39	8,995.49
21	110.40	2,406.31	3,759.38	47	672.52	5,534.51	6,428.77	73	4,096.77	8,662.71	9,098.16
22	118.35	2,526.62	3,862.05	48	720.93	5,654.82	6,531.44	74	4,391.61	8,783.02	9,200.83
23	126.86	2,646.94	3,964.72	49	772.81	5,775.14	6,634.11				
24	135.99	2,767.25	4,067.39	50	828.43	5,895.45	6,736.78				
25	145.78	2,887.57	4,170.05	51	888.05	6,015.77	6,839.45				
26	156.27	3,007.88	4,272.72	52	951.96	6,136.08	6,942.12				

183

Table 1 (continues)

Initial Catalog of Tunings : D-29

Scale Deg.	HZ	Cts	TU	Scale Deg.	HZ	Cts	TU	Scale Deg.	HZ	Cts	TU
1	27.50	0.00	1,706.00	28	168.32	3,136.50	4,382.47	55	1,030.30	6,272.99	7,058.95
2	29.41	116.17	1,805.13	29	180.01	3,252.66	4,481.60	56	1,101.81	6,389.16	7,158.07
3	31.45	232.33	1,904.26	30	192.50	3,368.83	4,580.73	57	1,178.27	6,505.33	7,257.20
4	33.63	348.50	2,003.39	31	205.86	3,485.00	4,679.86	58	1,260.05	6,621.49	7,356.33
5	35.97	464.67	2,102.51	32	220.15	3,601.16	4,778.99	59	1,347.50	6,737.66	7,455.46
6	38.46	580.83	2,201.64	33	235.43	3,717.33	4,878.12	60	1,441.02	6,853.83	7,554.59
7	41.13	697.00	2,300.77	34	251.77	3,833.50	4,977.24	61	1,541.03	6,969.99	7,653.72
8	43.99	813.17	2,399.90	35	269.24	3,949.66	5,076.37	62	1,647.98	7,086.16	7,752.85
9	47.04	929.33	2,499.03	36	287.92	4,065.83	5,175.50	63	1,762.36	7,202.33	7,851.97
10	50.30	1,045.50	2,598.16	37	307.91	4,182.00	5,274.63	64	1,884.67	7,318.49	7,951.10
11	53.80	1,161.67	2,697.29	38	329.28	4,298.16	5,373.76	65	2,015.47	7,434.66	8,050.23
12	57.53	1,277.83	2,796.41	39	352.13	4,414.33	5,472.89	66	2,155.35	7,550.83	8,149.36
13	61.52	1,394.00	2,895.54	40	376.57	4,530.50	5,572.02	67	2,304.94	7,666.99	8,248.49
14	65.79	1,510.17	2,994.67	41	402.70	4,646.66	5,671.14	68	2,464.91	7,783.16	8,347.62
15	70.36	1,626.33	3,093.80	42	430.65	4,762.83	5,770.27	69	2,635.98	7,899.33	8,446.75
16	75.24	1,742.50	3,192.93	43	460.54	4,879.00	5,869.40	70	2,818.92	8,015.49	8,545.87
17	80.46	1,858.66	3,292.06	44	492.50	4,995.16	5,968.53	71	3,014.56	8,131.66	8,645.00
18	86.05	1,974.83	3,391.19	45	526.68	5,111.33	6,067.66	72	3,223.78	8,247.83	8,744.13
19	92.02	2,091.00	3,490.32	46	563.24	5,227.49	6,166.79	73	3,447.52	8,363.99	8,843.26
20	98.41	2,207.16	3,589.44	47	602.33	5,343.66	6,265.92	74	3,686.79	8,480.16	8,942.39
21	105.23	2,323.33	3,688.57	48	644.13	5,459.83	6,365.05	75	3,942.66	8,596.32	9,041.52
22	112.54	2,439.50	3,787.70	49	688.84	5,575.99	6,464.17	76	4,216.30	8,712.49	9,140.65
23	120.35	2,555.66	3,886.83	50	736.64	5,692.16	6,563.30	77	4,508.92	8,828.66	9,239.78
24	128.70	2,671.83	3,985.96	51	787.77	5,808.33	6,662.43				
25	137.63	2,788.00	4,085.09	52	842.44	5,924.49	6,761.56				
26	147.19	2,904.16	4,184.22	53	900.91	6,040.66	6,860.69				
27	157.40	3,020.33	4,283.34	54	963.43	6,156.83	6,959.82				

Initial Catalog of Tunings : D-30

Scale Deg.	HZ	Cts	TU	Scale Deg.	HZ	Cts	TU	Scale Deg.	HZ	Cts	TU
1	27.50	0.00	1,706.00	29	169.08	3,144.24	4,389.08	57	1,039.56	6,288.48	7,072.16
2	29.34	112.29	1,801.82	30	180.41	3,256.54	4,484.91	58	1,109.22	6,400.78	7,167.99
3	31.31	224.59	1,897.65	31	192.50	3,368.83	4,580.73	59	1,183.56	6,513.07	7,263.81
4	33.41	336.88	1,993.47	32	205.40	3,481.12	4,676.55	60	1,262.87	6,625.37	7,359.64
5	35.65	449.18	2,089.30	33	219.16	3,593.42	4,772.38	61	1,347.50	6,737.66	7,455.46
6	38.03	561.47	2,185.12	34	233.85	3,705.71	4,868.20	62	1,437.80	6,849.95	7,551.28
7	40.58	673.77	2,280.95	35	249.52	3,818.01	4,964.03	63	1,534.15	6,962.25	7,647.11
8	43.30	786.06	2,376.77	36	266.24	3,930.30	5,059.85	64	1,636.96	7,074.54	7,742.93
9	46.21	898.35	2,472.59	37	284.09	4,042.60	5,155.68	65	1,746.66	7,186.84	7,838.76
10	49.30	1,010.65	2,568.42	38	303.12	4,154.89	5,251.50	66	1,863.71	7,299.13	7,934.58
11	52.61	1,122.94	2,664.24	39	323.44	4,267.18	5,347.32	67	1,988.60	7,411.43	8,030.41
12	56.13	1,235.24	2,760.07	40	345.11	4,379.48	5,443.15	68	2,121.87	7,523.72	8,126.23
13	59.89	1,347.53	2,855.89	41	368.24	4,491.77	5,538.97	69	2,264.06	7,636.01	8,222.05
14	63.91	1,459.83	2,951.72	42	392.92	4,604.07	5,634.80	70	2,415.78	7,748.31	8,317.88
15	68.19	1,572.12	3,047.54	43	419.25	4,716.36	5,730.62	71	2,577.67	7,860.60	8,413.70
16	72.76	1,684.42	3,143.37	44	447.34	4,828.66	5,826.45	72	2,750.41	7,972.90	8,509.53
17	77.63	1,796.71	3,239.19	45	477.32	4,940.95	5,922.27	73	2,934.73	8,085.19	8,605.35
18	82.84	1,909.00	3,335.01	46	509.31	5,053.25	6,018.09	74	3,131.40	8,197.49	8,701.18
19	88.39	2,021.30	3,430.84	47	543.44	5,165.54	6,113.92	75	3,341.24	8,309.78	8,797.00
20	94.31	2,133.59	3,526.66	48	579.86	5,277.83	6,209.74	76	3,565.15	8,422.08	8,892.82
21	100.63	2,245.89	3,622.49	49	618.71	5,390.13	6,305.57	77	3,804.06	8,534.37	8,988.65
22	107.37	2,358.18	3,718.31	50	660.18	5,502.42	6,401.39	78	4,058.99	8,646.66	9,084.47
23	114.57	2,470.48	3,814.14	51	704.42	5,614.72	6,497.22	79	4,330.99	8,758.96	9,180.30
24	122.25	2,582.77	3,909.96	52	751.62	5,727.01	6,593.04	80	4,621.23	8,871.25	9,276.12
25	130.44	2,695.06	4,005.78	53	801.99	5,839.31	6,688.87				
26	139.18	2,807.36	4,101.61	54	855.73	5,951.60	6,784.69				
27	148.51	2,919.65	4,197.43	55	913.08	6,063.89	6,880.51				
28	158.46	3,031.95	4,293.26	56	974.27	6,176.19	6,976.34				

Table 1 (continues)

Initial Catalog of Tunings : D-31

Scale Deg.	HZ	Cts	TU	Scale Deg.	HZ	Cts	TU	Scale Deg.	HZ	Cts	TU
1	27.50	0.00	1,706.00	29	159.46	3,042.81	4,302.53	57	924.62	6,085.63	6,899.06
2	29.28	108.67	1,798.73	30	169.79	3,151.49	4,395.26	58	984.52	6,194.30	6,991.79
3	31.18	217.34	1,891.47	31	180.79	3,260.16	4,488.00	59	1,048.30	6,302.97	7,084.53
4	33.20	326.02	1,984.20	32	192.50	3,368.83	4,580.73	60	1,116.21	6,411.64	7,177.26
5	35.35	434.69	2,076.93	33	204.97	3,477.50	4,673.46	61	1,188.52	6,520.32	7,269.99
6	37.64	543.36	2,169.67	34	218.25	3,586.17	4,766.20	62	1,265.52	6,628.99	7,362.73
7	40.08	652.03	2,262.40	35	232.39	3,694.85	4,858.93	63	1,347.50	6,737.66	7,455.46
8	42.67	760.70	2,355.13	36	247.44	3,803.52	4,951.66	64	1,434.80	6,846.33	7,548.19
9	45.44	869.38	2,447.87	37	263.47	3,912.19	5,044.40	65	1,527.75	6,955.00	7,640.93
10	48.38	978.05	2,540.60	38	280.54	4,020.86	5,137.13	66	1,626.72	7,063.68	7,733.66
11	51.52	1,086.72	2,633.33	39	298.72	4,129.53	5,229.86	67	1,732.10	7,172.35	7,826.39
12	54.85	1,195.39	2,726.07	40	318.07	4,238.21	5,322.60	68	1,844.31	7,281.02	7,919.13
13	58.41	1,304.06	2,818.80	41	338.67	4,346.88	5,415.33	69	1,963.79	7,389.69	8,011.86
14	62.19	1,412.74	2,911.53	42	360.61	4,455.55	5,508.06	70	2,091.02	7,498.36	8,104.59
15	66.22	1,521.41	3,004.27	43	383.98	4,564.22	5,600.80	71	2,226.48	7,607.04	8,197.33
16	70.51	1,630.08	3,097.00	44	408.85	4,672.89	5,693.53	72	2,370.72	7,715.71	8,290.06
17	75.08	1,738.75	3,189.73	45	435.34	4,781.57	5,786.26	73	2,524.30	7,824.38	8,382.79
18	79.94	1,847.42	3,282.46	46	463.54	4,890.24	5,879.00	74	2,687.83	7,933.05	8,475.53
19	85.12	1,956.09	3,375.20	47	493.57	4,998.91	5,971.73	75	2,861.96	8,041.72	8,568.26
20	90.64	2,064.77	3,467.93	48	525.55	5,107.58	6,064.46	76	3,047.37	8,150.40	8,660.99
21	96.51	2,173.44	3,560.66	49	559.59	5,216.25	6,157.19	77	3,244.79	8,259.07	8,753.73
22	102.76	2,282.11	3,653.40	50	595.84	5,324.92	6,249.93	78	3,454.99	8,367.74	8,846.46
23	109.42	2,390.78	3,746.13	51	634.45	5,433.60	6,342.66	79	3,678.82	8,476.41	8,939.19
24	116.50	2,499.45	3,838.86	52	675.55	5,542.27	6,435.39	80	3,917.14	8,585.08	9,031.92
25	124.05	2,608.13	3,931.60	53	719.31	5,650.94	6,528.13	81	4,170.91	8,693.75	9,124.66
26	132.09	2,716.80	4,024.33	54	765.91	5,759.61	6,620.86	82	4,441.12	8,802.43	9,217.39
27	140.65	2,825.47	4,117.06	55	815.53	5,868.28	6,713.59				
28	149.76	2,934.14	4,209.80	56	868.36	5,976.96	6,806.33				

Initial Catalog of Tunings : D-32

Scale Deg.	HZ	Cts	TU	Scale Deg.	HZ	Cts	TU	Scale Deg.	HZ	Cts	TU
1	27.50	0.00	1,706.00	30	160.40	3,053.00	4,311.22	59	935.56	6,106.00	6,916.45
2	29.22	105.28	1,795.84	31	170.46	3,158.28	4,401.06	60	994.22	6,211.28	7,006.28
3	31.06	210.55	1,885.67	32	181.14	3,263.55	4,490.89	61	1,056.55	6,316.56	7,096.12
4	33.00	315.83	1,975.51	33	192.50	3,368.83	4,580.73	62	1,122.80	6,421.83	7,185.95
5	35.07	421.10	2,065.34	34	204.57	3,474.11	4,670.57	63	1,193.19	6,527.11	7,275.79
6	37.27	526.38	2,155.18	35	217.39	3,579.38	4,760.40	64	1,268.00	6,632.38	7,365.62
7	39.61	631.66	2,245.01	36	231.02	3,684.66	4,850.24	65	1,347.50	6,737.66	7,455.46
8	42.09	736.93	2,334.85	37	245.51	3,789.93	4,940.07	66	1,431.98	6,842.94	7,545.30
9	44.73	842.21	2,424.68	38	260.90	3,895.21	5,029.91	67	1,521.76	6,948.21	7,635.13
10	47.54	947.48	2,514.52	39	277.26	4,000.49	5,119.74	68	1,617.17	7,053.49	7,724.97
11	50.52	1,052.76	2,604.35	40	294.64	4,105.76	5,209.58	69	1,718.57	7,158.76	7,814.80
12	53.68	1,158.04	2,694.19	41	313.12	4,211.04	5,299.41	70	1,826.31	7,264.04	7,904.64
13	57.05	1,263.31	2,784.02	42	332.75	4,316.31	5,389.25	71	1,940.82	7,369.32	7,994.47
14	60.63	1,368.59	2,873.86	43	353.61	4,421.59	5,479.08	72	2,062.50	7,474.59	8,084.31
15	64.43	1,473.86	2,963.69	44	375.78	4,526.87	5,568.92	73	2,191.81	7,579.87	8,174.14
16	68.47	1,579.14	3,053.53	45	399.34	4,632.14	5,658.75	74	2,329.23	7,685.14	8,263.98
17	72.76	1,684.42	3,143.36	46	424.38	4,737.42	5,748.59	75	2,475.27	7,790.42	8,353.81
18	77.32	1,789.69	3,233.20	47	450.98	4,842.69	5,838.42	76	2,630.46	7,895.70	8,443.65
19	82.17	1,894.97	3,323.04	48	479.26	4,947.97	5,928.26	77	2,795.38	8,000.97	8,533.48
20	87.32	2,000.24	3,412.87	49	509.31	5,053.25	6,018.10	78	2,970.64	8,106.25	8,623.32
21	92.79	2,105.52	3,502.71	50	541.24	5,158.52	6,107.93	79	3,156.89	8,211.52	8,713.15
22	98.61	2,210.79	3,592.54	51	575.17	5,263.80	6,197.77	80	3,354.81	8,316.80	8,802.99
23	104.79	2,316.07	3,682.38	52	611.23	5,369.07	6,287.60	81	3,565.15	8,422.08	8,892.83
24	111.36	2,421.35	3,772.21	53	649.56	5,474.35	6,377.44	82	3,788.67	8,527.35	8,982.66
25	118.35	2,526.62	3,862.05	54	690.28	5,579.62	6,467.27	83	4,026.21	8,632.63	9,072.50
26	125.77	2,631.90	3,951.88	55	733.56	5,684.90	6,557.11	84	4,278.64	8,737.90	9,162.33
27	133.65	2,737.17	4,041.72	56	779.55	5,790.18	6,646.94	85	4,546.90	8,843.18	9,252.17
28	142.03	2,842.45	4,131.55	57	828.43	5,895.45	6,736.78				
29	150.94	2,947.73	4,221.39	58	880.37	6,000.73	6,826.61				

185

Table 1 (continues)

Initial Catalog of Tunings : D-33

Scale Deg.	HZ	Cts	TU	Scale Deg.	HZ	Cts	TU	Scale Deg.	HZ	Cts	TU
1	27.50	0.00	1,706.00	31	161.29	3,062.57	4,319.39	61	945.96	6,125.15	6,932.78
2	29.17	102.09	1,793.11	32	171.09	3,164.66	4,406.50	62	1,003.42	6,227.23	7,019.89
3	30.94	204.17	1,880.23	33	181.48	3,266.74	4,493.62	63	1,064.37	6,329.32	7,107.01
4	32.82	306.26	1,967.34	34	192.50	3,368.83	4,580.73	64	1,129.02	6,431.40	7,194.12
5	34.82	408.34	2,054.45	35	204.19	3,470.92	4,667.84	65	1,197.60	6,533.49	7,281.23
6	36.93	510.43	2,141.57	36	216.60	3,573.00	4,754.96	66	1,270.34	6,635.57	7,368.35
7	39.17	612.51	2,228.68	37	229.75	3,675.09	4,842.07	67	1,347.50	6,737.66	7,455.46
8	41.55	714.60	2,315.79	38	243.71	3,777.17	4,929.18	68	1,429.35	6,839.75	7,542.57
9	44.08	816.69	2,402.90	39	258.51	3,879.26	5,016.30	69	1,516.17	6,941.83	7,629.69
10	46.75	918.77	2,490.02	40	274.21	3,981.34	5,103.41	70	1,608.26	7,043.92	7,716.80
11	49.59	1,020.86	2,577.13	41	290.87	4,083.43	5,190.52	71	1,705.94	7,146.00	7,803.91
12	52.61	1,122.94	2,664.24	42	308.53	4,185.52	5,277.63	72	1,809.56	7,248.09	7,891.03
13	55.80	1,225.03	2,751.36	43	327.27	4,287.60	5,364.75	73	1,919.48	7,350.17	7,978.14
14	59.19	1,327.11	2,838.47	44	347.15	4,389.69	5,451.86	74	2,036.07	7,452.26	8,065.25
15	62.79	1,429.20	2,925.58	45	368.24	4,491.77	5,538.97	75	2,159.74	7,554.35	8,152.36
16	66.60	1,531.29	3,012.70	46	390.61	4,593.86	5,626.09	76	2,290.92	7,656.43	8,239.48
17	70.64	1,633.37	3,099.81	47	414.33	4,695.94	5,713.20	77	2,430.07	7,758.52	8,326.59
18	74.94	1,735.46	3,186.92	48	439.50	4,798.03	5,800.31	78	2,577.67	7,860.60	8,413.70
19	79.49	1,837.54	3,274.03	49	466.19	4,900.12	5,887.43	79	2,734.24	7,962.69	8,500.82
20	84.31	1,939.63	3,361.15	50	494.51	5,002.20	5,974.54	80	2,900.32	8,064.77	8,587.93
21	89.44	2,041.72	3,448.26	51	524.55	5,104.29	6,061.65	81	3,076.49	8,166.86	8,675.04
22	94.87	2,143.80	3,535.37	52	556.41	5,206.37	6,148.76	82	3,263.35	8,268.95	8,762.16
23	100.63	2,245.89	3,622.49	53	590.20	5,308.46	6,235.88	83	3,461.57	8,371.03	8,849.27
24	106.74	2,347.97	3,709.60	54	626.05	5,410.55	6,322.99	84	3,671.83	8,473.12	8,936.38
25	113.23	2,450.06	3,796.71	55	664.08	5,512.63	6,410.10	85	3,894.86	8,575.20	9,023.49
26	120.10	2,552.14	3,883.83	56	704.42	5,614.72	6,497.22	86	4,131.43	8,677.29	9,110.61
27	127.40	2,654.23	3,970.94	57	747.20	5,716.80	6,584.33	87	4,382.37	8,779.38	9,197.72
28	135.14	2,756.32	4,058.05	58	792.59	5,818.89	6,671.44	88	4,648.56	8,881.46	9,284.83
29	143.35	2,858.40	4,145.16	59	840.73	5,920.97	6,758.56				
30	152.05	2,960.49	4,232.28	60	891.80	6,023.06	6,845.67				

Initial Catalog of Tunings : D-34

Scale Deg.	HZ	Cts	TU	Scale Deg.	HZ	Cts	TU	Scale Deg.	HZ	Cts	TU
1	27.50	0.00	1,706.00	31	153.11	2,972.50	4,242.53	61	852.48	5,944.99	6,779.05
2	29.12	99.08	1,790.55	32	162.13	3,071.58	4,327.08	62	902.69	6,044.08	6,863.60
3	30.84	198.17	1,875.10	33	171.68	3,170.66	4,411.63	63	955.86	6,143.16	6,948.15
4	32.65	297.25	1,959.65	34	181.79	3,269.75	4,496.18	64	1,012.16	6,242.24	7,032.71
5	34.57	396.33	2,044.20	35	192.50	3,368.83	4,580.73	65	1,071.78	6,341.33	7,117.26
6	36.61	495.42	2,128.75	36	203.84	3,467.91	4,665.28	66	1,134.91	6,440.41	7,201.81
7	38.77	594.50	2,213.31	37	215.85	3,567.00	4,749.83	67	1,201.76	6,539.49	7,286.36
8	41.05	693.58	2,297.86	38	228.56	3,666.08	4,834.38	68	1,272.54	6,638.58	7,370.91
9	43.47	792.67	2,382.41	39	242.02	3,765.16	4,918.93	69	1,347.50	6,737.66	7,455.46
10	46.03	891.75	2,466.96	40	256.28	3,864.25	5,003.48	70	1,426.87	6,836.74	7,540.01
11	48.74	990.83	2,551.51	41	271.37	3,963.33	5,088.04	71	1,510.92	6,935.83	7,624.56
12	51.61	1,089.92	2,636.06	42	287.36	4,062.41	5,172.59	72	1,599.91	7,034.91	7,709.11
13	54.65	1,189.00	2,720.61	43	304.28	4,161.50	5,257.14	73	1,694.15	7,133.99	7,793.66
14	57.87	1,288.08	2,805.16	44	322.21	4,260.58	5,341.69	74	1,793.94	7,233.08	7,878.21
15	61.28	1,387.17	2,889.71	45	341.18	4,359.66	5,426.24	75	1,899.61	7,332.16	7,962.77
16	64.89	1,486.25	2,974.26	46	361.28	4,458.75	5,510.79	76	2,011.50	7,431.24	8,047.32
17	68.71	1,585.33	3,058.81	47	382.56	4,557.83	5,595.34	77	2,129.98	7,530.33	8,131.87
18	72.76	1,684.42	3,143.37	48	405.09	4,656.91	5,679.89	78	2,255.44	7,629.41	8,216.42
19	77.04	1,783.50	3,227.92	49	428.96	4,756.00	5,764.44	79	2,388.29	7,728.49	8,300.97
20	81.58	1,882.58	3,312.47	50	454.22	4,855.08	5,848.99	80	2,528.97	7,827.58	8,385.52
21	86.39	1,981.66	3,397.02	51	480.98	4,954.16	5,933.54	81	2,677.93	7,926.66	8,470.07
22	91.48	2,080.75	3,481.57	52	509.31	5,053.25	6,018.09	82	2,835.66	8,025.74	8,554.62
23	96.86	2,179.83	3,566.12	53	539.31	5,152.33	6,102.65	83	3,002.69	8,124.83	8,639.17
24	102.57	2,278.91	3,650.67	54	571.07	5,251.41	6,187.20	84	3,179.55	8,223.91	8,723.72
25	108.61	2,378.00	3,735.22	55	604.71	5,350.49	6,271.75	85	3,366.84	8,322.99	8,808.27
26	115.01	2,477.08	3,819.77	56	640.33	5,449.58	6,356.30	86	3,565.15	8,422.08	8,892.82
27	121.78	2,576.16	3,904.32	57	678.05	5,548.66	6,440.85	87	3,775.14	8,521.16	8,977.38
28	128.96	2,675.25	3,988.87	58	717.98	5,647.74	6,525.40	88	3,997.51	8,620.24	9,061.93
29	136.55	2,774.33	4,073.42	59	760.27	5,746.83	6,609.95				
30	144.59	2,873.41	4,157.98	60	805.06	5,845.91	6,694.50				

Table 1 (continues)

Initial Catalog of Tunings: D-35

Scale Deg.	HZ	Cts	TU	Scale Deg.	HZ	Cts	TU	Scale Deg.	HZ	Cts	TU
1	27.50	0.00	1,706.00	31	145.78	2,887.57	4,170.05	61	772.81	5,775.14	6,634.11
2	29.07	96.25	1,788.14	32	154.12	2,983.82	4,252.19	62	816.99	5,871.39	6,716.24
3	30.73	192.50	1,870.27	33	162.93	3,080.07	4,334.32	63	863.70	5,967.64	6,798.38
4	32.49	288.76	1,952.41	34	172.24	3,176.33	4,416.46	64	913.08	6,063.89	6,880.51
5	34.35	385.01	2,034.54	35	182.09	3,272.58	4,498.59	65	965.28	6,160.15	6,962.65
6	36.31	481.26	2,116.68	36	192.50	3,368.83	4,580.73	66	1,020.47	6,256.40	7,044.78
7	38.39	577.51	2,198.81	37	203.51	3,465.08	4,662.87	67	1,078.81	6,352.65	7,126.92
8	40.58	673.77	2,280.95	38	215.14	3,561.33	4,745.00	68	1,140.49	6,448.90	7,209.05
9	42.90	770.02	2,363.08	39	227.44	3,657.59	4,827.14	69	1,205.69	6,545.16	7,291.19
10	45.36	866.27	2,445.22	40	240.44	3,753.84	4,909.27	70	1,274.63	6,641.41	7,373.32
11	47.95	962.52	2,527.35	41	254.19	3,850.09	4,991.41	71	1,347.50	6,737.66	7,455.46
12	50.69	1,058.78	2,609.49	42	268.72	3,946.34	5,073.54	72	1,424.54	6,833.91	7,537.60
13	53.59	1,155.03	2,691.62	43	284.09	4,042.60	5,155.68	73	1,505.98	6,930.16	7,619.73
14	56.65	1,251.28	2,773.76	44	300.33	4,138.85	5,237.81	74	1,592.08	7,026.42	7,701.87
15	59.89	1,347.53	2,855.89	45	317.50	4,235.10	5,319.95	75	1,683.11	7,122.67	7,784.00
16	63.32	1,443.78	2,938.03	46	335.65	4,331.35	5,402.08	76	1,779.33	7,218.92	7,866.14
17	66.94	1,540.04	3,020.16	47	354.84	4,427.61	5,484.22	77	1,881.06	7,315.17	7,948.27
18	70.76	1,636.29	3,102.30	48	375.13	4,523.86	5,566.35	78	1,988.60	7,411.43	8,030.41
19	74.81	1,732.54	3,184.43	49	396.57	4,620.11	5,648.49	79	2,102.30	7,507.68	8,112.54
20	79.09	1,828.79	3,266.57	50	419.25	4,716.36	5,730.62	80	2,222.49	7,603.93	8,194.68
21	83.61	1,925.05	3,348.70	51	443.22	4,812.61	5,812.76	81	2,349.55	7,700.18	8,276.81
22	88.39	2,021.30	3,430.84	52	468.56	4,908.87	5,894.89	82	2,483.88	7,796.44	8,358.95
23	93.44	2,117.55	3,512.97	53	495.34	5,005.12	5,977.03	83	2,625.89	7,892.69	8,441.08
24	98.78	2,213.80	3,595.11	54	523.66	5,101.37	6,059.16	84	2,776.02	7,988.94	8,523.22
25	104.43	2,310.05	3,677.24	55	553.60	5,197.62	6,141.30	85	2,934.73	8,085.19	8,605.35
26	110.40	2,406.31	3,759.38	56	585.25	5,293.88	6,223.43	86	3,102.51	8,181.44	8,687.49
27	116.71	2,502.56	3,841.51	57	618.71	5,390.13	6,305.57	87	3,279.89	8,277.70	8,769.62
28	123.39	2,598.81	3,923.65	58	654.09	5,486.38	6,387.70	88	3,467.41	8,373.95	8,851.76
29	130.44	2,695.06	4,005.78	59	691.48	5,582.63	6,469.84				
30	137.90	2,791.32	4,087.92	60	731.02	5,678.88	6,551.97				

Initial Catalog of Tunings: D-36

Scale Deg.	HZ	Cts	TU	Scale Deg.	HZ	Cts	TU	Scale Deg.	HZ	Cts	TU
1	27.50	0.00	1,706.00	31	139.18	2,807.36	4,101.61	61	704.42	5,614.72	6,497.22
2	29.03	93.58	1,785.85	32	146.91	2,900.94	4,181.46	62	743.54	5,708.30	6,577.07
3	30.64	187.16	1,865.71	33	155.07	2,994.52	4,261.32	63	784.84	5,801.87	6,656.92
4	32.34	280.74	1,945.56	34	163.68	3,088.09	4,341.17	64	828.43	5,895.45	6,736.78
5	34.14	374.31	2,025.41	35	172.77	3,181.67	4,421.02	65	874.44	5,989.03	6,816.63
6	36.03	467.89	2,105.27	36	182.37	3,275.25	4,500.88	66	923.01	6,082.61	6,896.48
7	38.03	561.47	2,185.12	37	192.50	3,368.83	4,580.73	67	974.27	6,176.19	6,976.34
8	40.15	655.05	2,264.98	38	203.19	3,462.41	4,660.58	68	1,028.38	6,269.77	7,056.19
9	42.38	748.63	2,344.83	39	214.48	3,555.99	4,740.44	69	1,085.50	6,363.35	7,136.05
10	44.73	842.21	2,424.68	40	226.39	3,649.57	4,820.29	70	1,145.79	6,456.92	7,215.90
11	47.22	935.79	2,504.54	41	238.96	3,743.14	4,900.14	71	1,209.42	6,550.50	7,295.75
12	49.84	1,029.36	2,584.39	42	252.24	3,836.72	4,980.00	72	1,276.60	6,644.08	7,375.61
13	52.61	1,122.94	2,664.24	43	266.24	3,930.30	5,059.85	73	1,347.50	6,737.66	7,455.46
14	55.53	1,216.52	2,744.10	44	281.03	4,023.88	5,139.71	74	1,422.34	6,831.24	7,535.31
15	58.61	1,310.10	2,823.95	45	296.64	4,117.46	5,219.56	75	1,501.34	6,924.82	7,615.17
16	61.87	1,403.68	2,903.80	46	313.12	4,211.04	5,299.41	76	1,584.72	7,018.40	7,695.02
17	65.30	1,497.26	2,983.66	47	330.51	4,304.62	5,379.27	77	1,672.74	7,111.97	7,774.87
18	68.93	1,590.84	3,063.51	48	348.86	4,398.19	5,459.12	78	1,765.65	7,205.55	7,854.73
19	72.76	1,684.42	3,143.37	49	368.24	4,491.77	5,538.97	79	1,863.71	7,299.13	7,934.58
20	76.80	1,777.99	3,223.22	50	388.69	4,585.35	5,618.83	80	1,967.22	7,392.71	8,014.44
21	81.06	1,871.57	3,303.07	51	410.28	4,678.93	5,698.68	81	2,076.48	7,486.29	8,094.29
22	85.57	1,965.15	3,382.93	52	433.07	4,772.51	5,778.53	82	2,191.81	7,579.87	8,174.14
23	90.32	2,058.73	3,462.78	53	457.12	4,866.09	5,858.39	83	2,313.55	7,673.45	8,254.00
24	95.34	2,152.31	3,542.63	54	482.51	4,959.67	5,938.24	84	2,442.04	7,767.02	8,333.85
25	100.63	2,245.89	3,622.49	55	509.31	5,053.25	6,018.09	85	2,577.67	7,860.60	8,413.70
26	106.22	2,339.47	3,702.34	56	537.59	5,146.82	6,097.95	86	2,720.84	7,954.18	8,493.56
27	112.12	2,433.04	3,782.19	57	567.45	5,240.40	6,177.80	87	2,871.96	8,047.76	8,573.41
28	118.35	2,526.62	3,862.05	58	598.97	5,333.98	6,257.66	88	3,031.47	8,141.34	8,653.26
29	124.92	2,620.20	3,941.90	59	632.24	5,427.56	6,337.51				
30	131.86	2,713.78	4,021.75	60	667.35	5,521.14	6,417.36				

Table 1 (continues)

Initial Catalog of Tunings : D-37

Scale Deg.	HZ	Cts	TU	Scale Deg.	HZ	Cts	TU	Scale Deg.	HZ	Cts	TU
1	27.50	0.00	1,706.00	31	133.21	2,731.48	4,036.86	61	645.30	5,462.97	6,367.72
2	28.98	91.05	1,783.70	32	140.41	2,822.53	4,114.56	62	680.15	5,554.02	6,445.42
3	30.55	182.10	1,861.39	33	147.99	2,913.58	4,192.25	63	716.87	5,645.07	6,523.12
4	32.20	273.15	1,939.09	34	155.98	3,004.63	4,269.95	64	755.59	5,736.12	6,600.81
5	33.94	364.20	2,016.78	35	164.40	3,095.68	4,347.64	65	796.39	5,827.17	6,678.51
6	35.77	455.25	2,094.48	36	173.28	3,186.73	4,425.34	66	839.39	5,918.21	6,756.20
7	37.70	546.30	2,172.17	37	182.64	3,277.78	4,503.03	67	884.72	6,009.26	6,833.90
8	39.74	637.35	2,249.87	38	192.50	3,368.83	4,580.73	68	932.49	6,100.31	6,911.59
9	41.88	728.40	2,327.56	39	202.89	3,459.88	4,658.43	69	982.85	6,191.36	6,989.29
10	44.15	819.45	2,405.26	40	213.85	3,550.93	4,736.12	70	1,035.92	6,282.41	7,066.98
11	46.53	910.49	2,482.95	41	225.40	3,641.98	4,813.82	71	1,091.86	6,373.46	7,144.68
12	49.04	1,001.54	2,560.65	42	237.57	3,733.03	4,891.51	72	1,150.82	6,464.51	7,222.37
13	51.69	1,092.59	2,638.34	43	250.40	3,824.08	4,969.21	73	1,212.96	6,555.56	7,300.07
14	54.48	1,183.64	2,716.04	44	263.92	3,915.13	5,046.90	74	1,278.46	6,646.61	7,377.76
15	57.42	1,274.69	2,793.74	45	278.17	4,006.18	5,124.60	75	1,347.50	6,737.66	7,455.46
16	60.53	1,365.74	2,871.43	46	293.19	4,097.23	5,202.29	76	1,420.26	6,828.71	7,533.16
17	63.79	1,456.79	2,949.13	47	309.03	4,188.28	5,279.99	77	1,496.96	6,919.76	7,610.85
18	67.24	1,547.84	3,026.82	48	325.71	4,279.32	5,357.68	78	1,577.79	7,010.81	7,688.55
19	70.87	1,638.89	3,104.52	49	343.30	4,370.37	5,435.38	79	1,662.99	7,101.86	7,766.24
20	74.70	1,729.94	3,182.21	50	361.84	4,461.42	5,513.07	80	1,752.80	7,192.91	7,843.94
21	78.73	1,820.99	3,259.91	51	381.38	4,552.47	5,590.77	81	1,847.45	7,283.96	7,921.63
22	82.98	1,912.04	3,337.60	52	401.97	4,643.52	5,668.47	82	1,947.21	7,375.01	7,999.33
23	87.46	2,003.09	3,415.30	53	423.68	4,734.57	5,746.16	83	2,052.36	7,466.06	8,077.02
24	92.19	2,094.14	3,492.99	54	446.56	4,825.62	5,823.86	84	2,163.18	7,557.11	8,154.72
25	97.16	2,185.19	3,570.69	55	470.67	4,916.67	5,901.55	85	2,279.99	7,648.15	8,232.41
26	102.41	2,276.24	3,648.39	56	496.09	5,007.72	5,979.25	86	2,403.11	7,739.20	8,310.11
27	107.94	2,367.29	3,726.08	57	522.88	5,098.77	6,056.94	87	2,532.88	7,830.25	8,387.80
28	113.77	2,458.34	3,803.78	58	551.11	5,189.82	6,134.64	88	2,669.65	7,921.30	8,465.50
29	119.91	2,549.38	3,881.47	59	580.87	5,280.87	6,212.33				
30	126.39	2,640.43	3,959.17	60	612.24	5,371.92	6,290.03				

Initial Catalog of Tunings : D-38

Scale Deg.	HZ	Cts	TU	Scale Deg.	HZ	Cts	TU	Scale Deg.	HZ	Cts	TU
1	27.50	0.00	1,706.00	31	127.80	2,659.60	3,975.52	61	593.88	5,319.21	6,245.05
2	28.94	88.65	1,781.65	32	134.51	2,748.26	4,051.17	62	625.08	5,407.86	6,320.70
3	30.47	177.31	1,857.30	33	141.58	2,836.91	4,126.83	63	657.93	5,496.51	6,396.35
4	32.07	265.96	1,932.95	34	149.02	2,925.56	4,202.48	64	692.49	5,585.17	6,472.00
5	33.75	354.61	2,008.60	35	156.85	3,014.22	4,278.13	65	728.88	5,673.82	6,547.65
6	35.52	443.27	2,084.25	36	165.09	3,102.87	4,353.78	66	767.18	5,762.47	6,623.30
7	37.39	531.92	2,159.90	37	173.76	3,191.52	4,429.43	67	807.49	5,851.13	6,698.95
8	39.36	620.57	2,235.56	38	182.89	3,280.18	4,505.08	68	849.91	5,939.78	6,774.60
9	41.42	709.23	2,311.21	39	192.50	3,368.83	4,580.73	69	894.57	6,028.43	6,850.25
10	43.60	797.88	2,386.86	40	202.61	3,457.48	4,656.38	70	941.57	6,117.09	6,925.90
11	45.89	886.53	2,462.51	41	213.26	3,546.14	4,732.03	71	991.04	6,205.74	7,001.56
12	48.30	975.19	2,538.16	42	224.47	3,634.79	4,807.68	72	1,043.11	6,294.39	7,077.21
13	50.84	1,063.84	2,613.81	43	236.26	3,723.44	4,883.33	73	1,097.92	6,383.05	7,152.86
14	53.51	1,152.49	2,689.46	44	248.67	3,812.10	4,958.98	74	1,155.61	6,471.70	7,228.51
15	56.32	1,241.15	2,765.11	45	261.74	3,900.75	5,034.63	75	1,216.33	6,560.35	7,304.16
16	59.28	1,329.80	2,840.76	46	275.49	3,989.40	5,110.29	76	1,280.23	6,649.01	7,379.81
17	62.40	1,418.45	2,916.41	47	289.97	4,078.06	5,185.94	77	1,347.50	6,737.66	7,455.46
18	65.68	1,507.11	2,992.06	48	305.20	4,166.71	5,261.59	78	1,418.30	6,826.31	7,531.11
19	69.13	1,595.76	3,067.71	49	321.24	4,255.36	5,337.24	79	1,492.82	6,914.97	7,606.76
20	72.76	1,684.42	3,143.37	50	338.11	4,344.02	5,412.89	80	1,571.26	7,003.62	7,682.41
21	76.58	1,773.07	3,219.02	51	355.88	4,432.67	5,488.54	81	1,653.81	7,092.27	7,758.06
22	80.60	1,861.72	3,294.67	52	374.58	4,521.32	5,564.19	82	1,740.71	7,180.93	7,833.71
23	84.84	1,950.38	3,370.32	53	394.26	4,609.98	5,639.84	83	1,832.17	7,269.58	7,909.36
24	89.30	2,039.03	3,445.97	54	414.98	4,698.63	5,715.49	84	1,928.43	7,358.23	7,985.02
25	93.99	2,127.68	3,521.62	55	436.78	4,787.28	5,791.14	85	2,029.76	7,446.89	8,060.67
26	98.93	2,216.34	3,597.27	56	459.73	4,875.94	5,866.79	86	2,136.40	7,535.54	8,136.32
27	104.13	2,304.99	3,672.92	57	483.88	4,964.59	5,942.44	87	2,248.66	7,624.19	8,211.97
28	109.60	2,393.64	3,748.57	58	509.31	5,053.25	6,018.10	88	2,366.80	7,712.85	8,287.62
29	115.36	2,482.30	3,824.22	59	536.07	5,141.90	6,093.75				
30	121.42	2,570.95	3,899.87	60	564.23	5,230.55	6,169.40				

187

Table 1 (continues)

Initial Catalog of Tunings : D-39

Scale Deg.	HZ	Cts	TU	Scale Deg.	HZ	Cts	TU	Scale Deg.	HZ	Cts	TU
1	27.50	0.00	1,706.00	31	122.86	2,591.41	3,917.33	61	548.89	5,182.82	6,128.66
2	28.91	86.38	1,779.71	32	129.14	2,677.79	3,991.04	62	576.97	5,269.20	6,202.37
3	30.39	172.76	1,853.42	33	135.75	2,764.17	4,064.75	63	606.49	5,355.58	6,276.08
4	31.94	259.14	1,927.13	34	142.70	2,850.55	4,138.46	64	637.52	5,441.96	6,349.79
5	33.57	345.52	2,000.84	35	150.00	2,936.93	4,212.17	65	670.13	5,528.34	6,423.51
6	35.29	431.90	2,074.56	36	157.67	3,023.31	4,285.89	66	704.42	5,614.72	6,497.22
7	37.10	518.28	2,148.27	37	165.74	3,109.69	4,359.60	67	740.45	5,701.10	6,570.93
8	39.00	604.66	2,221.98	38	174.22	3,196.07	4,433.31	68	778.34	5,787.48	6,644.64
9	40.99	691.04	2,295.69	39	183.13	3,282.45	4,507.02	69	818.16	5,873.86	6,718.35
10	43.09	777.42	2,369.40	40	192.50	3,368.83	4,580.73	70	860.02	5,960.24	6,792.06
11	45.29	863.80	2,443.11	41	202.35	3,455.21	4,654.44	71	904.01	6,046.62	6,865.77
12	47.61	950.18	2,516.82	42	212.70	3,541.59	4,728.15	72	950.26	6,133.00	6,939.48
13	50.05	1,036.56	2,590.53	43	223.58	3,627.97	4,801.86	73	998.88	6,219.38	7,013.19
14	52.61	1,122.94	2,664.24	44	235.02	3,714.35	4,875.57	74	1,049.98	6,305.76	7,086.90
15	55.30	1,209.32	2,737.95	45	247.05	3,800.73	4,949.29	75	1,103.70	6,392.14	7,160.62
16	58.13	1,295.70	2,811.67	46	259.68	3,887.11	5,023.00	76	1,160.17	6,478.52	7,234.33
17	61.10	1,382.08	2,885.38	47	272.97	3,973.49	5,096.71	77	1,219.52	6,564.90	7,308.04
18	64.23	1,468.46	2,959.09	48	286.94	4,059.87	5,170.42	78	1,281.92	6,651.28	7,381.75
19	67.51	1,554.84	3,032.80	49	301.62	4,146.25	5,244.13	79	1,347.50	6,737.66	7,455.46
20	70.97	1,641.22	3,106.51	50	317.05	4,232.63	5,317.84	80	1,416.44	6,824.04	7,529.17
21	74.60	1,727.61	3,180.22	51	333.27	4,319.01	5,391.55	81	1,488.91	6,910.42	7,602.88
22	78.41	1,813.99	3,253.93	52	350.32	4,405.39	5,465.26	82	1,565.08	6,996.80	7,676.59
23	82.42	1,900.37	3,327.64	53	368.24	4,491.77	5,538.97	83	1,645.15	7,083.18	7,750.30
24	86.64	1,986.75	3,401.35	54	387.08	4,578.15	5,612.68	84	1,729.32	7,169.56	7,824.02
25	91.07	2,073.13	3,475.06	55	406.88	4,664.53	5,686.40	85	1,817.79	7,255.94	7,897.73
26	95.73	2,159.51	3,548.78	56	427.70	4,750.91	5,760.11	86	1,910.79	7,342.32	7,971.44
27	100.63	2,245.89	3,622.49	57	449.58	4,837.29	5,833.82	87	2,008.55	7,428.70	8,045.15
28	105.78	2,332.27	3,696.20	58	472.58	4,923.67	5,907.53	88	2,111.31	7,515.08	8,118.86
29	111.19	2,418.65	3,769.91	59	496.76	5,010.05	5,981.24				
30	116.88	2,505.03	3,843.62	60	522.17	5,096.44	6,054.95				

Initial Catalog of Tunings : D-40

Scale Deg.	HZ	Cts	TU	Scale Deg.	HZ	Cts	TU	Scale Deg.	HZ	Cts	TU
1	27.50	0.00	1,706.00	31	118.35	2,526.62	3,862.05	61	509.31	5,053.25	6,018.09
2	28.87	84.22	1,777.87	32	124.25	2,610.84	3,933.92	62	534.70	5,137.47	6,089.96
3	30.31	168.44	1,849.74	33	130.44	2,695.06	4,005.78	63	561.35	5,221.69	6,161.83
4	31.82	252.66	1,921.60	34	136.94	2,779.28	4,077.65	64	589.33	5,305.91	6,233.70
5	33.41	336.88	1,993.47	35	143.77	2,863.51	4,149.52	65	618.71	5,390.13	6,305.57
6	35.07	421.10	2,065.34	36	150.94	2,947.73	4,221.39	66	649.56	5,474.35	6,377.44
7	36.82	505.32	2,137.21	37	158.46	3,031.95	4,293.26	67	681.94	5,558.57	6,449.30
8	38.66	589.55	2,209.08	38	166.36	3,116.17	4,365.13	68	715.93	5,642.79	6,521.17
9	40.58	673.77	2,280.95	39	174.65	3,200.39	4,436.99	69	751.62	5,727.01	6,593.04
10	42.61	757.99	2,352.81	40	183.36	3,284.61	4,508.86	70	789.09	5,811.23	6,664.91
11	44.73	842.21	2,424.68	41	192.50	3,368.83	4,580.73	71	828.43	5,895.45	6,736.78
12	46.96	926.43	2,496.55	42	202.10	3,453.05	4,652.60	72	869.72	5,979.67	6,808.65
13	49.30	1,010.65	2,568.42	43	212.17	3,537.27	4,724.47	73	913.08	6,063.89	6,880.51
14	51.76	1,094.87	2,640.29	44	222.75	3,621.49	4,796.33	74	958.60	6,148.11	6,952.38
15	54.34	1,179.09	2,712.16	45	233.85	3,705.71	4,868.20	75	1,006.38	6,232.34	7,024.25
16	57.05	1,263.31	2,784.02	46	245.51	3,789.93	4,940.07	76	1,056.55	6,316.56	7,096.12
17	59.89	1,347.53	2,855.89	47	257.75	3,874.15	5,011.94	77	1,109.22	6,400.78	7,167.99
18	62.88	1,431.75	2,927.76	48	270.60	3,958.38	5,083.81	78	1,164.52	6,485.00	7,239.86
19	66.01	1,515.97	2,999.63	49	284.09	4,042.60	5,155.68	79	1,222.57	6,569.22	7,311.72
20	69.30	1,600.19	3,071.50	50	298.25	4,126.82	5,227.54	80	1,283.52	6,653.44	7,383.59
21	72.76	1,684.42	3,143.37	51	313.12	4,211.04	5,299.41	81	1,347.50	6,737.66	7,455.46
22	76.39	1,768.64	3,215.23	52	328.72	4,295.26	5,371.28	82	1,414.67	6,821.88	7,527.33
23	80.19	1,852.86	3,287.10	53	345.11	4,379.48	5,443.15	83	1,485.20	6,906.10	7,599.20
24	84.19	1,937.08	3,358.97	54	362.32	4,463.70	5,515.02	84	1,559.23	6,990.32	7,671.06
25	88.39	2,021.30	3,430.84	55	380.38	4,547.92	5,586.89	85	1,636.96	7,074.54	7,742.93
26	92.79	2,105.52	3,502.71	56	399.34	4,632.14	5,658.75	86	1,718.57	7,158.76	7,814.80
27	97.42	2,189.74	3,574.57	57	419.25	4,716.36	5,730.62	87	1,804.24	7,242.98	7,886.67
28	102.28	2,273.96	3,646.44	58	440.15	4,800.58	5,802.49	88	1,894.18	7,327.21	7,958.54
29	107.37	2,358.18	3,718.31	59	462.09	4,884.80	5,874.36				
30	112.73	2,442.40	3,790.18	60	485.12	4,969.02	5,946.23				

189

Table 1 (continues)

Initial Catalog of Tunings : D-41

Scale Deg.	HZ	Cts	TU	Scale Deg.	HZ	Cts	TU	Scale Deg.	HZ	Cts	TU
1	27.50	0.00	1,706.00	31	114.21	2,465.00	3,809.46	61	474.31	4,930.00	5,912.92
2	28.84	82.17	1,776.12	32	119.76	2,547.16	3,879.58	62	497.36	5,012.16	5,983.04
3	30.24	164.33	1,846.23	33	125.58	2,629.33	3,949.69	63	521.54	5,094.33	6,053.15
4	31.71	246.50	1,916.35	34	131.68	2,711.50	4,019.81	64	546.89	5,176.49	6,123.27
5	33.25	328.67	1,986.46	35	138.08	2,793.66	4,089.92	65	573.47	5,258.66	6,193.38
6	34.87	410.83	2,056.58	36	144.80	2,875.83	4,160.04	66	601.34	5,340.83	6,263.50
7	36.56	493.00	2,126.69	37	151.83	2,958.00	4,230.15	67	630.57	5,422.99	6,333.61
8	38.34	575.17	2,196.81	38	159.21	3,040.16	4,300.27	68	661.22	5,505.16	6,403.73
9	40.20	657.33	2,266.92	39	166.95	3,122.33	4,370.38	69	693.36	5,587.33	6,473.84
10	42.15	739.50	2,337.04	40	175.07	3,204.50	4,440.50	70	727.06	5,669.49	6,543.96
11	44.20	821.67	2,407.15	41	183.58	3,286.66	4,510.61	71	762.40	5,751.66	6,614.08
12	46.35	903.83	2,477.27	42	192.50	3,368.83	4,580.73	72	799.46	5,833.83	6,684.19
13	48.60	986.00	2,547.38	43	201.86	3,451.00	4,650.85	73	838.32	5,915.99	6,754.31
14	50.97	1,068.17	2,617.50	44	211.67	3,533.16	4,720.96	74	879.06	5,998.16	6,824.42
15	53.44	1,150.33	2,687.62	45	221.96	3,615.33	4,791.08	75	921.79	6,080.33	6,894.54
16	56.04	1,232.50	2,757.73	46	232.74	3,697.50	4,861.19	76	966.59	6,162.49	6,964.65
17	58.77	1,314.67	2,827.85	47	244.06	3,779.66	4,931.31	77	1,013.57	6,244.66	7,034.77
18	61.62	1,396.83	2,897.96	48	255.92	3,861.83	5,001.42	78	1,062.84	6,326.83	7,104.88
19	64.62	1,479.00	2,968.08	49	268.36	3,944.00	5,071.54	79	1,114.50	6,408.99	7,175.00
20	67.76	1,561.17	3,038.19	50	281.40	4,026.16	5,141.65	80	1,168.67	6,491.16	7,245.11
21	71.05	1,643.33	3,108.31	51	295.08	4,108.33	5,211.77	81	1,225.48	6,573.33	7,315.23
22	74.51	1,725.50	3,178.42	52	309.42	4,190.50	5,281.88	82	1,285.04	6,655.49	7,385.34
23	78.13	1,807.66	3,248.54	53	324.46	4,272.66	5,352.00	83	1,347.50	6,737.66	7,455.46
24	81.92	1,889.83	3,318.65	54	340.23	4,354.83	5,422.11	84	1,413.00	6,819.83	7,525.58
25	85.91	1,972.00	3,388.77	55	356.77	4,437.00	5,492.23	85	1,481.68	6,901.99	7,595.69
26	90.08	2,054.16	3,458.88	56	374.11	4,519.16	5,562.35	86	1,553.69	6,984.16	7,665.81
27	94.46	2,136.33	3,529.00	57	392.30	4,601.33	5,632.46	87	1,629.21	7,066.33	7,735.92
28	99.05	2,218.50	3,599.11	58	411.36	4,683.50	5,702.58	88	1,708.40	7,148.49	7,806.04
29	103.87	2,300.66	3,669.23	59	431.36	4,765.66	5,772.69				
30	108.91	2,382.83	3,739.35	60	452.32	4,847.83	5,842.81				

Initial Catalog of Tunings : D-42

Scale Deg.	HZ	Cts	TU	Scale Deg.	HZ	Cts	TU	Scale Deg.	HZ	Cts	TU
1	27.50	0.00	1,706.00	31	110.40	2,406.31	3,759.38	61	443.22	4,812.61	5,812.76
2	28.80	80.21	1,774.45	32	115.64	2,486.52	3,827.82	62	464.23	4,892.82	5,881.20
3	30.17	160.42	1,842.89	33	121.12	2,566.73	3,896.27	63	486.25	4,973.03	5,949.65
4	31.60	240.63	1,911.34	34	126.86	2,646.94	3,964.72	64	509.31	5,053.25	6,018.10
5	33.10	320.84	1,979.78	35	132.88	2,727.15	4,033.16	65	533.46	5,133.46	6,086.54
6	34.67	401.05	2,048.23	36	139.18	2,807.36	4,101.61	66	558.76	5,213.67	6,154.99
7	36.31	481.26	2,116.68	37	145.78	2,887.57	4,170.05	67	585.25	5,293.88	6,223.43
8	38.03	561.47	2,185.12	38	152.69	2,967.78	4,238.50	68	613.01	5,374.09	6,291.88
9	39.84	641.68	2,253.57	39	159.94	3,047.99	4,306.95	69	642.08	5,454.30	6,360.32
10	41.73	721.89	2,322.01	40	167.52	3,128.20	4,375.39	70	672.52	5,534.51	6,428.77
11	43.71	802.10	2,390.46	41	175.46	3,208.41	4,443.84	71	704.42	5,614.72	6,497.22
12	45.78	882.31	2,458.91	42	183.78	3,288.62	4,512.28	72	737.82	5,694.93	6,565.66
13	47.95	962.52	2,527.35	43	192.50	3,368.83	4,580.73	73	772.81	5,775.14	6,634.11
14	50.22	1,042.73	2,595.80	44	201.63	3,449.04	4,649.18	74	809.46	5,855.35	6,702.55
15	52.61	1,122.94	2,664.24	45	211.19	3,529.25	4,717.62	75	847.84	5,935.56	6,771.00
16	55.10	1,203.15	2,732.69	46	221.20	3,609.46	4,786.07	76	888.05	6,015.77	6,839.45
17	57.71	1,283.36	2,801.14	47	231.69	3,689.67	4,854.51	77	930.16	6,095.98	6,907.89
18	60.45	1,363.57	2,869.58	48	242.68	3,769.88	4,922.96	78	974.27	6,176.19	6,976.34
19	63.32	1,443.78	2,938.03	49	254.19	3,850.09	4,991.41	79	1,020.47	6,256.40	7,044.78
20	66.32	1,523.99	3,006.47	50	266.24	3,930.30	5,059.85	80	1,068.86	6,336.61	7,113.23
21	69.46	1,604.20	3,074.92	51	278.87	4,010.51	5,128.30	81	1,119.55	6,416.82	7,181.68
22	72.76	1,684.42	3,143.36	52	292.09	4,090.72	5,196.74	82	1,172.64	6,497.03	7,250.12
23	76.21	1,764.63	3,211.81	53	305.95	4,170.93	5,265.19	83	1,228.25	6,577.24	7,318.57
24	79.82	1,844.84	3,280.26	54	320.45	4,251.14	5,333.64	84	1,286.49	6,657.45	7,387.01
25	83.61	1,925.05	3,348.70	55	335.65	4,331.35	5,402.08	85	1,347.50	6,737.66	7,455.46
26	87.57	2,005.26	3,417.15	56	351.57	4,411.56	5,470.53	86	1,411.40	6,817.87	7,523.91
27	91.73	2,085.47	3,485.59	57	368.24	4,491.77	5,538.97	87	1,478.33	6,898.08	7,592.35
28	96.07	2,165.68	3,554.04	58	385.70	4,571.98	5,607.42	88	1,548.43	6,978.29	7,660.80
29	100.63	2,245.89	3,622.49	59	403.99	4,652.19	5,675.87				
30	105.40	2,326.10	3,690.93	60	423.15	4,732.40	5,744.31				

Table 1 (continues)

Initial Catalog of Tunings : D-43

Scale Deg.	HZ	Cts	TU	Scale Deg.	HZ	Cts	TU	Scale Deg.	HZ	Cts	TU
1	27.50	0.00	1,706.00	31	106.89	2,350.35	3,711.63	61	415.47	4,700.69	5,717.25
2	28.77	78.34	1,772.85	32	111.84	2,428.69	3,778.48	62	434.70	4,779.04	5,784.11
3	30.11	156.69	1,839.71	33	117.02	2,507.04	3,845.33	63	454.83	4,857.38	5,850.96
4	31.50	235.03	1,906.56	34	122.43	2,585.38	3,912.19	64	475.88	4,935.73	5,917.81
5	32.96	313.38	1,973.42	35	128.10	2,663.73	3,979.04	65	497.91	5,014.07	5,984.67
6	34.48	391.72	2,040.27	36	134.03	2,742.07	4,045.90	66	520.96	5,092.42	6,051.52
7	36.08	470.07	2,107.13	37	140.24	2,820.42	4,112.75	67	545.08	5,170.76	6,118.38
8	37.75	548.41	2,173.98	38	146.73	2,898.76	4,179.60	68	570.31	5,249.11	6,185.23
9	39.50	626.76	2,240.83	39	153.52	2,977.11	4,246.46	69	596.71	5,327.45	6,252.08
10	41.33	705.10	2,307.69	40	160.63	3,055.45	4,313.31	70	624.34	5,405.80	6,318.94
11	43.24	783.45	2,374.54	41	168.06	3,133.80	4,380.17	71	653.24	5,484.14	6,385.79
12	45.24	861.79	2,441.40	42	175.84	3,212.14	4,447.02	72	683.48	5,562.49	6,452.65
13	47.33	940.14	2,508.25	43	183.98	3,290.49	4,513.88	73	715.12	5,640.83	6,519.50
14	49.53	1,018.48	2,575.10	44	192.50	3,368.83	4,580.73	74	748.23	5,719.18	6,586.36
15	51.82	1,096.83	2,641.96	45	201.41	3,447.17	4,647.58	75	782.87	5,797.52	6,653.21
16	54.22	1,175.17	2,708.81	46	210.74	3,525.52	4,714.44	76	819.11	5,875.87	6,720.06
17	56.73	1,253.52	2,775.67	47	220.49	3,603.86	4,781.29	77	857.03	5,954.21	6,786.92
18	59.35	1,331.86	2,842.52	48	230.70	3,682.21	4,848.15	78	896.70	6,032.56	6,853.77
19	62.10	1,410.21	2,909.38	49	241.38	3,760.55	4,915.00	79	938.21	6,110.90	6,920.63
20	64.98	1,488.55	2,976.23	50	252.55	3,838.90	4,981.86	80	981.65	6,189.25	6,987.48
21	67.98	1,566.90	3,043.08	51	264.24	3,917.24	5,048.71	81	1,027.09	6,267.59	7,054.33
22	71.13	1,645.24	3,109.94	52	276.48	3,995.59	5,115.56	82	1,074.64	6,345.94	7,121.19
23	74.42	1,723.59	3,176.79	53	289.28	4,073.93	5,182.42	83	1,124.38	6,424.28	7,188.04
24	77.87	1,801.93	3,243.65	54	302.67	4,152.28	5,249.27	84	1,176.44	6,502.63	7,254.90
25	81.47	1,880.28	3,310.50	55	316.68	4,230.62	5,316.13	85	1,230.90	6,580.97	7,321.75
26	85.24	1,958.62	3,377.35	56	331.34	4,308.97	5,382.98	86	1,287.88	6,659.32	7,388.61
27	89.19	2,036.97	3,444.21	57	346.68	4,387.31	5,449.83	87	1,347.50	6,737.66	7,455.46
28	93.32	2,115.31	3,511.06	58	362.73	4,465.66	5,516.69	88	1,409.88	6,816.00	7,522.31
29	97.64	2,193.66	3,577.92	59	379.52	4,544.00	5,583.54				
30	102.16	2,272.00	3,644.77	60	397.09	4,622.35	5,650.40				

Initial Catalog of Tunings : D-44

Scale Deg.	HZ	Cts	TU	Scale Deg.	HZ	Cts	TU	Scale Deg.	HZ	Cts	TU
1	27.50	0.00	1,706.00	31	103.64	2,296.93	3,666.04	61	390.61	4,593.86	5,626.09
2	28.74	76.56	1,771.33	32	108.33	2,373.49	3,731.38	62	408.27	4,670.42	5,691.42
3	30.04	153.13	1,836.67	33	113.23	2,450.06	3,796.71	63	426.73	4,746.99	5,756.76
4	31.40	229.69	1,902.00	34	118.35	2,526.62	3,862.05	64	446.03	4,823.55	5,822.09
5	32.82	306.26	1,967.34	35	123.70	2,603.19	3,927.38	65	466.19	4,900.12	5,887.43
6	34.31	382.82	2,032.67	36	129.29	2,679.75	3,992.72	66	487.27	4,976.68	5,952.76
7	35.86	459.39	2,098.01	37	135.14	2,756.32	4,058.05	67	509.31	5,053.25	6,018.10
8	37.48	535.95	2,163.34	38	141.25	2,832.88	4,123.39	68	532.34	5,129.81	6,083.43
9	39.17	612.51	2,228.68	39	147.64	2,909.44	4,188.72	69	556.41	5,206.37	6,148.76
10	40.94	689.08	2,294.01	40	154.31	2,986.01	4,254.06	70	581.57	5,282.94	6,214.10
11	42.80	765.64	2,359.35	41	161.29	3,062.57	4,319.39	71	607.86	5,359.50	6,279.43
12	44.73	842.21	2,424.68	42	168.58	3,139.14	4,384.73	72	635.35	5,436.07	6,344.77
13	46.75	918.77	2,490.02	43	176.20	3,215.70	4,450.06	73	664.08	5,512.63	6,410.10
14	48.87	995.34	2,555.35	44	184.17	3,292.27	4,515.40	74	694.11	5,589.20	6,475.44
15	51.08	1,071.90	2,620.69	45	192.50	3,368.83	4,580.73	75	725.49	5,665.76	6,540.77
16	53.39	1,148.46	2,686.02	46	201.20	3,445.39	4,646.06	76	758.30	5,742.32	6,606.11
17	55.80	1,225.03	2,751.36	47	210.30	3,521.96	4,711.40	77	792.59	5,818.89	6,671.44
18	58.32	1,301.59	2,816.69	48	219.81	3,598.52	4,776.73	78	828.43	5,895.45	6,736.78
19	60.96	1,378.16	2,882.03	49	229.75	3,675.09	4,842.07	79	865.89	5,972.02	6,802.11
20	63.72	1,454.72	2,947.36	50	240.14	3,751.65	4,907.40	80	905.04	6,048.58	6,867.45
21	66.60	1,531.29	3,012.70	51	251.00	3,828.22	4,972.74	81	945.96	6,125.15	6,932.78
22	69.61	1,607.85	3,078.03	52	262.35	3,904.78	5,038.07	82	988.74	6,201.71	6,998.12
23	72.76	1,684.42	3,143.36	53	274.21	3,981.34	5,103.41	83	1,033.45	6,278.27	7,063.45
24	76.05	1,760.98	3,208.70	54	286.61	4,057.91	5,168.74	84	1,080.18	6,354.84	7,128.79
25	79.49	1,837.54	3,274.03	55	299.57	4,134.47	5,234.08	85	1,129.02	6,431.40	7,194.12
26	83.08	1,914.11	3,339.37	56	313.12	4,211.04	5,299.41	86	1,180.07	6,507.97	7,259.46
27	86.84	1,990.67	3,404.70	57	327.27	4,287.60	5,364.75	87	1,233.43	6,584.53	7,324.79
28	90.76	2,067.24	3,470.04	58	342.07	4,364.17	5,430.08	88	1,289.21	6,661.10	7,390.13
29	94.87	2,143.80	3,535.37	59	357.54	4,440.73	5,495.42				
30	99.16	2,220.37	3,600.71	60	373.71	4,517.29	5,560.75				

Table 1 (continues)

Initial Catalog of Tunings : D-45

Scale Deg.	HZ	Cts	TU	Scale Deg.	HZ	Cts	TU	Scale Deg.	HZ	Cts	TU
1	27.50	0.00	1,706.00	31	100.63	2,245.89	3,622.49	61	368.24	4,491.77	5,538.97
2	28.72	74.86	1,769.88	32	105.08	2,320.75	3,686.37	62	384.51	4,566.64	5,602.86
3	29.98	149.73	1,833.77	33	109.72	2,395.61	3,750.25	63	401.50	4,641.50	5,666.74
4	31.31	224.59	1,897.65	34	114.57	2,470.48	3,814.14	64	419.25	4,716.36	5,730.62
5	32.69	299.45	1,961.53	35	119.63	2,545.34	3,878.02	65	437.77	4,791.22	5,794.50
6	34.14	374.31	2,025.41	36	124.92	2,620.20	3,941.90	66	457.12	4,866.09	5,858.39
7	35.65	449.18	2,089.30	37	130.44	2,695.06	4,005.78	67	477.32	4,940.95	5,922.27
8	37.22	524.04	2,153.18	38	136.20	2,769.93	4,069.67	68	498.41	5,015.81	5,986.15
9	38.87	598.90	2,217.06	39	142.22	2,844.79	4,133.55	69	520.44	5,090.68	6,050.04
10	40.58	673.77	2,280.95	40	148.51	2,919.65	4,197.43	70	543.44	5,165.54	6,113.92
11	42.38	748.63	2,344.83	41	155.07	2,994.52	4,261.32	71	567.45	5,240.40	6,177.80
12	44.25	823.49	2,408.71	42	161.92	3,069.38	4,325.20	72	592.53	5,315.27	6,241.69
13	46.21	898.35	2,472.59	43	169.08	3,144.24	4,389.08	73	618.71	5,390.13	6,305.57
14	48.25	973.22	2,536.48	44	176.55	3,219.10	4,452.96	74	646.06	5,464.99	6,369.45
15	50.38	1,048.08	2,600.36	45	184.35	3,293.97	4,516.85	75	674.60	5,539.85	6,433.33
16	52.61	1,122.94	2,664.24	46	192.50	3,368.83	4,580.73	76	704.42	5,614.72	6,497.22
17	54.93	1,197.81	2,728.13	47	201.01	3,443.69	4,644.61	77	735.55	5,689.58	6,561.10
18	57.36	1,272.67	2,792.01	48	209.89	3,518.56	4,708.50	78	768.05	5,764.44	6,624.98
19	59.89	1,347.53	2,855.89	49	219.16	3,593.42	4,772.38	79	801.99	5,839.31	6,688.87
20	62.54	1,422.39	2,919.77	50	228.85	3,668.28	4,836.26	80	837.43	5,914.17	6,752.75
21	65.30	1,497.26	2,983.66	51	238.96	3,743.14	4,900.14	81	874.44	5,989.03	6,816.63
22	68.19	1,572.12	3,047.54	52	249.52	3,818.01	4,964.03	82	913.08	6,063.89	6,880.51
23	71.20	1,646.98	3,111.42	53	260.55	3,892.87	5,027.91	83	953.43	6,138.76	6,944.40
24	74.35	1,721.85	3,175.31	54	272.06	3,967.73	5,091.79	84	995.56	6,213.62	7,008.28
25	77.63	1,796.71	3,239.19	55	284.09	4,042.60	5,155.68	85	1,039.56	6,288.48	7,072.16
26	81.06	1,871.57	3,303.07	56	296.64	4,117.46	5,219.56	86	1,085.50	6,363.35	7,136.05
27	84.65	1,946.44	3,366.96	57	309.75	4,192.32	5,283.44	87	1,133.47	6,438.21	7,199.93
28	88.39	2,021.30	3,430.84	58	323.44	4,267.18	5,347.32	88	1,183.56	6,513.07	7,263.81
29	92.29	2,096.16	3,494.72	59	337.73	4,342.05	5,411.21				
30	96.37	2,171.02	3,558.60	60	352.66	4,416.91	5,475.09				

Initial Catalog of Tunings : D-46

Scale Deg.	HZ	Cts	TU	Scale Deg.	HZ	Cts	TU	Scale Deg.	HZ	Cts	TU
1	27.50	0.00	1,706.00	31	97.83	2,197.06	3,580.82	61	348.04	4,394.13	5,455.65
2	28.69	73.24	1,768.49	32	102.06	2,270.30	3,643.32	62	363.08	4,467.36	5,518.14
3	29.93	146.47	1,830.99	33	106.47	2,343.53	3,705.81	63	378.77	4,540.60	5,580.64
4	31.22	219.71	1,893.48	34	111.07	2,416.77	3,768.31	64	395.14	4,613.83	5,643.13
5	32.57	292.94	1,955.98	35	115.87	2,490.00	3,830.80	65	412.21	4,687.07	5,705.62
6	33.98	366.18	2,018.47	36	120.88	2,563.24	3,893.29	66	430.02	4,760.30	5,768.12
7	35.45	439.41	2,080.96	37	126.10	2,636.48	3,955.79	67	448.61	4,833.54	5,830.61
8	36.98	512.65	2,143.46	38	131.55	2,709.71	4,018.28	68	467.99	4,906.77	5,893.11
9	38.58	585.88	2,205.95	39	137.23	2,782.95	4,080.78	69	488.21	4,980.01	5,955.60
10	40.24	659.12	2,268.45	40	143.16	2,856.18	4,143.27	70	509.31	5,053.25	6,018.09
11	41.98	732.35	2,330.94	41	149.35	2,929.42	4,205.77	71	531.31	5,126.48	6,080.59
12	43.79	805.59	2,393.44	42	155.80	3,002.65	4,268.26	72	554.27	5,199.72	6,143.08
13	45.69	878.83	2,455.93	43	162.53	3,075.89	4,330.75	73	578.22	5,272.95	6,205.58
14	47.66	952.06	2,518.42	44	169.56	3,149.12	4,393.25	74	603.21	5,346.19	6,268.07
15	49.72	1,025.30	2,580.92	45	176.88	3,222.36	4,455.74	75	629.27	5,419.42	6,330.57
16	51.87	1,098.53	2,643.41	46	184.53	3,295.59	4,518.24	76	656.46	5,492.66	6,393.06
17	54.11	1,171.77	2,705.91	47	192.50	3,368.83	4,580.73	77	684.83	5,565.89	6,455.55
18	56.45	1,245.00	2,768.40	48	200.82	3,442.07	4,643.22	78	714.42	5,639.13	6,518.05
19	58.89	1,318.24	2,830.89	49	209.50	3,515.30	4,705.72	79	745.29	5,712.36	6,580.54
20	61.43	1,391.47	2,893.39	50	218.55	3,588.54	4,768.21	80	777.49	5,785.60	6,643.04
21	64.09	1,464.71	2,955.88	51	227.99	3,661.77	4,830.71	81	811.09	5,858.83	6,705.53
22	66.86	1,537.94	3,018.38	52	237.84	3,735.01	4,893.20	82	846.14	5,932.07	6,768.02
23	69.74	1,611.18	3,080.87	53	248.12	3,808.24	4,955.69	83	882.70	6,005.31	6,830.52
24	72.76	1,684.42	3,143.37	54	258.84	3,881.48	5,018.19	84	920.84	6,078.54	6,893.01
25	75.90	1,757.65	3,205.86	55	270.03	3,954.71	5,080.68	85	960.63	6,151.78	6,955.51
26	79.18	1,830.89	3,268.35	56	281.69	4,027.95	5,143.18	86	1,002.14	6,225.01	7,018.00
27	82.60	1,904.12	3,330.85	57	293.86	4,101.18	5,205.67	87	1,045.44	6,298.25	7,080.50
28	86.17	1,977.36	3,393.34	58	306.56	4,174.42	5,268.17	88	1,090.61	6,371.48	7,142.99
29	89.90	2,050.59	3,455.84	59	319.81	4,247.66	5,330.66				
30	93.78	2,123.83	3,518.33	60	333.63	4,320.89	5,393.15				

192

Table 1 (continues)

Initial Catalog of Tunings : D-47

Scale Deg.	HZ	Cts	TU	Scale Deg.	HZ	Cts	TU	Scale Deg.	HZ	Cts	TU
1	27.50	0.00	1,706.00	31	95.23	2,150.32	3,540.93	61	329.75	4,300.63	5,375.87
2	28.66	71.68	1,767.16	32	99.25	2,221.99	3,602.10	62	343.69	4,372.31	5,437.03
3	29.87	143.35	1,828.33	33	103.45	2,293.67	3,663.26	63	358.21	4,443.99	5,498.20
4	31.14	215.03	1,889.49	34	107.82	2,365.35	3,724.43	64	373.36	4,515.67	5,559.36
5	32.45	286.71	1,950.66	35	112.38	2,437.03	3,785.59	65	389.14	4,587.34	5,620.53
6	33.82	358.39	2,011.82	36	117.13	2,508.70	3,846.76	66	405.59	4,659.02	5,681.69
7	35.25	430.06	2,072.99	37	122.08	2,580.38	3,907.92	67	422.73	4,730.70	5,742.85
8	36.75	501.74	2,134.15	38	127.24	2,652.06	3,969.09	68	440.60	4,802.37	5,804.02
9	38.30	573.42	2,195.32	39	132.62	2,723.73	4,030.25	69	459.23	4,874.05	5,865.18
10	39.92	645.10	2,256.48	40	138.22	2,795.41	4,091.41	70	478.64	4,945.73	5,926.35
11	41.60	716.77	2,317.64	41	144.07	2,867.09	4,152.58	71	498.87	5,017.41	5,987.51
12	43.36	788.45	2,378.81	42	150.16	2,938.77	4,213.74	72	519.96	5,089.08	6,048.68
13	45.20	860.13	2,439.97	43	156.50	3,010.44	4,274.91	73	541.94	5,160.76	6,109.84
14	47.11	931.80	2,501.14	44	163.12	3,082.12	4,336.07	74	564.85	5,232.44	6,171.01
15	49.10	1,003.48	2,562.30	45	170.02	3,153.80	4,397.24	75	588.73	5,304.12	6,232.17
16	51.17	1,075.16	2,623.47	46	177.20	3,225.48	4,458.40	76	613.61	5,375.79	6,293.34
17	53.34	1,146.84	2,684.63	47	184.69	3,297.15	4,519.57	77	639.55	5,447.47	6,354.50
18	55.59	1,218.51	2,745.80	48	192.50	3,368.83	4,580.73	78	666.58	5,519.15	6,415.66
19	57.94	1,290.19	2,806.96	49	200.64	3,440.51	4,641.89	79	694.76	5,590.82	6,476.83
20	60.39	1,361.87	2,868.12	50	209.12	3,512.18	4,703.06	80	724.13	5,662.50	6,537.99
21	62.94	1,433.54	2,929.29	51	217.96	3,583.86	4,764.22	81	754.74	5,734.18	6,599.16
22	65.60	1,505.22	2,990.45	52	227.17	3,655.54	4,825.39	82	786.64	5,805.86	6,660.32
23	68.38	1,576.90	3,051.62	53	236.77	3,727.22	4,886.55	83	819.90	5,877.53	6,721.49
24	71.27	1,648.58	3,112.78	54	246.78	3,798.89	4,947.72	84	854.55	5,949.21	6,782.65
25	74.28	1,720.25	3,173.95	55	257.22	3,870.57	5,008.88	85	890.68	6,020.89	6,843.82
26	77.42	1,791.93	3,235.11	56	268.09	3,942.25	5,070.05	86	928.33	6,092.56	6,904.98
27	80.69	1,863.61	3,296.28	57	279.42	4,013.93	5,131.21	87	967.57	6,164.24	6,966.14
28	84.10	1,935.29	3,357.44	58	291.23	4,085.60	5,192.37	88	1,008.47	6,235.92	7,027.31
29	87.66	2,006.96	3,418.61	59	303.54	4,157.28	5,253.54				
30	91.36	2,078.64	3,479.77	60	316.37	4,228.96	5,314.70				

Initial Catalog of Tunings : D-48

Scale Deg.	HZ	Cts	TU	Scale Deg.	HZ	Cts	TU	Scale Deg.	HZ	Cts	TU
1	27.50	0.00	1,706.00	31	92.79	2,105.32	3,502.71	61	313.12	4,211.04	5,299.41
2	28.64	70.18	1,765.89	32	96.63	2,175.70	3,562.60	62	326.07	4,281.22	5,359.30
3	29.82	140.37	1,825.78	33	100.63	2,245.89	3,622.49	63	339.56	4,351.41	5,419.19
4	31.06	210.55	1,885.67	34	104.79	2,316.07	3,682.38	64	353.61	4,421.59	5,479.08
5	32.34	280.74	1,945.56	35	109.13	2,386.25	3,742.27	65	368.24	4,491.77	5,538.97
6	33.68	350.92	2,005.45	36	113.64	2,456.44	3,802.16	66	383.47	4,561.96	5,598.86
7	35.07	421.10	2,065.34	37	118.35	2,526.62	3,862.05	67	399.34	4,632.14	5,658.75
8	36.52	491.29	2,125.23	38	123.24	2,596.81	3,921.94	68	415.86	4,702.33	5,718.64
9	38.03	561.47	2,185.12	39	128.34	2,666.99	3,981.83	69	433.07	4,772.51	5,778.53
10	39.61	631.66	2,245.01	40	133.65	2,737.17	4,041.72	70	450.98	4,842.69	5,838.42
11	41.25	701.84	2,304.90	41	139.18	2,807.36	4,101.61	71	469.64	4,912.88	5,898.31
12	42.95	772.02	2,364.79	42	144.94	2,877.54	4,161.50	72	489.07	4,983.06	5,958.20
13	44.73	842.21	2,424.68	43	150.94	2,947.73	4,221.39	73	509.31	5,053.25	6,018.09
14	46.58	912.39	2,484.57	44	157.18	3,017.91	4,281.28	74	530.38	5,123.43	6,077.99
15	48.51	982.58	2,544.46	45	163.68	3,088.09	4,341.17	75	552.32	5,193.61	6,137.88
16	50.52	1,052.76	2,604.35	46	170.46	3,158.28	4,401.06	76	575.17	5,263.80	6,197.77
17	52.61	1,122.94	2,664.24	47	177.51	3,228.46	4,460.95	77	598.97	5,333.98	6,257.66
18	54.78	1,193.13	2,724.13	48	184.85	3,298.65	4,520.84	78	623.75	5,404.16	6,317.55
19	57.05	1,263.31	2,784.02	49	192.50	3,368.83	4,580.73	79	649.56	5,474.35	6,377.44
20	59.41	1,333.50	2,843.91	50	200.46	3,439.01	4,640.62	80	676.43	5,544.53	6,437.33
21	61.87	1,403.68	2,903.80	51	208.76	3,509.20	4,700.51	81	704.42	5,614.72	6,497.22
22	64.43	1,473.86	2,963.69	52	217.39	3,579.38	4,760.40	82	733.56	5,684.90	6,557.11
23	67.09	1,544.05	3,023.58	53	226.39	3,649.57	4,820.29	83	763.91	5,755.08	6,617.00
24	69.87	1,614.23	3,083.47	54	235.76	3,719.75	4,880.18	84	795.51	5,825.27	6,676.89
25	72.76	1,684.42	3,143.36	55	245.51	3,789.93	4,940.07	85	828.43	5,895.45	6,736.78
26	75.77	1,754.60	3,203.26	56	255.67	3,860.12	4,999.96	86	862.70	5,965.64	6,796.67
27	78.90	1,824.78	3,263.15	57	266.24	3,930.30	5,059.85	87	898.39	6,035.82	6,856.56
28	82.17	1,894.97	3,323.04	58	277.26	4,000.49	5,119.74	88	935.56	6,106.00	6,916.45
29	85.57	1,965.15	3,382.93	59	288.73	4,070.67	5,179.63				
30	89.11	2,035.33	3,442.82	60	300.68	4,140.85	5,239.52				

Table 2
Constant Increments in Cents and Tuning Units

Tuning	K Cts	K TU	Tuning	K Cts	K TU	Tuning	K Cts	K TU
Oct -5	240.00	204.80	A -8	237.75	202.88	B -12	232.19	198.13
Oct -6	200.00	170.67	A -9	211.33	180.33	B -13	214.33	182.89
Oct -7	171.43	146.29	A -10	190.20	162.30	B -14	199.02	169.83
Oct -8	150.00	128.00	A -11	172.91	147.55	B -15	185.75	158.51
Oct -9	133.33	113.78	A -12	158.50	135.25	B -16	174.14	148.60
Oct -10	120.00	102.40	A -13	146.30	124.85	B -17	163.90	139.86
Oct -11	109.09	93.09	A -14	135.85	115.93	B -18	154.80	132.09
Oct -12	100.00	85.33	A -15	126.80	108.20	B -19	146.65	125.14
Oct -13	92.31	78.77	A -16	118.87	101.44	B -20	139.32	118.88
Oct -14	85.71	73.14	A -17	111.88	95.47	B -21	132.68	113.22
Oct -15	80.00	68.27	A -18	105.66	90.17	B -22	126.65	108.07
Oct -16	75.00	64.00	A -19	100.10	85.42	B -23	121.14	103.37
Oct -17	70.59	60.24	A -20	95.10	81.15	B -24	116.10	99.07
Oct -18	66.67	56.89	A -21	90.57	77.29	B -25	111.45	95.10
Oct -19	63.16	53.89	A -22	86.45	73.77	B -26	107.17	91.45
Oct -20	60.00	51.20	A -23	82.69	70.57	B -27	103.20	88.06
Oct -21	57.14	48.76	A -24	79.25	67.63	B -28	99.51	84.91
Oct -22	54.55	46.55	A -25	76.08	64.92	B -29	96.08	81.99
Oct -23	52.17	44.52	A -26	73.15	62.42	B -30	92.88	79.25
Oct -24	50.00	42.67	A -27	70.44	60.11	B -31	89.88	76.70

Tuning	K Cts	K TU	Tuning	K Cts	K TU	Tuning	K Cts	K TU
C-12	258.50	220.58	D -12	280.73	239.57	D -31	108.67	92.74
C-13	238.61	203.62	D -13	259.14	221.14	D -32	105.28	89.84
C-14	221.57	189.07	D -14	240.63	205.34	D -33	102.08	87.12
C-15	206.80	176.47	D -15	224.59	191.65	D -34	99.08	84.55
C-16	193.87	165.44	D -16	210.55	179.68	D -35	96.25	82.14
C-17	182.47	155.71	D -17	198.16	169.11	D -36	93.58	79.86
C-18	172.33	147.06	D -18	187.16	159.71	D -37	91.05	77.70
C-19	163.26	139.32	D -19	177.31	151.31	D -38	88.65	75.65
C-20	155.10	132.35	D -20	168.44	143.74	D -39	86.38	73.71
C-21	147.71	126.05	D -21	160.42	136.90	D -40	84.22	71.87
C-22	141.00	120.32	D -22	153.13	130.67	D -41	82.17	70.12
C-23	134.87	115.09	D -23	146.47	124.99	D -42	80.21	68.45
C-24	129.25	110.29	D -24	140.37	119.78	D -43	78.34	66.86
C-25	124.08	105.88	D -25	134.75	114.99	D -44	76.56	65.34
C-26	119.31	101.81	D -26	129.57	110.57	D -45	74.86	63.88
C-27	114.89	98.04	D -27	124.77	106.47	D -46	73.23	62.50
C-28	110.78	94.54	D -28	120.31	102.67	D -47	71.68	61.17
C-29	106.96	91.28	D -29	116.17	99.13	D -48	70.18	59.89
C-30	103.40	88.23	D -30	112.29	95.83			
C-31	100.06	85.39						
C-32	96.94	82.72						
C-33	94.00	80.21						
C-34	91.23	77.85						
C-35	88.63	75.63						
C-36	86.17	73.53						
C-37	83.84	71.54						
C-38	81.63	69.66						
C-39	79.54	67.87						
C-40	77.55	66.18						

Table 3
Proximity of Tunings

Tuning	K Cts	K TU	Tuning	K Cts	K TU	Tuning	K Cts	K TU
Oct -24	50.00	42.67	A -20	95.10	81.15	D -24	140.37	119.78
Oct -23	52.17	44.52	B -29	96.08	81.99	C-22	141.00	120.32
Oct -22	54.55	46.55	D -35	96.25	82.14	A -13	146.30	124.85
Oct -21	57.14	48.76	C-32	96.94	82.72	D -23	146.47	124.99
Oct -20	60.00	51.20	D -34	99.08	84.55	B -19	146.65	125.14
Oct -19	63.16	53.89	B -28	99.51	84.91	C-21	147.71	126.05
Oct -18	66.67	56.89	Oct -12	100.00	85.33	Oct -8	150.00	128.00
D -48	70.18	59.89	C-31	100.06	85.39	D -22	153.13	130.67
A -27	70.44	60.11	A -19	100.10	85.42	B -18	154.80	132.09
Oct -17	70.59	60.24	D -33	102.08	87.12	C-20	155.10	132.35
D -47	71.68	61.17	B -27	103.20	88.06	A -12	158.50	135.25
A -26	73.15	62.42	C-30	103.40	88.23	D -21	160.42	136.90
D -46	73.23	62.50	D -32	105.28	89.84	C-19	163.26	139.32
D -45	74.86	63.88	A -18	105.66	90.17	B -17	163.90	139.86
Oct -16	75.00	64.00	C-29	106.96	91.28	D -20	168.44	143.74
A -25	76.08	64.92	B -26	107.17	91.45	Oct -7	171.43	146.29
D -44	76.56	65.34	D -31	108.67	92.74	C-18	172.33	147.06
C-40	77.55	66.18	Oct -11	109.09	93.09	A -11	172.91	147.55
D -43	78.34	66.86	C-28	110.78	94.54	B -16	174.14	148.60
A -24	79.25	67.63	B -25	111.45	95.10	D -19	177.31	151.31
C-39	79.54	67.87	A -17	111.88	95.47	C-17	182.47	155.71
Oct -15	80.00	68.27	D-30	112.29	95.83	B -15	185.75	158.51
D -42	80.21	68.45	C-27	114.89	98.04	D -18	187.16	159.71
C-38	81.63	69.66	B -24	116.10	99.07	A -10	190.20	162.30
D -41	82.17	70.12	D -29	116.17	99.13	C-16	193.87	165.44
A -23	82.69	70.57	A -16	118.87	101.44	D -17	198.16	169.11
C-37	83.84	71.54	C-26	119.31	101.81	B -14	199.02	169.83
D -40	84.22	71.87	Oct -10	120.00	102.40	Oct -6	200.00	170.67
Oct -14	85.71	73.14	D -28	120.31	102.67	C-15	206.80	176.47
C-36	86.17	73.53	B -23	121.14	103.37	D -16	210.55	179.68
D -39	86.38	73.71	C-25	124.08	105.88	A -9	211.33	180.33
A -22	86.45	73.77	D -27	124.77	106.47	B -13	214.33	182.89
C-35	88.63	75.63	B -22	126.65	108.07	C-14	221.57	189.07
D -38	88.65	75.65	A -15	126.80	108.20	D -15	224.59	191.65
B -31	89.88	76.70	C-24	129.25	110.29	B -12	232.19	198.13
A -21	90.57	77.29	D -26	129.57	110.57	A -8	237.75	202.88
D -37	91.05	77.70	B -21	132.68	113.22	C-13	238.61	203.62
C-34	91.23	77.85	Oct -9	133.33	113.78	Oct -5	240.00	204.80
Oct -13	92.31	78.77	D -25	134.75	114.99	D -14	240.63	205.34
B -30	92.88	79.25	C-23	134.87	115.09	C-12	258.50	220.58
D -36	93.58	79.86	A -14	135.85	115.93	D -13	259.14	221.14
C-33	94.00	80.21	B -20	139.32	118.88	D -12	280.73	239.57

195

Table 4
Originality of Expanded Tunings in Comparison to Octave-Based Tunings

Rank	Tuning	K Cts	Diff. From	Tuning	K Cts	Rank	Tuning	K Cts	Diff. From	Tuning	K Cts
1	D -12	280.73	40.73	Oct -5	240.00	54	A -14	135.85	2.52	Oct -9	133.33
2	D -13	259.14	19.14	Oct -5	240.00	55	C -40	77.55	2.45	Oct -15	80.00
3	C -12	258.50	18.50	Oct -5	240.00	56	B -31	89.88	2.43	Oct -13	92.31
4	C -14	221.57	18.43	Oct -5	240.00	57	B -25	111.45	2.36	Oct -11	109.09
5	D -15	224.59	15.41	Oct -5	240.00	58	C -21	147.71	2.29	Oct -8	150.00
6	B -13	214.33	14.33	Oct -6	200.00	59	A -8	237.75	2.25	Oct -5	240.00
7	B -15	185.75	14.25	Oct -6	200.00	60	D -41	82.17	2.17	Oct -15	80.00
8	D -18	187.16	12.84	Oct -6	200.00	61	C -29	106.96	2.13	Oct -11	109.09
9	A -9	211.33	11.33	Oct -6	200.00	62	D -33	102.08	2.08	Oct -12	100.00
10	C -17	182.47	11.04	Oct -7	171.43	63	B -26	107.17	1.93	Oct -11	109.09
11	D -16	210.55	10.55	Oct -6	200.00	64	C -37	83.84	1.88	Oct -14	85.71
12	D -21	160.42	10.42	Oct -8	150.00	65	A -26	73.15	1.85	Oct -16	75.00
13	A -10	190.20	9.80	Oct -6	200.00	66	D -17	198.16	1.84	Oct -6	200.00
14	A -12	158.50	8.50	Oct -8	150.00	67	D -46	73.23	1.77	Oct -16	75.00
15	C -19	163.26	8.17	Oct -7	171.43	68	A -21	90.57	1.74	Oct -13	92.31
16	B -12	232.19	7.81	Oct -5	240.00	69	C -28	110.78	1.69	Oct -11	109.09
17	C -22	141.00	7.66	Oct -9	133.33	70	C -33	94.00	1.69	Oct -13	92.31
18	B -17	163.90	7.53	Oct -7	171.43	71	D -43	78.34	1.66	Oct -15	80.00
19	D -24	140.37	7.03	Oct -9	133.33	72	C -38	81.63	1.63	Oct -15	80.00
20	C -15	206.80	6.80	Oct -6	200.00	73	D -44	76.56	1.56	Oct -16	75.00
21	B -22	126.65	6.65	Oct -10	120.00	74	C -23	134.87	1.53	Oct -9	133.33
22	A -15	126.80	6.54	Oct -9	133.33	75	D -40	84.22	1.49	Oct -14	85.71
23	C -16	193.87	6.13	Oct -6	200.00	76	A -11	172.91	1.48	Oct -7	171.43
24	B -20	139.32	5.98	Oct -9	133.33	77	D -25	134.75	1.42	Oct -9	133.33
25	D -19	177.31	5.88	Oct -7	171.43	78	C -13	238.61	1.39	Oct -5	240.00
26	C -27	114.89	5.11	Oct -10	120.00	79	D -36	93.58	1.27	Oct -13	92.31
27	C -20	155.10	5.10	Oct -8	150.00	80	D -37	91.05	1.26	Oct -13	92.31
28	B -18	154.80	4.79	Oct -8	150.00	81	B -23	121.14	1.14	Oct -10	120.00
29	D -27	124.77	4.77	Oct -10	120.00	82	A -16	118.87	1.13	Oct -10	120.00
30	C -24	129.25	4.09	Oct -9	133.33	83	D -47	71.68	1.09	Oct -17	70.59
31	C -25	124.08	4.08	Oct -10	120.00	84	A -25	76.08	1.08	Oct -16	75.00
32	B -24	116.10	3.90	Oct -10	120.00	85	C -34	91.23	1.07	Oct -13	92.31
33	D -29	116.17	3.83	Oct -10	120.00	86	B -14	199.02	0.98	Oct -6	200.00
34	D -32	105.28	3.82	Oct -11	109.09	87	D -34	99.08	0.92	Oct -12	100.00
35	B -29	96.08	3.77	Oct -13	92.31	88	C -18	172.33	0.90	Oct -7	171.43
36	D -26	129.57	3.76	Oct -9	133.33	89	A -24	79.25	0.75	Oct -15	80.00
37	D -35	96.25	3.75	Oct -12	100.00	90	A -22	86.45	0.74	Oct -14	85.71
38	A -13	146.30	3.70	Oct -8	150.00	91	C -26	119.31	0.69	Oct -10	120.00
39	D -23	146.47	3.53	Oct -8	150.00	92	D -39	86.38	0.67	Oct -14	85.71
40	A -18	105.66	3.43	Oct -11	109.09	93	B -21	132.68	0.65	Oct -9	133.33
41	C -30	103.40	3.40	Oct -12	100.00	94	D -14	240.63	0.63	Oct -5	240.00
42	B -19	146.65	3.35	Oct -8	150.00	95	B -30	92.88	0.57	Oct -13	92.31
43	D -30	112.29	3.20	Oct -11	109.09	96	B -28	99.51	0.49	Oct -12	100.00
44	B -27	103.20	3.20	Oct -12	100.00	97	C -39	79.54	0.46	Oct -15	80.00
45	D -22	153.13	3.13	Oct -8	150.00	98	C -36	86.17	0.45	Oct -14	85.71
46	C -32	96.94	3.06	Oct -12	100.00	99	D -31	108.67	0.42	Oct -11	109.09
47	D -20	168.44	2.99	Oct -7	171.43	100	D -48	70.18	0.40	Oct -17	70.59
48	D -38	88.65	2.94	Oct -14	85.71	101	D -28	120.31	0.31	Oct -10	120.00
49	C -35	88.63	2.91	Oct -14	85.71	102	D -42	80.21	0.21	Oct -15	80.00
50	A -20	95.10	2.79	Oct -13	92.31	103	A -27	70.44	0.15	Oct -17	70.59
51	A -17	111.88	2.79	Oct -11	109.09	104	D -45	74.86	0.14	Oct -16	75.00
52	B -16	174.14	2.72	Oct -7	171.43	105	A -19	100.10	0.10	Oct -12	100.00
53	A -23	82.69	2.69	Oct -15	80.00	106	C -31	100.06	0.06	Oct -12	100.00

Table 5
Foreign Chroma Interference in the Family A-n

		First 6 powers of 2		
Rank	Tuning	Diff.	Scale Degree.	Cts
1	A-12	22.54	16	2,377.45
2	A-10	13.72	20	3,613.72
3	A-24	11.27	16	1,188.73
3	A-16	11.27	11	1,188.73
3	A-8	11.27	6	1,188.73
6	A-17	10.84	44	4,810.84
7	A-22	10.33	15	1,210.34
8	A-11	10.33	8	1,210.34
9	A-15	9.14	20	2,409.15
10	A-20	8.82	64	5,991.17
11	A-18	7.40	35	3,592.59
11	A-9	7.40	18	3,592.59
13	A-25	7.06	64	4,792.94
14	A-27	2.46	18	1,197.53
15	A-23	1.87	30	2,398.12
16	A-26	1.51	83	5,998.49
16	A-13	1.51	42	5,998.49
18	A-19	1.23	13	1,201.24
19	A-14	0.27	54	7,200.28
20	A-21	0.18	54	4,800.18

Table 6
Foreign Chroma Interference in the Family B-n

		First 6 powers of 2			First 4 powers of 3			Smaller
Rank	Tuning	Diff.	Scale Degree.	Cts	Diff.	Scale Degree.	Cts	Approx.
1	B-15	14.80	14	2,414.80	44.42	11	1,857.54	14.80
2	B-16	19.01	8	1,219.01	13.63	12	1,915.59	13.63
3	B-27	11.88	36	3,611.88	14.36	38	3,818.28	11.88
4	B-23	11.43	11	1,211.44	12.12	48	5,693.76	11.43
5	B-25	7.54	44	4,792.45	7.27	18	1,894.69	7.27
6	B-20	9.43	44	5,990.57	6.06	42	5,711.94	6.06
7	B-28	5.86	13	1,194.13	11.25	20	1,890.71	5.86
7	B-14	5.86	7	1,194.13	22.50	20	3,781.42	5.86
9	B-17	5.81	23	3,605.81	30.64	36	5,736.52	5.81
10	B-31	4.76	41	3,595.24	14.46	22	1,887.50	4.76
11	B-19	12.56	42	6,012.56	4.46	14	1,906.42	4.46
12	B-30	7.40	14	1,207.40	4.04	42	3,807.96	4.04
13	B-22	6.35	20	2,406.36	2.20	16	1,899.76	2.20
14	B-12	2.03	32	7,197.97	44.42	9	1,857.54	2.03
15	B-29	1.99	26	2,401.99	19.63	21	1,921.59	1.99
16	B-18	1.35	32	4,798.65	21.54	38	5,727.42	1.35
17	B-26	1.28	57	6,001.28	26.09	54	5,679.79	1.28
17	B-13	1.28	29	6,001.28	27.02	10	1,928.98	1.28
19	B-24	1.01	32	3,598.98	17.16	50	5,688.72	1.01
20	B-21	5.86	10	1,194.13	0.58	44	5,705.30	0.58

Table 7
Foreign Chroma Interference
in the Family C-n

Rank	Tuning	First 6 Powers of 2			First 4 Powers of 3			First 2 Powers of 5			Smaller
		Diff.	Scale Degree	Cts	Diff.	Scale Degree	Cts	Diff.	Scale Degree	Cts	Approx.
1	C-17	21.45	34	6,021.45	27.91	22	3,831.83	49.29	16	2,737.02	21.45
2	C-12	18.95	15	3,618.95	18.95	23	5,686.93	57.15	12	2,843.46	18.95
3	C-21	18.30	9	1,181.70	18.30	14	1,920.26	20.23	20	2,806.54	18.30
4	C-14	17.64	28	5,982.35	37.25	18	3,766.67	33.41	26	5,539.21	17.64
5	C-24	17.81	38	4,782.19	18.95	45	5,686.93	14.94	44	5,557.68	14.94
6	C-23	13.81	10	1,213.81	13.81	15	1,888.15	43.04	42	5,529.58	13.81
7	C-27	12.63	22	2,412.64	12.64	34	3,791.28	29.01	25	2,757.30	12.63
8	C-32	10.04	63	6,010.05	13.36	60	5,719.24	24.84	30	2,811.15	10.04
8	C-16	10.04	32	6,010.05	36.76	11	1,938.73	49.68	30	5,622.30	10.04
10	C-38	8.25	45	3,591.74	8.26	71	5,714.14	10.87	35	2,775.44	8.25
10	C-19	8.25	23	3,591.74	8.26	36	5,714.14	10.87	18	2,775.44	8.25
12	C-34	7.49	80	7,207.50	13.96	22	1,915.92	7.34	62	5,565.28	7.34
13	C-35	7.05	28	2,392.94	7.06	44	3,810.98	10.91	64	5,583.53	7.05
14	C-26	6.93	11	1,193.06	6.94	17	1,908.90	34.77	48	5,607.39	6.93
14	C-13	6.93	6	1,193.06	6.94	9	1,908.90	77.04	13	2,863.35	6.93
16	C-36	6.31	15	1,206.32	6.32	23	1,895.64	28.14	66	5,600.76	6.31
16	C-18	6.31	8	1,206.32	6.32	12	1,895.64	29.01	17	2,757.30	6.31
18	C-33	6.06	52	4,793.94	21.98	21	1,879.98	26.69	60	5,545.93	6.06
19	C-20	8.03	32	4,808.04	32.75	38	5,738.63	5.45	19	2,791.76	5.45
20	C-29	10.00	57	5,989.99	23.39	19	1,925.35	5.24	27	2,781.07	5.24
21	C-37	4.98	44	3,604.98	4.98	69	5,700.90	19.70	34	2,766.61	4.98
22	C-40	4.01	32	2,404.02	4.02	50	3,799.90	5.45	37	2,791.76	4.01
23	C-22	3.03	18	2,396.97	3.03	28	3,806.95	33.65	21	2,819.96	3.03
24	C-30	2.87	59	5,997.12	18.95	56	5,686.93	5.45	28	2,791.76	2.87
24	C-15	2.87	30	5,997.12	40.78	10	1,861.18	10.91	28	5,583.53	2.87
26	C-39	6.93	16	1,193.06	6.94	25	1,908.90	2.50	36	2,783.81	2.50
27	C-25	1.72	30	3,598.27	1.73	47	5,707.61	10.91	46	5,583.53	1.72
28	C-28	0.97	66	7,200.98	18.63	18	1,883.33	16.70	26	2,769.61	0.97
29	C-31	0.75	13	1,200.76	0.76	20	1,901.20	15.46	29	2,801.77	0.75

Table 8
Foreign Chroma Interference in the Family D-n

Rank	Tun.	First 6 Powers of 2 Scale			First 4 Powers of 3 Scale			First 2 Powers of 5 Scale			First 2 Powers of 6 Scale			Smaller Approx.
		Diff.	Degr.	Cts	Diff.	Degr.	Cts	Diff.	Degr.	Cts	Diff.	Degr.	Cts	
1	D-20	20.90	8	1,179.09	21.13	35	5,727.01	14.05	34	5,558.57	70.01	19	3,031.95	14.05
2	D-12	27.49	18	4,772.51	63.19	8	1,965.15	21.05	11	2,807.36	13.87	12	3,088.09	13.87
3	D-24	13.74	18	2,386.25	13.99	28	3,789.93	21.05	21	2,807.36	13.87	23	3,088.09	13.74
4	D-19	12.71	28	4,787.28	32.06	33	5,673.82	50.60	17	2,836.91	87.74	18	3,014.22	12.71
5	D-34	11.00	13	1,189.00	19.38	20	1,882.58	11.98	29	2,774.33	30.38	32	3,071.58	11.00
5	D-17	11.00	7	1,189.00	38.76	20	3,765.16	11.98	15	2,774.33	68.70	17	3,170.66	11.00
7	D-27	10.96	49	5,989.03	30.39	16	1,871.57	41.34	23	2,744.97	17.33	26	3,119.29	10.96
7	D-18	10.96	33	5,989.03	30.39	11	1,871.57	21.05	16	2,807.36	79.71	18	3,181.67	10.96
9	D-16	20.61	18	3,579.38	6.99	10	1,894.97	49.14	14	2,737.17	56.32	16	3,158.28	6.99
10	D-48	6.87	18	1,193.13	6.99	28	1,894.97	21.05	41	2,807.36	13.87	45	3,088.09	6.87
11	D-30	6.58	33	3,593.42	7.04	18	1,909.00	21.05	26	2,807.36	42.28	29	3,144.24	6.58
11	D-15	6.58	17	3,593.42	14.09	18	3,818.01	42.10	26	5,614.72	42.28	15	3,144.24	6.58
13	D-21	6.30	16	2,406.31	23.09	13	1,925.05	42.10	36	5,614.72	53.97	20	3,047.99	6.30
14	D-37	7.09	80	7,192.91	10.08	22	1,912.04	18.60	62	5,554.02	6.28	35	3,095.68	6.28
15	D-35	6.30	26	2,406.31	23.09	21	1,925.05	5.01	30	2,791.32	21.89	33	3,080.07	5.01
16	D-13	27.97	15	3,627.97	4.78	23	5,701.10	64.24	12	2,850.55	7.73	13	3,109.69	4.78
17	D-43	3.86	47	3,603.86	13.30	74	5,719.18	10.13	72	5,562.49	31.84	41	3,133.80	3.86
18	D-42	3.15	16	1,203.15	10.95	72	5,694.93	21.05	36	2,807.36	26.24	40	3,128.20	3.15
18	D-28	3.15	11	1,203.15	23.09	17	1,925.05	19.06	24	2,767.25	26.24	27	3,128.20	3.15
18	D-14	3.15	6	1,203.15	23.09	9	1,925.05	38.11	24	5,534.51	26.24	14	3,128.20	3.15
21	D-22	2.95	48	7,197.05	24.30	26	3,828.22	29.99	19	2,756.32	39.39	21	3,062.57	2.95
22	D-25	12.77	10	1,212.78	15.42	15	1,886.54	43.51	22	2,829.82	2.64	24	3,099.32	2.64
23	D-36	5.55	78	7,205.55	2.42	62	5,708.30	21.05	31	2,807.36	13.87	34	3,088.09	2.42
24	D-47	2.37	68	4,802.37	5.03	54	3,798.89	9.10	40	2,795.41	19.84	44	3,082.12	2.37
25	D-45	2.19	17	1,197.81	14.09	52	3,818.01	16.38	38	2,769.93	32.58	42	3,069.38	2.19
26	D-46	5.30	83	6,005.31	2.16	27	1,904.12	3.36	39	2,782.95	26.07	43	3,075.89	2.16
26	D-23	5.30	42	6,005.31	2.16	14	1,904.12	3.36	20	2,782.95	26.07	22	3,075.89	2.16
28	D-33	1.96	48	4,798.03	10.92	57	5,716.80	29.99	28	2,756.32	39.39	31	3,062.57	1.96
29	D-41	1.83	74	5,998.16	12.13	24	1,889.83	7.35	35	2,793.66	20.37	39	3,122.33	1.83
30	D-39	9.32	15	1,209.32	1.59	23	1,900.37	22.14	33	2,764.17	7.73	37	3,109.69	1.59
31	D-44	1.47	48	3,598.52	12.15	26	1,914.11	16.58	74	5,589.20	37.18	42	3,139.14	1.47
32	D-29	1.16	32	3,601.16	13.72	50	5,692.16	1.69	25	2,788.00	34.54	28	3,136.50	1.16
33	D-26	5.89	38	4,794.10	4.78	45	5,701.10	1.09	44	5,571.53	7.73	25	3,109.69	1.09
34	D-38	6.35	28	2,393.64	8.18	44	3,812.10	12.55	64	5,585.17	0.91	36	3,102.87	0.91
35	D-32	0.72	58	6,000.73	6.99	19	1,894.97	7.00	54	5,579.62	48.96	30	3,053.00	0.72
36	D-40	0.58	58	4,800.58	13.99	46	3,789.93	7.03	34	2,779.28	14.21	38	3,116.17	0.58
37	D-31	4.60	12	1,195.39	0.40	36	3,803.52	30.35	52	5,542.27	49.53	30	3,151.49	0.40

Table 9
Chroma Originality

Chroma Originality Rank	Tuning	Smallest Difference	Chroma Originality Rank	Tuning	Smallest Difference
1	A-12	22.54	54	B-17	5.81
2	C-17	21.45	55	C-20	5.45
3	C-12	18.95	56	C-29	5.24
4	C-21	18.30	57	D-35	5.01
5	C-14	17.64	58	C-37	4.98
6	C-24	14.94	59	D-13	4.78
7	B-15	14.80	60	B-31	4.76
8	D-20	14.05	61	B-19	4.46
9	D-12	13.87	62	B-30	4.04
10	C-23	13.81	63	C-40	4.01
11	D-24	13.74	64	D-43	3.86
12	A-10	13.72	65	D-42	3.15
13	B-16	13.63	66	D-28	3.15
14	D-19	12.71	67	D-14	3.15
15	C-27	12.63	68	C-22	3.03
16	B-27	11.88	69	D-22	2.95
17	B-23	11.43	70	C-30	2.87
18	A-24	11.27	71	C-15	2.87
19	A-16	11.27	72	D-25	2.64
20	A-8	11.27	73	C-39	2.50
21	D-34	11.00	74	A-27	2.46
22	D-17	11.00	75	D-36	2.42
23	D-27	10.96	76	D-47	2.37
24	D-18	10.96	77	B-22	2.20
25	A-17	10.84	78	D-45	2.19
26	A-22	10.33	79	D-46	2.16
27	A-11	10.33	80	D-23	2.16
28	C-32	10.04	81	B-12	2.03
29	C-16	10.04	82	B-29	1.99
30	A-15	9.14	83	D-33	1.96
31	A-20	8.82	84	A-23	1.87
32	C-38	8.25	85	D-41	1.83
33	C-19	8.25	86	C-25	1.72
34	A-18	7.40	87	D-39	1.59
35	A-9	7.40	88	A-26	1.51
36	C-34	7.34	89	A-13	1.51
37	B-25	7.27	90	D-44	1.47
38	A-25	7.06	91	B-18	1.35
39	C-35	7.05	92	B-26	1.28
40	D-16	6.99	93	B-13	1.28
41	C-26	6.93	94	A-19	1.23
42	C-13	6.93	95	D-29	1.16
43	D-48	6.87	96	D-26	1.09
44	D-30	6.58	97	B-24	1.01
45	D-15	6.58	98	C-28	0.97
46	C-36	6.31	99	D-38	0.91
47	C-18	6.31	100	C-31	0.75
48	D-21	6.30	101	D-32	0.72
49	D-37	6.28	102	D-40	0.58
50	C-33	6.06	103	B-21	0.58
51	B-20	6.06	104	D-31	0.40
52	B-28	5.86	105	A-14	0.27
53	B-14	5.86	106	A-21	0.18

Table 10
Total Originality

Rank	Tuning	Chroma Originality Rank	Comparative Originality	Tuning	Aver. Rank	Rank	Tuning	Chroma Originality Rank	Comparative Originality	Aver. Rank
1	C-12	3	3	C-12	3.0	54	A-22	26	90	58.0
2	C-14	5	4	C-14	4.5	55	B-31	60	56	58.0
3	D-12	9	1	D-12	5.0	56	C-29	56	61	58.5
4	C-17	2	10	C-17	6.0	57	C-25	86	31	58.5
5	B-15	7	7	B-15	7.0	58	B-29	82	35	58.5
6	A-12	1	14	A-12	7.5	59	C-40	63	55	59.0
7	A-10	12	13	A-10	12.5	60	B-18	91	28	59.5
8	D-24	11	19	D-24	15.0	61	D-23	80	39	59.5
9	D-18	24	8	D-18	16.0	62	C-13	42	78	60.0
10	C-24	6	30	C-24	18.0	63	C-33	50	70	60.0
11	D-19	14	25	D-19	19.5	64	C-34	36	85	60.5
12	C-27	15	26	C-27	20.5	65	A-25	38	84	61.0
13	A-9	35	9	A-9	22.0	66	C-37	58	64	61.0
14	C-19	33	15	C-19	24.0	67	A-13	89	38	63.5
15	D-15	45	5	D-15	25.0	68	D-29	95	33	64.0
16	D-16	40	11	D-16	25.5	69	D-37	49	80	64.5
17	C-16	29	23	C-16	26.0	70	B-24	97	32	64.5
18	D-27	23	29	D-27	26.0	71	C-26	41	91	66.0
19	A-15	30	22	A-15	26.0	72	D-26	96	36	66.0
20	D-20	8	47	D-20	27.5	73	C-18	47	88	67.5
21	D-21	48	12	D-21	30.0	74	D-43	64	71	67.5
22	B-27	16	44	B-27	30.0	75	D-32	101	34	67.5
23	D-13	59	2	D-13	30.5	76	A-23	84	53	68.5
24	C-21	4	58	C-21	31.0	77	B-14	53	86	69.5
25	B-16	13	52	B-16	32.5	78	D-48	43	100	71.5
26	B-17	54	18	B-17	36.0	79	C-36	46	98	72.0
27	C-32	28	46	C-32	37.0	80	D-33	83	62	72.5
28	A-18	34	40	A-18	37.0	81	D-41	85	60	72.5
29	B-20	51	24	B-20	37.5	82	D-46	79	67	73.0
30	A-17	25	51	A-17	38.0	83	D-38	99	48	73.5
31	A-8	20	59	A-8	39.5	84	B-28	52	96	74.0
32	A-20	31	50	A-20	40.5	85	D-25	72	77	74.5
33	C-20	55	27	C-20	41.0	86	A-26	88	65	76.5
34	C-23	10	74	C-23	42.0	87	D-36	75	79	77.0
35	C-22	68	17	C-22	42.5	88	B-26	92	63	77.5
36	D-30	44	43	D-30	43.5	89	B-30	62	95	78.5
37	D-17	22	66	D-17	44.0	90	D-47	76	83	79.5
38	C-35	39	49	C-35	44.0	91	A-14	105	54	79.5
39	C-15	71	20	C-15	45.5	92	D-14	67	94	80.5
40	B-25	37	57	B-25	47.0	93	D-44	90	73	81.5
41	D-35	57	37	D-35	47.0	94	D-28	66	101	83.5
42	B-12	81	16	B-12	48.5	95	D-42	65	102	83.5
43	B-23	17	81	B-23	49.0	96	C-28	98	69	83.5
44	B-22	77	21	B-22	49.0	97	C-39	73	97	85.0
45	B-13	93	6	B-13	49.5	98	A-21	106	68	87.0
46	A-16	19	82	A-16	50.5	99	A-27	74	103	88.5
47	A-11	27	76	A-11	51.5	100	D-40	102	75	88.5
48	B-19	61	42	B-19	51.5	101	D-39	87	92	89.5
49	C-38	32	72	C-38	52.0	102	D-45	78	104	91.0
50	A-24	18	89	A-24	53.5	103	B-21	103	93	98.0
51	D-34	21	87	D-34	54.0	104	A-19	94	105	99.5
52	C-30	70	41	C-30	55.5	105	D-31	104	99	101.5
53	D-22	69	45	D-22	57.0	106	C-31	100	106	103.0

INDEX

Blackwood, Easley
16, 103

Carlos, Wendy
65, 103

Carrillo, Julián
16

Chroma
definitions, 26, 27
expanded, 35, 36, 59, 96
-originality factor, 46
perception of, 28, 31, 34, 47

Contracted Tunings
see *Semi-expanded Tunings*

Consonance
28, 34, 45, 61, 62

Computer
-assisted tuning, 38, 49
music, 93, 102
-assisted notation, 54

Dissonance
and harmony, 88
and tuning, 61, 67, 98, 108
passing, 87
in Western music, 90

Equal Temperaments
in acoustics, 108
formula for, 4
graphical functions of, 18
in relationship to
the harmonic series, 4
in Western music, 87, 88, 95, 99,
101, 113

Haba, Alois
16

Harmonic
analysis, 53, 60
functions, 61, 68, 89, 96, 97
location theorem, 8
interval, 11, 35
new systems, 100, 101, 102

organization, 23, 28, 56, 57, 85
periodic vibrations, 88
properties, 75, 81
series, 7, 9, 10, 12, 26, 33, 34,
tension, 65
coincidence, 29, 30

Intervals
consonant/dissonant, 65, 67
in different tunings, 46, 50, 61, 66, 69
foreign chroma, 45, 71, 73
learning of, 29, 31, 34, 36
primary lemma, 7
problem, 75, 76, 77, 79
redundancy theorem, 13

Mathews, Max
20

Microtonal Music
16, 103

Morenoctave
definition, 18
terminology, 22

Nettl, Bruno
27

Notation
color, 54
symbols, 61
tablatures, 49, 50, 51

Octave
ambiguity, 33
-based tunings, see :
Semi-expanded Tunings
circularity, 26
generalization, 25, 26
octave-morenoctave
hierarchy, 35

powers of two, 7
similarity, 27, 60, 82
terminology, 22
uniqueness, 33

Partials
coincidence of, 28, 29, 33, 34
in complex tones, 31,

Pedagogy
-cal establishment, 107
innovations, 110

Performance
implementation, 37
live, 105

Pierce, John
16, 20, 21, 22

Pitch
class, 26, 28, 53, 55, 96
neural mapping of, 27

Repetition Rate
31, 34

Risset, J. Claude
28

Roederer, Juan
28, 30, 31

Russolo, Luigi
92

Scales
calculation of, 5
expanded, 94
non-Western, 91

Schaeffer, Pierre
92

Schubert, Earl
22

Shepard, Roger
25

Semi-expanded/Contracted Tunings
caveats, 66, 85
definition, 16
notation, 51
classification, 56,

Stravinsky, Igor
92, 113, 114

Tape Music
103, 105

Timbre
and tuning, 38, 65, 66
control of, 50, 57, 98
problems of, 104, 105

Tunings
definitions of:
    equal, 6,
    expanded, 23.
    fully expanded, 15
    original, 102
    poor, 74
    pseudo-expanded, 102
    redundant, 13
    repeated, 14, 15,
    truly expanded, 70, 101
historical forms of, 92, 107, 108

Yasser, Joseph
16

STUDIES IN THE HISTORY AND INTERPRETATION OF MUSIC

1. Hugo Meynell, **The Art of Handel's Operas**
2. Dale A. Jorgenson, **Moritz Hauptmann of Leipzig**
3. Nancy van Deusen (ed.), **The Harp and The Soul: Essays in Medieval Music**
4. James L. Taggart, **Franz Joseph Haydn's Keyboard Sonatas: An Untapped Gold Mine**
5. William E. Grim, **The Faust Legend in Music and Literature, Volume I**
6. Richard R. LaCroix, **Augustine on Music: An Interdisciplinary Collection of Essays**
7. Clifford Taylor, **Musical Idea and the Design Aesthetic in Contemporary Music: A Text for Discerning Appraisal of Musical Thought in Western Culture**
8. Mary Gilbertson, **The Metaphysics of Alliteration in** *Pearl*
9. Geary Larrick, **Musical References and Song Texts in the Bible**
10. Felix-Eberhard von Cube, **The Book of the Musical Artwork: An Interpretation of the Musical Theories of Heinrich Schenker**, David Neumeyer, George R. Boyd and Scott Harris (trans.)
11. Robert C. Luoma, **Music, Mode and Words in Orlando Di Lasso's Last Works**
12. John A. Kimmey, Jr., **A Critique of Musicology: Clarifying the Scope, Limits, and Purposes of Musicology**
13. Kent A. Holliday, **Reproducing Pianos Past and Present**
14. Gloria Shafer, **Origins of the Children's Song Cycle as a Musical Genre with Four Case Studies and an Original Cycle**
15. Bertil H. van Boer, Jr., **Dramatic Cohesion in the Music of Joseph Martin Kraus: From Sacred Music to Symphonic Form**
16. William O. Cord, **The Teutonic Mythology of Richard Wagner's** *The Ring of The Nibelung,* **Volume One: Nine Dramatic Properties**
17. William O. Cord, **The Teutonic Mythology of Richard Wagner's** *The Ring of The Nibelung,* **Volume Two: The Family of Gods**
18. William O. Cord, **The Teutonic Mythology of Richard Wagner's** *The Ring of The Nibelung,* **Volume Three: The Natural and Supernatural Worlds**

19. Victorien Sardou, *La Tosca* (The Drama Behind the Opera), W. Laird Kleine-Ahlbrandt (trans.)

20. Herbert W. Richardson (ed.), **New Studies in Richard Wagner's** *The Ring of The Nibelung*

21. Catherine Dower, **Yella Pessl, First Lady of the Harpsichord**

22. Margaret Scheppach, **Dramatic Parallels in Michael Tippett's Operas: Analytical Essays on the Musico-Dramatic Techniques**

23. William E. Grim, **Haydn's** *Sturm Und Drang* **Symphonies: Form and Meaning**

24. To be announced.

25. Harold E. Fiske, **Music and Mind: Philosophical Essays on the Cognition and Meaning of Music**

26. Anne Trenkamp and John G. Suess (eds.), **Studies in the Schoenbergian Movement in Vienna and the United States: Essays in Honor of Marcel Dick**

27. Harvey J. Stokes, **A Selected Annotated Bibliography on Italian Serial Composers**

28. Julia Muller, **Words and Music in Henry Purcell's First Semi-Opera,** *Dioclesian:* **An Approach to Early Music Through Early Theatre**

29. Ronald W. Holz, **Erik Leidzen: Band Arranger and Composer**

30. Enrique Moreno, **Expanded Tunings in Contemporary Music: Theoretical Innovations and Practical Applications**

31. Charles H. Parsons (compiler), **A Benjamin Britten Discography**

32. Denis Wilde, **The Development of Melody in the Tone Poems of Richard Strauss: Motif, Figure, and Theme**

33. William Smialek, **Ignacy Feliks Dobrzynski and Musical Life in Nineteenth-Century Poland**

34. Judith A. Eckelmeyer, **The Cultural Context of Mozart's Magic Flute: Social, Aesthetic, Philosophical** (2 Volume Set)

35. Joseph Coroniti, **Poetry as Text in Twentieth Century Vocal Music: From Stravinsky to Reich**

36. William E. Grim, **The Faust Legend in Music and Literature, Volume II**